GUINNESS WORLD RECORDS 2009

★ABOUT THIS BOOK

This year's typeface of choice is Franklin Gothic, designed by the prolific American typographer Morris Fuller Benton (1872–1948) at the start of the 20th century. The term "gothic" (or "grotesque") is an archaic term that simply means the face is *sans serif* – that is, without serifs, the short horizontal or vertical lines occuring at the tips of strokes in "roman" typefaces such as Times.

Our cover is a metal foil with a 3D effect that has been created using a diamond engraving process. This book represents the first commercial use of the process, which produces a smooth, satin-like finish while at the same time giving the appearance of great depth and movement.

Peppered throughout this book is a selection of 3D images. You'll spot them from the 3D-glasses symbol, above, and from what look like printing errors – the red and blue parts of the photos will be offset. Use the 3D glasses provided to see the images in all their glory.

This "anaglyph" (from the Greek "to carve") photography is based on the fact that our left eye sees the world from a slightly different angle to the right eye. The brain processes the two images to create a 3D view of the world. With anaglyphs, the same effect is achieved using two offset colours: each eye sees a different colour and the brain processes this as 3D (binocular) vision.

British Library Cataloguing-in-Publication Data:
A catalogue record for this book is available from the British Library

ISBN: 978-1-904994-36-7

For a complete list of credits and acknowledgements, turn to p.278

If you wish to make a record claim, find out how on p.10. Always contact us before making a record attempt.

Check the official website www.guinnessworldrecords.com regularly for record-breaking news, plus video footage of record attempts. You can also sign up for the official GWR mobile phone services.

Sustainability
The trees that are harvested to print Guinness World Records are carefully selected from managed forests to avoid the devastation of the landscape. For every tree harvested, at least one other is planted.

The paper contained within this book is manufactured by UPM Kymi, Finland. The production site has been awarded the EU Flower licence, is Chain-of-Custody certified, and operates environmental systems certified to both ISO 14001 and EMAS in order to ensure sustainable production.

The European Eco-label distinguishes products that meet high standards of both performance and environmental quality. Every product awarded the European Eco-label must pass rigorous environmental fitness trials, with results verified by an independent body.

Made of paper awarded the European Union Eco-label reg.nr FI/11/1

Pictured opposite is Rosi, the world's **largest spider**. She's a Goliath bird-eating spider (Theraphosa blondi) weighing 175 g (6.17 oz) and belonging to Walter Baumgartner of Andorf, Austria.

THE JIM PATTISON GROUP

Dinosaur artwork: © BBC Books/The Random House Group Ltd

GUINNESS WORLD RECORDS 2009

CONTENTS

3D GLASSES

Tear out and build the free 3D glasses that came with this book. You'll find that some pages can be viewed in 3D, so where you see the logo, put on your glasses and discover a whole new exciting way of viewing our amazing records!

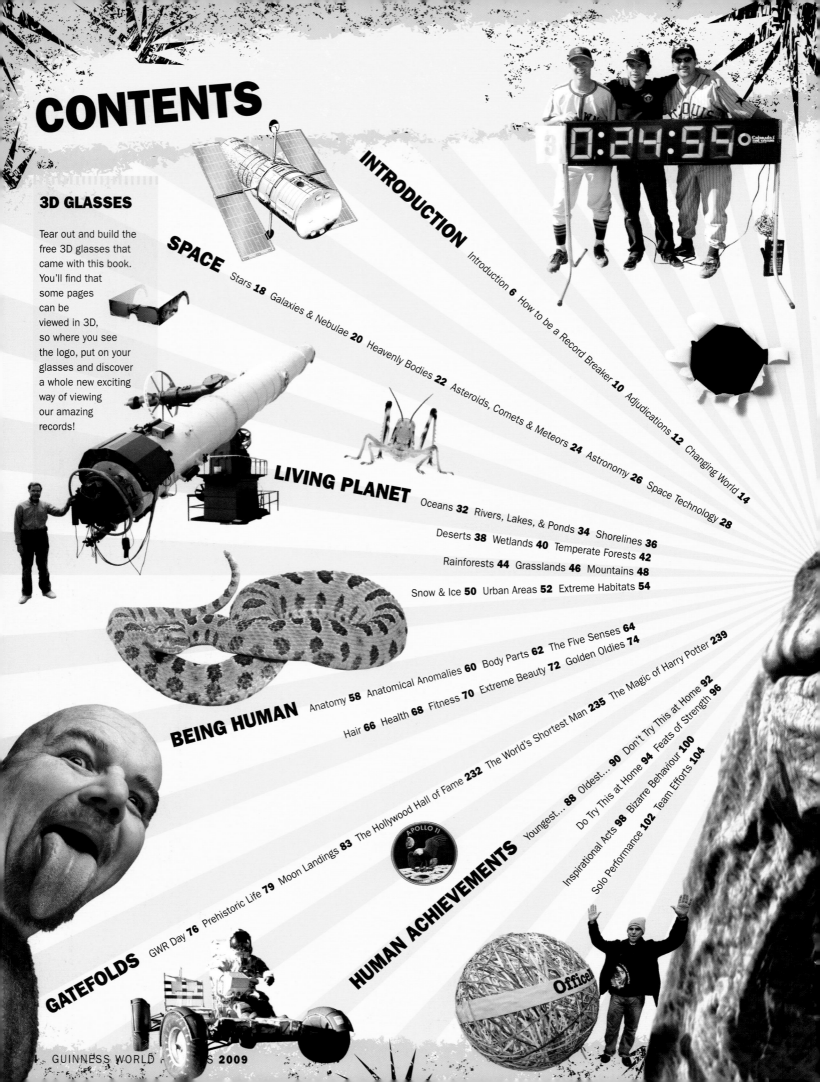

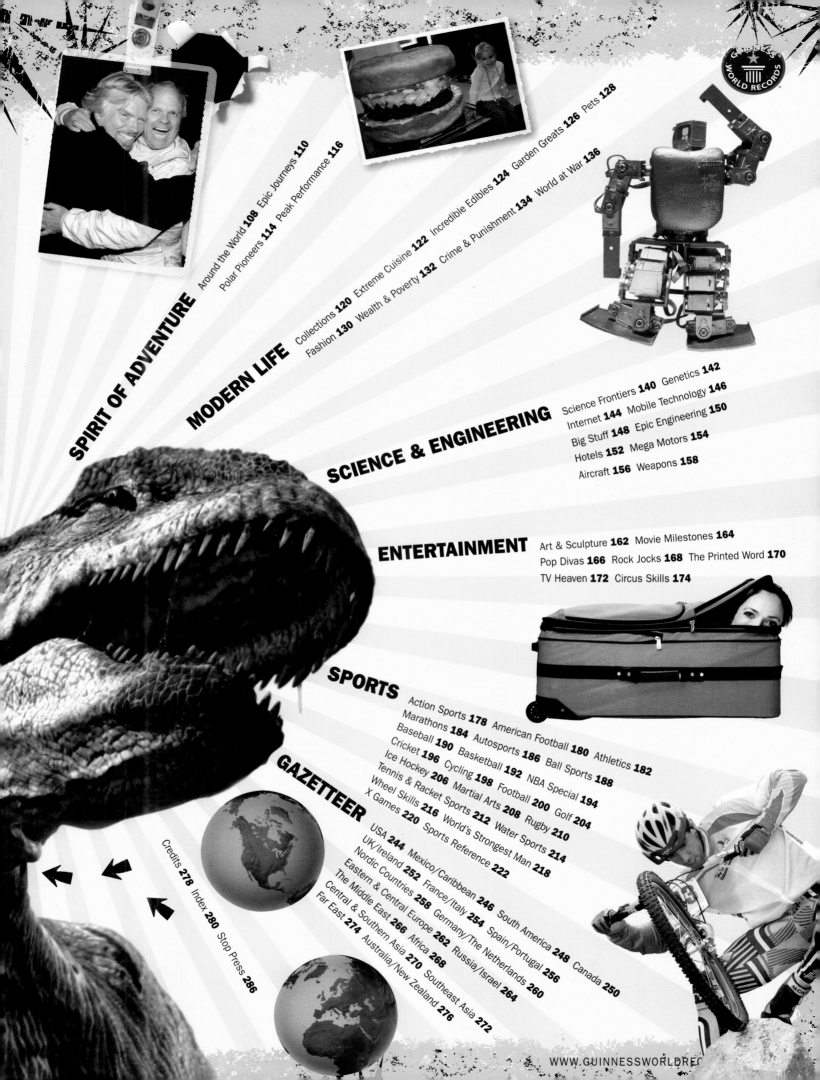

INTRODUCTION

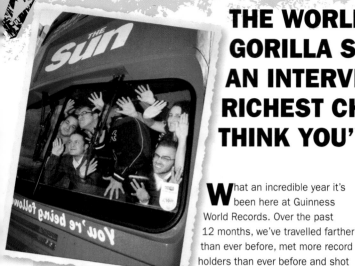

THE WORLD'S DEADLIEST CHEESE, A GIANT GORILLA SCULPTED FROM COAT HANGERS, AN INTERVIEW WITH A DARK JEDI AND THE RICHEST CHIMPANZEE ON WALL STREET. THINK YOU'VE SEEN IT ALL? THINK AGAIN...

What an incredible year it's been here at Guinness World Records. Over the past 12 months, we've travelled farther than ever before, met more record holders than ever before and shot more fantastic images than ever before to bring the 2009 edition of the world's best-selling copyright book to life. This edition is truly the result of the most action-packed, varied and exciting year we've ever had at GWR.

So what's new? Well, as ever, we've pushed Keren and Lisa at Itonic, our design agency, to develop and improve upon last year's book, and they've responded with a cool, funky new look for the 2009 edition. The concept behind the design is urban/skateboard/graffiti, and I hope you'll agree it certainly brightens up the pages.

Next, our tireless Picture Editor, Michael Whitty, had the job of filling the beautifully designed pages with the world's most extreme photography. Michael and his gang of first-class photographers toured the globe, shooting record holders in their homes and local areas. And, as always, each shot in the book is seen here for the first time!

Achievements make it into the *Guinness World Records* book in one of two ways. The first is via our carefully selected board of consultants, all of whom are experts in their particular fields. They spend their year hunting down superlatives just for

SUN BUS

Once again, we are indebted to the UK's biggest-selling daily newspaper, *The Sun*, for all its support throughout the year. Pictured here is their attempt at the ★ **most people crammed on a modified bus** record. They succeeded in cramming 88 people on to the lower deck of *The Sun* Battle Bus!

GWR DAY

Where else would you find a contortionist, a Victorian-style housewife, a samurai sword master and a karate black belt all in one place... except at the launch of a *Guinness World Records* book!? Many thanks to Leslie Tipton, Cathie Jung, Kenneth Lee and Narve Laeret (pictured left to right) for visiting London for the 2008 launch. And apologies for continually being arrested by the police – the Buckingham Palace guards don't take too kindly to people hanging around outside the Queen's residence with big samurai swords!

SMASHING TIME ON TOP GEAR

Records are just some of the things that get smashed on BBC TV's *Top Gear* – you can usually expect a few cars, and plenty of caravans, to end up in pieces by the time the credits role! We've had a great time adjudicating at some of the record-breaking stunts for the new series, and we salute you, *Top Gear* Stunt Man, for your many record attempts!

Read the interview with Christopher Lee in full and unedited, at www.guinnessworldrecords.com/2009

CHRISTOPHER LEE

One of the highlights of the year for me as Editor-in-Chief was having tea with screen legend Christopher Lee. Despite playing the likes of Dracula, Saruman and Count Dooku, Mr Lee, in person, is polite, absolutely fascinating and generous with his time. The exclusive interview marked his induction into the **GWR Hollywood Hall of Fame** – find out more on p.232.

★ NEW RECORD
☆ UPDATED RECORD

BLUE PETER

This year marks the 50th anniversary of *Blue Peter* (BBC), the **longest-running children's magazine TV programme**. To mark the event – and to say thank you for regularly featuring our record holders on air – I paid a visit to the set and presented the current team (below) with their own Guinness World Records certificate (and in the process, earned the much-desired *Blue Peter* badge!).

Here are just a few of the many records set on the show over the years:

● **Fastest time to peel and eat a lemon** – first set back in 2005 by host Gethin Jones (UK) at 51.2 seconds

● **Most gyrator spins in one minute** – 29, set by Sam Foakes (UK) on 11 March 2002

● **Fastest time to pop 1,000 balloons** – 1 min 44 sec, by a team of 37 from Oakthorpe Primary School

● **Most yoyo tricks in one minute** – 51, by Hans Van Dan Helzen (USA) on 17 May 2004

● **Most shoelaces tied in a bow in one minute** – 14, achieved by Andy Akinwolere (Nigeria) on GWR Day 2006.

us, and supply about two thirds of the material you'll see in the book. They also help the Records Management Team – led by Marco Frigatti, our Director of Records Management – to write the guidelines for records, and to help us decide if a claim is a genuine record. Many thanks to all our consultants – the book would be impossible to create without your help!

The second route is via Marco's team of Records Managers. It's their job to investigate the thousands of emails and letters we receive every year and process the claims efficiently and professionally. Sadly, they spend most of their day rejecting claims that are either inappropriate or just not up to the mark. Thanks, too, to this hard-working team for all their efforts over the past year.

So, with the help of our consultants and our Records Managers – and, of course, you, the record claimants! – we've explored some fascinating new territory for record categories this year. For example, check out how the world has moved on and how much records have changed over the years (or not!) in **Changing World** (pp.14–15); keep up to date with the latest technological developments in **Mobile Technology** (pp.146–47); and marvel at the many different records associated with **Hair** (pp.66–67). Oh, and be sure not to miss our feature on the **World's Strongest Man** competition (pp.218–19) – surprisingly, it's the first time we've ever used this popular annual event as a source for records, so expect a whole spread of new categories!

If you've already had a flick through the book, you'll have noticed that some parts of it can be viewed in 3D! This is another new feature we're proud of, as it really does add a thrilling new dimension to the photography. Simply tear out and build the free 3D glasses provided, then cast your eyes over any photos accompanied by a logo of the glasses with their distinctive red and blue lenses. We're indebted to David Burder for his innovative work and ideas in 3D photography.

GWR'S GOT SATTITUDE

The ☆ **most bananas snapped in a minute** (achieved by Declan Wolfe, Ireland, below) was just one of the records attempted on RTÉ's *Sattitude* show! Thanks to the cast and crew for their support...

GWR: THE VIDEO GAME

Look out for **Guinness World Records – The Video Game** this Christmas. It's your chance to break a world record – such as turkey plucking or balancing a vehicle on your head (above) – on the Wii or DS Lite. Go head-to-head against family and friends, and try to break records on a household, city, national or global scale!

ON THE ROAD

Countries visited this year by GWR adjudicators: UK, China, USA, Mexico, Spain, India, Germany, UAE, Kuwait, Italy, Romania, Portugal, Japan, France, Belgium, Austria, Turkey, Sweden, Russia, Qatar, Poland, Peru, Nigeria, Ireland, Greece, Croatia, Bahrain, Albania, Brazil, Bulgaria, the Netherlands, Thailand, Uruguay, the Philippines, Vietnam, Taiwan, Australia and New Zealand (for the ★ **most people in a snowboard race**, see box below right).

DOH!-NUT STACKING

To celebrate the British premiere of *The Simpsons Movie* (USA, 2007), we headed for the offices of Capital Radio in Leicester Square, London, to adjudicate the record for the ★ **tallest stack of doughnuts**. A team of eight from 20th Century Fox and Capital Radio built a pyramid of 1,764 ring doughnuts, reaching a record height of 110.5 cm (43.5 in).

The gatefold sections this year are of a celebratory nature: to mark the publication of the final book in J. K. Rowling's phenomenal boy wizard series, we explore **The Magic of Harry Potter**; we celebrate the 40th anniversary of the first Apollo **Moon landings** and have even included an interview with Gene Cernan, the last man to walk on the Moon! And we hope you'll be blown away by the fantastic four-page **3D dinosaurs** feature.

This year's subject for the **Hall of Fame** is Hollywood and specifically its greatest record-breaking actors. Turn to p.232 to find out why the likes of Brad Pitt, Angelina Jolie, Jack Nicholson and Johnny Depp have been inducted into the prestigious GWR Hall of Fame, and read an extract from our exclusive interview with screen legend Christopher Lee.

We've also inducted a couple of Hollywood figures who aren't actors but whom we considered particularly worthy of mention. One is director Tim Burton (USA) and the other is the unluckiest man in Tinseltown! Turn to the gatefold to find out more.

60-MINUTE MAKEOVER

We've rarely been off your TV screens this year and even turned up on the home-improvement show *60 Minute Makeover*. Could there be a better show on which to attempt the record for the ★ **fastest time to hang three strips of wallpaper by a team of two**? Kevin Patten and Rolandas Paulauskas would say not – they achieved a record time of 1 min 42.19 sec.

IT'S A RECORD!

GWR adjudicator Chris Sheedy confirmed the record for ★ **most people in a snowboard race** on 6 October 2007. In total, 88 people gathered at Mount Hutt in Christchurch, New Zealand, for the race!

The final fold-out is particularly special to us as it welcomes into the Guinness World Records "family" an important new member: He Pingping, the world's ★ **shortest living man**! I had the experience of a lifetime travelling to Inner Mongolia to meet and measure Pingping, and I hope you enjoy him in all his glory in 3D – and at actual size – on pp.235–38!

This year, we've also added an entirely new section at the back of the book called the **Gazetteer**. This feature explores the record-breaking achievements of all the major countries and territories in which Guinness World Records is available. It's a cross between a travel guide and a record book, and helpful if you're either visiting

CHILDREN IN NEED

Thousands – if not millions – of pounds are raised every year by charities and their supporters carrying out record-breaking events. Among such events are the Flora London Marathon (see pp.184–85) and Children in Need, which this year saw the creation of the ★ **longest human teddy-bear chain**! A total of 631 schoolchildren and teachers from Grangemouth, Scotland, gathered on a cold November morning in an ASDA car park, each with a teddy bear, smashing the record of 430 set in 2006 in Vienna, Austria.

PAUL O'GRADY

Many thanks are due to TV star Paul O'Grady (below) for all his support over the past 12 months. If you get the chance to watch his teatime TV show, you'll find regular record-breaking attempts happening – not just by members of the public, but by Paul and his (usually) willing guests! Among the records set this year on the show were:

★ **Most éclairs filled with cream in one minute** (13, by Andy Collins, UK)

HE PINGPING

With the death in 2006 of Nelson de la Rosa (Dominican Republic), we found ourselves with a gap in our database: who was the new ★ **shortest living man**? The answer, incredibly, came from the same remote region within Inner Mongolia in which we'd found the **tallest living man**, Bao Xi Shun (China). His name was He Pingping, and to confirm his actual size

and age (all candidates for this record must be over 18), I travelled to Hohhot, the capital city of Inner Mongolia, and spent a couple of days with him and his family. It was an unforgettable experience to meet this fascinating character and having his record-breaking height confirmed in a local hospital. Pingping eventually measured up to the record – find out about his amazing achievement on pp.235–38.

You may also be interested to know that Xi Shun has officially been renamed the **tallest living man**. Last year's entrant, Leonid Stadnyk, has had his record suspended pending a new investigation into his height (we have still not been able to measure him in person). Watch this space!

somewhere new or investigating a part of the world for a school homework project.

I really hope that this year's edition inspires you to tackle a Guinness World Record of your own! Without the public and their passion and inventiveness, we'd be nothing, so start thinking about what you can break – perhaps for the next GWR Day? Or to raise money for charity? Or just to push yourself to new limits? Whatever the reason, good luck!

Editor-in-Chief
Guinness World Records

★ **Most kilts worn in one minute** (three, by Lorraine Kelly, UK, *above*)

★ **Most eggs smashed with head in one minute** (40, by Osi Anyanwu, UK)

★ **Most eggs thrown and caught in one minute by a team of two** (31, by Hadley Jones and James Abram, both UK).

HOW TO BE A RECORD BREAKER

1. CONTACT US

Got an idea? Then contact us via our website: **www.guinnessworldrecords. com**. Simply click on "Break a Record" and follow the instructions. We need to know as much as possible about your claim, and this is your chance to tell us every detail. *LEFT: Robert T. Natoli (USA) receives his certificate for the ★ **most chin-ups in one minute** (a phenomenal 53!) from GWR's Laura.*

IS THERE A COST INVOLVED?

No! Trying for a Guinness World Record won't cost a thing – just commitment and time. Anyone can apply, but under-18s must get approval from a parent or guardian first.

2. FOLLOW THE RULES

If your application is for an existing record, we'll send you the guidelines that the current record holder followed; if it's for a new record, and we like it, we'll write new guidelines for you. Once you receive these, you're ready to make your attempt. *BELOW: Sweet-toothed GWR judge Jane gets her job of a lifetime – weighing the ★ **largest chocolate** (13,852 kg; 30,540 lb)!*

LARGEST PHONE GATHERING

*ABOVE: GWR's Kaoru found herself surrounded by giant mobile phones at the world's ★ **largest gathering of people dressed as mobile phones**, in San Juan, Puerto Rico, in November 2007.* Have you got a few friends who could help you beat this or a similar record? Let us know by visiting our website **www. guinnessworld records.com**.

MARCO FRIGATTI

Marco, Guinness World Records' Director of Records Management, heads up a multilingual team that processes thousands of record claims each year. Here, he gives his advice on getting your name into the records book.

I always recommend looking through the book or watching our TV shows for the kinds of records we like. A record must fulfil four criteria. One, it has to be measureable – that is, you can take a tape measure to it, or weigh it or count it. So you can't have the ugliest dog or most beautiful girlfriend but you can have a dog that's won the most "ugly dog" competitions or a girlfriend who's won the most beauty contests. Two, it has to be singularly quantifiable – so, we're looking for just one superlative... we're not interested in the fastest tallest man, or the heaviest fastest accordion player. Three, it has to be breakable – unless it's a "significant first", by which we mean it has to be *really* significant, such as **first man on the moon** or **first movie to gross over $1 billion**. Four, it has to be interesting to as wide a range of people as possible. Also, remember that securing a record does *not* guarantee you a place in the book – that decision is the Editor's – but follow these basic pointers and you'll have a much better chance of success.

3. PROVE IT

The guidelines we send you will contain details of the evidence we need: expect to film video evidence, take photographs and collect two written independent witness statements. *ABOVE: members of the Scout Association – the world's ★largest youth organization*.

FACTS
● Last year, we received 35,692 claims – but only 2,017 made it on to our database
● The database holds around 40,000 live and rested records
● The book has room for just 4,000 entries!

4. POST IT

Next, send us your evidence. If you want a GWR adjudicator present at your event, see p.12. Otherwise, we'll get back to you in due course. *BELOW: Câmara Municipal de Gondomar and Montepio (Portugal) achieve the record for the ★most footballs released – an amazing 5,071 balls!*

★ **NEW RECORD**
⭑ **UPDATED RECORD**

5. WAIT

If you've requested an adjudicator, he or she can ratify your record immediately. Otherwise, once we receive your package of evidence, our researchers will assess it to make sure that you've followed the rules correctly. This process can take a few months, so please be patient! *ABOVE: GWR's Michael celebrates with the St Louis Chapter of the Men's Senior Baseball League (USA) for their record-breaking ★longest baseball marathon (see p.191).*

CHOOSING A RECORD? PLEASE AVOID:

● **Non-records** – your claim *must* involve a record! Is it the tallest, longest, smelliest? What is the "-est"? You may be able to lick your own elbow but it's not a record!
● **Animal cruelty** – don't overfeed your pets to make them the heaviest. Not cool.
● **Breaking the law** – driving at high speeds on public roads is dangerous and illegal, so don't do it.
● **Teenage surgery** – teenagers performing medical operations is not on: you're a danger to society. As are **speedy house builders** who try to erect homes in record time! They come down just as fast...

X GAMES

You'll find Guinness World Records out and about at various events throughout the world every year, including the X Games, where we adjudicate records, organize signings with record holders and stage competitions. *RIGHT: GWR's own Stuart is joined by Danny Way (USA), holder of several X Games world records (see p.220).*

6. CELEBRATE

If your attempt is a success, you'll receive your official GWR certificate in the post. If not, better luck next time! *LEFT: Gary Cole (USA) celebrates achieving the record for the **most faces painted in an hour** (217).*

ADJUDICATIONS

THROUGHOUT THE YEAR, GWR'S ADJUDICATORS TRAVEL THE WORLD TO SEEK OUT NEW RECORDS. HERE'S THE INSIDE STORY ON THEIR UNIQUE ROLE.

ADJUDICATORS AT YOUR SERVICE!

After registering your record idea, you can arrange for a GWR adjudicator to be present at your event. The advantages of this include:

• Instant verification of your record and an official certificate presentation.

• An article about your record on our website. See **www. guinness worldrecords.com/ register/login.aspx**.

• Support in the build-up to your event.

• International media coverage for your record attempt.

★ **NEW RECORD**
☆ **UPDATED RECORD**

LEFT: GWR's Patricia Magill celebrates the ★**tightest frying pan roll of two pans**. *TOP: Adjudicator Gareth Deaves monitors the* ★**fastest lap time on Project Gotham 4 (Xbox 360)**: *47.53 seconds. ABOVE: Carlos Martinez takes note of the* ★**largest chestnut roaster**: *5 m (16 ft 4 in) in diameter.*

ANDREA BÁNFI

As Guinness World Records Adjudications Manager, Andrea Bánfi leads a team of multilingual adjudicators located in London, New York, Beijing and Sydney. So what is it like to attend record-breaking attempts for a living?

People often ask me how I became an adjudicator. Well, it wasn't easy! GWR has a strict recruitment process involving a variety of tests, and successful applicants need to have expertise in a number of different areas, such as sports, music and science.

After I joined GWR, records that up until then had been just numbers and facts suddenly came alive. Every GWR adjudication is different. Record attempts are always full of emotions and excitement – whether they are successful or not. Some people do extreme sports to get their adrenaline levels going; I get a buzz from record attempts, and not too long after officiating at my first event, I realized I was becoming addicted to them!

Of all the adjudications I've attended, my favourite so far has been the ★**most people reading aloud simultaneously in one location**: 13,839 people read a Taoist text together in a rugby stadium in Hong Kong. They were so well rehearsed that they read as if they were one person; when they paused, the silence was stunning.

We officiate at hundreds of record attempts every year and the demand is growing continuously, as a result of our adjudicators' dedication, support and professionalism. If you are thinking of having us present at your record attempt, get in touch via our website and I'll get back to you by phone or email.

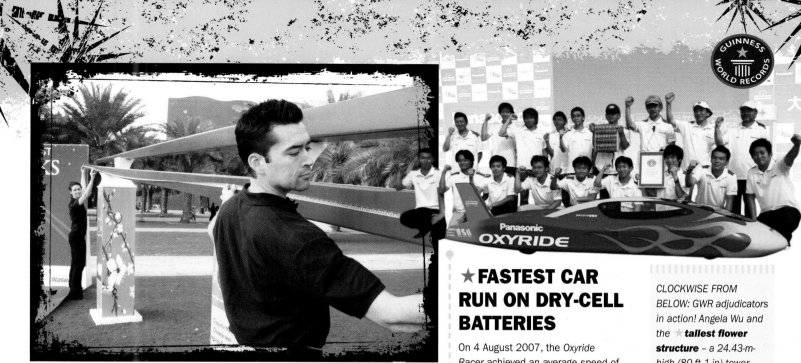

★ LARGEST CHOPSTICKS

Andrea Bánfi and fellow Guinness World Records adjudicator Danny Girton measure the largest chopsticks – 6.73 m (22 ft 1 in) – manufactured by the Marco Polo Hotel in Dubai, UAE, and certified at the Dubai Shopping Festival on 23 February 2008.

★ FASTEST CAR RUN ON DRY-CELL BATTERIES

On 4 August 2007, the *Oxyride Racer* achieved an average speed of 105.95 km/h (65.83 mph) at JARI Shirosato Test Centre in Ibaraki, Japan. This dry-cell-battery-powered vehicle was created by the Oxyride Speed Challenge Team, consisting of Matsushita Electric Industrial Co., Ltd, and Osaka Sangyo University (both Japan).

*CLOCKWISE FROM BELOW: GWR adjudicators in action! Angela Wu and the ★ **tallest flower structure** – a 24.43-m-high (80-ft 1-in) tower of chrysanthemums; Rob Molloy receives evidence for the ★ **longest boom (truck-mounted)**, made by SANY Heavy Industry Co., Ltd, China; our adjudicators are all experienced at working with the media – here, Amarilis Espinoza breaks the news of another GWR record; Kim Lacey and the ★ **largest toilet roll**: 1.68 m (5 ft 6 in).*

• Availability of the adjudicator for interviews and press conferences.

Please note: GWR charges a fee for adjudicators to attend record attempts. Visit **www.guinnessworldrecords.com/ member** to find out more about this premium service.

We carry out on-site adjudications for corporate activities, charity functions, product launches, marketing and PR events, sports events and to raise awareness for good causes.

With the publication of *Guinness World Records: Gamer's Edition*, GWR now carries out a wide range of PC, console and arcade game adjudications, from international shows to local arcades. So, if you're aiming for a record-breaking high score, why not have a GWR adjudicator there to make it official?

CHANGING WORLD

RECORD BREAKING IS AS OLD AS HUMANITY ITSELF. IT'S AMAZING TO SEE HOW MUCH SOME WORLD RECORDS HAVE CHANGED OVER THE YEARS – AND HOW LITTLE SOME HAVE ALTERED...

MOST EXPENSIVE PAINTINGS

The Magdalen Reading
Artist: Unknown
Date painted: Unknown
Date of sale: 1746
£6,500 (2008: £911,970)

The Sistine Madonna (above)
Artist: Raphael
Date painted: 1513–14
Date of sale: 1759
£8,500 (2008: £1,134,552)

Adoration of the Lamb (right)
Artist: Van Eyck
Date painted: 1432
Date of sale: 1821
£16,000 (2008: £1,116,255)

The Immaculate Conception
Artist: Murillo
Date painted: 1660–65
Date of sale: 1852
£24,600 (2008: £2,041,762)

FASTEST 100 M

Don Lippincott (USA)
Date: 6 July 1912
Location: Stockholm, Sweden
10.6 SEC

Jesse Owens (USA, pictured)
Date: 20 June 1936
Location: Chicago, Illinois, USA
10.2 SEC

Armin Hary (West Germany)
Date: 21 June 1960
Location: Zürich, Switzerland
10.0 SEC

Jim Hines (USA, pictured)
Date: 14 October 1968
Location: Mexico City, Mexico
9.95 SEC

Leroy Burrell (USA)
Date: 14 June 1991
Location: New York City, USA
9.9 SEC

PROGRESSIVE SPEED

Sledge
Date: ca. 6500 BC
Location: Heinola, Finland
40 KM/H (25 MPH)

Horse
Date: ca. 1400 BC
Location: Anatolia, Turkey
55 KM/H (35 MPH)

Ice yacht
Date: ca. AD 1600
Location: The Netherlands
80 KM/H (50 MPH)

Downhill skier
Date: March 1873
Location: La Porte, California, USA
Tommy Todd (USA)
141.3 KM/H (87.8 MPH)

Midland Railway 4-2-2
Date: March 1897
Location: Ampthill, Bedford, UK
144.8 KM/H (90 MPH)

Messerschmitt 163V-1
Date: 2 October 1941
Location: Peenemunde, Germany
Heinz Dittmar (Germany)
1,004 KM/H (623.85 MPH)

LARGEST CONURBATIONS

YEAR	CITY/PRESENT LOCATION	POPULATION
ca. 27000 BC	Dolní Věstonice, Czechoslovakia	>100
3000 BC	Uruk (Erech; now Warka), Iraq	50,000
2200 BC	Greater Ur (now Tell el-Muqayyar), Iraq	250,000
133 BC	Rome, Italy	1,100,000
AD 900	Angkor, Cambodia	1,500,000
1578	Peking (now Beijing), China	707,000
1801	Greater London, UK	1,117,290
1925	New York City, USA	7,774,000
1939	Greater London, UK	8,615,050
1985	Tokyo, Japan	11,600,069
2003	Tokyo, Japan	26,546,000
2020 (projection)	Tokyo, Japan	>37,000,000

TALLEST STRUCTURES

Djoser Step Pyramid
Location: Saqqâra, Egypt
Built: ca. 2650 BC
62 M (204 FT)

Great Pyramid of Cheops
Location: El Gizeh, Egypt
Built: ca. 2580 BC
146.5 M (480 FT 10 IN)

St Paul's Cathedral
Location: London, UK
Built: 1315–1561
149 M (489 FT)*

*Original spire destroyed by lightning, 4 June 1561

BEST-SELLING SINGLE

Although no exact figures are available, it has been estimated that sales of the song "White Christmas", written by Irving Berlin (USA, b. Israel Baline, Russia), exceed 100 million copies worldwide when 78s, 45s and albums are taken into account.

"White Christmas" was listed as the world's **best-selling single** in the first-ever Guinness Book of Records (published in 1955) and – remarkably – still retains the title more than 50 years later.

Bing Crosby (USA, pictured) is the artist most closely associated with the song. He originally recorded it on 29 May 1942, but his re-recording (on 18 March 1947) has become the best-known version. The song has been a Yuletide favourite ever since.

The Colonna Altarpiece
Artist: Raphael
Date painted: 1503–05
Date of sale: 1901
£100,000
(2008: £7,783,708)

Irises
Artist: Van Gogh
Date painted: 1889
Date of sale: 1987
$53,900,000
(2008: $98,377,938

Garçon à la Pipe*
Artist: Picasso
Date painted: 1905
Date of sale: 2004 (above)
$104,200,000
(2008: $114,372,876)

*In November 2006, it was reported that Jackson Pollock's painting *No.5* (1948) had been sold by David Geffen (USA) for $140 million (£70 million). However, as there has still been no definitive confirmation of the sale, the sale price or even the buyer, GWR still recognizes *Garçon à la Pipe* as history's most expensive painting.

Carl Lewis
(USA, pictured)
Date: 25 August 1991
Location: Tokyo, Japan
9.86 SEC

Donovan Bailey (Canada)
Date: 29 July 1996
Location: Atlanta, Georgia
9.84 SEC

Maurice Greene (USA)
Date: 16 June 1999
Location: Athens, Greece
9.79 SEC

Asafa Powell
(Jamaica, right)
Date: June 14, 2005
Location: Athens, Greece
9.77 SEC

Usain Bolt (Jamaica)
Date: 31 May 2008
Location: New York, USA
9.72 SEC

USAF Bell XS-1
Date: 14 October 1947
Location: Murdoc Dry Lake, California, USA
Capt. C. E. Yeager (USA)
1,078 KM/H (670 MPH)

North American X-15
Date: 7 March 1961
Location: Murdoc Dry Lake, California, USA
Maj. R. M. White (USA)
4,675.1 KM/H (2,905 MPH)

Vostok 1
Date: 12 April 1961
Location: Earth orbit
Maj. Y. A. Gagarin (USSR)
CA. 28,260 KM/H (17,560 MPH)

Apollo 10
Date: 26 May 1969
Location: Re-entry into Earth's atmosphere
Crew of *Apollo 10* (USA)
39,897 KM/H (24,790.8 MPH)

Eiffel Tower
Location: Paris, France
Built: 1887–89
300.5 M (985 FT 10 IN)

Chrysler Building
Location: New York City, USA
Built: 1929–30
318 M (1,046 FT)

Empire State Building
Location: New York City, USA
Built: 1929–30
381 M (1,250 FT)

Warszawa Radio Mast
Location: Plock, Poland
Built: 1974
646 M (2,120 FT)*

Ursa Tension Leg Platform
Location: Gulf of Mexico
Built: 1998
1,306 M (4,285 FT)

*Fell during renovation, 1991

ALTITUDE
(SINCE 1900)

400,171 KM (248,655 MILES)
Holder/vehicle: crew of US *Apollo 13*: Capt. James A. Lovell, Jr; Frederick W. Haise, Jr; John L. Swigert, Jr (all USA). Date: 15 April 1970

377,667 KM (234,672 MILES)
Holder/vehicle: crew of US *Apollo 8* command module: Col Frank Borman; Capt. James A. Lovell, Jr; Maj. William A. Anders (all USA). Date: 25 December 1968

327 KM (203.2 MILES)
Holder/vehicle: Maj. Yuri A. Gagarin (USSR) in *Vostok 1*. Date: 12 April 1961

51,694 M (169,600 FT)
Holder/vehicle: Joseph Walker (USA) in US *X-15* rocket plane. Date: 30 March 1961

38,465 M (126,200 FT)
Holder/vehicle: Capt. Iven C. Kincheloe, Jr (USA) in US *Bell X-2* rocket plane. Date: 7 September 1956

24,262 M (79,600 FT)
Holder/vehicle: William B. Bridgeman (USA) in US Douglas D558-11 *Skyrocket*. Date: 15 August 1951

22,066 M (72,395 FT)
Holder/vehicle: Capt. Orvill A. Anderson and Capt. Albert W. Stevens (both USA) in US *Explorer II* helium balloon. Date: 11 November 1935

15,837 M (51,961 FT)
Holder/vehicle: Prof. Auguste Piccard and Paul Kipfer (both Switzerland) in *FNRS 1* balloon. Date: 27 May 1931

11,145 M (36,565 FT)
Holder/vehicle: Sadi Lecointe (France) in Nieuport aircraft. Date: 30 October 1923

SPACE

LARGEST PLANET IN THE SOLAR SYSTEM

Jupiter's Great Red Spot appears as a white oval in this image of the largest planet in the Solar System. The gas giant has an equatorial diameter of 143,884 km (89,405 miles) and a mass of more than 300 Earths. Despite its size, Jupiter also has the shortest day of any planet in the Solar System, completing a full rotation in just 9 hrs 55 min.

In the foreground is the rocky moon Io, complete with blue aurora at its north pole and an orange glow from incandescent molten lava on its surface. This montage was assembled from images taken by NASA's New Horizons spacecraft. It passed through the Jupiter system in February 2007 and is now in interplanetary space en route to its encounter with Pluto in July 2015.

CONTENTS

STARS

FLATTEST STAR

The least spherical star studied to date in our galaxy is the southern star Achenar (Alpha Eridani). Observations made using the VLT Interferometer at the European Southern Observatory's Paranal Observatory, Atacama, Chile, have revealed that Achenar is spinning so rapidly that its equatorial diameter is more than 50% greater than its polar diameter.

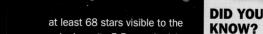

LARGEST DIAMOND

Observations of pulsations from the carbon white dwarf star BPM 37093 have allowed astronomers from the Harvard-Smithsonian Center for Astrophysics, Cambridge, Massachusetts, USA, to deduce that it had crystallized into a

diamond some 4,000 km (2,500 miles) across. BPM 37093 is around 50 light years from Earth in the constellation of Centaurus.

★ OLDEST STAR IN THE MILKY WAY

The star HE1327-2326 is located 4,000 light years from Earth. Its age is measured by its composition. When the universe was formed, it consisted of hydrogen with some helium. As it evolved, the rest of the chemical elements appeared, formed by nuclear synthesis in stars. HE1327-2326 has almost no metal content in it (just 1/300,000th of the metal content of our own Sun), so must have formed from clouds of almost pure hydrogen and helium gas when the universe was young. It may date back to just after the very start of the universe, around 13.7 billion years ago.

★ NEW RECORD
★ UPDATED RECORD

★ LARGEST STAR

Owing to the physical difficulties in directly measuring the size of a distant star, the identity of the largest star is a matter for debate among astronomers. The current most likely candidate is VY Canis Majoris, a red supergiant some 5,000 light years away. Estimates of its size give it a diameter of 2.5–3 billion km (1.55–1.86 billion miles), or 1,800–2,100 times that of the Sun. If placed at the centre of the Solar System, the star's outer surface would reach beyond the orbit of Jupiter.

LARGEST CONSTELLATION

Of the 88 constellations, Hydra (the Sea Serpent) is the largest, covering 3.16% of the whole sky and containing at least 68 stars visible to the naked eye (to 5.5 magnitude). The constellation Centaurus (Centaur), which ranks ninth in area, embraces at least 94 such stars.

★ MOST STARS IN A STAR SYSTEM

The greatest number of stars in a single star system is six. There are a few known examples but the most famous is Castor, the second brightest star in the constellation of Gemini.

★ MOST COMMON TYPE OF STAR

By far the most common class of star in our galaxy and the Universe are red dwarfs. These are weak, dim stars with no more than 40% of the mass of the Sun, and the brightest of them shines at only 10% of the Sun's luminosity. Because they burn their fuel so slowly they have life spans much longer than our own star, of at

least 10 billion years. Around 80% of all stars in our local neighbourhood are red dwarfs.

★ NEAREST RED SUPERGIANT

Betelgeuse, in the constellation of Orion, lies just 427 light years from the Solar System. Like all red supergiants, it is a massive star nearing the end of its relatively short life span of perhaps just a few million years in total. It has a mass of around 14 times that of the Sun and varies in size between around 400 and 600 times the Sun's diameter.

NEAREST STAR VISIBLE TO THE NAKED EYE

The nearest star visible to the naked eye is the southern-hemisphere binary Alpha Centauri (4.40 light years distant).

★ SHORTEST-LIVED STARS

With masses of around 100 times that of the Sun, "blue supergiants" (seen right in a computer simulation) burn through their fuel extremely quickly and can last for as little as 10 million years. Their blue colour is a consequence of their very high surface temperatures of around 20,000–50,000°C (36,032–90,032°F).

One of the best known is Rigel in the constellation of Orion. It is the sixth brightest star in the sky, even though it is around 900 light years away.

Antares

Reigel   Sirius A   Sun

BRIGHTEST SUPERNOVA

In April 1006, the supernova SN 1006 was noted near the star Beta Lupi; it flared for two years and reached a magnitude of -9.5. This titanic cosmic explosion could be seen with the naked eye for 24 months and, at its brightest, was 1,500 times brighter than Sirius A.

In 1987, a giant star in the Large Magellanic Cloud, a satellite galaxy of our own Milky Way, exploded in the **brightest supernova of modern times**. Its peak brightness was magnitude 2.3 – easily visible without a telescope.

★ MOST MAGNETIC OBJECTS

A magnetar is a type of neutron star (a body created from the remains of a collapsed star) that possesses a stupendously powerful magnetic field of around 10 thousand million teslas. (Earth has a magnetic field of around 50 microteslas.) Measuring around 20 km (12 miles) across, a magnetar should theoretically be able to wipe the data from a credit card at a distance equivalent to halfway to the Moon.

DENSEST OBJECTS IN THE UNIVERSE

Black holes are the remnants of stars that ended their lives as supernovae. They are characterized by a region of space in which gravity is so strong that not even light can escape. The boundary of a black hole is known as the "event horizon". At its centre is the "singularity", where the mass of the dead star is compressed to a point of zero size and infinite density, generating the black hole's powerful gravitational field.

HOTTEST PLACE IN THE SOLAR SYSTEM

The temperature at the centre of the Sun has been estimated at 15,600,000°C (28,080,000°F). The pressure at the heart of the Sun is huge – around 250 billion times the pressure at sea level on Earth – and it is here that around 600 million tonnes of hydrogen are fused into helium every second. This ongoing nuclear reaction is what makes the Sun shine.

BRIGHTEST OPEN STAR CLUSTER

Located in the constellation of Taurus, the Pleiades (M45) – also known as the Seven Sisters – contains approximately 500 individual stars in a region of space roughly 20 light years across, and at an average distance of around 380 light years from Earth. Even from a major light-polluted city, around six of the Pleiades can be seen with the naked eye.

• The nearest brown dwarf to the Earth is Epsilon Indi B, a companion to the star Epsilon Indi, 11.8 light years away.

BRIGHTEST STAR VIEWED FROM EARTH

Sirius A (alpha Canis Majoris), located 8.64 light years from Earth, is the brightest star in the night sky, with an apparent magnitude of -1.46. It has a diameter of 2.33 million km (1.45 million miles), a mass 2.14 times that of the Sun and is visually 24 times brighter than the Sun.

NEAREST BROWN DWARF

Brown dwarfs are often referred to as "failed stars". Like other stars, they form from clouds of galactic gas and dust, which collapse under their own gravity. If the resulting star is less than 0.08 times the mass of the Sun, its core never becomes hot enough to initiate hydrogen fusion and the star is never "born". Brown dwarfs represent the missing link between stars and planets.

GALAXIES & NEBULAE

SPACE STATS

The Solar System is located in a spiral arm of the Milky Way galaxy, some 26,000 light years from the centre. The Milky Way is around 100,000 light years across, 12,000 light years thick and contains between 200 billion and 400 billion stars.

The Andromeda Galaxy is similar to our own and, at 2.2 million light years' distance, is one of the closest galaxies to ours. Because of the time it takes light from the galaxy to reach Earth, we are seeing Andromeda as it was 2.2 million years ago.

The Milky Way and Andromeda galaxies belong to a collection of around 35 galaxies known as the "Local Group". It is part of the Virgo Supercluster of around 100 groups and clusters of galaxies.

It is thought there are about 130 billion galaxies in the universe, which is around 13.8 billion years old.

It is possible for two galaxies to collide without a single star hitting another.

★ LARGEST SATELLITE GALAXY

To date, some 15 minor satellite galaxies have been discovered orbiting our Milky Way galaxy, the most recent of which was discovered in 2006. Of these, the largest and brightest is the Large Magellanic Cloud, some 160,000 light years from the centre of the Milky Way. It is classed as a dwarf irregular galaxy and measures around 20,000 light years across, with a mass of around 10 billion solar masses.

★ LARGEST SPIRAL GALAXY

Discovered in 1986, Malin 1 is a spiral galaxy some 1.1 billion light years away. In terms of its diameter, it is the largest known spiral galaxy in the Universe, measuring around 650,000 light years across – several times the size of our Milky Way.

★ YOUNGEST PLANETARY NEBULA

The Stingray Nebula, located 18,000 light years away in the southern constellation of Ara, was observed as a star in the 1970s. In 1996, the Hubble Space Telescope imaged it and found that, in the intervening 20 years, its central star had heated up enough to make the ejected gas shells that surround it glow as a planetary nebula.

★ LONGEST GALACTIC JET

In December 2007, astronomers announced their discovery of an energetic jet of matter that was being emitted from a supermassive black hole in the centre of the active galaxy CGCG 049-033. Measuring some 1.5 million light years long, the high-energy jet happens to be pointed directly at a nearby galaxy. Any planets in that galaxy in the line of fire would have their atmospheres ionized, extinguishing any life there.

COLDEST PLACE IN THE MILKY WAY

The coldest place in the universe is in the Boomerang Nebula, a cloud of dust and gases 5,000 light years from Earth. It has a temperature of -272°C (-457.6°F) and is formed by the rapid expansion of gas and dust flowing away from its central ageing star.

★ CLOSEST ACTIVE GALAXY

Galaxies that contain a compact highly luminous core that emits intense radiation are known as active galaxies. The source of the radiation is believed to be a vast disc of shredded stars and other matter being swallowed by a central supermassive black hole. At just 11 million light years away, the enormous elliptical galaxy Centaurus A is the closest of these active galaxies to our own.

"Our galaxy is only one of some hundred thousand million that can be seen using modern telescopes."

Professor Stephen W. Hawking

CLOSEST PLANETARY NEBULA

At a distance of around 400 light years, the Helix Nebula (also known as NGC 7293) is the closest planetary nebula to the Earth. It formed when a dying star threw off its outer layers, which are gradually expanding into space. They are called planetary nebulae because astronomers originally believed they were new planets, due to their often spherical shapes. The Helix Nebula is around 100 times more distant than the nearest stars (excluding the Sun).

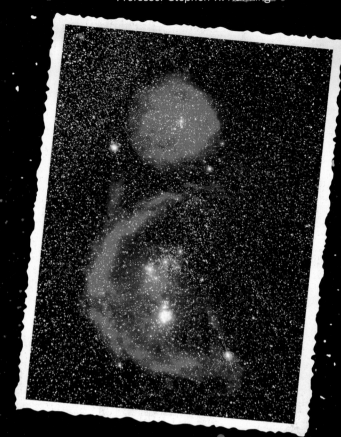

★ CLOSEST GALAXY TO THE MILKY WAY

The Canis Major dwarf galaxy was only discovered in 2003 by a team of French, Italian, British and Australian astronomers. It lies an average of just 42,000 light years from the centre of our galaxy. It was hard to detect because it is behind the plane of our spiral galaxy as seen from Earth. The shape of the dwarf galaxy indicates it is in the process of being ripped apart and absorbed by the gravity of the Milky Way.

The galaxy contains a high percentage of red giant stars and is thought to contain around 1 billion stars in total.

★ LARGEST NEBULAE SEEN FROM EARTH

As seen from Earth, the vast cloud of molecular hydrogen known as Barnard's Loop is a faintly glowing arc only visible in long-exposure images. At an average distance of around 1,600 light years and measuring around 300 light years across, it contains the famous Orion and Horsehead nebulae. If it were visible to the naked eye, Barnard's Loop would fill most of the entire constellation of Orion in the night sky.

BRIGHTEST SUPERNOVA REMNANT

The Crab Nebula (M1), in the constellation of Taurus (the Bull), is the brightest supernova remnant in the sky, with a magnitude of 8.4.

HEAVENLY BODIES

SUPERLATIVE SATELLITES

PLANET WITH THE MOST MOONS

As of 2008, astronomers had discovered 63 natural satellites for the planet Jupiter. Saturn has the second greatest number of moons, with 60. Most of these moons are small irregularly shaped bodies of ice and rock, and many are almost certainly captured asteroids.

CLOSEST MOON TO A PLANET

The tiny Martian moon Phobos orbits Mars at an altitude of 9,378 km (5,827 miles) from the planet's centre – or 5,981 km (3,716 miles) above Mars' surface.

MOST DISTANT MOON FROM A PLANET

On 3 September 2003, the International Astronomical Union announced the discovery of the moon S/2003 N1, which orbits Neptune at an average distance of almost 49.5 million km (31 million miles). It has an orbital period of approximately 26 years and measures around 38 km (24 miles) across.

TALLEST RIDGE IN THE SOLAR SYSTEM

Observations of Saturn's moon Iapetus by the NASA/ESA spacecraft *Cassini-Huygens*, on 31 December 2004, revealed an enormous ridge, at least 1,300 km (800 miles) long, which reaches an altitude of around 20 km (12 miles) above the surface. Iapetus is 1,400 km (890 miles) across.

MOST DISTANT IMAGE OF EARTH

On 4 February 1990, NASA's *Voyager 1* spacecraft turned its camera back towards the Sun and the planets. After 12.5 years in space, travelling away from Earth, *Voyager 1*'s camera took a picture of our home planet from a distance of almost 6.5 billion km (4 billion miles).

TALLEST NON-VOLCANIC MOUNTAINS IN THE SOLAR SYSTEM

Boosaule Montes, on Jupiter's active moon Io, are up to 16,000 m (52,493 ft) tall. Rather than being built up by volcanic eruptions, like Olympus Mons (the **tallest mountain in the Solar System** – see opposite page), they were formed by tectonic activity generated by huge stresses in Io's crust.

MOST VOLCANICALLY ACTIVE BODY

When NASA's *Voyager 1* probe passed by the giant planet Jupiter in 1979, its camera imaged Jupiter's moon Io. The photographs revealed enormous volcanic eruption plumes, some reaching hundreds of kilometres into space. This activity is driven by tidal energy inside Io, created as a result of gravitational interactions between Io, Jupiter and one of the other moons, Europa.

DEEPEST CRATER

The largest impact basin on the Moon is the far-side South Pole-Aitken, which is 2,250 km (1,400 miles) in diameter and on average 12,000 m (39,000 ft) deep below its rim. This is the largest and deepest such crater known in the Solar System.

DID YOU KNOW?

The NASA/ESA Cassini-Huygens spacecraft was launched on 15 October 1997. At 5,655 kg (12,467 lb), this unmanned probe is the heaviest ever launched to the outer Solar System.

★TALLEST NITROGEN GEYSERS

When *Voyager 2* encountered Neptune and its large moon Triton in 1989, its cameras discovered active cryovolcanism in the form of geysers of nitrogen gas and snow.

Reaching heights of up to 8 km (5 miles), these eruptions are believed to be brought about by weak sunlight heating nitrogen ice located just below the moon's surface.

MOST REFLECTIVE BODY

The most reflective body in the Solar System is Enceladus, a small moon of Saturn with a surface composed mainly of icy material. It reflects some 90% of the sunlight that illuminates it, making it more reflective than freshly fallen snow.

★ LARGEST MARTIAN FROZEN LAKE

While scientists are certain that Mars holds vast amounts of frozen water at its poles and under ground, the discovery of a lake of frozen water in 2005 represents a first in the 40-year history of Martian exploration. Sitting in an unnamed crater near the Martian north pole, the lake, which is around 15 km (9 miles) across, was discovered by ESA's *Mars Express* spacecraft.

★ TALLEST VENUSIAN MOUNTAIN

Maxwell Montes, on the Ishtar Terra plateau (pictured below in a computer simulation) is the highest point on Venus, reaching 11 km (6.8 miles) above the planet's average surface altitude (the Venusian equivalent of sea level). It is named after UK physicist James Maxwell, who devised laws that related electricity to magnetism – the basis for radar.

★ LARGEST MOLTEN CORE

Relative to its size, the planet Mercury has the largest molten metallic core of all the planets in the Solar System. With a radius of around 1,800 km (1,118 miles), the core takes up around 42% of the planet's volume, compared with just 15% for the Earth's core. Being only around 6% the mass of Earth, Mercury's core was previously believed to have cooled billions of years ago.

NASA's *Messenger* spacecraft, which is currently studying the planet, will hopefully provide data that explains Mercury's molten interior.

★ LEAST ROUND PLANET

A combination of its low density (less than water) and rapid rotation (once every 10.6 hours) gives Saturn the most oblate shape of all the planets. Its equatorial diameter is 120,536 km (74,897.5 miles); its polar diameter is just 108,728 km (67,560 miles).

★ LARGEST PLANETARY RING

The outermost major ring of Saturn, the E ring, is a tenuous and ethereal sheet of countless tiny particles. It extends from roughly the orbit of the moon Mimas out to roughly the orbit of the moon Rhea – a width of around 340,000 km (211,260 miles). Recent discoveries by the *Cassini* spacecraft have revealed that the E ring is being constantly replenished by water ice eruption plumes from the active moon Enceladus.

★ SMALLEST BODY WITH A RING SYSTEM

In March 2008, scientists announced the discovery of what seems to be a ring along with a debris disc around Saturn's moon Rhea. All four gas giant planets in the Solar System have a ring system but, at just 1,530 km (950 miles) across, Rhea is the smallest world with one.

FARTHEST RESTING PLACE

On 31 July 1999, America's *Lunar Prospector* spacecraft crashed into the lunar surface after 18 months of successful mission operations. This orbiter contained a small (3.8-cm; 1.5-in) polycarbonate container holding one ounce of the remains of planetary science pioneer Dr Eugene Shoemaker.

LARGEST CHAOTICALLY ROTATING OBJECT

Saturn's moon Hyperion measures 410 x 260 x 220 km (254 x 161 x 136 miles) and is the largest highly irregularly shaped body in the Solar System. It is one of only two bodies in the Solar System discovered to have completely chaotic rotation, essentially randomly tumbling in its orbit around Saturn. The other is asteroid 4179 Toutatis, measuring 4.5 x 2.4 x 2.9 km (2.7 x 1.5 x 1.8 miles).

TALLEST MOUNTAIN IN THE SOLAR SYSTEM

The peak of Martian mountain Olympus Mons towers 25 km (15 miles) – nearly three times the height of Mt Everest – above its base. Because of its shape, it is termed a shield volcano.

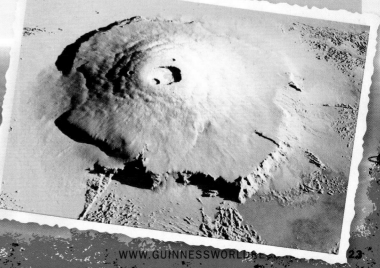

ASTEROIDS, COMETS, & METEORS

GREATEST RECORDED IMPACT IN THE SOLAR SYSTEM

Between 16 and 22 July 1994, more than 20 fragments of comet Shoemaker-Levy 9 collided with the giant planet Jupiter, leaving a series of colossal bruises in its atmosphere. The greatest impact was that of the "G" fragment, which exploded with the energy of roughly 600 times the world's nuclear arsenal, equivalent to 6 million megatons of TNT.

to a combination of the brightness of its surface, its size (576 km, or 357.9 miles, across) and the fact that it can approach Earth as close as 177 million km (110 million miles).

★ MOST COMET TAILS ENCOUNTERED BY A SPACECRAFT

In February 2007, the NASA/European Space Agency (ESA) spacecraft *Ulysses* unexpectedly flew through the tail of Comet McNaught, some 260 million km (160 million miles) distant from the comet's core. This was the spacecraft's third passage through a cometary tail – in 1996 and 2004, *Ulysses* flew through the tails of comets Hyakutake and McNaught-Hartley respectively.

COLOSSAL COMETS

LARGEST COMET

Discovered in May 1977, Centaur 2060 Chiron has a 182-km (113-mile) diameter.

CLOSEST APPROACH TO EARTH BY A COMET

On 1 July 1770, Lexell's Comet, travelling at a speed of 138,600 km/h (86,100 mph) relative to the Sun, came to within 2,200,000 km (1,360,000 miles) of the Earth.

BRIGHTEST ASTEROID

Asteroid 4 Vesta, discovered on 29 March 1807, is the only asteroid visible to the naked eye. This is owing

★ FIRST IMPACT ON A COMET

On 4 July 2005, a 350-kg (771-lb) copper "bullet" ejected from NASA's *Deep Impact* spacecraft hit the surface of comet Tempel 1 at a velocity of 10.3 km/sec (6.4 miles/sec). The impact, which was the equivalent of 4.7 tonnes (10,360 lb) of TNT, created a huge ejecta plume and a crater on the comet around 100 m (328 ft) wide and 30 m (98 ft) deep.

★ FIRST LANDING ON AN ASTEROID

On 12 February 2001, NASA's *NEAR Shoemaker* spacecraft touched down on the asteroid Eros, after 12 months of orbital observations. The landing was considered a mission bonus as the spacecraft had no landing gear but still survived after an impact velocity of 1.5–1.8 m/sec (4 ft 10 in/sec– 5 ft 10 in/sec).

SMALLEST OBJECT LANDED ON

On 20 November 2005, the Japanese spacecraft *Hayabusa* made the first of two touchdowns on asteroid Itokawa in an attempt to collect samples to take back to Earth. Itokawa measures just 500 m (1,600 ft) across its longest axis.

GREATEST NUMBER OF ASTEROIDS DISCOVERED BY AN INDIVIDUAL

Dr Eugene Shoemaker (USA, 1928–97) was one of the most eminent geologists of the 20th century. Best known for his work on extraterrestrial impacts, he discovered 1,125 asteroids, many in partnership with his wife, Caroline.

★ **NEW RECORD**
★ **UPDATED RECORD**

METEORIC MARVELS

History's **greatest meteor shower** occurred on the night of 16–17 November 1966, when the Leonid meteors (so called as they appear from the direction of the constellation of Leo) were visible between western North America and eastern Russia (then USSR). Meteors passed over Arizona, USA, at a rate of 2,300 per minute for 20 minutes from 5 a.m. on 17 November 1966.

The Leonids are also the **fastest annual meteor shower**: they enter Earth's atmosphere at a speed of around 71 km/sec (44 miles/sec).

on our planet. The scientists had studied ancient rock samples from Australia and South Africa and analysed spherules (tiny spherical particles) contained within. They discovered that the impacting body had a diameter of approximately 20 km (12 miles).

LARGEST ASTEROID IN THE MAIN ASTEROID BELT

The largest asteroid is 1 Ceres (the first discovered, by G. Piazzi at Palermo, Sicily, on 1 January 1801) with an average diameter of 941 km (584.7 miles).

★ LARGEST COLLECTION OF ASTEROIDS

The main asteroid belt lies between the orbits of Mars and Jupiter. It contains between 700,000 and 1,700,000 asteroids that are at least 1 km (0.6 miles) across, and many millions of smaller bodies.

The total mass of the asteroid belt is equivalent to just 4% of the mass of Earth's Moon, with around half the mass of the whole belt accounted for by the four largest asteroids.

X-REF
The story of mankind's sojourns in space is a heady mix of scientific savvy and sheer heroism. Discover the amazing history of the **Moon Landings** for yourself: take off for p.83 now!

GREATEST RECORDED IMPACT ON EARTH

An explosion recorded over the basin of the Podkamennaya Tunguska River, Russia, on 30 June 1908 was equivalent to 10–15 megatons of high-explosive and resulted in the devastation of an area of 3,900 km^2 (1,500 miles^2). The shock wave was felt up to 1,000 km (620 miles) away. The cause is thought to have been the energy released following the total disintegration, at an altitude of 10 km (6 miles), of a common type of stony meteoroid 30 m (100 ft) in diameter.

The **oldest recorded impact on Earth** was revealed on 23 August 2002. A team of US scientists led by Gary Byerly (Louisiana State University) and Donald Lowe (Stanford University) announced their discovery of a 3.47-billion-year-old asteroid impact

★ LARGEST SOURCE OF COMETS

Beyond the orbit of Neptune lie the Kuiper Belt, the Scattered Disc and the Oort Cloud, collectively known as Trans-Neptunian Objects. The Oort Cloud is a spherical cloud of thousands of billions of cometary nuclei. It surrounds the Sun at a distance of around 50,000 Astronomical Units (1 AU = the distance from the Earth to the Sun), which is around 1,000 times the distance from the Sun to Pluto. It is believed to be the source of most of the comets that visit the inner Solar System.

★ LARGEST TRANS-NEPTUNIAN OBJECT

Sedna, discovered in 2003, is an icy world measuring between 1,180 km and 1,800 km (733–1,118 miles). It takes an estimated 12,000 years for Sedna to orbit the Sun once.

★ FIRST SAMPLE RETURNED FROM A COMET

An engineer carries out final checks on NASA's *Stardust* spacecraft prior to its launch on 7 January 1999. *Stardust* encountered the comet Wild 2 on 2 January 2004, sweeping up tiny, precious samples of its dust in an aerogel collector.

ASTRONOMY

★ LARGEST REFRACTING TELESCOPE

The largest refractor, which uses a lens instead of a mirror to gather and focus light, is at the Yerkes Observatory in Wisconsin, USA. Built in 1897, it has a primary lens diameter of 1.02 m (3 ft 4 in).

MOST EXPENSIVE TELESCOPE SOLD AT AUCTION

A very rare type of binocular telescope signed and dated in 1720 was sold at Christie's, London, UK, in December 1998 for £155,500 ($256,591).

★ LARGEST LIQUID MIRROR

The Large Zenith Telescope in Canada uses a mirror made from liquid mercury. By spinning the 3-tonne (6,613-lb), 6-m-diameter (19-ft 8-in) mercury mirror, the liquid forms a concave mirror shape perfect for astronomical observations.

LARGEST...

AIRBORNE TELESCOPE

NASA's Stratospheric Observatory for Infrared Astronomy is a Boeing 747SP fitted with an infrared telescope bearing a 2.7-m-wide (8-ft 10-in) primary mirror. Its "first light" occurred on 18 August 2004.

★ COSMIC RAY TELESCOPE

The Pierre Auger Observatory is a vast array of some 1,600 particle detectors arranged across 3,000 km^2 (1,158 miles^2) of western Argentina. It was designed to detect very high-energy cosmic ray particles produced by supermassive black holes.

FULLY ROBOTIC TELESCOPE

Owned by the Astrophysics Research Institute (ARI) of Liverpool John Moores University (UK), the Liverpool Telescope is located on La Palma, Canary Islands, Spain, and has a main mirror with a diameter of 2 m (6 ft 6 in). It was designed for observing visible and near-infrared wavelengths, and achieved "first light" on 27 July 2003.

FACT
The Large Binocular Telescope is the world's **highest-resolution and most technologically advanced optical telescope**. It is capable of creating images in the near infrared with 10 times the resolution of the Hubble Space Telescope.

★ LARGEST BINOCULAR TELESCOPE

The Large Binocular Telescope comprises two identical telescopes, each with an 8.4-m-diameter (27-ft 6-in) main mirror. Working in tandem, they have an equivalent light-gathering power of a single mirror 11.8 m (38 ft 8 in) across. The telescope – which is located on a mountain top in Arizona, USA – became fully functional in March 2008.

LARGEST LAND-BASED TELESCOPE

The twin Keck Telescopes, on the summit of Hawaii's dormant Mauna Kea volcano, are the world's largest land-based optical and infrared telescopes.

Each Keck telescope is eight stories tall and weighs 300 tons (600,000 lb), and each has a 10-m (32-ft) mirror, made up of 36 hexagonal segments which act together to create a single reflective surface. With these telescopes, you would be able to see a golf ball 150 km (93.2 miles) away.

★ NEW RECORD
☆ UPDATED RECORD

LENS

The world's largest refracting optical lens measures 1.827 m (5 ft 11 in) in diameter. It was built by a team led by Thomas Peck (USA), at the Optics Shop of the Optical Sciences Center of the University of Arizona in Tucson, Arizona, USA, and completed in January 2000. It was built as a test for the secondary mirror of the 6.5-m (21-ft 4-in) MMT Telescope on Mt Hopkins, Arizona, USA.

RADIO TELESCOPE DISH

The world's largest dish radio telescope is the partially steerable ionospheric assembly built over a natural bowl at Arecibo, Puerto Rico, completed in November 1963. The dish is 305 m (1,000 ft) in diameter and covers 7.48 ha (18.5 acres) in area – similar to 14 football fields.

★ SOLAR TELESCOPE

The McMath-Pierce Solar Telescope on Kitt Peak, Arizona, USA, opened in 1962. Light from the Sun is collected via a 152-m-long (498-ft) slanted shaft, which directs sunlight on to a 1.6-m (5-ft 3-in) mirror 50 m (164 ft) below ground. It forms an 85-cm-wide (33-in) high-resolution image of the Sun.

★ SUBMILLIMETRE TELESCOPE

Beyond the red end of the visible spectrum of light lies infrared radiation, microwaves and radio waves. The largest telescope designed to study the universe at the wavelengths between the far infrared and microwaves – the submillimetre region – is the James Clerk Maxwell Telescope, on Mauna Kea, Hawaii. Rather than an optical mirror, it uses a massive 15-m (49-ft) dish to collect submillimetre radiation.

★ LARGEST SINGLE OPTICAL TELESCOPE

The Gran Telescopio Canarias (GTC) achieved "first light" on 13 July 2007. Located on the island of La Palma, it has a main mirror made up of 36 hexagonal segments and a diameter of 10.4 m (34 ft). The huge telescope and its 35-m (114-ft) dome took seven years to build.

★ LARGEST GATHERING OF MAJOR TELESCOPES

Kitt Peak, a 2,096-m-high (6,876-ft) mountain in Arizona, USA, is home to the Kitt Peak National Observatory. Its excellent seeing conditions and atmospheric clarity have attracted the construction of 23 major telescopes on its summit since 1958.

SPACE TELESCOPES

• The **most powerful gamma ray telescope** was the Compton Gamma Ray Observatory, launched in 1991. After nine years of observations, it re-entered the Earth's atmosphere and burned up on 4 June 2000.

• The Chandra X-Ray Telescope, launched in July 1999, is the world's **most powerful X-ray telescope**. It has a resolving power equivalent to the ability to read a stop sign at a distance of 19 km (12 miles).

• NASA's Spitzer Space Telescope – the **largest infrared space telescope** – was launched into Earth's orbit on 25 August 2003. It is the best tool astronomers have for observing the heat emissions from objects in deep space as well as our own Solar System. The instrument has a total mass of 950 kg (2,094 lb).

SPACE TECHNOLOGY

LARGEST SPACE FUNERAL

The ashes of 24 space pioneers and enthusiasts, including *Star Trek* creator Gene Roddenberry (above), were sent into orbit on 21 April 1997 at a cost of $4,900 (£3,000) each. The ashes stayed in orbit for up to five years before burning up in Earth's atmosphere.

★ LONGEST SPACE TETHER

The *Young Engineers Satellite 2* (YES2) was launched on 14 September 2007. On 25 September, *YES2* unwound an experimental package on a 0.5-mm-thick cable to test the principle of returning payloads to Earth without the use of retrorockets. The cable extended to its full length of 31.7 km (9.6 miles) – the longest man-made structure in space.

★ LARGEST AUTOMATED EUROPEAN SPACECRAFT

The European Space Agency's (ESA) Automated Transfer Vehicle is an unmanned cargo freighter designed to resupply astronauts on the International Space Station (ISS). Its cylindrical body measures 10.3 m (33 ft 9 in) long by 4.5 m (14 ft 9 in) across, with a mass of 20 tonnes (44,092 lb). Its cargo capacity of 7.5 tonnes (16,534 lb) is around three times that of the Russian *Progress* unmanned freighter. Its maiden launch was on 8 March 2008.

★ MOST DURABLE MARS ORBITER

NASA's *Mars Global Surveyor* was launched in 1996 and entered Martian orbit on 11 September 1997. It was due to spend just two years mapping and monitoring the planet but, due to the success of the mission and the quality of the information gathered, it was granted multiple extensions. Contact was lost with the spacecraft on 2 November 2006 – it had sent over 250,000 images of the red planet back to Earth after more than nine years in orbit.

★ LARGEST MILITARY SATELLITE CONSTELLATION

America's Global Positioning System is a coordinated constellation of at least 24 satellites in orbit around the Earth. They provide, via radio signals, precise

LARGEST SPACE STATION

The International Space Station (ISS) has been under construction since its first component, the *Zarya* module, was launched in November 1998. The latest element to be added was ESA's *Columbus* module, on 11 February 2008, bringing the total mass of the ISS so far to 245,735 kg (541,753 lb).

3D navigation data coverage for the whole world, enabling users to quickly pinpoint their location using a receiver. The GPS constellation is operated by the US Air Force 50th Space Wing and was restricted to military use until 1996.

SIGNIFICANT SPACECRAFT

Since the days of the first satellite, *Sputnik 1*, and the first manned spaceflight, *Vostok 1*, spacecraft have taken on a range of forms and uses. From manned capsules, shuttles and space stations, to Earth-orbiting satellites, unmanned planetary probes and landers, spacecraft have provided mankind with global communications and environmental monitoring, as well as being our eyes and ears as we reach out and explore the Universe at large.

VOSTOK 1
Length (of capsule and equipment module): 4.6 m (15 ft 1 in)
Mass: 4,730 kg (10,427 lb)
Launched: 12 April 1961
Duration: 1 hr 48 min
Crew: Yuri Gagarin (USSR)
First manned spaceflight

PIONEER 10
Dish diameter: 2.74 m (8 ft 11 in)
Mass: 258 kg (568 lb)
Launched: 3 March 1972
Duration: Last contact on 23 January 2003
First spacecraft to reach the outer Solar System

SPIRIT MARS ROVER
Height: 1.5 m (4 ft 11 in) with mast up
Mass: 174 kg (383 lb)
Launched: 10 June 2003
Landed (on Mars): 4 January 2004
Duration: Still operating
Longest-lasting Mars rover

EARLIEST HOMINID TO SURVIVE A SPACE FLIGHT

The first hominid to survive a space flight was Ham, a four-year-old chimpanzee who was launched by NASA on a sub-orbital test flight from Cape Canaveral, Florida, USA, on 31 January 1961. At its peak, the rocket he was travelling in reached 254 km (158 miles) above Earth, before returning to land – 16.5 minutes after launch – where Ham was recovered alive, but with a bruised nose.

FACT

Before the flight, Ham was trained to push a lever within five seconds of seeing a flashing light. Failure to do so would result in a punishment in the form of a mild electric shock to the soles of his feet, while the correct response was rewarded with a banana pellet.

★ LARGEST COMBAT SATELLITE

The Soviet *Polyus* satellite was a prototype orbital weapons platform measuring 37 m (121 ft 4 in) long, 4.1 m (13 ft 5 in) in diameter and with a mass of 80 tonnes (176,369 lb). It was equipped with an anti-satellite recoilless cannon, a sensor-blinding laser to confuse hostile satellites and a nuclear space mine launcher. Only one was ever launched, on 15 May 1987, but it failed to reach orbit and crashed into the Pacific Ocean.

MOST DURABLE SPACE STATION

Mir, the central core module of the *Mir* space station (USSR/Russia), was launched into orbit on 20 February 1986. Over the following 10 years, five modules and a docking port for US space shuttles were added to the complex. On 23 March 2001, the space station was deorbited and destroyed in a controlled re-entry over the Pacific Ocean. More than 100 people visited the *Mir* space station in its 15-year operational history.

★ NEW RECORD
★ UPDATED RECORD

LONGEST SHUTTLE FLIGHT

Space shuttle *Columbia* was launched on its 21st mission, STS80, with a crew of five (four men and one woman) on 19 November 1996. The flight lasted 17 days 15 hr 53 min 26 sec to main gear shutdown.

APOLLO 11 LUNAR MODULE
Height: 6.37 m (20 ft 10 in)
Mass: 16,488 kg (36,349 lb)
Launched: 16 July 1969
Duration: Five days
First manned lunar landing

CASSINI-HUYGENS
Length: body and dish 6.8 m (22 ft 3 in)
Mass: 2,500 kg (5,511 lb)
Launched: 15 October 1997
Duration: Still operating
First spacecraft to orbit Saturn

HUBBLE
Length: 13.2 m (43 ft 4 in)
Mass: 11,000 kg (24,250 lb)
Launched: 24 April 1990
Duration: Still operating
Most powerful optical space telescope

LIVING PLANET

CONTENTS

LARGEST LAND CARNIVORE

The largest of all land carnivores is the polar bear (*Ursus maritimus*). Adult males typically weigh 400–600 kg (880–1,320 lb) and have a nose-to-tail length of 2.4–2.6 m (7 ft 10 in–8 ft 6 in). The male Kodiak bear (*U. arctos middendorffi*), a sub-species of brown bear found on Kodiak Island and the adjacent Afognak and Shuyak islands in the Gulf of Alaska, USA, is usually shorter in length than the polar bear and more robustly built.

OCEANS

★ COUNTRY WITH THE GREATEST NUMBER OF SEAWEED SPECIES

With almost 3,000 different species, Australia boasts the greatest number of seaweed species of any country. The majority occur in the more temperate, nutrient-rich southern waters, and a large number of those are endemic to Australia, occurring nowhere else in the world.

★ RAREST PENGUIN

The yellow-eyed penguin *Megadyptes antipodes* is found only in New Zealand. Also claimed to be the most ancient species of modern-day penguin, as well as the world's third largest, its total population probably does not exceed 4,500–5,000 individuals. Its survival is threatened by habitat loss and predation by non-native mammals, such as ferrets, cats and stoats.

★ MOST MARINE SPIDER

Spiders are not normally sea-living creatures. *Desis marina* is classed as semi-marine, as it lives on exposed coral reefs and intertidal rocks in Australia and New Zealand. When the tide comes in, it hides away inside disused seaworm burrows, blocking the water out with a lid woven from silk, and it can survive there under water for several days.

LARGEST FISH

The **heaviest cartilaginous fish**, and also the **largest fish** of all, is the whale shark (*Rhincodon typus*). The largest recorded example measured 12.65 m (41 ft 6 in) long, 7 m (23 ft) round the thickest part of the body and weighed an estimated 15–21 tonnes (33,000–46,200 lb). It was caught near Karachi, Pakistan, in 1949.

LARGEST AREA OF CALM WATER

The Sargasso Sea in the north Atlantic Ocean covers about 6.2 million km² (2.4 million miles²) of relatively still water. Its surface is largely covered by sargassum seaweed.

★ SMALLEST SQUID

Currently known only from two specimens, the world's smallest squid is *Parateuthis tunicata*, collected by the German South Polar Expedition of 1901–03. The larger of these two specimens measured 1.27 cm (0.5 in) long, including its tentacles.

★ SMALLEST OCTOPUS

Sri Lanka's *Octopus arborescens* has an arm-span of less than 5.1 cm (2 in).

★ LONGEST RECORDED
JOURNEY BY A SHARK

On 7 November 2003, a team of researchers led by Dr Ramón Bonfil from the Wildlife Conservation Society (USA) electronically tagged four sharks in South Africa, one of whom was nicknamed Nicole (after actress and shark-lover Nicole Kidman). In August 2004, Nicole was identified off the coast of South Africa, yet her timed-release tag was recovered in Australia six months earlier in February, where a satellite recorded its transmission. Thus, within nine months, this great white had swum 20,000 km (12,400 miles) across an entire ocean, from South Africa to Australia and back, and in doing so completed the longest recorded journey by a shark.

SLOWEST FISH

Sea horses (family Syngnathidae) are incapable of swimming against the current and, to avoid being swept away, hang on to coral and marine plants with their prehensile tails. Their swimming ability is severely limited by a rigid body structure. The major source of propulsion is the wave motion of the dorsal fin: this makes a ripple, which drives the fish forward in an erect posture. Some of the smaller species such as the dwarf sea horse (*Hippocampus zosterae*), which reaches a maximum length of only 4.2 cm (1.7 in), probably never attain speeds of more than 0.016 km/h (0.001 mph).

★ **NEW RECORD**
★ **UPDATED RECORD**

MOST VENOMOUS FISH

The most venomous fish in the world are the stonefish (family Synanceiidae) that inhabit the tropical waters of the Indo-Pacific. Direct contact with the spines of their fins, which contain a strong neurotoxic venom, can prove fatal. Pictured is the reed stonefish (*Synanceia verrucosa*), camouflaged like a rock.

DID YOU KNOW?

Puffer fish of the genus *Tetraodon* of the Red Sea and Indo-Pacific region deliver a fatally poisonous toxin called tetrodotoxin. These fish are the **most poisonous fish edible by humans**.

★ FIRST METHANE-SUSTAINED ANIMALS

In July 1997, Professor Charles Fisher led a team of scientists from Pennsylvania State University, Pennsylvania, USA, in a mini-submarine down 548 m (1,800 ft) to the Gulf of Mexico's ocean floor. Here they observed mushroom-shaped mounds of yellow and white methane ice (gas hydrates), 1.8–2.4 m (6–8 ft) across. These mounds were assumed to be too noxious to support any form of animal life, but Fisher's team discovered large numbers of a hitherto unknown species of pink, flat-bodied polychaete worms thriving on and burrowing into these mounds. They have been grazing upon chemosynthetic bacteria growing on the methane ice.

★ MOST COMMON SHARK

The spiny dogfish (*Squalus acanthias*) occurs in cold and temperate marine waters worldwide. Supporting important fisheries in several countries, the record catch for this species probably occurred in 1904–05, when some 27 million spiny dogfishes were caught off the coast of Massachusetts, USA, alone.

DEEPEST DIVE BY A PINNIPED

In May 1989, scientists testing the diving abilities of northern elephant seals (*Mirounga angustirostris*, juvenile pictured) off the coast of San Miguel Island, California, USA, measured a maximum depth of 1,529 m (5,017 ft).

★ SMALLEST SHARK

Because it is difficult to determine precisely when a small species is sexually mature (i.e., an adult and fully grown), there are three contenders for the smallest species of shark. Adult males of the dwarf lantern shark (*Etmopterus perryi*) measure a total length of 16–17.5 cm (6.3–6.8 in) with one confirmed male adult specimen collected measuring 19 cm or 7.4 in long, and mature females are typically 19–20 cm (7.4–7.8 in) long.

Prior to the discovery of the dwarf lantern shark, the record-holder was the spined pygmy shark (*Squaliolus laticaudus*), males of which measure 15 cm (6 in), and females 17–20 cm (6.7–7.8 in). A third rival, the pygmy ribbontail catshark (*Eridacnis radcliffei*), has males measuring 18–19 cm (7–7.4 in) and females possibly mature at 15–16 cm (6–6.3 in).

RIVERS, LAKES & PONDS

★ MOST POISONOUS SALAMANDER

The skin, blood and muscles of the California newt (*Taricha torosa*) all contain tetrodotoxin – an extremely toxic substance that acts as a powerful nerve poison. Laboratory experiments have shown that just a single tiny drop is poisonous enough to kill several thousand mice. The newt itself, however, is immune to even extremely high concentrations of it.

★ NEW RECORD
★ UPDATED RECORD

ACTUAL SIZE

MOST ELECTRIC FISH

The electric eel or paroque (*Electrophorus electricus*) that lives in rivers in Brazil and the Guianas, is not an eel at all, but a relative of the piranha. Up to 1.8 m (6 ft) in length, the fish is live from head to tail with its electrical apparatus consisting of two pairs of longitudinal organs. The shock, which can measure up to 650 volts, is used to immobilize prey and is strong enough to light an electric bulb or to stun an adult human.

– an alga that had formed as a layer of scum over the surface of the lake. This blue-green algal species produces nodularin, a hepatotoxin, which causes blood to collect in the liver. This, in turn, induces circulatory shock and often brings about the animal's death by internal haemorrhaging (bleeding).

★ LARGEST FRESHWATER BLUE-GREEN ALGAL BLOOM

The largest ever recorded blue-green algal bloom occurred during 1991–92 along the Barwon-Darling River in Australia. Dominated by *Anabaena circinalis*, which secretes dangerous neurotoxins, the bloom spread for over 1,000 km (620 miles) along the river, killing domesticated livestock that drank the river's contaminated water.

★ DEEPEST LIVING INSECT

Larvae of the non-biting midge *Sergentia koschowi* have been found thriving at a depth of 1,360 m (4,462 ft) within Siberia's Lake Baikal, the world's **deepest lake**. This is the greatest water depth recorded for any insect.

★ FIRST ANIMAL POISONING BY A FRESHWATER BLUE-GREEN ALGAL BLOOM

In the late 19th century, dogs, sheep, pigs, horses and cattle all died after drinking water from Lake Alexandrina in South Australia. The cause of death was poisoning from *Nodularia spumigene*

LARGEST RIVER TO DRY UP

The Yellow River (Huang He) is China's second longest river. It is known as China's Sorrow because of the millions of people killed in disastrous seasonal floods, while suffering from too little water the rest of the time. In 1997 and 1998, the Yellow River ran completely dry along its lower section for over 140 days in each year, leaving farmland parched and threatening the autumn harvest. For several months a year, the 5,460-km (3,390-mile) river now dries up in the Henan Province some 400 km (250 miles) before it reaches the sea.

FARTHEST RANGE OF AN ARCHER FISH

The archer fish (*Toxotes jaculator*) is found in Thailand's rivers. It lurks near the banks, waiting for a suitable insect to alight on a water plant within its amazing 1.5-m (5-ft) range. The fish shoots a jet of water at the prey from its tubulated (tube-shaped) mouth. If the fish misses its prey, it is able to attempt again in quick succession.

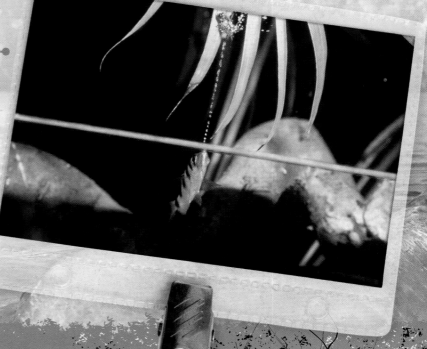

MOST PATERNAL AMPHIBIAN

The West European midwife toad (*Alytes obstetricans*) takes its name from the behaviour of the male. When the female lays her eggs, the male fertilizes them and then winds the string of eggs, which can be 1–1.2 m (3–4 ft) long, around his thighs and back. The male – itself only 7.5 cm (3 in) in length – carries the eggs around in this manner for up to four weeks. When the eggs are ready to hatch, the toad swims into suitable water for the tadpoles to be released.

★ INSECT MOST TOLERANT OF DESICCATION

Living in small pools on unshaded rocks in northern Nigeria and Uganda, the larvae of *Polypedilum vanderplanki*, a non-biting midge, withstand an environment that is alternately dry and flooded, and are the only insects capable of enduring cryptobiosis. This is defined as the state an organism enters when it shows no visible signs of life, when its metabolic activity comes to a virtual halt and is hardly measurable. Laboratory experiments have revealed that this midge's larvae can survive drying to less than 3% moisture.

ONLY TREE-CLIMBING FISH

The climbing perch (*Anabas testudineus*), which is found in south Asia, is remarkable for its habit of taking to the land and climbing palm trees. It even walks some distance across country in search of better habitat. The species has a special adaptation of its gills, which allows it to absorb atmospheric oxygen.

LARGEST WATER LILY

The gigantic floating leaves of the water lily *Victoria amazonica* measure up to 3 m (9 ft) across and are held in place upon an underwater stalk 7–8 m (23–26 ft) long. The undersurface of its leaves are supported by a series of rib-like ridges to keep the leaves flat and also prevent them from collapsing. The plant is native to shallow freshwater lakes and bayous in the Amazon basin.

MOST ENERGETIC ANIMAL BRAIN

In 1996, scientist Goran Nilsson (Norway) revealed that the brain of the African elephant-trunk fish (*Gnathonomus petersi*) equals 3.1% of its body mass and uses more than 50% of the oxygen that its body takes in. By contrast, the human brain uses a mere 20% of the oxygen that the body takes in.

RIVETING RIVERS

At 6,695 km (4,160 miles) long, the Nile in Africa is officially the planet's **longest river**. Its closest contender is South America's Amazon. The third longest is the Yangtze in China.

While not in flood (i.e., not including its tidal reaches where an estuary/delta can be much wider), the main stretches of the **widest river** – the Amazon – can reach widths of up to 11 km (7 miles).

LARGEST SPECIES OF RIVER DOLPHIN

The largest species of river dolphin is the boto (*Inia geoffrensis*), famed for its pink colouration. Inhabiting the Amazon and Orinoco rivers of South America, it attains a total length of up to 2.6 m (9 ft).

SHORELINES

★ LONGEST SPECIES OF SEAWEED

The giant kelp *Macrocystis pyrifera* lives near rocky shores in the Pacific Ocean. The longest verified specimen measured 60 m (197 ft) in total, but there are unauthenticated reports of even longer examples.

This kelp is also the ★ **fastest growing seaweed** – it grows up to 34 cm (13.3 in) per day, a growth speed of 0.0003 km/h (0.0002 mph). Indeed, it is the **fastest growing marine plant** on Earth. It is also a leading but often overlooked contender for the world's fastest growing plant of any kind.

★ ANIMAL WITH THE MOST CHROMOSOMES

Chromosomes are small, thread-like bodies within the nucleus of cells. They contain DNA, the body's hereditary information. Humans have 23 pairs of chromosomes in each cell, but the animals with the most are the hermit crabs of the superfamily Paguroidea with 254, or 127 pairs per cell.

LARGEST CROCODILIAN

The estuarine, or saltwater, crocodile (*Crocodylus porosus*) is found throughout the tropical regions of Asia and the Pacific. The Bhitarkanika Wildlife Sanctuary in Orissa State, India, houses four measuring more than 6 m (19 ft 8 in) in length, the largest being over 7 m (23 ft) long. There are several unauthenticated reports of specimens up to 10 m (33 ft) in length. Adult males average 4.2–4.8 m (14–16 ft) in length and weigh about 408–520 kg (900–1,150 lb).

★ LARGEST COASTAL MANGROVE FOREST

The Sundarbans forest stretches for almost 15,540 km² (6,000 miles²) across India and Bangladesh and acts as a natural barrier against tsunamis and cyclones. With saltwater-tolerant roots, this forest's mangrove trees sometimes exceed 21 m (70 ft) in height above islands of layered sand and grey clay, which have been deposited by rivers that flow for over 1,609 km (1,000 miles) from the Himalayas to the Bay of Bengal.

★ LARGEST SPECIES OF SPITTING COBRA

The giant spitting cobra (*Naja ashei*), discovered in 2004, lives in the coastal region of Kenya. Measuring almost 3 m (10 ft) long, it is the world's second-longest species of venomous snake (only the king cobra exceeds it) and possesses sufficient poison to kill at least 15 people.

DENSEST FUR

The sea otter (*Enhydra lutris*) has the densest fur of any mammal, with over 100,000 hairs per 1 cm² (650,000 hairs per 1 in²). Most of the world's sea otter population is found off the coast of Alaska, USA.

Sea otters are also the **smallest marine mammals**.

DID YOU KNOW?

Unlike other marine mammals, sea otters do not have a fat layer to keep them warm. Instead, they rely on their dense, water-resistant fur and an increased metabolism to trap and generate warmth.

ACTUAL SIZE

★ LARGEST WOODLOUSE

The largest species of woodlouse is the common sea slater (*Ligia oceanica*), an aquatic species that is abundant on rocky coasts within the terrestrial and littoral (shoreline) fringe around the UK, particularly in rock pools and crevices and under stones. Up to 3 cm (1 in) long in total, it has a flattened body that is twice as long as it is broad, and varies in colour from grey to olive.

★ LARGEST MINK EVER

The sea mink (*Mustela macrodon*) is a scarcely known species that measured up to 82.6 cm (2 ft 8.5 in) long – half as long again as the longest specimens of the common American mink (*M. vison*) and also much fatter. It inhabited the rocky coasts of New England and Canada's Atlantic coastline as far north as Nova Scotia, but owing to its highly prized pale-reddish fur, it was hunted into extinction. The last known specimen was killed on an island off Maine in 1889, but there is an unconfirmed report of a sea mink taken on New Brunswick's Campobello Island during the mid-1890s.

★ MOST BIOLUMINESCENT CTENOPHORE

The sea walnut (*Mnemiopsis leidyi*), a species of ctenophore, or comb jelly, is native to the waters around the east coast of North America, the Gulf of Mexico and north-eastern South America. (Comb jellies are not true jellyfish, belonging instead to a totally separate phylum, Ctenophora.) It grows to 100–120 mm (3.9–4.7 in) and features four rows of ciliated combs running along its body, which are iridescent by day and glow green at night.

★ LONGEST BIRD'S NEST BURROW

The rhinoceros auklet (*Cerorhinca monocerata*) is a puffin-related seabird. Nesting on small grass-covered islands in the North Pacific, its nesting burrows typically measure 2–3 m (6.5–10 ft) long, but examples twice this length are not unusual, and one exceptional burrow measured 8 m (26 ft).

LARGEST GREY SEAL COLONY

Every winter, as many as 100,000 grey seals (*Halichoerus grypus*) arrive at Sable Island off Nova Scotia, Canada, to breed.

LARGEST...

CLAM

Marine giant clam (*Tridacna gigas*): weight 333 kg (734 lb); length 115 cm (3 ft 9.25 in).

OYSTER

Common oyster (*Ostrea edulis*): weight 3.7 kg (8.1 lb); length 30.5 cm (12 in); width 14 cm (5.5 in).

LARGEST CHELONIAN

The widely distributed leatherback turtle (*Dermochelys coriacea*) averages 1.83–2.13 m (6–7 ft) from the tip of the beak to the end of the tail, with a carapace (shell) around 1.52–1.67 m (5–5 ft 6 in) long, and about 2.13 m (7 ft) across the front flippers. It weighs up to 450 kg (990 lb).

The largest specimen ever recorded is a male found on the beach at Harlech, Gwynedd, UK, in September 1988. It measured 2.91 m (9 ft 5.5 in) in total length over the carapace, 2.77 m (9 ft) across the front flippers and weighed 961.1 kg (2,120 lb). Although most museums refuse to exhibit large turtles because they can drip oil for up to 50 years, this specimen was put on display at the National Museum of Wales, Cardiff, UK, on 16 February 1990.

The leatherback is also the **fastest chelonian** in water, with a speed of up to 35 km/h (22 mph) recorded.

DESERTS

MOST DANGEROUS LIZARD

The Gila monster (*Heloderma suspectum*) is a heavily built, brightly coloured lizard that lives in arid parts of Mexico and the southwestern USA, and measures up to 60 cm (24 in). It has eight well-developed venom glands in its lower jaws and carries enough venom to kill two adult humans. The venom is not injected but seeps into the wound caused when the Gila monster bites its victim with its sharp, fragile teeth. Because of this, a lizard may continue to hang on after it has bitten and actively chew for several minutes. The lizard's teeth may even become embedded in the victim's wound after it has let go. It only attacks when provoked.

★ RAREST CACTUS

Knowlton's miniature cactus (*Pediocactus knowltonii*) is a tiny pink-flowered species that is critically endangered owing to over-exploitation by collectors, and is found only in New Mexico and Colorado, USA.

LONGEST LEAF LIFE-SPAN

The longest-lived leaves of all plants belong to the welwitschia (*Welwitschia mirabilis*), named after botanist Dr Friedrich Welwitsch (Austria), who discovered the plant in 1859 in its native Namib Desert of Namibia and Angola. The welwitschia has an estimated life-span of between 400 and 1,500 years, with some specimens carbon-dated to 2,000 years old. Each plant produces two leaves per century and never sheds them. Ancient individuals sprawl out over 10 m (33 ft) in circumference, with enough foliage to cover a 400-m (1,312-ft) athletics field.

★ LARGEST MODERN-DAY EXTINCT BIRD

The biggest bird to become extinct in modern times was the Arabian ostrich *Struthio camelus syriacus*, which was common in the desert regions of Syria and Arabia until World War I. After the war it was hunted for its plumes, and was also pursued by hunters in jeeps and shot for sport. The only type of ostrich found outside Africa, the last confirmed specimen of the Arabian ostrich was shot in Bahrain in 1941, but there is a controversial record of one allegedly being discovered drowned in a flash flood as recently as 1966.

★ LARGEST POPULATION OF WILD CAMELS

Intriguingly, the world's largest population of camels in the wild, numbering over 200,000 individuals, is found neither in Arabia nor in Mongolia – the traditional homelands of wild camels – but instead in the Australian desert. Camels were imported into Australia

★ LARGEST INDOOR DESERT

The Desert Dome in Omaha, USA, is housed under the world's **largest glazed geodesic dome**, and spans 7,840 m² (84,000 ft²) on two levels – that is 3,920 m² (42,000 ft²) on each level. It exhibits flora and fauna from three major deserts – southern Africa's Namib Desert, Mexico's Sonora Desert and Australia's Red Centre.

from the 1840s until the early 1900s, principally for transportation purposes in Australia's very hot, arid deserts, but as technology advanced, the camels were not needed as much. Consequently, many were released or escaped into the desert and have thrived and bred there ever since.

★ MOST SPECIALIZED LIZARD DIET

Australia's desert-dwelling moloch or thorny devil (*Moloch horridus*) lives exclusively on ants belonging to the genus *Iridomyrmex*.

MOST DESTRUCTIVE INSECT

The single most destructive insect is the desert locust (*Schistocerca gregaria*, pictured above right) from the dry and semi-arid regions of Africa, the Middle East and western Asia. Individuals are only 4.5–6 cm (1.8–2.4 in) long but can eat their own weight in food every day. Certain weather conditions induce unimaginable numbers to gather in huge swarms that devour almost all vegetation in their path. In a single day, a "small" swarm of about 50 million locusts can eat food that would sustain 500 people for a year. Pictured above is a man standing in a cloud of these locusts on 29 November 2004 around Corralejo in the north of the island of Fuerteventura, Canary Islands, about 100 km (60 miles) off the Moroccan coast.

MOST HEAT-TOLERANT LAND-BASED ANIMAL

The most heat-tolerant animal (thermophile) is *Cataglyphis bicolor*, a desert-dwelling scavenger ant that lives in the Sahara desert and forages at temperatures of over 55°C (131°F).

LARGEST GROUND NEST

The mallee fowl (*Leipoa ocellata*) constructs massive nests containing up to 229 m³ (8,100 ft³) of matter and weighing 300 tonnes (661,386 lb) and are unique in the bird world. Males work on the nest most months of the year, digging out a hole, then scraping leaf litter into it and covering it with sandy soil. Alternatively, an existing mound is used year after year and can reach a diameter of 5 m (16 ft). Once the eggs are laid and covered, they are ignored by both parents, as are the chicks, which hatch in 50–90 days.

★ FASTEST INVERTEBRATE

Solifugids of the genus *Solpuga* inhabit the arid areas of North Africa and the Middle East and have a burst sprint capability estimated at 16 km/h (10 mph), making them the fastest of all invertebrates. Despite their alternative names of camel spider and sun spider, solifugids are not true spiders (although they are arachnids), as their bodies are divided into separate head, thorax and abdomen sections, whereas in spiders the head and thorax comprise a single section.

★ FIRST CAMEL/ LLAMA HYBRID

On 14 January 1998, at the Camel Reproduction Centre (CRC) in the Arabian desert in Dubai, UAE, a project headed by chief scientific officer Dr Julian A. (Lulu) Skidmore (UK, below) finally came to fruition with the birth of Rama, the world's first hybrid of camel and llama, known as a cama. His father was an Arabian camel, or dromedary (*Camelus dromedarius*), and his mother was a South American guanaco (*Lama huanacos*), from which the domestic llama *L. glama* is descended. They would never have met in the wild. The camel is over six times heavier than the guanaco, so Rama was conceived by artificial insemination. This breeding project was funded by Dubai's Crown Prince and the Defence Minister H.H. Sheik Mohamed bin Rashed al-Maktoum.

TALLEST...

WILD CACTUS

A cardon (*Pachycereus pringlei*) found in the Sonora Desert, Baja California, Mexico, by Marc Salak and Jeff Brown in April 1995, measured 19.2 m (63 ft) – almost the combined height of four giraffes!

★ HERBA CISTANCHES

A herba cistanches (*Cistanche deserticola*) collected from the desert of Inner Mongolia, China, by Yongmao Chen on 15 August 2006 measured 1.95 m (6 ft 4 in). This plant is used extensively in Chinese herbal medicine.

WETLANDS

SMALLEST HIPPO

The pygmy hippopotamus (*Hexaprotodon liberiensis*) found mainly in Liberia, west Africa, has an average head–body length of 1.5–1.85 m (5–6 ft) plus a tail length of approximately 15–21 cm (6–8.25 in), a shoulder height of 70–100 cm (27.5–39.25 in) and a weight of 160–275 kg (353–606 lb).

★ LARGEST RODENT EVER

Displacing *Phoberomys pattersoni*, the previous record-holder, the world's largest rodent is now a newly named 2-million-year-old fossil species called *Josephoartigasia monesi*. Although it is currently known only from a single skull measuring 53 cm (21 in) long, scientists estimate from its immense size that the complete animal probably weighed a massive 1 tonne (2,000 lb) in weight. Related to today's much smaller pacaraca (*Dinomys branickii*), it lived in coastal Uruguay, in what was then lush forested swampland but is today an arid region, and probably fed upon soft vegetation as its jaws, though huge, lacked much chewing power.

★ MOST SPECIALIZED BIRD DIET

The southern Florida sub-species of the Everglades kite (*Rostrhamus sociabilis plumbeus*) lives exclusively upon a single species of snail, the large freshwater apple snail (*Pomacea paludosa*).

★ LARGEST AMPHIBIAN EVER

Far bigger than any modern-day amphibian, the largest amphibian of all time was *Mastodonsaurus*, inhabiting swamplands around 200 million years ago during the late Triassic period. This huge-headed, long-tailed creature vaguely resembled a crocodile and was as big as one too, attaining a total length of 4 m (13 ft), which included a skull length of 1.25 m (49 in).

★ INSECT WITH GREATEST SALINITY TOLERANCE

The larvae of the brine fly (*Ephydrella marshalli*) inhabit salt lagoons, and under laboratory conditions have withstood salinities of up to 5,848 mOsm per litre (by comparison, the salinity of seawater is 1,197 mOsm per litre). The unit "mOsm" stands for "milliOsmole". An Osmole is the molecular weight of a solute (a mixture of two or more substances), in grams, divided by the number of ions, or particles, into which it dissociates in solution.

TALLEST FLYING BIRD

The tallest of the flying birds are cranes, belonging to the family Gruidae. The largest can stand almost 2 m (6 ft 6 in) high. In the picture above, a sarus crane (*Grus antigone*) is performing a mating dance in the Keoladeo National Park, Rajasthan, India.

★ HEAVIEST ARTIODACTYL

The heaviest artiodactyl (even-toed ungulate mammal) is the common hippo *Hippopotamus amphibius* of sub-Saharan Africa, which can weigh up to 3,630 kg (8,000 lb).

LARGEST DELTA
IN ONE COUNTRY

The whole of the Okavango Delta is contained in Botswana, in southern Africa. With a total area of over 10,000 km² (3,861 miles²), this highly significant area of wetland includes a 1,578-km² (609-mile²) wildlife refuge, with over 400 species of bird and 65 species of fish as well as a herd of red lechwe antelopes numbering around 20,000. Pictured is one of the delta's male red lechwe (*Kobus leche leche*).

The fruit in the *Wolffia augusta* is only 0.25 mm long (1/100th of an inch). It would take 14,286 such fruit to weigh 1 gram (400,000 to weigh an ounce).

The **smallest toad** is the sub-species *Bufo taitanus beiranus* of Africa, the largest specimen of which measured 24 mm (0.94 in) long.

The **smallest dragonfly** is *Agriocnemis naia* of Burma. One specimen in the British Museum had a wing spread of 17.6 mm (0.69 in) and a body length of 18 mm (0.71 in).

LARGEST SWAMP

Located principally in southwestern Brazil but with small areas within neighbouring Bolivia and Paraguay, the Pantanal (which is Spanish for "marshland") covers a surface area of at least 150,000 km² (57,915 miles²). This is greater than the total surface area of England! During the rainy season (December to May), 80% of the Pantanal is flooded, and it contains the **greatest diversity of water plants in the world**.

DID YOU KNOW?

The Sudd swamp in Sudan has sometimes been referred to as the world's largest. However, even in high flood waters, its total area only slightly exceeds 30,000 km² (11,585 miles²), and thus falls short of the Pantanal's surface area.

SMALLEST PLANTS AND ANIMALS

The world's ★ **smallest flowering plants** are the watermeals, species of the genus *Wolffia*. Related to duckweed (*Lemna*), watermeal is an aquatic plant and forms a mat on the surface of ponds and quiet streams. An individual plant is less than 1 mm long and only 0.3 mm wide, and produces a minuscule flower that later develops into the world's **smallest fruit**! Since the entire plant body of the species is less than 1 mm long, the mature fruit takes up a large proportion of its parent plant body.

SHORTEST LIFE SPAN

Mayflies are insects belonging to the order Ephemeroptera. (In Greek, *ephemeros* means "short-lived" and *pteron* means "wing", referring to the short life span of adults.) Mayflies may spend two to three years as nymphs at the bottom of lakes and streams, and then live for as little as one hour as winged adults.

SMALLEST RATTLESNAKE

The pygmy rattlesnake *Sistrurus miliarius* inhabits wooded areas, preferably close to rivers or lakes, in the southeastern USA. Even adult specimens are less than 45 cm (18 in) long. The rattle is so tiny that it makes a faint buzzing sound only audible for up to 1 m (3 ft) or so away. Despite its small size, however, this species is very venomous and frequently bites humans. Pictured is the red pygmy rattlesnake (*Sistrurus miliarius miliarius*).

TEMPERATE FORESTS

LARGEST CONIFEROUS FOREST

The vast coniferous forests of northern Russia lie between latitude 55°N (shown below in yellow) and the Arctic Circle (red). The total wooded area covers 4 million km² (1,544,408 miles²). In this satellite image, water is blue,

vegetation green, arid areas brown and snow and ice white. The boreal forest "biome", or ecosystem, known as the Taiga, extends across Russia, Scandinavia, Canada and Alaska.

★ LARGEST BIOLUMINESCENT ORGANISM

The largest glowing organism is a single gigantic specimen of honey mushroom (*Armillaria ostoyae*) – discovered in the Malheur National Forest, Oregon, USA – which measures 5.6 km (3.5 miles) across and occupies a total area of 890 ha (2,200 acres): equivalent to 1,220 football fields. The honey mushroom is well known for its glowing surface, caused by bioluminescent bacteria, although most of its tissue is 1 m (3 ft) underground, in the form of root-like mycelia. Its age is calculated to be at least 2,400 years old, and it also holds the record for the world's **largest fungus**.

LARGEST LIVING TREE

The world's largest living tree is General Sherman, a giant sequoia (*Sequoiadendron giganteum*) growing in the Sequoia National Park, California, USA. It stands 82.6 m (271 ft) tall, has a diameter of 8.2 m (27 ft 2 in) and a circumference of approximately 25.9 m (85 ft). This tree is estimated to contain the equivalent of 630,096 board feet of timber, enough to make over 5 billion matches, and its red-brown bark may be up to 61 cm (24 in) thick in parts.

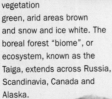

ACTUAL SIZE

★ LARGEST BADGER SETT

The European badger (*Meles meles*) spends more than half its life underground and builds the biggest setts of any badger species. The largest sett on record was estimated to contain a tunnel network 879 m (2,883 ft) long, containing 50 underground chambers and no less than 178 entrances.

DID YOU KNOW?

A sett is an underground network of tunnels, usually located in pasture or woodland, in soil that is easy to dig. It can take years to excavate. Badgers are nocturnal animals; they usually retreat to their setts at daybreak and emerge at dusk.

★ INSECT WITH THE GREATEST NUMBER AND RANGE OF FOODPLANTS

The insect that feeds on the greatest number of plant species, over the widest range, is the caterpillar of the fall webworm moth (*Hyphantria cunea*), a member of the tiger moth family, Arctiidae. It has been estimated that its caterpillars feed on 636 species of plant worldwide, including over 200 in the USA, 219 in Europe, over 300 in Japan and 65 in Korea (some of these plant species are found in more than one of the above regions).

★ LARGEST GROUSE

The capercaillie (*Tetrao urogallus*), native to northern European pine forests, became extinct in Scotland during the 17th century, but was successfully reintroduced from Sweden during the 1830s. Adult males of this species weigh up to 4 kg (8 lb), while adult females weigh up to around 2 kg (4 lb).

SMALLEST CARNIVORE

The least, or dwarf, weasel (*Mustela nivalis*) has a head-body length of 110–260 mm (4.3–10.2 in), a tail length of 13–87 mm (0.5–3.4 in) and weighs 30–200 g (1–7 oz). They are most commonly found in deciduous forests of the northern parts of Europe, Asia and North America, and usually feed on rodents, moles and bird's eggs.

★ LARGEST FERN FRONDS

The Australian giant fern *Angiopteris evecta*, which produces an immense woody trunk measuring as much as 1 m (3.25 ft) in diameter and up to 3 m (10 ft) tall, grows the world's largest fronds. These can measure up to 8 m (26 ft) long.

SLOWEST GROWING TREE

The slowest growing tree is the white cedar (*Thuja occidentalis*), one of which was located on a cliffside in the Great Lakes area of Canada and grew to a height of less than 10.2 cm (4 in) in 155 years! This same plant weighed only 17 g (0.5 oz) and averaged a growth rate of 0.11 g (0.003 oz) of wood each year.

HEAVIEST FUNGI

A single living clonal growth of the soil-fungus *Armillaria bulbosa*, reported on 2 April 1992 to be covering approximately 15 ha (37 acres) of forest in Michigan, USA, was calculated to weigh over 100 tonnes (220,462 lb) – the weight of a blue whale. The organism is thought to have originated from a single fertilized spore at least 1,500 years ago.

RAREST BIRD

The North American ivory-billed woodpecker (*Campephilus principalis principalis*) is currently the world's most endangered bird. North America's second biggest woodpecker (only the imperial woodpecker is bigger), it was believed extinct since the 1940s, until a Big Woods Conservation Partnership expedition, led by Cornell University's Cornell Laboratory of Ornithology and the Nature Conservancy, released a video filmed on 25 April 2005 that shows a single male specimen, discovered during their intensive year-long search for the species in the Cache River and White River national wildlife refuges of Arkansas, USA.

Diagnostic double-raps and tin-horn-like calls, again characteristic of the ivory-bill, were also recorded there by the expedition, whose team members hope that other specimens exist still undetected in this locality's vast wilderness. The ivory-bill's Cuban sub-species was briefly rediscovered in 1986, but no confirmed sightings have been reported since then, leading to speculation that it is now extinct.

★ NEWEST TREE

The Tahina palm tree (*Tahina spectabilis*) was not officially named and described until January 2008, although it had been discovered accidentally by a picnicking family in a remote, hilly, wooded area of northwestern Madagascar in 2006. It was only recognized to be a dramatically new species and genus following DNA analysis a year later. What makes the belated scientific discovery of this species so surprising is its huge size, standing over 18 m (58 ft) tall – with fan-like leaves 5 m (16 ft) across – and its bizarre, suicidal life cycle. Taking decades to bloom, when it does it produces an explosion of hundreds of nectar-rich flowers towering above its crown, each of which develops into fruit, but in so doing the tree's nutrients become so depleted that as soon as it has fruited, the tree collapses and dies.

★ FASTEST GROWING TREE

The fastest growing tree by volume of biomass is a giant sequoia (*Sequoiadendron giganteum*), nicknamed General Grant, in Grant Grove, Kings Canyon National Park, California, USA. The tree's trunk volume increased from 1,218 m³ (43,038 ft³) in 1931 to 1,319 m³ (46,608 ft³) in 1976 when it was measured by Wendell Flint (USA). This amount of wood growth could easily build an average three-bedroomed house. The tree is approximately 1,700 years old, which is quite young for a giant sequoia.

SMALLEST PRIMATE

The smallest true primate (excluding tree shrews, which are normally classified separately) is the pygmy mouse lemur (*Microcebus myoxinus*), discovered in the deciduous forests of western Madagascar in 1993. It has a head-body length of about 62 mm (2.4 in), a tail length of 136 mm (5.4 in) and an average weight of 30.6 g (1.1 oz).

ACTUAL SIZE

RAINFORESTS

VANISHING WORLD

According to data from the United Nations Food and Agriculture Organization's (FAO) *State of the World's Forests* 2007 report, of all 44 countries that, combined, represent 90% of the world's forests, the country that pursues the world's ★ **highest rate of deforestation** is Indonesia, with 1.8 million ha (4,447,896 acres) per year between 2000 and 2005 – a rate of 2% of its forest destroyed each year. This equates to an area measuring approximately 51 km² (20 miles²) each day or 300 football fields every hour!

The **fastest decrease in forested area** is an average rate of 9% every year between 1990 and 2000 in Burundi, Central Africa. If this rate were permanently sustained, Burundi's forested area would be completely cleared in just over 11 years.

★ LARGEST RAT

The largest species of rat is the slender-tailed cloud rat *Phloeomys cumingi* of Luzon, an island in the Philippines. This tree-climbing, densely furred species inhabits Luzon's cloud forests and measures almost 1 m (3 ft 3 in) long including the tail.

However, in 2007, during a visit by a scientific team to the remote, scarcely known Foja Mountains in Irian Jaya (Indonesian New Guinea), a huge, previously unknown species of furry rat was observed and captured alive (pictured below). With a head-and-body length of 70 cm (2 ft 3.5 in) plus its tail, this newly discovered species is the size of a cat and is already being referred to as the biggest rat known. When further specimens are recorded, it may well dethrone the slender-tailed cloud rat.

★ STRONGEST VERTEBRATE

In terms of watts of power generated per kilogram of muscle, the giant palm salamander (*Bolitoglossa dofleini*) of Central America is the strongest vertebrate species. Its tongue explodes outwards at 18,000 watts per 1 kg (818 watts per pound) of muscle. It is believed that the power is stored in the elastic tissue of the tongue, prior to release, much like a rubber band.

★ HIGHEST SOUND BY AN ARTHROPOD

The highest frequency of ultrasound of any known arthropod is produced by the male of the *Arachnoscelis* genus of katydids (cricket-like insects) from the family Tettigoniidae, which inhabit the tropical rainforests of Colombia, particularly in the National Park Isla Gorgona. Fernando Montealegre-Z (Colombia/Canada), Glenn K. Morris and Andrew C. Mason (both Canada) of the University of Toronto discovered the source was a "scraper" on the insect's right wing – as it rubs its wings together, the scraper is distorted then springs back into shape, generating the sound. These results were published in the *Journal of Experimental Biology* in December 2006. In November 2007, the "chirp" was measured at 133 kilohertz (133,000 Hz).

★ LARGEST MANTIS

Toxodera denticulata (pictured) from Java has a body length of 20 cm (7.8 in), making it officially the world's largest mantis. However, a larger, newly discovered and currently undescribed species from the Cameroon jungle has begun to appear in the pet trade, where it has been dubbed the "mega-mantis". Moreover, there are unconfirmed reports of a still longer species inhabiting the rainforests of Bolivia and Peru.

DID YOU KNOW?

Mantises (order Mantodea) number around 2,300 species and are popularly referred to as "praying mantises" (from their praying-like stance, not from the word "preying", although they are notorious predators). Captive females are also infamous for biting the heads off male partners during mating!

★ SMALLEST ARTIODACTYL MAMMAL

The world's smallest artiodactyl (even-toed hoofed mammal) is the lesser Malay chevrotain, or lesser mouse deer (*Tragulus javanicus*). This tiny ungulate is no bigger than a rabbit, sporting in the adult male (smaller than the female) a head-and-body length of only 44–48 cm (1 ft 5.3 in–1 ft 6.8 in), a tail length of 6.5–8 cm (2.5–3.1 in) and a shoulder height of 20–25 cm (7.8–9.8 in). It weighs just 1.7–3 kg (3 lb 12 oz–6 lb 9 oz).

This minuscule mammal inhabits the tropical rainforests and mangrove swamps of southeast Asia.

LARGEST TROPICAL RAINFOREST

The Amazon tropical rainforest is the largest of its kind, covering an area of 6.475 million km² (2.5 million miles²) across nine different south American countries: Brazil, Colombia, Peru, Venezuela, Ecuador, Bolivia, Guyana, Suriname and French Guiana.

★ LARGEST PECCARY

The giant peccary (*Pecari maximus*) is native to the Brazilian Amazon rainforested region of the Rio Aripuana basin. Discovered by Dr Marc van Roosmalen (Netherlands), it is superficially similar to the collared peccary (*Pecari tajacu*), but is notably larger though slimmer, with much longer legs. It has a total length of about 1 m (3 ft 3 in), a shoulder height of 0.85 m (2 ft 9 in), and weighs around 40 kg (88 lb). It has thinly bristled hair, with brown and white fur rather than dark blackish-grey. Until now, the largest recorded peccary species was the Chacoan peccary (*Catagonus wagneri*), discovered alive in 1974 after being known to science only from Ice Age fossil specimens.

★ SMELLIEST BIRD

Native to the Colombian rainforest, the world's smelliest bird is undoubtedly the hoatzin (*Opisthocomus hoazin*), a bizarre-looking creature variously classified with pheasants, cuckoos, touracos and even in a taxonomic group entirely of its own. It stinks like cow manure, and even its local name, *pava hedionda*, translates as "stinking pheasant". The noxious odour is believed to derive from a combination of its exclusive diet of green leaves and, for birds, its uniquely bovine digestive system that involves a kind of foregut fermentation.

TALLEST ORCHID

A height of 15 m (49 ft) has been recorded for the orchid (*Galeola foliata*), a saprophyte of the vanilla family that grows in the decaying rainforests of Queensland, Australia.

ACTUAL SIZE

GRASSLANDS

FASTEST LAND MAMMAL (SHORT DISTANCES)

When measured over a short distance on level ground, the cheetah (*Acinonyx jubatus*) – found in the open plains of sub-Saharan Africa, Iran, Turkmenistan and Afghanistan – can maintain a steady top speed of approximately 100 km/h (62 mph). But research by Prof. Craig Sharp of Brunel University, London, UK, in 1965 recorded accurate speeds of 104.4 km/h (64.3 mph) for a 35-kg (77-lb) adult female over a distance of 201.2 m (660 ft).

*(For the **fastest mammal on land over long distances**, see p.246.)*

LARGEST GRASSLANDS

The largest area of natural grasslands is the Great Plains of North America, which stretch along the USA for 3 million km² (1,158,300 miles²) from southern Canada to northern Mexico. The Great Plains are found inland and experience warm, dry summers. They have a temperate climate, without extremes of heat or cold.

The **largest tropical grasslands** (which grow nearer the coast, have higher rainfall and often include woodland) are the savannah grasslands of northern Australia, covering 1.2 million km² (463,320 miles²).

The ★**largest area of dry steppe** land is the Kazakh Steppe of Central Asia, which measures 804,500 km² (310,600 miles²). Steppe land is treeless, savannah grassland with hot, dry summers and cold, snowless winters.

★ MOST COMMON GRASS

Cogon grass (*Imperata cylindrica*) is a perennial rhizomatous species – that is, a tough, year-round plant with a creeping horizontal stem from which the grass shoots. Native to east and southeast Asia, India, Micronesia and Australia, it is an aggressively invasive weed and has successfully colonized great swathes of Europe, Africa, the Americas and northern Asia, as well as numerous islands around the world. The grass's rhizome has become particularly infamous in the USA for its ability to kill pine seedlings and usurp native plants. The grass is also very flammable in nature, rendering it a major fire hazard and a risk to the habitat of endangered species.

TALLEST MAMMAL

Giraffes (*Giraffa camelopardalis*) live in the dry savannah and open woodland areas of sub-Saharan Africa. An adult bull typically measures 4.6–5.5 m (15–18 ft) tall. Its long neck has no more than the usual seven vertebrae found in most mammals, but each is greatly elongated. Giraffes have such long legs that they have to spread out their fore legs and bend their knees in order to drink. They also have long, extensible tongues and lengthy, sensitive lips with which they can delicately pick leaves from the trees and shrubs on which they browse. The horns of giraffes are unique. Present in both sexes, they have a bony core fused to the skull and are covered by skin and hair.

The giraffe is the **tallest artiodactyl** or even-toed ungulate mammal. The **tallest specimen ever recorded** was a 5.8-m (19-ft) Masai bull (*G. c. tippelskirchi*) measured at Chester Zoo, UK, in 1959.

★ LARGEST EGG FROM A LIVING BIRD

The largest egg laid by a living bird (pictured) weighed 2.58 kg (5 lb 11 oz) and was laid by an ostrich on the farm of Kerstin and Gunnar Sahlin (both Sweden) on 30 August 2007.

The ★**toughest egg** is that of the ostrich (*Struthio camelus*), which can withstand the weight of a person weighing 115 kg (253 lb 8 oz; 18 st).

The **largest living bird** is the North African ostrich (*Struthio camelus camelus*). Male examples of this ratite (flightless) sub-species have been recorded up to 2.75 m (9 ft) tall and weighing 156.5 kg (345 lb; 24 st 9 lb).

FASTEST...

PRIMATE

The patas monkey (*Erythrocebus patas*) of western and eastern Africa can reach speeds of 55 km/h (34 mph). With their long slender limbs, they are sometimes referred to as "primate cheetahs".

LAND SNAKE

The aggressive black mamba (*Dendroaspis polylepis*) of southeastern Africa can reach speeds of 16–19 km/h (10–12 mph) in short bursts over level ground.

CATERPILLAR

The larvae of the mother-of-pearl moth (*Pleuroptya ruralis*) can travel 38.1 cm (15 in) in a second or 1.37 km/h (0.8 mph) – the caterpillar equivalent of 241 km/h (150 mph).

★ HEAVIEST FLYING BIRD

The male kori bustard (*Ardeotis kori*) of southern and eastern Africa can weigh up to 18.2 kg (40 lb) – the weight of the largest confirmed specimen, as documented in 1936 after being shot in South Africa by H. T. Glynn. Pictured is a kori bustard with a carmine bee-eater on its back.

DID YOU KNOW?

The largest species of South American bird is the ostrich-related flightless common rhea (*Rhea americana*), inhabiting the grasslands of Argentina, Bolivia, Brazil, Paraguay and Uruguay. Adults average 129 cm (51 in) in length and 27 kg (60 lb) in weight.

★ MOST POPULOUS BIRD'S NEST

Native to southwestern Africa's dry grasslands, the sociable weaver (*Philetairus socius*) builds an immense communal nest that can be up to 8 m (26 ft) long and 2 m (6 ft 6 in) high. Resembling a giant haystack that hangs from a tree or telegraph pole, it contains up to 300 individual nests. Each of these nests in turn houses a pair of weavers and their brood. Not surprisingly, these enormous communal nests can get so heavy that the tree on which they are built sometimes collapses under the weight!

★ SWEETEST INSECTS

As many as 5 billion aphids can be supported in a single hectare of vegetation (2.4 acres), and these in turn can saturate the soil each day with 2 tonnes (4,410 lb) of sugar in the form of honeydew. This is the **largest sugar secretion by insects**.

★ FASTEST MUSCLE MOVEMENT

The muscular contraction-expansion cycle of the tiny *Forcipomyia* midge, which occurs in 0.00045 seconds (1/2,218th of a second) – yielding 62,760 wing-beats per minute (1,046 wing-beats per second) under natural conditions – is the **fastest wing-beat** documented for any animal.

MOUNTAINS

MOST NORTHERLY PRIMATES

Japanese macaques (*Macaca fuscata*) live in the mountainous Jigokudani area of Honshu, Japan, near Nagano (36°40N, 138°10E). Humans aside, they are the northernmost population of primates. Also known as snow monkeys, they survive the -15°C (5°F) winters by warming themselves in hot volcanic springwater.

HIGHEST MOUNTAIN TABLETOP

Monte Roraima is a sandstone plateau that marks the border of Brazil, Venezuela and Guyana, although more than 75% of it is in Venezuela. This tabletop mountain, or tepui, measures 2,810 m (9,220 ft) in height. Its harsh environment has resulted in around one third of its plant species being unique to the mountain. Monte Roraima is believed to have been the inspiration for Arthur Conan Doyle's novel *The Lost World*.

★ SMALLEST HOME RANGE FOR A BEAR

The smallest home range of female giant pandas (*Ailuropoda melanoleuca*) studied in the Qinling Mountains, Shaanzi Province, China, is a mere 4.2 km² (1.6 miles²).

The giant panda also has the ★ **most restricted distribution of any bear**, being limited to six small mountainous areas in the Sichuan, Shaanzi and Gansu Provinces along the eastern rim of the Tibetan Plateau in southwestern China, yielding a total range of only 5,900 km² (2,277 miles²).

★ GREATEST RESURRECTION FROM EXTINCTION FOR A MARSUPIAL

The mountain pygmy possum (*Burramys parvus*) was known to science only from fossils dating back 10,000–15,000 years until one day in August 1966 when zoologist Dr Kenneth Shortman discovered an unfamiliar-looking possum, resembling a large dormouse, hiding in a corner of the Melbourne University Ski Lodge, high on the slopes of Mt Hotham, Victoria, Australia. Studies of this puzzling creature revealed it to be a living mountain pygmy possum, and others have since been found alive elsewhere in Victoria and also in New South Wales, Australia, thereby resurrecting the species from many thousands of years of supposed extinction.

LARGEST SPECIES OF WASP

The Asian giant hornet (*Vespa mandarinia*) is native to the mountains of Japan and can grow to be 5.5 cm (2.2 in) long, with a wing-span of approximately 7.6 cm (3 in). Its sting is about 0.6 cm (0.25 in) long and can inject a venom so powerful that it dissolves human tissue.

HIGHEST FLYING INSECT

The greatest height reported for migrating butterflies is 5,791 m (19,000 ft) for a flock of small tortoiseshells (*Aglais urticae*) seen flying over the Zemu Glacier in the eastern Himalayas. This is also the **highest migrating butterfly**.

In comparison, the highest altitude recorded for a bird is 11,300 m (37,000 ft) for a Rüppell's vulture (*Gyps rueppellii*), which collided with a commercial aircraft over Abidjan, Ivory Coast, on 29 November 1973.

ACTUAL SIZE

★ LONGEST TONGUE

Relative to body size, the nectar bat (*Anoura fistulata*) of the Andes, Ecuador, has the longest mammalian tongue. It has a reach of 8.49 cm (3.34 in) – that is, 150% of its body length. According to Nathan Muchhala of the University of Miami, Florida, USA, who published these measurements in *Nature* in 2006, it is no coincidence that *A. fistulata* is the sole pollinator of *Centropogon nigricans*, with corolla tubes measuring 8–9 cm (3–3.5 in) in length. Pictured is a nectar bat drinking from a glass tube.

If your tongue was as long as a nectar bat's, you'd be able to lick your own toes while standing upright!

★ NEW RECORD
★ UPDATED RECORD

HIGHEST-LIVING PLANTS AND ANIMALS

Ermania himalayensis (belonging to the crucifer or cabbage family) and *Ranunculus lobatus* (buttercup family) grow on Mt Kamet in the Himalayas at 6,400 m (21,000 ft) – the **highest altitude for flowering plants**.

The large-eared pika (*Ochtona macrotis*) has been recorded at a height of 6,130 m (20,100 ft) in mountain ranges in Asia, making it the **highest-living mammal**. The yak (*Bos mutus*) of Tibet and the Sichuanese Alps, China, climbs to an altitude of 6,100 m (20,000 ft), but only when foraging.

The **highest-living fish** is the Tibetan loach (family Cobitidae). It has been found at an altitude of 5,200 m (17,060 ft) in the Himalayas.

The Himalayan pit viper (*Agkistrodon himalayanus*) is a venomous species that has been found at altitudes up to 4,900 m (16,072 ft), making it the ★ **highest-living snake**.

The vicuña (*Vicugna vicugna*) from South America's high Andes is the ★ **highest-living wild camelid**. It lives at altitudes of up to 4,800 m (15,750 ft), as does the alpaca, a domestic camelid.

The ★ **highest altitude at which trees have been discovered** is 4,600 m (15,000 ft) for a silver fir (*Abies squamata*) found in southwestern China. Himalayan birch trees (*Betula utilis*) have also been discovered at this altitude. Specimens of *A. spectabilis*, a species closely related to *A. squamata*, have been found at an altitude of 4,267 m (14,000 ft) in the Himalayas.

★ LARGEST HERB

The puya (*Puya raimondii*) is a rare species of giant bromeliad growing high in the Bolivian mountains. Although it is a herbaceous plant, it has a trunk up to 4 m (13 ft) high.

The puya takes around 150 years to bloom, making it the **slowest plant to flower**.

★ LARGEST ELEPHANT SHREW

The grey-faced elephant shrew (*Rhynchocyon udzungwensis*) was discovered in March 2006 in two high-altitude forest blocks in the mountains of south-central Tanzania. Weighing approximately 700 g (1 lb 6 oz), it is more than 25% heavier than any previously known elephant shrew (or sengi) species. Confined entirely to Africa and known as elephant shrews on account of their long trunk-like snout and superficial resemblance to true shrews, sengis are now known to constitute a totally separate taxonomic order of mammals more closely related to elephants, sea cows and aardvarks than to true shrews.

With a bright chestnut-red body and grey face, as well as its large size, this new species is very distinctive, making its late discovery by science all the more surprising.

★ HIGHEST-LIVING PREDATOR ON LAND

The range of the snow leopard (*Uncia uncia*) extends across 12 countries in the mountainous regions of central and southern Asia. This rarely seen cat has been photographed by hidden cameras at altitudes as high as 5,800 m (19,000 ft). Moving footage of a snow leopard hunting a markhor (a species of ibex-related wild goat) was famously captured by a camera crew in remote mountains on the Afghan/Pakistan border for the *Planet Earth* series (BBC, 2006).

SNOW & ICE

★ LARGEST ANTARCTIC LAND ANIMAL

The biggest – and only – species of Antarctic insect is the Antarctic midge *Belgica antarctica*. At 12 mm (0.47 in), it is slightly larger than a grain of rice, but is nevertheless the largest animal species that has adapted to live on land on Antarctica all year long (seals and penguins spend much of their time in the water). It lives in penguin colonies, feeding on waste matter and algae.

★ LARGEST SPECIES OF FALCON

The largest species of falcon is the gyrfalcon (*Falco rusticolus*), indigenous to Arctic and subarctic regions. Adult birds can reach maximum lengths of 64 cm (25 in), with wing-spans of 123 cm (48 in) and weights of 800–2,100 g (28–74 oz).

★ **NEW RECORD**
★ **UPDATED RECORD**

MOST DANGEROUS PINNIPED

The carnivorous leopard seal (*Hydrurga leptonyx*) is the only species with a reputation for apparently unprovoked attacks on people. There are a number of documented cases of leopard seals suddenly lunging through cracks in the ice to snap at human feet. Divers have also been attacked and there are instances of several people being chased across the ice over distances of up to 100 m (330 ft). Pictured is a leopard seal resting on the rocky shore at Port Lockroy on Wiencke Island, Antarctica.

★ LARGEST PETREL

Native to Antarctica, the world's largest species of petrel is the giant petrel (*Macronectes giganteus*), with a length of approximately 90 cm (3 ft) and a wing-span exceeding 2 m (6.5 ft), thus approaching the size of a small albatross. Foraging here both on land and at sea for carrion, these formidable birds will also attack and kill other creatures as large as king penguins and isolated seal pups.

★ SMALLEST PETREL

Also native to Antarctica is Wilson's storm petrel (*Oceanites oceanicus*). It weighs a mere 40 g (1.4 oz) and is no bigger than a house martin or swallow.

★ LARGEST POPULATION OF KILLER WHALES

The world's largest population of the killer whale, or orca (*Orcinus orca*), exists in the waters off Antarctica, where around 160,000 individuals occur. (Pictured is a South American sea lion pup being attacked by an orca.)

On 12 October 1958, a bull killer whale was timed at 55.5 km/h (34.5 mph) in the northeastern Pacific, making it the **fastest marine mammal**. Similar speeds have been reported for Dall's porpoise (*Phocoenoides dalli*), but only in short bursts.

★ LARGEST CRUSTACEAN GENOME

Although only a tiny animal, the genome of the Arctic-dwelling amphipod *Ampelisca macrocephala* contains 63.2 billion base pairs, which is roughly 20 times more than in the human genome.

★ SHORTEST ARCTIC TREE

The dwarf willow *Salix herbacea* is a tiny species that rarely exceeds 6.4 cm (2.5 in) tall and has been found growing on frozen tundra in the Arctic.

No plant survives farther north than Lat. 83°N or farther south than Lat 86°09'S.

★ MOST NORTHERLY SEAL

The common (ringed) seal (*Phoca hispida*) is the most abundant seal species in the Arctic, and also the world's most northerly seal species. Occurring wherever there is enough open water in the more permanent high Arctic ice, this hardy species has even been recorded as far north as the North Pole itself.

★ LONGEST FAST FOR A BIRD

The longest continuous fast on record for any bird was 134 days for a male emperor penguin (*Aptenodytes forsteri*). Once a male emperor penguin arrives on land from the sea, it does not usually eat while travelling overland to the breeding colony, courting a female, incubating their single egg for 62–67 days (a job that the female takes no part in), waiting for the female to return and travelling back to the sea. Only when it reaches the sea once more does it feed again. It is able to survive this enforced fast (during which period its body weight falls by 50%) by surviving on plentiful reserves of subcutaneous fat, which can be 3–4 cm (1.2–1.6 in) thick.

PENGUINS APLENTY

The **largest penguin colony** in the world is on Zavodovski Island in the South Sandwich Islands. Approximately 2 million chinstrap penguins (*Pygoscelis antarctica*) breed on the slopes of the island, which is an active volcano.

★ LARGEST SPECIES OF PENGUIN

Anthropornis nordenskjöldi lived in the Antarctic about 24 million years ago, during the lower Miocene epoch. This human-sized penguin stood approximately 1.5–1.8 m (5–5 ft 10 in) tall and may have weighed 90–135 kg (200–300 lb). By comparison, today's largest penguin species, the emperor penguin (*Aptenodytes forsteri*), stands just 1 m (3 ft 3 in) tall, has a total length of 1.15 m (3 ft 9 in) and weighs up to 43 kg (95 lb).

The **most southerly bird tracks** ever recorded were those of an emperor penguin, which were chanced upon over 400 km (248 miles) from the nearest sea by a team of Antarctic explorers on 31 December 1957.

LOWEST MAMMALIAN BODY TEMPERATURE

A body temperature of -3°C (26°F) was measured for the Arctic ground squirrel (*Spermophilus parryii*) of Alaska and north-west Canada. Its body temperature drops below freezing when in a state of suspended animation during its hibernation period in the Arctic winter. Its normal body temperature in the summer months is 37°C (98°F).

Its hibernation, which can last up to nine months, is the **longest hibernation by a rodent** in the wild.

REMOTEST TREE

The most remote tree is believed to be a solitary Norwegian spruce on Campbell Island, Antarctica, whose nearest companion would be over 222 km (119.8 nautical miles) away on the Auckland Islands.

★ MOST SOUTHERLY TREE FERN

Cyathea smithii, a large species of tree fern with a slender trunk, stands up to 8 m (26 ft) tall and sports fronds that attain a length of up to 2.5 m (9 ft) when mature. This species is native not only to the cool mountain forests of New Zealand but also to the subantarctic Auckland Islands, and, as might be expected, is one of New Zealand's cold-hardiest tree ferns.

The **southernmost recorded flowering plant** is Antarctic hair grass (*Deschampsia antarctica*), found in Lat. 68°21'S on Refuge Island, Antarctica, on 11 March 1981.

URBAN AREAS

HIGHEST FREQUENCY HEARING

Bats (order Chiroptera) have the most acute hearing of any non-aquatic animal, owing to their ultrasonic echolocation. Most species use frequencies in the 20–80 kHz range, although some are able to hear frequencies as high as 120–250 kHz, compared to almost 20 kHz for humans and 280 kHz for that of dolphins. Pictured is a parti-coloured bat (*Vespertilio murinus*).

MOST LEGS

Despite their names, centipedes do not have 100 legs and millipedes do not have 1,000, although millipedes do have more legs than centipedes. They have two pairs per body segment compared with just one pair per body segment in centipedes. Normally millipedes have about 300 pairs of legs, although a millipede called *Illacme plenipes* found in California, USA, had 375 pairs (equalling 750 legs).

★ LOWEST DWELLING BIRDS

From the northern hemisphere summer of 1975 to spring 1978, three house sparrows (*Passer domesticus*) lived in Frickley Colliery, Yorkshire, UK, at a depth of 640 m (2,100 ft), making them the lowest known resident population of wild birds. Two of these three sparrows even nested and raised three chicks, but the chicks died not long afterwards.

★ LARGEST FLOCK OF BIRDS TO INVADE A HOUSE

Many people have discovered the odd sparrow or blackbird in their chimney, but the feathered invasion of a house in Pasadena, California, USA, on the evening of 4 May 1998 resembled a scene from Alfred Hitchcock's film *The Birds* (USA, 1963). Fortunately, the owners weren't home, because when neighbours called out the Fire Department to investigate, the firefighters discovered that more than a thousand swifts (family Apidae) had flown down the chimney, spreading soot everywhere. Some of the swifts were dead, having apparently flown headlong into the walls in panic, and it took the firefighters over two hours to shoo the rest of the flock out through windows and doors. It is unclear why the swifts flew down the chimney en masse.

DID YOU KNOW?

Echolocation is a method of sensory perception by which bats orient themselves to their surroundings, detect obstacles, communicate with each other and find food. Bats send out sound waves using their mouth or nose; when the sound hits an object, an echo comes back. The echolocation system is so accurate that bats can detect insects the size of gnats and objects as fine as a human hair.

LONGEST PARASITIC FASTS

The common bedbug (*Cimex lectularius*), which feeds upon human blood, is able to survive without feeding for more than a year. The soft tick (*Ornithodoros turicata*) that spreads the spirochaete causing relapsing fever can survive without food for periods of up to five years.

★ FIRST MAN-MADE BIOLUMINESCENT FISH

Created in 2001 by Prof H. J. Tsai of National Taiwan University, the world's first man-made bioluminescent fish (dubbed Frankenfish) are green-glowing specimens of the zebra fish, a popular aquarium species, whose bioluminescence is the result of the introduction of jellyfish DNA.

SMALLEST SPIDER EGG

A tiny pink spider that lives on the walls of houses in Europe and is called *Oonops domesticus* lays eggs that measure only a fraction of a millimetre across. This spider also lays the **fewest eggs by any spider in a single batch** – only two.

LONGEST EARTHWORM

In 1967, a giant specimen of the earthworm *Microchaetus rappi* was found on the road between Alice and King William's Town, KwaZulu-Natal, South Africa. It was 6.7 m (21 ft) long when naturally extended and 20 mm (0.8 in) in diameter. (This was a prize specimen as the average length of this species is approximately 1.8 m [6 ft] when naturally extended.)

The **shortest earthworm** is *Chaetogaster annandalei* – it measures less than 0.5 mm (0.02 in) long.

● ACTUAL SIZE

★ OLDEST MARSUPIAL

The longest-living marsupial whose age has been reliably recorded was a common wombat (*Vombatus ursinus*) that was 26 years 22 days old when it died on 20 April 1906 at London Zoo, UK. Although the hypothesis has not been verified, it is possible that larger species of kangaroo live up to 28 years in the wild.

SLEEPIEST MAMMAL

In October 2007, University of New England zoologist Dr Fritz Geiser (USA) announced a new world record for the sleepiest mammal. After an extensive feed, an Australian eastern pygmy possum (*Cercartetus nanus*) curled up and hibernated for 367 days – the first time any mammal has been known to hibernate non-stop for more than a year. During its marathon sleep, the possum used just one fortieth of the energy it consumes when awake.

Prior to this, the record holder had been a western jumping mouse (*Zapus princeps*) that hibernated for 320 days in a laboratory.

ACTUAL SIZE

★ LONGEST YUCA ROOT

On 24 December 2000, Camilo Outerino (USA) pulled a yuca (cassava) root from the ground in his garden in Hialeah, Florida, USA. It was a surprising 2.46 m (8 ft 10 in) long.

LARGEST INDOOR SPIDER WEB

A cobweb 5.08 m (16 ft 8 in) long and 3.8 m (12 ft 6 in) wide, covering an area of 19.3 m² (208 ft²), was discovered in an outhouse belonging to David Hyde (UK) in Newent, Gloucestershire, UK, in January 1999.

Discovered by Ken Thompson (UK) in 1998, the **largest outdoor web** (made by thousands of black money spiders) covered an entire 4.54-ha (11.23-acre) playing field in Warwick, UK.

MOST BEE STINGS REMOVED

The greatest number of bee stings sustained by any surviving human is 2,443 by Johannes Relleke at the Kamativi tin mine, Gwaii River, Wankie District, Zimbabwe (then Rhodesia), on 28 January 1962. All the stings were removed and counted.

MOST DANGEROUS BEE

The Africanized honey bee (*Apis mellifera scutellata*) will generally only attack when provoked, but is persistent and aggressive in pursuit, and protective of territories. Although its venom is no more potent than that of other bees, because it attacks in swarms the result can be death due to the number of stings inflicted.

★ FIRST DOMESTICATED ELEPHANTS

The earliest known records of domesticated elephants relate to the Asian species (*Elephas maximus*). They tell of tamed animals being used as beasts of burden at least 4,000 years ago during the Indus Valley civilization (in the region of present-day Pakistan and India).

EXTREME HABITATS

LARGEST CAVE DWELLERS

Although they do not live there permanently, the salt-mining African elephants (*Loxodonta africana*) of Kitum Cave on Mount Elgon, Kenya, regularly enter the cave and travel underground in search of salt, which they need for dietary purposes. They dig the mineral out with their tusks and have done so for generations.

★ FIRST PLANT SPECIES TO FLOWER IN SPACE

In 1982, the then Soviet Union's Salyut-7 space station grew some *Arabidopsis* on board. During their 40-day life cycle, they became the first plants to flower and produce seeds in the zero gravity of space.

HIGHEST MICROBE

In April 1967, NASA reported that bacteria had been discovered at an altitude of 41.13 km (25 miles).

MOST HEAT-TOLERANT ANIMAL

The most heat-tolerant multicellular animals are the tardigrades or water bears, a group of tiny, near-indestructible animals that are able to survive temperatures exceeding 150°C (302°F).

DEEPEST PLANT

Algae found by Mark and Diane Littler (both USA) off San Salvador Island, The Bahamas, in October 1984 grew at a depth of 269 m (882 ft). These maroon-coloured plants survived, despite the fact that 99.9995% of sunlight was filtered out.

MOST ACID-RESISTANT LIFE-FORM

The most acidic conditions in which microbial (or any) life has been discovered to survive is pH 0, equivalent to hydrochloric acid. Several organisms are known to thrive in these conditions, including *Cyanidium caldarium*, which lives in volcanic vents.

MOST ALKALI-RESISTANT LIFE-FORM

A bacterium discovered in 2003 near Chicago, Illinois, USA, lives in groundwater contaminated by more than a century of industrial iron-slag tipping, where it can survive pH levels of up to 12.8.

MOST COLD-TOLERANT TREES

The most cold-tolerant trees are the larches (genus *Larix*). These include the tamarack larch *L. laricina* (pictured), native to northern North America – and commonly occurring at the arctic tree line at the edge of the tundra – which can survive winter temperatures down to at least -65°C (-85°F).

★ MOST PARASITICALLY CONTROLLED MOLLUSC

In January 1998, scientists at Vrije University, Amsterdam, the Netherlands, revealed that specimens of the freshwater snail *Lymnaea stagnalis* parasitized by the digenean fluke *Trichobilharzia ocellata* develop an aversion to sex. Instead, they grow more quickly, allowing their parasites to thrive. Studying this behavioural change in the host species revealed that levels of certain types of a nucleic acid (messenger RNA) responsible for producing proteins affecting snail behaviour were much higher in parasitized snails than in non-parasitized snails. In other words, *T. ocellata* was directly affecting the gene expression of *Lymnaea* – seemingly the first time that this type of parasite control over its host has been shown.

DID YOU KNOW?

Parasitism is an association between two different species in which one, the parasite, gains an advantage whereas the other, the host, suffers. Parasites usually live on or inside their host, which they use as a source of nutrition while reproducing, often causing illness in the host.

LARGEST PARASITE

The broad, or fish, tapeworm (*Diphyllobothrium latum*), inhabiting the small intestine of fish and sometimes humans too, attains a length of 9.1–12.1 m (30–40 ft) but can exceptionally reach 18 m (60 ft). If a specimen survived for 10 years, it could measure almost 8 km (5 miles) long and contain 2 billion eggs!

Another human parasite, the pork tapeworm (*Taenia solium*), can exceed 6 m (20 ft), while the beef tapeworm (*Taeniarhynchus saginatus*) can reach up to 15.25 m (50 ft). One extreme *Taeniarhynchus* specimen was 22.86 m (75 ft) long – three times as long as the entire human intestine!

MOST BLOODTHIRSTY PARASITE

The indistinguishable eggs of the hookworms *Ancylostoma duodenale* and *Necator americanus* are found in the faeces of 1.3 billion people worldwide. Around 10 million litres (2.2 million gallons) of blood is extracted worldwide daily as a result of the worms' feeding.

MOST ADAPTABLE FLUKE

Most flukes (comprising two classes of flatworms) infect very few different organisms, but the liver fluke (*Fasciola hepatica*) has been found as an adult in the liver, gall bladder and associated ducts in sheep, cattle, goats, pigs, horses, rabbits, squirrels, dogs and humans.

★ LARGEST CAVE-DWELLING BAT

The world's largest cave-dwelling bat is Bulmer's fruit bat (*Aproteles bulmerae*), native to Papua New Guinea. Adult females have a wing-span of around 1 m (3 ft 3 in) and weigh approximately 600 g (21 oz). It was known to science only from 9,000-year-old fossils until 1977, when some modern-day preserved specimens were unexpectedly uncovered in a museum. Living specimens were later discovered in a huge cave within western Papua's Hindenburg mountain range.

★ MOST HEAT-TOLERANT WORM

Only scientifically described as recently as 1980, and living in association with deep-sea hydrothermal vents sited on the Pacific ocean bed just off the Galapagos Islands, the world's most heat-tolerant worm is the Pompeii worm (*Alvinella pompejana*). This small polychaete (meaning "many bristled") worm attaches itself to "black smoker" vents and thrives at temperatures of up to 80°C (176°F). Only the tardigrades can tolerate higher temperatures.

★ DEEPEST BAT COLONY

The world's deepest bat colony – comprising approximately 1,000 little brown bats (*Myotis lucifrugus*) – spends each winter in a New York zinc mine at a record depth for any bat species of 1,160 m (3,805 ft) – almost six times deeper than their normal roosting depth.

★ NEW RECORD
★ UPDATED RECORD

PARASITIC PESTS

Also known as roundworms, the **largest parasitic nematode**, inhabiting the placenta of sperm whales, is *Placentonema gigantissimus*. It can reach a length of 7.62 m (25 ft).

The **largest parasitic fluke**, a species of didymozoid digenean, encysted in the giant oceanic sunfish *Mola mola*, can attain a length of 6–9 m (20–30 ft).

MOST COSMETIC SURGERY

Cindy Jackson (USA) has spent over $100,000 (£51,000) on more than 50 cosmetic procedures, including nine full-scale surgical operations, since 1988. The Midwestern farmer's daughter is the pioneer of the "Extreme Makeover" and has been dubbed a "Living Barbie Doll" by the world's media. Her treatments have included facelifts, a nose job, breast implants, liposuction, chemical peels, oxygen facials, Botox, chin-bone reduction, cheek implants, filler injections, microdermabrasion, dermal vitamin injections, and tattooed lipstick and eyeliner! She is pictured here with cosmetic surgeon Dr Jose Campo and assistants at the Xanit hospital near Malaga, Spain. You can visit Cindy online at www.cindyjackson.com.

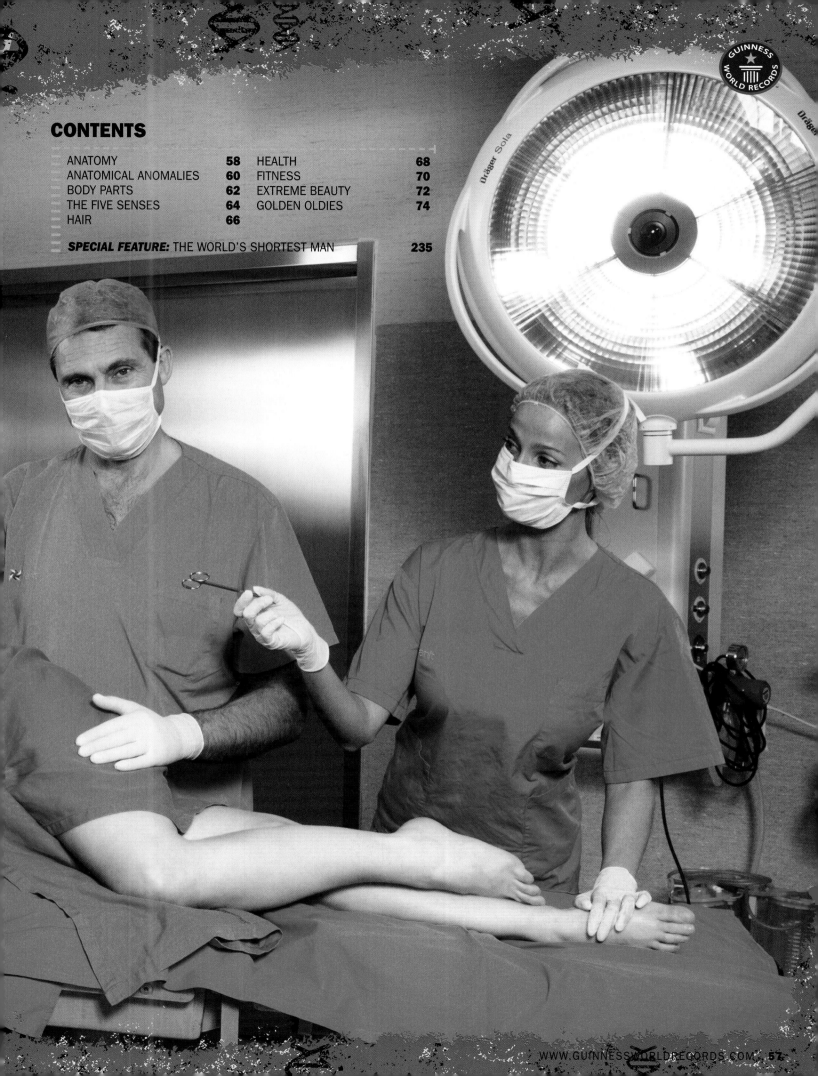

CONTENTS

Being Human
Anatomy

Stapes (stirrup)

The smallest bone in the body is the stapes (or stirrup) found in the ear. It measures just 2.6–2.7 mm (0.1–0.12 in) long.

Head
Neck
Anterior crus
Posterior crus
Base

A
B

Great wing of sphenoid

Shoulder

The shoulder is the most mobile joint in the body — and as a result is the joint that is easiest to dislocate.

Liver

The largest internal organ, the adult liver can weigh 1.2–1.5 kg (2 lb 10 oz–3 lb 7 oz), or about 1/36th of total body weight.

Eye muscles

The most active muscles are those of the eye, which move an estimated 100,000 times every day.

Jaw

The strongest muscle in the human body is the masseter (there is one masseter on each side of the mouth). See left for more notes on jaw strength.

Inner ear

The smallest muscle in the body is the stapedius, which controls the stapes (stirrup) bone (see illustration far right). It is around 0.12 cm (0.05 in) long!

Bite marks

In August 1986, Richard Hofmann (USA) achieved a bite strength of 442 kg (975 lb) for approximately two seconds in a research test using a gnathodynamometer at the College of Dentistry, University of Florida, USA. This is SIX times greater than the average biting strength!

liver

The liver can measure up to 22 cm (8.6 in) long and 10 cm (3.9 in) wide. Located behind the lower ribs and below the diaphragm, it performs over 100 functions.

Skin

An organ is defined loosely as any part of an animal or plant that is adapted for a particular function, such as respiration, digestion or protection. Skin, therefore, is the largest organ in the body.

Bones

Excluding a variable number of sesamoid bones, adult humans have 206 bones. Children have about 200 — some bones fuse together over time.

Longest bone ever

The longest recorded bone was a femur measuring 76 cm (2 ft 6 in), which belonged to Constantine, a German giant.

Femur

The longest human bone is the femur, which constitutes 27.5% of a person's stature normally and may be expected to be 50 cm (19.75 in) long in a man measuring 180 cm (6 ft) tall.

Patella (knee cap)

The patella, or knee cap, is the largest sesamoid bone in the human body. Sesamoid bones are only a few millimetres in diameter and are shaped like seeds of the sesame plant. They are usually embedded in tendons close to joints.

Sartorius muscle

The longest muscle in the human body is the sartorius, which is a narrow ribbon-like muscle running from the pelvis and across the front of the thigh to the top of the tibia below the knee.

Hip

The hip joint is the most difficult to dislocate, making it the strongest joint in the human skeleton. This is because the head of the femur fits almost perfectly into the socket of the pelvis.

Anatomy of a font

The font used on these pages is 822 da Vinci. It is based on the distinctive handwriting found in the journals, manuscripts and codices of the famous Italian artist, inventor, anatomist and visionary Leonardo da Vinci.

CAPSULAR LIG.
COTYLOID LIG.
ACETABULUM
LIGAMENTES
CAPSULAR LIG.

Quadriceps femoris

Ligamentum patellae

Femur

Tibia

Fibular collateral ligament
Tendon of Popliteus
Lateral meniscus

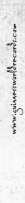

www.guinnessworldrecords.com

ANATOMICAL ANOMALIES

TALLEST MAN LIVING

Bao Xi Shun (China, b. 1951) is the tallest living man whose height has been fully ratified by GWR. His height, 2.36 m (7 ft 8.95 in), was confirmed at Chifeng City Hospital, Inner Mongolia, China, on 15 January 2005. The Ukraine's Leonid Stadnyk, whose height of 2.57 m (8 ft 5.5 in) made international news last year, is currently back under investigation, as he continues to reject requests to measure him.

TALLEST TWINS

Identical twins Michael and James Lanier (USA) of Troy, Michigan, both stand 2.235 m (7 ft 3 in) in height, making them the **tallest male twins**.

Ann and Claire Recht (USA, b. 9 February 1988) are the ★ **tallest female twins**. Measured on 10 January 2007 in Oregon, USA, both sisters registered an average overall height of 2.01 m (6 ft 7 in).

TALLEST MARRIED COUPLE

Anna Hanen Swan (Canada) measured 2.27 m (7 ft 5.5 in) in height. On 18 June 1871, she married 2.2-m (7-ft 2.5-in) Martin van Buren Bates (USA), giving the couple a combined height of 4.46 m (14ft 8 in).

ANATOMICAL MILESTONES

TALLEST MAN EVER

The tallest man in medical history for whom there is irrefutable evidence is Robert Pershing Wadlow (b. 6:30 a.m., on 22 February 1918, at Alton, Illinois, USA). When last measured, on 27 June 1940, he was found to be 2.72 m (8 ft 11.1 in) tall. Robert died on July 15, 1940.

HEAVIEST MAN EVER

Jon Brower Minnoch (USA, 1941–83) suffered from obesity since childhood. He was 185 cm (6 ft 1 in) tall and weighed 178 kg (392 lb; 28 st) in 1963, 317 kg (700 lb; 50 st) in 1966 and 442 kg (975 lb; 70 st) in September 1976. In March 1978, Minnoch was admitted to University Hospital, Seattle, USA, where consultant endocrinologist Dr Robert Schwartz calculated that Minnoch must have weighed more than 635 kg (1,400 lb; 100 st), a great deal of which was water accumulation due to his congestive heart failure.

HEAVIEST WOMAN

Rosalie Bradford (USA, b. 27 August 1943) claimed to have registered a peak weight of 544 kg (1,200 lb; 86 st) in January 1987. In August of that year, she developed congestive heart failure and was rushed to hospital. She was then put on a carefully controlled diet and by February 1994 weighed 128 kg (283 lb; 20 st).

LARGEST WAIST

Walter Hudson's (USA) waist measured 302 cm (119 in) at his peak weight of 545 kg (1,197 lb; 86 st).

TALLEST WOMAN EVER

Zeng Jinlian (China, b. 26 June 1964) of Yujiang village, Hunan Province, measured 2.48 m (8 ft 1.75 in) when she died on 13 February 1982.

TALLEST WOMAN

When last measured, Sandy Allen (USA, b. 18 June 1955) was 2 m 31.7 cm (7 ft 7.25 in). When she was born, she weighed 2.95 kg (6 lb 7 oz) and her abnormal growth began soon after. She stood 1 m 90.5 cm (6 ft 3 in) by the age of 10 and was 2.16 m (7 ft 1 in) by 16.

★ **NEW RECORD**
☆ **UPDATED RECORD**

SHORTEST WOMAN EVER

Pauline Musters (Netherlands, b. 26 February 1876) measured 30 cm (1 ft) at birth. At nine years of age, she was 55 cm (1 ft 9.5 in) tall and weighed only 1.5 kg (3 lb 5 oz). She died of pneumonia with meningitis on 1 March 1895 in New York City, USA, at the age of 19. A post mortem revealed her to be 61 cm (2 ft) tall – there was some elongation after death.

ANATOMICAL MILESTONES

SHORTEST MAN EVER

The shortest mature human of whom there is independent evidence was Gul Mohammed (India, 1957–97). On 19 July 1990, he was examined at Ram Manohar Hospital, New Delhi, India, and found to have a height of just 57 cm (1 ft 10.5 in).

SHORTEST PEOPLE LIVING

Madge Bester (South Africa, b. 26 April 1963), is only 65 cm (2 ft 1.5 in) tall. However, she suffers from osteogenesis imperfecta (characterized by brittle bones and other skeletal deformities) and is confined to a wheelchair. Her mother, Winnie, is just 70 cm (2 ft 2.5 in) tall.

The **shortest living man** is Taiwan's Lin Yih-Chih at 67.5 cm (27 in). He, too, is confined to a wheelchair because of osteogenesis imperfecta.

The **shortest living mobile man** is He Pingping (China) – see the "Shortest Man" gatefold to see him actual size and in glorious 3D!

SHORTEST TWINS

Matyus and Béla Matina (b. 1903– ca. 1935) of Budapest, Hungary – who later became American citizens – both measured 76 cm (2 ft 6 in) tall.

GREATEST HEIGHT DIFFERENCE BETWEEN A MARRIED COUPLE

Fabien Pretou (France, b. 15 June 1968), who stood 188.5 cm (6 ft 2 in) tall, married Natalie Lucius (France, b. 19 January 1966), measuring 94 cm (3 ft 1 in) tall, at Seyssinet-Pariset, France, on 14 April 1990. Their height difference was 94.5 cm (3 ft 1 in).

GREATEST WEIGHT DIFFERENCE BETWEEN A MARRIED COUPLE

On their wedding day in March 1978, Jon Brower Minnoch (USA) – the **heaviest human being who ever lived** (see panel on p.60) – weighed ca. 635 kg (1,400 lb; 100 st) and his wife Jeannette (USA) just 50 kg (110 lb; 8 st). This is a difference of 585 kg (1,289 lb; 91 st).

MOST VARIABLE STATURE

Adam Rainer (Austria, 1899– 1950) measured just 1.18 m (3 ft 10.5 in) at the age of 21 but suddenly started growing at a rapid rate. By 1931, he had nearly doubled to 2.18 m (7 ft 1.75 in). He became so weak that he was bedridden for the rest of his life. At the time of his death, he measured 2.34 m (7 ft 8 in) and was the only person in medical history to have been both a dwarf and a giant.

X-REF

How well do you know your own body? If you've ever been curious about what your longest bone or largest organ is, flip back to **Anatomy** on p.58. And remember: you're never too young (or old) to be a record breaker. Don't believe us? Then fast forward to **Youngest...** (p.88) and **Oldest...** (p.90).

HEAVIEST MAN ALIVE?

In January 2006, when he first made a television appeal for help with his size, Manuel Uribe Garza (Mexico) weighed 560 kg (1,232 lb) and was the world's heaviest living human. Since then, with medical assistance and The Zone diet, the bed-bound behemoth has been losing weight at a spectacular rate. Just two years after Manuel's initial appeal, his weight was down to an impressive 299.3 kg (660 lb; 47 st 2 lb) – leaving the title of world's heaviest living man wide open for new applicants!

MANUEL URIBE'S WEIGHT LOSS

JAN 08

468.1 kg (1,032 lb) (73 st 10 lb)

558.8 kg (1,232 lb) (88 st)

382.8 kg (844 lb) (60 st 4 lb)

408.2 kg (900 lb) (64 st 4 lb)

299.3 kg (660 lb) (47 st 2 lb)

374.2 kg (825 lb) (58 st 13 lb)

FEB 06

The heaviest living man is Manuel Uribe (Mexico), who weighed 560 kg (1,235 lb; 88 stone) in January 2006

GUINNESS WORLD RECORDS
CERTIFICATE
GUINNESS WORLD RECORDS LTD.

BEING HUMAN
BODY PARTS

★ NEW RECORD
★ UPDATED RECORD

★ MOST TOES AND FINGERS ON A LIVING PERSON

Two individuals possess 25 digits. Pranamya Menaria (India, above) has 12 fingers and 13 toes as a result of the conditions polydactyly and syndactyly. Devendra Harne (India) has also grown 12 fingers and 13 toes as a result of polydactyly.

A coroner's inquest held on a baby boy at Shoreditch in east London, UK, on 16 September 1921 confirmed that he had 14 fingers and 15 toes, the **most fingers and toes ever** recorded on a human being.

FEWEST TOES

Some members of the Wadomo tribe of the Zambezi Valley, Zimbabwe, and the Kalanga tribe of the eastern Kalahari Desert, Botswana, have two toes on each foot, owing to a single mutated, hereditary gene.

LARGEST HANDS

Robert Wadlow (USA), the **tallest man ever**, (see p.60) had hands that measured 32.3 cm (12.75 in) from the wrist to the tip of his middle finger. He wore a size-25 ring.

Hussain Bisad (UK, b. Somalia) has hands measuring 26.9 cm (10.5 in) from wrist to tip of middle finger, the **largest hands on a living person**.

LARGEST FEET

Robert Wadlow (USA) wore US size 37AA shoes (UK size 36; European size 75), equivalent to 47 cm (18.5 in) in length.

The **tallest woman ever**, Zeng Jinlian (China, see also p.60) had feet measuring 35.5 cm (14 in) in length.

★ LONGEST LEGS (FEMALE)

Svetlana Pankratova's (Russia) legs were measured at 132 cm (51.9 in) long in Torremolinos, Spain, on 8 July 2003. Her unique gift presents certain challenges – she has to have some clothes specially made, ducks through most doorways, and needs lots of legroom in cars and aeroplanes. But that's a small price to pay if you're the "Queen of the Longest Legs"!

★ OLDEST PERSON WITH A NEW TOOTH

In March 2007, Mária Magdolna Pozderka (Hungary, b. 19 July 1938, above) – then 68 – had an upper right canine tooth erupt.

The **oldest man to grow a new tooth** is Mark Tora (UK, above centre), who was 61 years old when a lower right third molar (wisdom tooth) erupted in February 2002. (Wisdom teeth normally erupt between the ages of 15 and 25.)

DID YOU KNOW?

On 24 October 2002, Matthew Adams (USA) had two wisdom teeth removed at the age of just 9 years 339 days, making him the **youngest person to have a wisdom tooth extracted**.

The **longest human tooth extracted** measured 2.53 cm (0.99 in). It was removed from 12-year-old Philip Puszczalowski (Canada) in 1993.

★ MOST TEETH

Meriano Luca (Italy) had 35 adult teeth as of 15 January 2004. (By way of comparison, it is normal to have up to 32 adult teeth.)

★ LONGEST MILK TOOTH

Ahmed Afrah Ismail (Maldives) had a milk tooth that measured 2.3 cm (0.9 in), with a crown length of 1 cm (0.39 in) and a root length of 1.3 cm (0.5 in).

★ FARTHEST EYEBALL POP

In Istanbul, Turkey, on 2 November 2007, Kim Goodman (USA) popped her eyeballs 12 mm (0.47 in) beyond her eye sockets.

★ LONGEST TIME TO KEEP THE EYEBALLS PROTRUDED

Keith Smith (USA) kept his eyes popped out of their sockets for 43 seconds on the set of *Lo Show dei Record*, in Madrid, Spain, on 9 February 2008.

★ LOWEST HEART RATE

Martin Brady (UK) had a resting heartbeat of 27 beats per minute when he was tested at the Guernsey Chest and Heart Unit, Channel Islands, UK, on 11 August 2005.

★ LARGEST KIDNEY STONE

Vilas Ghuge (India) had a stone removed from his left kidney on 18 February 2004 by Dr Hemendra Shah (India) at R. G. Stone Urological Research Institute, Mumbai, India. The stone was 13 cm (5.1 in) at its widest point.

LONGEST TONGUE

Stephen Taylor's (UK) tongue measures 9.5 cm (3.7 in) from the tip to the centre of his closed top lip. The awesome organ was measured on the set of *Lo Show dei Record* in Milan, Italy, on 5 January 2006.

STRETCHIEST SKIN

Owing to a rare condition called Ehlers-Danlos syndrome, Garry Turner (UK) has exceptionally malleable skin – so much so that he is able to perform the "human turtleneck" by pulling his neck skin up over his mouth!

THE FIVE SENSES

FASTEST TALKER

Sean Shannon (Canada) recited Hamlet's soliloquy "To be or not to be" (260 words) in a time of 23.8 seconds (655 words per minute) in Edinburgh, UK, on 30 August 1995.

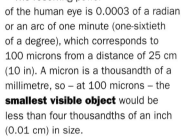

HOTTEST SPICE

The hottest of all spices is believed to be the chili pepper Bhut Jolokia, belonging to the species *Capsicum chinense*, which was measured at 1,001,304 Scoville Heat Units (SHU) at the New Mexico State University, Las Cruces, New Mexico, USA, on 9 September 2006.

HEARING

The intensity of noise or sound is measured in terms of pressure. The pressure of the **lowest pitch** that can be detected by a person of normal hearing at the most sensitive frequency of around 2,750 Hz is 2×10^{-5} pascal. One-tenth of the logarithm to this standard provides a unit termed a decibel (dB). A noise of 30 dB is negligible.

• The limit for the **highest detectable pitch** is accepted to be 20,000 Hz (cycles per sec), although it has been alleged that children with asthma can detect sounds of 30,000 Hz.

• According to a year-long online survey by Trevor Cox, Professor of Acoustic Engineering at Salford University, UK, the ★ **most repellent sound to the human ear** is that of someone vomiting, which beat the jarring sounds of a baby's wailing, a dentist's drill and microphone feedback (among many others) to reach the top spot.

SIGHT

The **most distant object visible with the naked eye** is the Andromeda Galaxy in the constellation of Andromeda (mag. 3.47), known as Messier 31. It is a spiral galaxy situated about 2.2 million light years away from Earth.

• The resolving power of the human eye is 0.0003 of a radian, or an arc of one minute (one-sixtieth of a degree), which corresponds to 100 microns from a distance of 25 cm (10 in). A micron is a thousandth of a millimetre, so – at 100 microns – the **smallest visible object** would be less than four thousandths of an inch (0.01 cm) in size.

LOUDEST SCREAM

Classroom assistant Jill Drake (UK) had a scream that reached 129 dB when measured at the Halloween festivities held in the Millennium Dome, London, UK, in October 2000.

NEW RECORD
UPDATED RECORD

TASTE

The ★ **sweetest substance** is Thaumatin, also known as Thalin®, obtained from arils (appendages found on certain seeds) of the katemfe plant (*Thaumatococcus daniellii*). It is 3,250 times sweeter than sugar (compared to a 7.5% sucrose solution).

• The **bitterest substances** are based on the denatonium cation and have been produced commercially as benzoate and saccharide. Taste detection levels are as low as one part in 500 million.

TOUCH

Our skin contains a variety of touch receptors with differing functions. Meissner's corpuscles react to light touch and are located in sensitive areas of the skin, such as our fingertips. Our fingers are so sensitive that they can detect a vibration with a movement of just 0.02 microns (0.000019 mm).

★ SMELLIEST CHEESE

According to research conducted by Cranfield University, UK, in November 2004, the smelliest cheese is Vieux Boulogne. This soft cheese, matured for seven to nine weeks, is made from cow's milk by cheesemaker Philippe Olivier (France).

★ LONGEST FULL-BODY ICE-CONTACT ENDURANCE

On 17 April 2008, Wang Jintu (China) set a new world record when he spent 1 hour 30 minutes in direct, full-body contact with blocks of ice. The record was set at the Beijing Fu Li Cheng Building, Beijing, China.

SMELL

Ethyl mercaptan (C_2H_5SH) and butyl seleno-mercaptan (C_4H_9SeH) are the **smelliest molecules** in the world with an odour reminiscent of a combination of rotting cabbage, garlic, onions, burnt toast and sewer gas.

• The **smelliest substances** are the man-made "Who-Me?" and "US Government Standard Bathroom Malodor", which have five and eight chemical ingredients respectively. Bathroom Malodor smells mainly of human faeces and becomes repellent to the human nose at just two parts per million. It was originally created to test the power of deodorising products.

• Madeline Albrecht (USA) was employed at the Hill Top Research Laboratories in Cincinnati, Ohio, USA, a testing lab for products by Dr. Scholl. She worked there for 15 years and had to smell thousands of feet and armpits. During her career, she sniffed approximately 5,600 feet and an indeterminate number of armpits, giving her the record for **most feet and armpits sniffed**.

LOUDEST BURPS

Paul Hunn (UK) delivered a burp that read 104.9 dB on a certified and calibrated class 1 precision measuring noise level meter, from a distance of 2.5 m (8 ft 2 in) and 1 m (3 ft 3 in) high, at the offices of Guinness World Records, London, UK, on 20 July 2004.

The ★ **loudest burp by a woman**, measured under the same conditions, read 104.75 dB and was achieved by Jodie Parks (USA, above) on the set of *Lo Show dei Record*, in Madrid, Spain, on 16 February 2008.

HAIR

MOST EXPENSIVE HAIR SOLD

A mass of hair cuttings from the head of Elvis Presley were sold by his personal barber, Homer Gilleland, for $115,120 (£72,791, including buyer's premium) to an anonymous bidder during an online auction held by MastroNet Inc, Oak Brook, Illinois, USA, on 15 November 2002. Here Presley is pictured with army barber James Peterson after his induction into the US Army.

HAIR RAZORS

On 11 September 2004, Trevor Mitchell (UK) cut a full head of hair in a time of 1 min 11 sec at ITV London Studios, London, UK – **the fastest haircut ever**.

The ★**highest hairstyle** measured 92.5 cm (3 ft) and was achieved by Mirre Hammarling (Sweden) in Haningen, Sweden, on 2 November 2007.

LONGEST...

ARM HAIR

Robert Starrett (USA) had an arm hair that had grown to a length of 13.5 cm (5.3 in) when measured in Mequon, Wisconsin, USA, on 7 December 2006.

BEARD ON A LIVING WOMAN

Vivian Wheeler (USA), who first started to shave at the age of seven, finally grew a full beard in 1990. The longest strand of hair, from the follicle to the tip, measured 27.9 cm (11 in) in 2000.

★ CHEST HAIR

The longest chest hair ever measured was 22.8 cm (9 in) long and belonged to Richard Condo (USA). The length was verified on 29 April 2007.

EAR HAIR

Radhakant Bajpai (India) has hair sprouting from the tragus – the skin covering a small cartilage flap just in front of the ear hole – that measures 13.2 cm (5.19 in) at its longest point.

★ EYEBROW HAIR

Toshie Kawakami (Japan) had an eyebrow hair 15.1 cm (5.94 in) in length when measured at the Guinness World Records Museum, Tokyo, Japan, on 22 January 2008.

★ LEG HAIR

Wesley Pemberton (USA) had a leg hair measuring 12.7 cm (5 in) in Tyler, Texas, USA, on 10 August 2007.

MOUSTACHE

The moustache of Kalyan Ramji Sain (India) has been growing since 1976. By July 1993 it had a span of 3.39 m (11 ft 1.5 in) – the right side 1.72 m (5 ft 7.75 in) and the left side 1.67 m (5 ft 5.75 in).

★ NIPPLE HAIR

A nipple hair belonging to Douglas Williams (USA) was 12.9 cm (5.07 in) long on 26 May 2007 in New York City, USA.

LONGEST BEARD

On 18 August 1997, the beard of Shamsher Singh (India) was measured in Punjab, India. From the end of his chin to the tip of the beard, it was an amazing 1.83 m (6 ft) long.

★ MOST SCISSORS USED TO CUT HAIR

Zedong Wang (China) used 10 pairs of scissors in one hand, controlling each pair independently, to style a head of hair on the set of *Zheng Da Zong Yi – Guinness World Records Special* in Beijing, China, on 31 October 2007.

★ LARGEST BEARD AND MOUSTACHE CHAMPIONSHIPS

The latest World Beard and Moustache Championships – held in Brighton, UK, on 1 September 2007 – drew 250 entrants and 3,000 spectators. Overall winner Mr Elmar Weisser of the Swabian Beard Club, Germany, sculpted his facial hair into the shape of London's Tower Bridge. Most competitors strive to complement their extravagant facial fuzz with suitably eye-catching costumes.

LONGEST HAIR

Xie Qiuping (China) has been growing her hair from the age of 13 in 1973. When measured on 8 May 2004, her hair was 5.627 m (18 ft 5.54 in) long.

MOST...

★ EXPENSIVE HAIRCUT

A haircut by Stuart Phillips in Covent Garden, London, UK, on 29 October 2007 cost £8,000 ($16,420).

★ HAIR DONATED TO CHARITY IN 24 HOURS

On 21 May 2007, 881 people donated hair in Clinton, Mississippi, USA, in support of the Pantene Beautiful Lengths charity campaign. It weighed a whopping 48.72 kg (107 lb).

★ PEOPLE SHAVING IN ONE VENUE

On 3 March 2007, 1,580 people shaved simultaneously at the Gillette Fusion Shave for History and Charity event organized by P&G Singapore Private Ltd. at the Fountain of Wealth in Suntec City, Singapore.

★ SHAVED HEADS

A team of five hairstylists from Sears Hair Studio at Notre Dame College, Sudbury, Ontario, Canada, shaved 662 heads in four hours on 8 April 2006.

SPLITS TO A SINGLE HAIR

In 1976, Alfred West (UK) succeeded in splitting a human hair 17 times into 18 parts on eight occasions. All the divisions were made from the same point, using a razor.

HAIRIEST FAMILY

Victor "Larry" Ramos Gomez (Mexico) is one of a family of 19, spanning five generations and all suffering from the rare condition known as congenital generalized hypertrichosis, characterized by excessive facial and torso hair. The women of the family are covered with a light-to-medium coating of hair, while the men have thick hair on approximately 98% of their body, apart from the palms of their hands and the soles of their feet.

HEALTH

HEALTH & DISEASE

Lowest rate of death
United Arab Emirates:
1.3 deaths per 1,000 (2005)

Highest rate of death
Swaziland: 31.2 deaths per
1,000 of the population (2005)

Lowest rate of infant mortality
Singapore: 3 deaths per
1,000 live births (2005)

Highest rate of infant mortality
Sierra Leone: 159.8 deaths
per 1,000 live births (2005)

Most survivable cancer
Non-melanoma skin cancer:
97% survival rate

Most lethal cancer
Lung cancer: responsible for
17.8% of all cancer deaths
in 2000. Followed by
stomach cancer
(10.4%) and
liver cancer
(8.8%)

★ MOST BLOOD PRESSURE READINGS TAKEN IN 24 HOURS

The organization Novartis Pharma K.K.
(Japan) took 2,109 blood pressure
readings at the Chiba Marines Stadium
in Chiba, Japan, on 17 May 2007.

★ MOST VACCINATIONS IN A WORKING DAY

A total of 3,271 flu shots were
administered by Florida Hospital
Centra Care, working with Get Healthy
Florida and Seminole County Health
Department, at Florida Hospital
Centra Care in Sanford, Florida,
USA, on 9 November 2006.

★ LARGEST BODY-MASS INDEX (BMI) CHECK

On 5 September 2004, the body-mass
index of 3,594 participants were
recorded as part of the Singapore
Ministry of Health's National Healthy
Lifestyle Campaign Day, which
took place at Sentosa
Island, Singapore.
The body-
mass index
(BMI) is a
measure of
your body's
fat and
muscle
content. To calculate your BMI,
divide your weight in kilograms
by the square of your height in
metres. A figure of 20–25 is
considered acceptable; below
this and you are underweight;
above this, you are overweight
(25–30), obese (30–35) or
severely obese (35+).

HEALTH BUDGETS

According to a World Health
Organization (WHO) report for 2002
(the most recent data available),
the US government has the **highest
health budget** per capita. In 2002,
the equivalent allocation per person
amounted to $5,274 (£3,480).

By contrast, North Koreans received
the equivalent of just $0.30 (£0.18)
per person on health care in 2002, the
lowest health budget per capita,
according to the WHO.

DID YOU KNOW?

The world record
for the **most
bone marrow
donors recruited
in 24 hours** is
266 by Leben
Spenden – KMT
in Götzendorf,
Austria, on
2 September 2007.

★ LIFE EXPECTANCY

As of 2007, Andorrans had the
highest life expectancy, with
an average of 83.52 years:
80.62 years for males and
86.62 years for females.

The **lowest life expectancy**
is just 32.23 in Swaziland:
31.82 years for men and
32.62 years for women.

★ HAPPIEST AND UNHAPPIEST NATIONS

According to the World Database of
Happiness, the **happiest country** during
1995–2005 was Denmark, which scored
an average of 8.2 out of 10 (where 10
was the highest level of contentment).
By contrast, with an average score of
3.2, Tanzania ranked lowest, making it
the **least happy country** in the world.
The survey assessed how people in
95 different countries rated their
enjoyment of life as a whole.

★ LARGEST SKIN-CANCER SCREENING

The most extensive simultaneous skin-
cancer screening involved 10,359
participants at 123 different
locations across the USA for an
event organized by the American
Academy of Dermatology on
6 May 2006.

> *If appropriate action is not taken, by 2015 an estimated 20 million people will die from cardiovascular disease.*
> World Health Organization report

★ HIGHEST CIGARETTE CONSUMPTION PER CAPITA

The Greeks smoke an average of 8.5 cigarettes per person per day, according to *The Economist*. In a similar study, the World Health Organization puts the annual total of cigarettes smoked in Greece at 3,230 per person.

MOST URGENT HEALTH PROBLEM

The WHO estimates that by 2020, tobacco-related illness such as heart disease, cancer and respiratory disorders will be the world's leading killer, responsible for more deaths than AIDS, tuberculosis, road accidents, murder and suicide combined.

DEADLIEST DISEASE

Based on estimates from the United Nations Health Report 2004, 57 million people died of numerous causes in 2002. Of this total, the disease that killed the most people was ischaemic heart disease, with an estimated 7.2 million deaths (12.6% of the total).

Among communicable diseases, HIV/AIDs caused the highest number of fatalities, with 2.8 million deaths (4.9% of the total).

★ **NEW RECORD**
★ **UPDATED RECORD**

★ MOST WIDESPREAD ZOONOSIS

Leptospirosis is the most widespread zoonosis – that is, a disease naturally transmitted from vertebrate animals such as rats, cattle, foxes and other wild or domestic animals to humans through cuts or mucous membranes during contact with urine in contaminated soil or water. The disease can occur everywhere, but typical outbreaks are in tropical and sub-tropical areas, such as Nicaragua (pictured).

The World Health Organization (WHO) estimates the annual incidence of infection in these humid areas to be as high as 100 per 100,000.

★ MOST COMMON CAUSE OF DEATH

According to the latest WHO figures, the most common cause of death, globally, is cardiovascular disease, which in 2005 caused the deaths of approximately 17.5 million people (equivalent to 30% of all deaths). Of this figure, 7.6 million were the result of heart attacks and 5.7 million were caused by strokes.

In 1998, the **most common cause of death among children** (defined by the WHO as aged between 0 and 4 years old) was infectious diseases, which accounted for 63% of all fatalities. The term "infectious diseases" refers to all communicable diseases, including parasitic and zoonotic diseases, and some forms of respiratory and diarrhoeal diseases.

MOST PEOPLE MASSAGED

At Potters Fields Park in London, UK, on 21 October 2007, 154 people received a massage at the same time. All participants sat on inflatable chairs and were massaged for at least 15 minutes by qualified practitioners to celebrate the launch of a new range of offers from the Nectar (UK) loyalty-points card system.

BEING HUMAN
FITNESS

PADDY POWERS TO NEW HEIGHTS

Fitness and endurance champion Paddy Doyle (UK) had a record-breaking day at Stamina's Boxing Self Defence Gym in Erin Go Bragh Sports Centre, Birmingham, UK, on 8 November 2007, when he powered his way to three new world records:

Paddy established a new mark for the **most full contact kicks in one hour** when he completed 5,750 kicks.

He also completed the **most push-ups using the backs of the hands in one hour** with a record 1,940 repetitions.

Finally, the strongman pulled off the **most squats in one hour** with 4,708 squats in the 60-minute time limit.

MOST... IN ONE MINUTE

★ BODY SKIPS
Brittany Boffo (Australia) was able to "skip" with her arms (stepping through her arms and bringing them up and over her head) a total of 68 times in a minute on the set of *Lo Show dei Record* in Madrid, Spain, on 9 February 2008.

★ KNEE BENDS ON A SWISS BALL
Stephen Buttler (UK) performed 54 knee bends in one minute while standing on a Swiss ball in Shropshire, UK, on 28 October 2007.

★ ROUNDHOUSE KICKS
Mark Scott (UK) performed a total of 148 roundhouse kicks in one minute at the Griphouse Gym, Glasgow, UK, on 18 November 2007.

★ SIT-UPS USING AN ABDOMINAL FRAME
On 14 April 2006, at the New York Sports Club in Forest Hills, New York, USA, Ashrita Furman (USA) completed a total of 177 sit-ups using an abdominal frame in one minute.

MOST PARALLEL BAR DIPS IN ONE HOUR
Simon Kent (UK) completed 3,989 parallel bar dips in one hour at Farrahs Health Centre, Lincoln, UK, on 5 September 1998.

★ SIDE JUMPS
Alastair Galpin (New Zealand) made 90 side jumps (alternating each leg) in one minute at The Warehouse shop in Sylvia Park, Auckland, New Zealand, on 27 October 2007.

★ SKIPS
Olga Berberich (Germany) completed 251 skips on the set of *Guinness World Records: Die Größten Weltrekorde*, in Cologne, Germany, on 1 September 2007.

★ SQUAT THRUSTS
Craig De-Vulgt (UK) did 70 squat thrusts in one minute at the Wave for Wales event in Margam Country Park, UK, on 24 June 2007.

FACT
Simon Kent (UK, see above) also holds the record for the **most parallel bar dips in one minute**. Simon managed 173 dips within the 60-second time limit at Lincoln University, Lincoln, UK, on 15 November 2006.

★ STAR JUMPS
Ashrita Furman (USA) completed 51 star jumps in one minute in front of the Gateway Arch in St Louis, Missouri, USA, on 28 January 2008.

★ CARTWHEELS
Ivan Koveshnikov (USA) completed 54 cartwheels in a minute at the Multnomah Athletic Club, Portland, Oregon, USA, on 13 August 2007.

PUSH-UPS (USING BACKS OF HANDS)
John Morrow (USA) completed 123 push-ups using the backs of his hands in one minute at Saint Ambrose University in Davenport, Iowa, USA, on 5 May 2006.

★ MOST FULL CONTACT PUNCH STRIKES IN ONE HOUR
Paddy Doyle (UK) made 29,850 full contact punch strikes in one hour at Stamina's Gym, Erin Go Bragh Sports Centre, Erdington, Birminghham, UK, on 21 January 2008.

GREATEST DISTANCE STATIC CYCLING IN 24 HOURS
Brian O. Pedersen (Denmark) clocked up a distance of 1,377.79 km (856.11 miles) on a static cycle in 24 hours at Club La Santa, Lanzarote, Canary Islands, Spain, on 10–11 June 2004.

> *Sumo squats work every major muscle group in the body.*
>
> Dr Thienna Ho, sumo squat record holder

MOST... IN ONE HOUR

BENCH PRESSES

Michael Williams (UK) achieved 1,438 repetitions of his bodyweight of 67 kg (147.7 lb) in one hour by bench presses at Don Styler's Gymnasium, Gosport, UK, on 17 April 1989.

★ CHIN-UPS

Stephen Hyland (UK) completed 812 chin-ups in one hour in Stoneleigh, Surrey, UK, on 18 October 2007.

PUSH-UPS

The greatest number of push-ups in one hour is 3,416 by Canadian Roy Berger at the Central Canada Exhibition, Ottawa, Canada, on 30 August 1998.

★ VAULTS

The 10–man Blue Falcons Gymnastic Display Team (all UK) carried out 5,685 vaults in Chelmsford, Essex, UK, on 13 September 2003.

ENDURANCE

★ TREADMILL – GREATEST DISTANCE COVERED IN ONE WEEK

Daniel Bocuze (France) ran 732.5 km (455.15 miles) on a treadmill in a week at the Casino Le Lion Blanc in St-Galmier, Rhône-Alpes, France, between 1 and 8 December 2007.

★ GREATEST AVERAGE DISTANCE RUN DAILY OVER ONE YEAR

Tirtha Kumar Phani (India) ran an average of 61.87 km (38.44 miles) every day from 30 June 2006 to 29 June 2007. He achieved this feat in Calcutta, India, running 22,581.09 km (14,031.15 miles) in total.

MOST SIT-UPS IN 24 HOURS

Jack Zatorski (USA) did 130,200 sit-ups using an abdominal frame in 24 hours at Accelerated Physical Therapy, Fort Lauderdale, USA, on 24–25 September 2005.

★ MOST ROTATIONS ON A VERTICAL ROPE IN ONE MINUTE

Brandon Pereyda (USA) completed 13 rotations on a vertical rope in one minute on the set of *Guinness World Records: Die Größten Weltrekorde* in Cologne, Germany, on 23 November 2007.

★ NEW RECORD
★ UPDATED RECORD

★ MOST SUMO SQUATS IN ONE HOUR

Dr Thienna Ho (Vietnam) performed 5,135 sumo squats in an hour at the San Francisco State University in San Francisco, California, USA, on 16 December 2007. Thienna said the record was in honour of her father, a judo master, who had inspired her to practise sumo squats when she was in her twenties.

EXTREME BEAUTY

★ LONGEST
FINGERNAILS
(FEMALE)

Lee Redmond (USA), who hasn't cut her nails since 1979, has grown and carefully manicured them to reach a total combined length of 8.65 m (28 ft 4.5 in).

LONGEST FINGERNAILS (MALE)

Melvin Boothe (USA) has a set of fingernails that had a combined length of 9.05 m (29 ft 8.3 in) when measured in Troy, Michigan, USA, on 2 June 2007.

LONGEST TOENAILS

Louise Hollis (USA) hasn't cut her toenails since 1982. When measured at their longest in 1991, their combined length was 2.2 m (7 ft 3 in).

PLASTIC SURGERY

★ MOST PLASTIC SURGERY PROCEDURES (COUNTRY)

Nearly 11.5 million cosmetic surgical and non-surgical procedures took place in the USA in 2006 – 92% on women. The American Society for Aesthetic Plastic Surgery (ASAPS) records 3,181,592 Botox injections for that year, making this the ★ **most popular non-surgical procedure**.

ACTUAL SIZE

SMALLEST WAIST (LIVING PERSON)

SMALLEST WAIST (EVER)

The smallest waist of a person with normal stature was 33 cm (13 in) and was recorded on Ethel Granger (UK, 1905–82). Ethel was 60 years old, 160 cm (5 ft 3 in) tall and weighed 54 kg (119 lb) when her corseted waist measured 33 cm (13 in). Her bust measurement was 86.3 cm (34 in) and her hips 101.6 cm (40 in). She did not commence waist reduction until she was 25, after the birth of her daughter. A measurement of 33 cm (13 in) was also claimed for the actress Mlle Polaire (b. Emile Marie Bouchand, France, 1881–1939).

15 IN (38.1 CM)

Cathie Jung (USA, left), who stands 1.72 m (5 ft 8 in) tall, has a corseted waist measuring 38.1 cm (15 in).

I'm just taking a very old tradition, that to my knowledge is not practiced anymore.

Dennis Avner aka Cat Man

★ MOST PIERCED WOMAN

Since having her first piercing in January 1997, Elaine Davidson (UK) has had 4,225 piercings over her body as of 8 June 2006.

LONGEST PENIS EXTENSION

A patient of Dr Bayard Olle Fischer Santos (Brazil) has had his penis enhanced by 16 cm (6.29 in) through surgery and physiotherapy. The first treatment was administered on 20 February 1995, and the patient's full distension of 27 cm (10.62 in) was achieved by 28 March 2000.

PIERCINGS

MOST PIERCINGS IN ONE SESSION

In a single session lasting 7 hr 55 min, Charlie Wilson (UK) pierced Kam Ma (UK) with 1,015 temporary metal rings at Sunderland Body Art, Tyne and Wear, UK, on 4 March 2006.

MOST PIERCED MAN

Luis Antonio Agüero, from Havana, Cuba, sports 230 permanent piercings on his body and head. His face alone carries more than 175 rings.

TATTOOS

MOST TATTOOED PERSON

Lucky Diamond Rich (Australia, born New Zealand), has spent over 1,000 hours having his body modified by hundreds of tattoo artists. His "body suit" of colourful designs has been entirely blacked in – including eyelids, the delicate skin between the toes, down into the ears and even his gums – and he is now being tattooed with white designs on top of the black, and coloured designs on top of the white!

MOST TATTOOED WOMAN

The world's most decorated woman is strip artiste Krystyne Kolorful (Canada). Tattoos cover 95% of her body and took 10 years to complete.

LONGEST SESSION

The record for the longest tattoo session stands at 43 hr 50 min and was achieved by Stephen Grady and Melanie Grieveson (both Australia) at the Twin City Tattoo and Body Piercing, Wodonga, Victoria, Australia, from 26 to 28 August 2006.

★ NEW RECORD
★ UPDATED RECORD

★ MOST SURGICAL PROCEDURES TO LOOK LIKE AN ANIMAL

Dennis Avner (USA), aka Cat Man, has undergone 14 separate surgical procedures in order to give cat-like features to his face, ears and teeth. His feline feat was verified on the set of *Lo Show dei Record*, in Madrid, Spain, on 9 February 2008.

DID YOU KNOW?

Dennis Avner's feline transformations included three operations on the ears, five implants on the forehead, cheekbones and chin, one modification of the upper lip, one modification of the nose and four dental modifications.

The ★ **most popular surgical procedure for women** in 2006 was breast augmentation, with 383,885 operations performed. The ★ **most popular surgical procedure for men** in that year was liposuction, with a total of 53,263 operations performed.

MOST BREAST AUGMENTATION PROCEDURES

The late Lolo Ferrari (b. Eve Valois, France, 1962–2000) had a bust measurement of 180 cm (5 ft 11 in) and a bra size of 54G – the result of at least 22 breast enlargement procedures over the course of five years from 1990.

★ LARGEST AUGMENTED BREASTS

When measured on 4 February 2005, Maxi Mounds (USA) had an under-breast measurement of 91.44 cm (36 in), an around-chest-over-nipple measurement of 153.67 cm (60.5 in) and a US bra size of 42M. She had her first implants (350 cc silicone) in 1991, which were replaced in 1993 with 700 cc saline. These were then inflated to 1,000 cc and, in 1998, replaced with 2,000 cc saline expander bags. In 1999, she had 1,100 cc of fluid and 2,000 cc of string implants added.

BEING HUMAN
GOLDEN OLDIES

★ **NEW RECORD**
☆ **UPDATED RECORD**

OLDEST PERSON

The greatest confirmed age to which any human has lived is 122 years 164 days by Jeanne Louise Calment (France). Born on 21 February 1875 to Nicolas and Marguerite (née Gilles), Jeanne died at a nursing home in Arles, France, on 4 August 1997.

OLDEST TWINS

Kin Narita (left) and Gin Kanie (both Japan, b. 1 August 1892), whose names mean "gold" and "silver" respectively, were the **oldest female twins** recorded to date. Kin died of heart failure on 23 January 2000 at the age of 107 years 175 days.

☆ OLDEST PERSON BAPTISED

Phyllis Nina Stewart (UK) was christened on 14 April 2002, aged 91 years 114 days, at Bishops Tawton Parish Church, Barnstaple, Devon, UK. She was born on 21 December 1910.

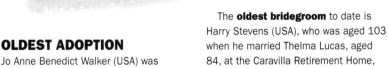

OLDEST ADOPTION

Jo Anne Benedict Walker (USA) was aged 65 years 224 days when she was officially adopted by Frances Ensor Benedict (USA) on 5 April 2002 in Putnam County, Tennessee, USA.

Frances (b. 11 May 1918) was 83 years 329 days old when she adopted Jo Anne, making Ms Benedict the **oldest adoptive parent**.

OLDEST BRIDE

Minnie Munro (Australia) was 102 years old when she married Dudley Reid, aged 83, at Point Clare, New South Wales, Australia, on 31 May 1991.

The **oldest bridegroom** to date is Harry Stevens (USA), who was aged 103 when he married Thelma Lucas, aged 84, at the Caravilla Retirement Home, Wisconsin, USA, on 3 December 1984.

☆ OLDEST LIVING MAN

Tomoji Tanabe was born in Miyakonojo, Miyazaki Prefecture, Japan, on 18 September 1895, and became the world's oldest living man on 24 January 2007 (upon the death of Emiliano Mercado Del Toro of Puerto Rico), aged 111 years 128 days.

OLDEST TRIPLETS

The longest-lived triplets recorded to date were Faith, Hope and Charity Cardwell, who were born on 18 May 1899 at Elm Mott, Texas, USA. Faith died on 2 October 1994, aged 95 years 137 days.

DID YOU KNOW?

The Ottman quadruplets of Munich, Germany – Adolf, Anne-Marie, Emma and Elisabeth – were born on 5 May 1912. All four quads lived to the age of 79, making them the **oldest quadruplets**.

OLDEST PERSON TO GET DIVORCED

On 21 November 1980, at the age of 101, Harry Bidwell of East Sussex, UK, divorced his 65-year-old wife.

OLDEST DIVORCED COUPLE – AGGREGATE AGE

On 2 February 1984, a divorce was granted in Milwaukee, Wisconsin, USA, to Ida Stern, aged 91, and her husband Simon, 97. Their combined age was 188.

OLDEST MALE TWINS

The oldest male twins authenticated were Glen and Dale Moyer (USA), both of whom reached the age of 105. Born on 20 June 1895, they became the oldest living twins on 23 January 2000.

The youngest of four children born to Mahlon and Anna Moyer, Dale was a retired farmer and was 20 minutes older than his brother Glen, a retired teacher. Glen passed away on 16 April 2001, aged 105 years, 9 months and 26 days.

OLDEST MOTHERS

Maria del Carmen Bousada Lara (Spain, b. 5 January 1940) gave birth by Caesarean section to twin boys – Christian and Pau, aged 66 years 358 days – at the Sant Pau Hospital, Barcelona, Spain, on 29 December 2006. This makes her both the **oldest mother** and the ★ **oldest person to give birth to twins**.

The **oldest mother to have quadruplets** is Australia's Merryl Thelma Fudel (née Coward), who gave birth to three girls and one boy on 18 April 1998, aged 55 years 286 days.

★ OLDEST WOMAN LIVING WITH DOWN'S SYNDROME

Joyce Greenman (UK, b. 14 March 1925) became the oldest living woman with Down's Syndrome on 12 December 2007, aged 82 years 273 days.

Peter Davison (UK, b. 20 October 1939) is currently the ★ **oldest living man with Down's Syndrome**. Mr Davison was 67 years 216 days old as of 24 May 2007.

★ MOST SIBLINGS TO REACH RETIREMENT AGE

The 19 siblings (seven sons and 12 daughters) born to Canadians Eugene (1892–1962) and Alice Theriault (1896–1967) between 1920 and 1941 were all claiming a government pension in 2007. They ranged in age from 66 to 87.

OLDEST LIVING PERSON

On 13 August 2007, Edna Parker (USA) became the oldest living person, aged 114 years 115 days.

THE TEN OLDEST OLDIES

1. **Jeanne Calment (France):** 122 years 164 days
2. **Shigechiyo Izumi (Japan):** 120 years 237 days*
3. **Sarah Knauss (USA):** 119 years 97 days
4. **Lucy Hannah (USA):** 117 years 248 days
5. **Marie-Louise Meilleur (Canada):** 117 years 230 days
6. **María Esther de Capovilla (Ecuador):** 116 years 347 days
7. **Tane Ikai (Japan):** 116 years 175 days
8. **Elizabeth Bolden (USA):** 116 years 118 days
9. **Carrie White (USA):** 116 years 88 days*
10. **Kamato Hongo (Japan):** 116 years 45 days*

There is some doubt about the authenticity of these cases

★ OLDEST BRIDESMAID

Edith Gulliford (UK, b. 12 October 1901) served as bridesmaid at the wedding of Kyra Harwood and James Lucas (both UK) on 31 March 2007 at Commissioner's House, Chatham, UK, at the age of 105 years 171 days.

GUINNESS WORLD RECORDS DAY

★ LONGEST WHEELIE ON A SKATEBOARD (FLAT SURFACE)

Stefan Akesson (Sweden) performed a one-wheel manual (wheelie) measuring 68.54 m (224 ft 10 in) on a flat surface at the Gallerian Shopping Centre, Stockholm, Sweden, on 2 November 2007.

★ MOST RATTLESNAKES (BATHTUB)

Jackie Bibby (USA), a.k.a. The Texas Snake Man, shared a bathtub with 87 snakes for 45 minutes on 5 November 2007 in Dublin, Texas, USA, as part of GWR Day.

★ MOST CANS COLLECTED

The most steel cans collected in one month is 1,971,026, weighing 61,443 kg (135,458 lb). The event was organized by Collect-a-Can, MySchool and Pan Macmillan in South Africa between 1 and 31 October 2007.

★ MOST BARS JUMPED ON A TRIAL BIKE

In celebration of GWR Day 2007, Vittorio Brumotti, a.k.a. "100%" (Italy), jumped 20 gapping bars on the back wheel of his trial bike in Milan, Italy (above).

Brumotti subsequently broke his own record by achieving 24 jumps on the set of Lo show dei record, in Madrid, Spain, on 9 February 2008.

MOST KISSES IN ONE MINUTE

Adrian Chiles (UK) received 78 kisses in one minute on BBC 1's The One Show, London, UK, on 8 November 2007 in celebration of GWR Day.

★ LARGEST HANDHELD GAME CONSOLE PARTY

K-Zone magazine and Nintendo held a party at which 381 gamers played their own Nintendo DS consoles for 10 minutes in Parramatta, Australia.

★ FASTEST 100 M BIKE SLED RACE (FOUR DOGS, ON SAND)

The record for the fastest 100 m on a dog sled pulled by four dogs on sand is 11.65 seconds by Suzannah Sorrell (UK) at Holkham National Nature Reserve in Holkham, Norfolk, UK, on 6 November 2007. On the same day, she also broke the record with six and eight dogs in times of 11.53 seconds and 10.65 seconds respectively.

★ LARGEST DULCE DU LECHE

A dulce de leche – a "caramelized milk candy" popular throughout Latin America – made by Rosario Olvera in Loreto, Zacatecas, Mexico, weighed a record 1,419.65 kg (3,129 lb 12 oz). And if you fancy making it, here's the ingredients list:

- **milk**: 1,750 litres (462 gallons)
- **sugar**: 1,800 litres (475 gallons)
- **cinnamon**: 12 kg (26 lb) cane and 10 kg (22 lb) powder
- **carbonated powder**: 3 kg (6 lb 9 oz)
- **walnuts**: 100 kg (220 lb)
- **almonds**: 100 kg (220 lb)

The final dessert measured: 20 cm wide by 258.93 m long (8 in by 850 ft).

★ MOST LETTERS TO SANTA IN A XMAS SEASON

During Christmas 2006, Santa received 1.06 million letters and 44,166 emails (each one responded to with the help of Santa's very special *Canada Post* elves). More than 11,000 *Canada Post* volunteers helped respond to these letters in 11 languages, including Braille. They were presented with their certificate on GWR Day 2007.

1,060,000 children wrote to Santa. He wrote back!

★ FARTHEST LEANING TOWER

The leaning tower of the Protestant church in Suurhusen, Germany, was unveiled as an official record to the world on GWR Day 2007. It leans at an angle of inclination of 5.1939 degrees.

US
RS

"beast-footed")
fearsome *T. rex*,
and the even bigger
saurus (pictured), which
grow to an estimated 13 m
ft 7 in) long with a weight of
tonnes (13,227 lb).

PREHISTORIC LIFE

LONGEST CLAWS

The therizinosaurids ("scythe lizards") from the Late Cretaceous period, found in the Nemegt Basin, Mongolia, had the largest claws of any known animal. In the case of *Therizinosaurus cheloniformis*, they measured up to 91 cm (3 ft) along the outer curve. It has been suggested that these talons were designed for grasping and tearing apart large victims, but this creature had a feeble skull, partially or entirely lacking teeth, and probably lived on termites.

TALLEST DINOSAUR

Dinosaur remains discovered in 1994 in Oklahoma, USA, belong to what is believed to be the largest creature to have ever walked the earth. The Sauroposeidon stood at 18 m (60 ft) tall and weighed 60 tonnes (132,277 lb). The length of its neck is about a third larger than that of the Brachiosaurus, its nearest competitor. It lived about 110 million years ago, during the mid-Cretaceous period.

LARGEST LAND-BASED CARNIVORO DINOSAUR

The therapods included the Allosaurus Giganot could (42 6

WIDEST DINOSAUR

Anklyosaurs, distinguished by a large club at the end of the tail, were up to 5 m (16 ft 4 in) wide and included the most heavily armoured dinosaurs of all the "tanks" of the Cretaceous world. The entire back was covered with bony plates, studs and spikes, and the head – right down to the eyelids – were also heavily armoured.

GUINNESS
WORLD
RECORDS
DAY NOVEMBER 2007

LARGEST & SMALLEST DOGS

Gibson, the world's tallest living dog (measuring 107 cm; 42.2 in tall) and Boo Boo, the smallest living dog (at 10.16 cm; 4 in) met for a photo shoot in Sacramento, USA, on GWR Day 2007. Read more about them on page 128.

★ MOST CONSECUTIVE ONE-GAME WINS OF WII SPORTS TENNIS

Staš Kostrzewski (France) had 21 consecutive one-game wins of Wii Sports Tennis at the Virgin Megastore, Paris, France, on 7 November 2007 as part of GWR Day. This is the most wins by an individual against multiple players.

BUS PULLING

One of Britain's strongest men pulled a double-decker bus over a distance of 5 m (16 ft 4.8 in) using only his ears. Manjit Singh managed to get the giant 7.5-tonne Routemaster moving, but unfortunately he failed in his bid to break a world record. He had hoped to pull the bus 10 m (33 ft) to kick off the third annual Guinness World Records Day, but only succeeded in moving the vehicle half of the way.

MISSED OUT ON GWR DAY? THERE'S ALWAYS NEXT YEAR

If you didn't take part in the last GWR Day, you can always try again next year. We're always keen to hear about your ideas, but you need to get in touch with our Records Management Team in plenty of time – preferably a couple of months before. Find out more by visiting: **www.guinness worldrecords.com/gwrday**

★ LONGEST LINE OF RIVERDANCERS

During the Guinness World Records Day 2007 celebrations on 8 November, 216 dancers from CLRG Dance Schools, Leinster Province, Ireland, danced in a "Riverdance" line. The event was held at St Stephen's Green, Dublin, Ireland.

GET INVOLVED IN GWR DAY...

Want to set or break a record on the next Guinness World Records Day? Find out how to register at **www.guinnessworldrecords. com/gwrday**. Good luck!

MOON LANDINGS

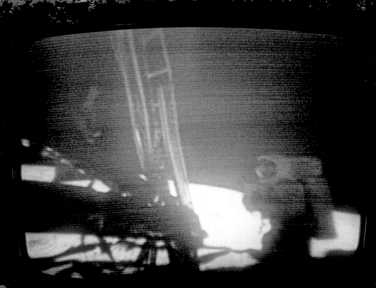

LARGEST TV AUDIENCE FOR A SPACE EVENT

The first moonwalk by the Apollo 11 astronauts was watched on TV by an estimated 600 million people, a fifth of the world's population at the time. The astronauts – Neil Armstrong, Edwin "Buzz" Aldrin and Michael Collins (all USA) – were the stars of a parade through New York City, USA, on 14 August 1969 to celebrate their historic achievement.

MOST REMOTE GOLF SHOT

In February 1971, astronaut Alan Shepard Jr (USA) struck two golf balls in the Fra Mauro region on the surface of the Moon. He used a club made from a sampling tool with a six-iron attached. One of the balls travelled a distance of around 15 m (50 ft).

★ NEW RECORD
★ UPDATED RECORD

CAPTAIN GENE CERNAN, THE LAST MAN ON THE MOON

US astronaut Captain Gene Cernan orbited the Moon in Apollo 10 and, as Commander of Apollo 17, was the last man to walk on its surface. He talked to Guinness World Records about his experience...

Can you describe the launch of the Saturn V?

I'm one of three people who had the chance to ride the Saturn V twice. I called it "my mistress", it was an unbelievable experience. During lift-off, if the booster guidance failed I could flip a switch and manually control 7.6 million lb [3,440 tonnes] of rocket thrust into Earth orbit and on to the Moon. I literally almost dared it to fail. I didn't want it to fail but I thought, "If you fail, sweetheart, I can handle you!"

What was it like to fly the lunar module?

People are going to look back in 50 or 100 years and say how the hell did they get to the Moon in that thing? Any movement you input you had to take back out, because it would continue until you stopped it as there were no aerodynamic effects in space to damp them out. When we were landing, if we didn't like what we saw, we could throttle up the descent engine or jettison it and use the ascent engine and get out of there. But once you're on the Moon, you have to put all your confidence in the ascent engine.

What impressed you most about the Moon?

The thing that impressed me when I made my first steps was that for the first time I was stepping on something that wasn't the Earth. You could climb the highest mountain on this planet of ours or go to the depths of the deepest ocean but you're still on Earth! But all of a sudden I was on something else out there in the Universe, with magnificent mountains. People would love me on this Earth of ours if I could turn everything into 1/6th gravity. It's just wonderful and there were only 12 people who ever experienced it! After three days on the Moon, standing on the ladder looking down at my last footprint, looking over my shoulder at the Earth in all its splendour, I realized I was not coming this way again. I literally wanted to stop the clock and press the freeze button. I wanted that moment to last forever.

When will we return to the Moon?

Some of my final words on the Moon were "May America's challenge of today lead to man's destiny of tomorrow." When I talk to 4th and 5th graders in school, I look them in the eye and say, "If I can go to the Moon before your mom and dad were born, you can tell me what you can do in your lifetime if you want to do it badly enough."

MOST
SUCCESSFUL
DINOSAUR GROUP

In terms of longevity and diversity, the most successful group of dinosaurs were the therapods. They were bipedal and mainly carnivorous and dominated the land from around 200 million years ago right up to the extinction of the dinosaurs some 65 million years ago. Allosaurus (pictured) grew up to around 10 m (32 ft 9 in) long and was the largest land-based carnivore of the late Jurassic period (144–150 million years ago) and existed some 85 million years before *Tyrannosaurus rex*.

LARGEST
PREHISTORIC INSECT

The dragonfly *Meganeura monyi*, which existed about 280 million years ago, was the largest insect that ever lived. Fossil remains (impressions of the creature's wings) discovered at Commentry, France, indicate a wing-span of up to 70 cm (2 ft 3.5 in).

LONGEST
DINOSAUR

The suborder of dinosaurs called the sauropoda were herbivorous land animals that first appeared in the late Triassic period, around 200 million years ago. They included the well-known Diplodocus and Brachiosaurus, but the longest of all was Amphicoelias, which is estimated to have been around 60 m (196 ft 10 in) long.

LARGEST
DINOSAUR SKULLS

The Ceratopsids were herbivorous dinosaurs characterized by their beaks, huge skull frills and horns, and included Triceratops and Torosaurus (pictured). A Pentaceratops skull on display in the USA measures 3.2 m (10 ft 5 in) in height.

APOLLO 11

Crew: Neil Armstrong, Commander; Edwin "Buzz" Aldrin Jr, Lunar Module Pilot; Michael Collins, Command Module Pilot
During landing, Armstrong took manual control of the lunar module to avoid a boulder field. The extra manoeuvres meant that when Apollo 11 finally touched down, less than 30 seconds of fuel remained in the descent engine's tank, the ★**least amount of fuel upon landing**.

APOLLO 15

Crew: David R. Scott, Commander; James B. Irwin, Lunar Module Pilot; Alfred M. Worden, Command Module Pilot
Apollo 15, as the first of the more extensive "J" missions, was the ★**first lunar mission to include a lunar rover** when it landed on 7 August 1971.

APOLLO 16

Crew: John W. Young, Commander; Charles M. Duke Jr, Lunar Module Pilot; Thomas K. Mattingly II, Command Module Pilot
The **highest lunar speed** record was set by the manned Apollo 16 Rover, driven by Commander John Young, with 18 km/h (11.2 mph) achieved downhill.

APOLLO 12

Crew: Charles Conrad, Commander; Alan L. Bean, Lunar Module Pilot; Richard F. Gordon, Command Module Pilot
Apollo 12 was to bring back samples of the robotic *Surveyor 3*, which landed on the Moon in April 1967. The Apollo 12 lander, crewed by Charles Conrad and Alan Bean, touched down on 19 November 1969 less than 200 m (656 ft) from *Surveyor 3*, the ★**nearest landing to an unmanned probe**.

APOLLO 14

Crew: Alan B. Shepard Jr, Commander; Edgar D. Mitchell, Lunar Module Pilot; Stuart A. Roosa, Command Module Pilot
Alan Shepard Jr became the ★**oldest person to land on the Moon**, aged 47 years old, when he touched down on 4 February 1971.

APOLLO 17

Crew: Gene A. Cernan, Commander (seated); Harrison H. Schmitt, Lunar Module Pilot (left); Ronald E. Evans, Command Module Pilot (standing, right)
Cernan and Schmitt spent 74 hr 59 min 40 sec on the lunar surface, the **longest time spent on the surface of any celestial body**. They also achieved the **longest moonwalk** in an extra-vehicular activity (EVA) that lasted 7 hr 37 min.

LARGEST ROCKET

The Saturn V rocket was the largest rocket launched. It stood 110.6 m (363 ft) tall with the *Apollo* spacecraft on top and weighed around 3,000 tonnes (6,613,000 lb) on the launch pad, depending upon the specific mission. The Saturn V had a lift-off thrust of 3,447 tonnes (7,600,000 lb). The five main engines had a combined thrust equivalent to 40 jumbo jets, and burned 3 tonnes (6,613 lb) of fuel per second. The first Saturn V launch, pictured left, took place on 9 November 1967 and the 13th (and last) on 14 May 1973.

LAUNCH ESCAPE TOWER

Capable of yanking the command module off the top of the rocket if it malfunctioned, aborting the mission.

COMMAND MODULE

Home to the crew during launch and splashdown, this is the only part of the spacecraft that returns to Earth.

SERVICE MODULE

Remains connected to the command module until just before re-entry and splashdown. Contains propulsion and life-support systems.

LUNAR EXCURSION MODULE

Lunar lander for two of the three crew. It has one engine for the lunar landing and another for lift-off. Third crew member remains in the command module.

SATURN V ROCKET

Everything below the Lunar Excursion Module is the massive rocket itself.

FIRST MEN ON THE MOON

Neil Alden Armstrong (USA), Commander of the Apollo 11 mission, became the first man to set foot on the Moon, at 02:56 GMT on 21 July 1969. He was followed out of the lunar module *Eagle* by Edwin Eugene "Buzz" Aldrin Jr (USA, pictured below).

THE SATURN V ROCKET

The Saturn V was a multi-stage rocket whose sections can be seen to the right. The bottom section, or "stage", had five main engines that propelled the rocket and spacecraft to an altitude of 61 km (37.9 miles) until the fuel in the tank above it ran out. Then this first stage was jettisoned, allowing the engines of the second stage to fire up, which accelerated the spacecraft to speeds approaching Earth orbital velocity. After the second stage was jettisoned, the third stage was used to boost the spacecraft to orbital velocity, and then again to break away from Earth orbit into a trajectory to the Moon.

HUMAN ACHIEVEMENTS

★ **MOST PEOPLE PERFORMING FULL-BODY BURNS**

Thomas Hangarter and his team (all Germany) performed 10 simultaneous full-body burns on the set of *Guinness World Records – Die Größten Weltrekorde* in Cologne, Germany, on 1 September 2007.

CONTENTS

YOUNGEST...

★ HEAD OF STATE

At the age of 26 years, on 30 April 1992, Valentine Strasser (Sierra Leone) assumed control of his country following a military coup. Strasser became head of state on 7 May 1992 and ruled until he was ousted from power on 16 January 1996.

YOUNGEST SPORTSPEOPLE

NAME (NAT.)	YOUNGEST...	AGE
Kim Yun-Mi (South Korea)	Team Olympic gold medallist	13 years 85 days
Marjorie Gestring (USA)	Individual Olympic gold medallist	13 years 268 days
Souleymane Mamam (Togo)	World Cup footballer (qualifier)	13 years 310 days
Hasan Raza (Pakistan)	Test match cricketer	14 years 227 days
Charlotte Dod (UK)	Wimbledon ladies' singles tennis champion	15 years 285 days
Martina Hingis (Switzerland)	Australian Open ladies' singles tennis champion	16 years 117 days
Monica Seles (USA, b. Yugoslavia)	French Open ladies' singles tennis champion	16 years 169 days
Tracy Austin (USA)	US Open ladies' singles tennis champion	16 years 271 days
Rodney W. Heath (Australia)	Australian Open men's singles tennis champion	17 years
Norman Whiteside (UK)	World Cup footballer (finals)	17 years 41 days
Michael Chang (USA)	French Open men's singles tennis champion	17 years 109 days
Boris Becker (Germany)	Wimbledon men's singles tennis champion	17 years 227 days
Jermaine O'Neal (USA)	NBA player	18 years 53 days
Fred Lindstrom (USA)	World Series Baseball player	18 years 339 days
Pete Sampras (USA)	US Open men's singles tennis champion	19 years 28 days
Marco Andretti (USA)	Indycar race winner	19 years 167 days
Henri Cornet (France)	Tour de France winner	19 years 350 days

★ ALPINE SKIER TO WIN OLYMPIC GOLD

Kjetil André Aamodt (Norway) won the first of his four career Olympic golds in Albertville, France, on 16 February 1992, aged 20 years 167 days.

F1 WORLD CHAMPION

Fernando Alonso (Spain) won his first Formula One World Championship title on 25 September 2005, at Interlagos, Brazil, aged 24 years 59 days.

★ GOLFER TO WIN A PRO TOURNAMENT

Ryo Ishikawa (Japan) was 15 years 245 days old when he won the Munsingwear Open KSB Cup at Tojigaoka Marine Hills Golf Club, Okayama, Japan, on 20 May 2007.

X-REF

Does golf suit you to a tee? Then putter across to p.204 in the Sports section for more golf stats.

★ HOLE-IN-ONE GOLFER (FEMALE)

Soona Lee-Tolley (USA) was only 5 years 103 days old when she hit a hole-in-one at the par 3 seventh at Manhattan Woods Golf Club, West Nyack, New York, USA, on 1 July 2007.

★ PROFESSOR

Alia Sabur (USA, b. 22 February 1989), was appointed as a full-time faculty Professor of the Department of Advanced Technology Fusion at Konkuk University, Seoul, South Korea, with effect from 19 February 2008, aged 18 years 362 days.

★ KITESURFING WORLD CHAMPION (FEMALE)

Gisela Pulido (Spain) won her first Kiteboard Pro World Tour (KPWT) World Championship on 4 November 2004, aged 10 years 294 days. She won her first Professional Kiteboard Riders Association Championship on 26 August 2007, aged 13 years 224 days.

★ CLUB DJ

DJ Jack Hill (UK, b. 20 May 2000) played at CK's Bar and Club in Weston-super-Mare, UK, on 26 August 2007, aged 7 years and 98 days. Jack, who started DJing when he was only three, has his own full-size decks, but has to stand on a box to reach the controls.

> *Facebook has 52 million active users, and could have 200 million users by the end of 2008*
>
> *www.portfolio.com, November 2007*

★ **NEW RECORD**
★ **UPDATED RECORD**

★ BILLIONAIRE

The youngest US dollar billionaire is Mark Zuckerberg (USA, b. 14 May 1984), who had an estimated net worth of $1.5 billion (£756 million) when listed on Forbes.com on 5 March 2008, aged 23 years 296 days. Mr Zuckerberg is the CEO of the social networking site Facebook, which he founded in February 2004.

WINNER OF THE NOBEL PEACE PRIZE

In 1992, Rigoberta Menchú Tum (Guatemala) was awarded the Nobel Peace Prize "in recognition of her work in social justice and ethnocultural reconciliation based on respect for the rights of indigenous people". At 33, she was the first indigenous person, and the youngest person ever, to receive this honour.

POOL WORLD CHAMPION

Chia-ching Wu (Taiwan) was 16 years 121 days old when he won the World Championship pool title in Kaohsiung, Taiwan, on 10 June 2005.

RODEO WORLD CHAMPION

After more than four decades, Anne Lewis's (USA) rodeo record still stands. She was 10 years old when she won the WPRA barrel racing title in 1968. In this event, the rider has to successfully manoeuvre their horse in a clover-leaf pattern around three barrels.

★ WEARER OF A FULL SET OF DENTURES

Daniel Sanchez-Ruiz (UK) was given a full set of dentures on 25 February 2005 at the age of 3 years and 301 days. He lost his teeth owing to a condition called hypohidrotic ectodermal dysplasia.

TRAVELLER TO ALL SEVEN CONTINENTS

Thomas Lucian Staff (UK) was born on 14 January 2006. On 4 January 2007, aged 355 days, he visited Antarctica – the seventh continent since his birth. With his parents, Neil Staff and Susan Crawford, Thomas visited Asia (14–19 Apr), North America (8–13 Jun), Australia (2–9 Sep), Europe (20–22 Oct), Africa (30 Nov–12 Dec), South America (29 Dec 2006–11 Jan 2007 and Antarctica (4–8 Jan).

OLDEST...

★ OLDEST PRIMARY SCHOOL STUDENT

Kimani Ng'ang'a Maruge (Kenya) enrolled at Kapkenduiyo Primary School, Eldoret, Kenya, on 12 January 2004, aged 84. On 6 April 2004, Ng'ang'a passed his first end-of-term exams with straight As in English, Kiswahili and maths.

★ ALPINE SKIING OLYMPIC GOLD MEDALLIST

Kjetil André Aamodt (Norway, b. 2 September 1971) won his fourth Alpine skiing Olympic gold medal in Turin, Italy, on 18 February 2006, aged 34 years 169 days.

PROFESSIONAL BULL RIDER

Adriano Moraes (Brazil, b. 10 April 1970) competed in the 2005 Professional Bull Riders World Finals aged 35.

SPORT RECORD BREAKER

Gerhard Weidner (West Germany, b. 15 March 1933) set a record 20-mile-walk time of 2 hr 30 min 38.6 sec on 25 May 1974, aged 41 years 71 days. He is the oldest sportsperson to set an official world record that is open to all ages and recognized by an international governing body.

★ PERSON TO SKI TO BOTH POLES

Norbert H. Kern (Germany, b. 26 July 1940) skied to the South Pole on 18 January 2007 and the North Pole on 27 April 2007, aged 66 years 275 days.

★ LIFEGUARD

Edwin McCarthy (USA, b. 8 April 1925) has worked as a lifeguard since 1992.

★ CURRENT MONARCH

Abdullah bin Abdulaziz Al-Saud, the King of Saudi Arabia, was born in August 1924 and became the oldest living monarch on 11 May 2007, aged 82 years 253 days.

NEWLY APPOINTED CHIEF OF STATE

After the German invasion of France in 1940, Henri Philipe Pétain (1856–1951) was recalled to active military service as adviser to the minister of war. On 16 June 1940, aged 84, he succeeded Paul Reynaud as premier of France.

★ OLDEST BALLET DANCER (MALE)

The oldest male ballet dancer is Frank Russell Galey (USA, b. 7 September 1932) who was aged 74 years and 101 days at this latest performance in The Nutcracker with Mendocino Ballet, Ukiah, California, USA on 17 December 2006.

NOBEL LAUREATE

In 1966, Professor Francis Peyton Rous (USA, 1879–1970) shared in the Physiology or Medicine prize, aged 87.

OLDEST HOLE-IN-ONE GOLFER

Otto Bucher (Switzerland, b. 12 May 1885) achieved a hole-in-one on the 119-m (130-yd) 12th hole at La Manga GC, Spain, on 13 January 1985. At the time, he was aged 99 years 244 days.

★ OLDEST SHOWGIRL

Dorothy Kloss (USA, b. 27 October 1923) regularly performs in the chorus line of The Fabulous Palm Springs Follies, Palm Springs, California, USA.

★ GRADUATE

Allan Stewart (Australia, b. 7 March 1915) received a Bachelor of Laws degree aged 91 years and 214 days when he graduated from the University of New England, New South Wales, Australia, on 7 October 2006.

BANK ROBBER

J. L. Hunter Rountree (USA, b. 1911) admitted stealing $1,999 (£1,243.08) from a bank in Texas, USA, and was sentenced to 151 months in prison on 3 January 2004, aged 92.

OLDEST SPORTSPEOPLE

NAME/NATIONALITY	OLDEST...	AGE
Firmin Lambot (Belgium)	Tour de France winner	36 years 4 months
Kenneth Robert Rosewall (Australia)	Australian Open men's singles tennis champion	37 years 62 days
William Larned (USA)	US Open men's singles tennis champion	38 years 242 days
P. J. "Babe" McDonald (USA)	Olympic athletics gold medallist (25.4 kg weight throw)	42 years 26 days
Albert Roger Milla (Cameroon)	FIFA World Cup player and scorer	42 years 39 days
Robert Parish (USA)	NBA basketball player	43 years 231 days
W. H. "Billy" Meredith (UK)	International football player	45 years 229 days
Juan Manuel Fangio (Argentina)	F1 world champion	46 years 41 days
Martina Navratilova (USA)	Wimbledon tennis champion	46 years 261 days
Tebbs Lloyd Johnson (UK)	Olympic athletics medallist (50,000 m walk)	48 years 115 days
Wilfred Rhodes (UK)	Test cricket player	52 years 165 days
Louis Alexandre Chiron (Monaco)	F1 Grand Prix driver	55 years 292 days
Leroy "Satchel" Page (USA)	Baseball player	59 years 80 days
Oscar Swahn (Sweden)	Olympic gold medallist (Running Deer shooting team)	64 years 258 days
Julia Jones (UK)	Hockey player	71 years
Tércio Mariano de Rezende (Brazil)	Football player	b. 31 December 1921
Arthur Sweeney (UK)	Table tennis player	88 years
Dimitrion Yordanidis (Greece)	Marathon runner	98 years
José Guadalupe Leal Lemus (Mexico)	Tennis player	b. 13 December 1902

Rountree, nicknamed Red, said he had robbed his first bank when he was around 80 years of age because he wanted revenge on banks for sending him into a financial crisis.

★ BEST MAN
Gerald W. Pike (USA, b. 12 October 1910) was best man at the marriage of Nancy Lee Joustra and Clifford Claire Hill (both USA), aged 93 years 166 days, on 26 March 2004 at Kent County, Michigan, USA.

★ BILLIONAIRE
The oldest living US dollar billionaire is John Simplot (USA, b. 4 January 1909), who had a net worth valued at $3.2 billion (£1.6 billion) when listed on Forbes.com on 8 March 2007, aged 98 years 63 days. Mr Simplot, of Boise, Idaho, USA, made his fortune in agriculture, notably in potato products.

★ PROFESSIONAL ARTIST
Moses Aleksandrovich Feigin (Russia, b. 23 October 1904) held his last exhibition at the Central House of the Artist in Moscow, Russia, from 27 April to 10 May 2007. At the time, he was 102 years 199 days old.

★ OLDEST BAND
The Peace Old Jazz band comprises six veteran musicians whose average age is 76 (as of November 2007). They have performed every night for over 20 years in Shanghai, China.

Dirty, badly dressed and disagreeable!
Jeanne Louise Calment, the oldest person ever, on the artist Vincent van Gogh, whom she knew

PRISONER
Bill Wallace (Australia, 1881–1989) was the oldest prisoner on record, having spent the final 63 years of his life in Aradale Psychiatric Hospital at Ararat, Victoria, Australia, after killing a man in December 1925. He remained there until his death on 17 July 1989, shortly before his 108th birthday. Once asked why he was in prison, he replied: "There was a man... Well, to tell you the truth, I don't know."

★ OLDEST BARBER
Anthony Mancinelli (USA, b. 2 March 1911) has been a practising barber since 1924. Mr Mancinelli continues to work today at the age of 97 years.

ACTRESS
Jeanne Louise Calment (France, 1875–1997) portrayed herself at the age of 114 in the film *Vincent and Me* (Canada, 1990) – a modern-day fantasy about a young girl who travels back through time to the 19th century to meet the artist Vincent van Gogh. Calment, the **oldest person** whose age has been fully authenticated (see p.74), is regarded as the last living person to have known van Gogh.

★ NEW RECORD
★ UPDATED RECORD

DON'T TRY THIS AT HOME

★ HIGHEST STACK OF CHAIRS

Luo Jun (China), from the Zun Yi Acrobatic Group, successfully balanced on 11 stacked chairs on the set of *Zheng Da Zong Yi – Guinness World Records Special* in Beijing, China, on 15 September 2007.

★ LONGEST UNDERWATER SUBMERGENCE

Ronny Frimann (Norway) remained under water for 4 days and 4 hours (100 hours in total), from 14 to 18 June 2007 to raise funds for the World Wildlife Fund. During the submergence in a water tank at the Central Station, in Oslo, Norway, he wore a diving drysuit and helmet equipped with a catheter and tubes for nutritional fluids and air supply. During the feat, he lost 7.5 kg (16 lb 8 oz).

★ SHARING A BATHTUB WITH THE MOST RATTLESNAKES

Jackie Bibby (USA), a.k.a. The Texas Snake Man, sat in a bathtub with 87 snakes on 5 November 2007 in Dublin, Texas, USA, for 45 minutes as part of GWR Day.

★ LONGEST TIME TO HOLD ONE'S BREATH

On 23 February 2008, Tom Sietas (Germany) held his breath voluntarily for 16 min 13 sec in a swimming pool on the set of *Lo Show dei Record* in Madrid, Spain.

★ LONGEST TIME SPENT ON A BED OF NAILS

The duration record for lying on a bed of nails – with sharp 15.2 cm (6 in) nails placed 5 cm (2 in) apart – is 300 hours by Ken Owen (UK) between 3 and 14 May 1986. The longest uninterrupted stretch of lying down lasted 132 hr 30 min!

X-REF

Still got an appetite for eccentricity? Then seek out **Bizarre Behaviour** (pp.100–101). But if you're in search of truly heroic acts, our **Spirit of Adventure** chapter (pp.106–117) boasts a host of admirable feats.

★ MOST TIMES HIT BY A CAR

Dietmar Löffler (Germany) was hit eight times by a car in two minutes on the set of *Guinness World Records: Die Größten Weltrekorde* in Cologne, Germany, on 23 November 2007.

★ HEAVIEST WEIGHT LIFTED WITH GLUE

A Ford pick-up truck weighing 4,140 kg (9,127 lb 2 oz) was lifted for one hour by a crane, suspended on a 7-cm-diameter (2-in) steel cylinder, which had been glued together one hour earlier using nine drops of the commercially available household adhesive "UHU Alleskleber Super Strong & Safe" in Bühl, Germany, on 11 October 2007.

★ HEAVIEST TRAIN PULLED BY RICE-BOWL SUCTION ON THE STOMACH

By pressing a rice bowl on to his abdominal muscles, Zhang Xingquan (China) created enough suction to pull a 36.15-tonne (79,700-lb) train for 40 m (131 ft 2 in) in Dehai City, Jilin Province, China, on 3 August 2007.

★ MOST IRON BARS BROKEN BY THE HEAD

Wang Xianfa (China) broke 26 iron bars on his head on the set of *Zheng Da Zong Yi – Guinness World Records Special* in Beijing, China, on 18 September 2007.

★ GREATEST WEIGHT LIFTED BY BEARD

Antanas Kontrimas (Lithuania) lifted a 63.2-kg (139-lb 5-oz) woman 10 cm (4 in) off the ground on the set of *Zheng Da Zong Yi – Guinness World Records Special* in Beijing, China, on 16 September 2007.

★ NEW RECORD
★ UPDATED RECORD

> *Over a period of 40 years, Michel Lotito literally ate about 9 tons of metal*
> Craig Glenday, Editor-in-Chief, Guinness World Records

STRANGEST DIET

Michel Lotito (France, 1950–2006), a.k.a, Monsieur Mangetout, started eating metal and glass in 1959. Gastroenterologists X-rayed his stomach and described his ability to consume 900 g (2 lb) of metal per day as unique.

His diet since 1966 included 18 bicycles, 15 supermarket trolleys, seven TV sets, six chandeliers, two beds, a pair of skis, a computer and even a Cessna light aircraft! He is said to have provided the only example in history of a coffin (handles and all) ending up *inside* a man. Despite his strong stomach – the lining was twice as thick as normal – he couldn't bear to eat boiled eggs!

★ POWER DRILL ROTATIONS

The Guy Hiang (Germany) performed 141 rotations in one minute, while hanging from a power drill, on the set of *Guinness World Records: Die Größten Weltrekorde* in Cologne, Germany, on 1 September 2007.

LONGEST MOTORCYCLE RIDE THROUGH A TUNNEL OF FIRE

Clint Ewing (USA) successfully rode a motorcycle through a 60.96-m-long (200-ft) tunnel of fire at Universal City, Los Angeles, USA, on 27 January 2008. The daredevil record was being staged for the NBC TV special *Guinness World Records Live – The Top 100*.

GREATEST WEIGHT TO BALANCE ON TEETH

On 17 May 2007, Frank Simon (USA) balanced a refrigerator weighing 63.5 kg (140 lb) on his teeth for a duration of 10 seconds on the set of the *Circo Massimo Show* in Rome, Italy.

DEADLIEST MAGIC TRICK

At least 12 people have been killed during the bullet catching trick, in which a gun loaded with a marked bullet is fired at the magician, who apparently catches the bullet in his teeth. Even though the feat involves illusionary elements, it is fraught with danger.

★ LONGEST WALL OF FIRE

On 16 September 2007, Rich's Incredible Pyro (USA) created a wall of fire 2,022 m (6,636 ft) long during the Terre Haute Air Fair in Terre Haute, Indiana, USA.

HIGHEST FLAME BLOWN BY A FIRE-BREATHER

Tim Black (Australia) blew a flame 7.2 m (23 ft 7 in) high on the set of *Zheng Da Zong Yi – Guinness World Records Special* in Beijing, China, on 15 September 2007.

★ FARTHEST FIRE-WALK

Trever McGhee (Canada) walked 181.9 m (597 ft) over embers with a temperature of between 657.67°C and 853.33°C (1,214–1,307°F) at Symons Valley Rodeo Grounds, Calgary, Alberta, Canada, on 9 November 2007.

★ MOST PEOPLE FIRE-BREATHING AT ONCE

At an event organized by TSV D'artagnan and De Rooie Sok, 115 people performed a simultaneous display of fire-breathing on the Heuvelplein in Tilburg, the Netherlands, on 14 March 2007.

DO TRY THIS AT HOME

PEERLESS PUZZLERS

RUBIK'S CUBE
★ **Fastest time to solve:** 9.55 seconds, by Ron van Bruchem (Netherlands), on 24 November 2007.

★ **Fastest time to solve blindfolded:** 41.16 seconds, by Chen Danyang (China), on 28 October 2007.

BEDLAM CUBE
★ **Fastest time to assemble:** 7.77 seconds, by Aleksander Iljasov (Norway) on 28 September 2007.

★ **Fastest time to assemble blindfolded:** 36.41 seconds, by Danny Bamping (UK) on 8 November 2007.

GWR HASBRO PUZZLE
★ **Fastest completion:** 14 min 58 sec, by Elaine Lewis (UK) on 11 June 2007.

TETRIS
★ **Smallest game:** played (with a microscope) using tetraminoes made of tiny glass spheres at Vrije University, Amsterdam, the Netherlands, in November 2002. Each block measured 1 micrometre (0.001 mm; 0.00003 in) across.

★ **NEW RECORD**
★ **UPDATED RECORD**

★ MOST DECKS OF PLAYING CARDS MEMORIZED

Dave Farrow (Canada) memorized, on a single sighting, a random sequence of 59 separate card packs (3,068 cards in all) at CTV Studios, The Daily Planet, Toronto, Canada, on 2 April 2007.

FASTEST TIME TO...

★ POP 1,000 BALLOONS
A team of 40 people from OC&C Strategy Consultants (UK) popped 1,000 balloons in 8.78 seconds during their annual International Training Week in Barcelona, Spain, on 8 September 2007.

★ MODEL FIVE BALLOON SCULPTURES BLINDFOLDED
On 16 February 2008, Daniele Bottalico, a.k.a. "Mago Ciccio" (Italy), created five balloon sculptures while blindfolded in 1 min 24 sec on the set of the Guinness World Records programme, *Lo show dei record*, in Madrid, Spain.

★ HOP 100 M ON ONE LEG
Rommell Griffith (Barbados) hopped 100 m in 15.57 seconds at the Barbados World Record Festival at the Barbados National Stadium in St Michael on 31 March 2007.

X-REF
The human body is a fantastic creation, whether or not it's performing crazy feats. For some absolutely amazing anatomical facts and statistics, check out the **Being Human** chapter (pp.56–75).

MOST YO-YOS SPUN AT ONCE

Eric Lindeen (Sweden) was able to keep a total of nine yo-yos spinning simultaneously on hooks at the Gallerian Shopping Centre, Stockholm, Sweden, on 4 November 2006.

★ LARGEST RUBBER-BAND BALL

Bryce and Steve Milton (USA) created a rubber-band ball that weighed 2,083.8 kg (4,594 lb). The outsize orb was measured in Chicago, Illinois, USA, on 21 November 2006.

★ COMPLETE A 100 M PIGGYBACK RACE

The record time for the fastest piggyback race over 100 m is 16.97 seconds. It was set by Rommell Griffith carrying Ulinda Griffith (both Barbados), as part of the Barbados World Record Festival at the Barbados National Stadium on 31 March 2007.

★ BANANAS PEELED AND EATEN IN ONE MINUTE

Christopher "Big Black" Boykin (USA) successfully peeled and ate three bananas on MTV's *The Rob & Big Show* in Los Angeles, California, USA, on 17 September 2007.

★ LONGEST STRING OF APPLE PIPS

The largest string of apple pips is 250 m (820 ft) long and was completed by Zdzislawa Szydlowska (Poland) on 28 May 2001.

★ EGGS HELD IN THE HAND

On 20 December 2007, Zdenek Bradac (Czech Republic) managed to hold a total of 20 eggs in one hand at the same time at Sheffield Castle College, in South Yorkshire, UK.

★ BALLOON SCULPTURES IN AN HOUR

John Cassidy (USA) made 747 balloon shapes in one hour at Buck County Community College in Newtown, Pennsylvania, USA, on 14 November 2007.

★ SPOONS TWISTED IN ONE MINUTE

On 18 December 2006, Kong Tai (China) twisted five spoons 180 degrees in one minute, bare-handed, in Beijing, China.

★ MOST T-SHIRTS WORN AT ONCE

Charlie Williams (UK) put on a combined total of 224 T-shirts in an attempt organized by itiswhatitis Ltd, at St Antony's Catholic Primary School in Woodford Green, Essex, UK, on 14 September 2007.

MOST...

★ APPLES BOBBED IN ONE MINUTE

Ashrita Furman (USA) bobbed 32 apples in one minute in Jamaica, New York City, USA, on 11 June 2007.

LONGEST TIME TO SPIN A FRYING PAN ON ONE FINGER

Anders Björklund (Sweden) was able to spin a frying pan on his finger for 14 minutes on the set of *Guinness Rekord TV* in Stockholm, Sweden, on 29 November 2001.

FEATS OF STRENGTH

MANJIT'S MANY STRENGTHS

Manjit Singh (UK) holds several records, all of which involve great strength and stamina. He enjoys setting records not only for a sense of personal achievement but also to raise money for charity. These are his latest achievements:

FASTEST 10-M DASH CARRYING A TABLE AND WEIGHT IN THE MOUTH

Letting only his teeth take the strain, Georges Christen (Luxembourg) successfully carried a woman sitting on a table over a distance of 10 m (32 ft 9 in) in 7.5 seconds on the set of *L'Été de Tous Les Records* in La Tranche Sur Mer, France, on 28 July 2004.

GREATEST WEIGHT LIFTED WITH TEETH

Walter Arfeuille (Belgium) lifted weights totalling 281.5 kg (620 lb 10 oz) a distance of 17 cm (6.75 in) off the ground with his teeth in Paris, France, on 31 March 1990.

★ GREATEST WEIGHT LIFTED BY THE NECK

Frank Ciavattone (USA) lifted a weight of 366.5 kg (808 lb), supported by his neck, at the New England Weightlifting Club in Walpole, Massachusetts, USA, on 15 November 2005.

★ HEAVIEST BOAT PULLED

George Olesen (Denmark) pulled a 10,300-tonne (22.7 million-lb) passenger ferry for 5.1 m (16 ft 8.8 in) at Gothenburg Ferry Terminal, Gothenburg, Sweden, in June 2000.

★ BUS PULLING WITH THE EARS

Manjit pulled a single-decker bus a record 6.1 m (20 ft) on cables attached to his ears, to raise money for the Manjit Fitness Academy at the Loughborough Tesco in Loughborough, UK, on 31 March 2008.

★ SQUAT LIFTING

Manjit also set the record for the **most weight squat lifted in one hour** by an individual, achieving 30,390 kg (66,998.48 lb) at Montee Hair and Beauty Salon in Leicester, UK, on 20 December 2007.

★ GREATEST WEIGHT LIFTED WITH AN EAR

Zafar Gill (Pakistan) lifted gym weights totalling 61.7 kg (136 lb), which were hanging from a clamp attached to his right ear, during the event Vienna Recordia, in Vienna, Austria, on 30 September 2007.

★ NEW RECORD
★ UPDATED RECORD

★ LONGEST TIME RESTRAINING A CAR ON FULL THROTTLE

Franz Müllner (Austria) restrained a Lamborghini Diablo – a car with an output of over 400 hp – driving away from him at full throttle, for seven seconds, on the set of *Die Größten Weltrekorde* in Cologne, Germany, on 1 September 2007.

CONCRETE BLOCK-BUSTER

The record for the ★ **most concrete blocks broken in one minute** is 386, achieved by Eduardo Estrada (Mexico) at the University of Coahuila in Saltillo, Coahuila, Mexico, on 22 November 2007.

HIGHEST BEER-KEG TOSS

Heini Koivuniemi (Finland, pictured) threw a 12.3-kg (27-lb 1-oz) beer keg over a bar set at a height of 3.46 m (11 ft 4.2 in) on the set of *Guinness World Records* in Helsinki, Finland, on 9 August 2001 – the **highest beer-keg toss by a woman**. Juha Rasanen (Finland) threw a 12.3-kg (27-lb 1-oz) beer keg over a bar at a height of 7.1 m (23 ft 3 in) on 26 August 2005 – the **highest beer-keg toss by a man**.

★ HEAVIEST DEADLIFT

Andy Bolton (UK) deadlifted 455 kg (1,003 lb) at the World Powerlifting Organization Semi-Finals in Lake George, New York, USA, on 4 November 2006.

★ HEAVIEST DEADLIFT WITH THE LITTLE FINGER

Using just his little finger, Kristian Holm (Norway) deadlifted 95.38 kg (210 lb 3 oz) in Herefoss, Norway, on 24 March 2007.

HEAVIEST ELEPHANT LIFTED

In 1975, while performing with Gerry Cottle's Circus (UK), Khalil Oghaby (Iran) lifted an elephant that weighed approximately 2 tonnes (4,409 lb) off the ground. He stood on a platform above the animal and raised it by means of a harness.

★ HEAVIEST VEHICLE PULLED OVER 100 FT

Powerlifting pastor Rev. Kevin Fast (Canada) pulled a vehicle weighing 57,000 kg (125,680 lb) over a level 100-ft (30.48-m) course in Cobourg, Ontario, Canada, on 12 May 2007.

HEAVIEST WEIGHT DANGLED FROM A SWALLOWED SWORD

Matthew Henshaw (Australia) swallowed a non-retractable 40.5-cm (1-ft 3.9-in) long sword and then held a sack of potatoes weighing 20.1 kg (44 lb 5 oz) attached to the handle of the sword for five seconds at the studios of *Guinness World Records* in Sydney, New South Wales, Australia, on 16 April 2005.

★ Franz Müllner (Austria) also holds the record for the **longest time restraining a truck at full throttle**. On 3 November 2007, Franz held back a 400 hp truck for 8.40 seconds on the set of *Zheng Da Zong Yi – Guinness World Records Special* in Beijing, China.

INSPIRATIONAL ACTS

MOST MONEY RAISED BY A CHARITY RUN

The greatest amount of money raised by a charity run or walk is Can$24.7 million ($20.7 million; £9.1 million) by Terry Fox (Canada, 1958–1981). Terry, who had an artificial leg, ran from St John's, Newfoundland, to Thunder Bay, Ontario, Canada, in 143 days from 12 April to 2 September 1980. He covered 5,373 km (3,339 miles).

★ MOST MONEY RAISED BY A MARATHON RUNNER

Steve Chalke (UK) raised £1,841,138 ($3,669,325) for the Oasis UK charity by completing the Flora London Marathon, in London, UK, on 22 April 2007.

CHARITY AUCTIONS: MOST EXPENSIVE...

CALENDAR

"To Touch an Angel's Wings", a wall calendar designed for the Muir Maxwell Trust epilepsy charity, sold at a charity auction for £15,000 ($26,100) on 10 December 2005 to Stephen Winyard (UK) of Stobo Castle Health Spa, Peeblesshire, UK.

TELEPHONE NUMBER

An anonymous Qatari bidder paid 10 million QAR ($2.75 million; £1.46 million) for the mobile (cell) phone number 666-6666 during a charity auction hosted by Qatar Telecom in Doha, Qatar, on 23 May 2006.

GUITAR

A Fender Stratocaster guitar signed by a host of music legends including Mick Jagger, Eric Clapton and Paul McCartney (all UK) fetched $2.7 million (£1.6 million) at a charity auction for Reach Out To Asia at the Ritz-Carlton Hotel, Doha, Qatar, on 17 November 2005. The Reach Out To Asia campaign seeks to support worthy causes around the world, with particular emphasis on the Asian continent.

CHARITY WORK

★ LARGEST FUND-RAISING EVENT HELD ANNUALLY

Held every year around the streets of London, UK, the Flora London Marathon is the largest annual charity fundraiser. The 2007 race, held on 22 April, generated the most money to date, with £46.5 million ($91.9 million) accumulated by 24,750 runners for numerous charities.

In the 11 London Marathons held between 1996 and 2006, the average amount raised per event was £28,027,550 ($53,318,770).

★ MOST BREAST MILK DONATED

Erica Hines from Port Orange, Florida, USA, has donated 135.5 litres (4,581 fl oz) of breast milk to WakeMed Mother's Milk Bank in Raleigh, North Carolina, USA, as of 8 June 2007.

LONGEST CONCERT BY A GROUP

The Comaganin Raaga Priya Light Music Orchestra played continuously for 50 hours for the visually impaired in Chennai, India, from 27 to 29 April 2007.

OLDEST LIFE-SAVING ORGANIZATION

The Royal National Lifeboat Institution (RNLI), a British lifesaving society, was formed by royal edict in March 1824 and celebrated its 180th anniversary in 2004. In 2006, an average of 22 people were rescued each day.

I ran my first marathon aged 71, and will keep going as long as my legs keep carrying me!

Jenny Wood-Allen, oldest female to complete a marathon (91!)

★ NEW RECORD
★ UPDATED RECORD

MOST LIVES SAVED BY A PARROT

In December 1999, a grey parrot named Charlie woke up his owner, Patricia Tunnicliffe (UK), when her home in Durham, UK, caught fire. The bird began to squawk frantically as the flames in the front room took hold, which woke up Ms Tunnicliffe and gave her time to get her five children out of the house unharmed. Sadly, Charlie was not so lucky and died in the inferno.

RESCUERS

MOST PEOPLE RESCUED AT SEA (CIVILIANS)

On 23 January 1946, the crew of the cargo ship USS *Brevard* (AK-164), commanded by Lt John Elliott (USA), rescued 4,296 Japanese civilians whose ship, the *Enoshima Maru*, was sinking after hitting a mine off Shanghai, China.

MOST DECORATED WAR HERO

Audie Murphy (USA, 1924–71) was the most decorated soldier in American history, winning 24 medals from the Congressional Medal of Honor down. His exploits were the subject of the film *To Hell and Back* (USA, 1956), in which he starred as himself (below).

MOST CELEBRATED CANINE RESCUER

The most famous canine rescuer of all time is a St Bernard called Barry, who lived from 1800 to 1814. Barry rescued more than 40 people during a career on the Swiss Alps that spanned 12 years. One of the life-saving dog's more celebrated rescues was that of a boy who lay half frozen under an avalanche in which his mother had died. Barry spread himself across the boy's body to warm him, licked the youngster's face until he woke up and then carried him to the nearest dwelling.

FACT
The **largest live audience for a simultaneous rock concert** is an estimated one million people for Live 8 held at venues around the world in 10 cities, including London, Philadelphia, Paris, Johannesburg, Berlin, Rome and Moscow on 2 July 2005.

LARGEST SIMULTANEOUS ROCK CONCERT TV AUDIENCE

Live Aid, the world's largest simultaneous charity rock concert in terms of viewers, was organized by Bob Geldof (Ireland). Held in London, UK, and Philadelphia, USA, on 13 July 1985, over 60 of rock's biggest acts played for free to 1.5 billion TV viewers throughout the world in order to raise money for African famine relief.

LARGEST FUND-RAISING CHARITY

The Salvation Army, USA, has raised more funds annually than any other charity for 10 consecutive years. In 2001 alone, the charity raised $1.39 billion (£889 million), down from $1.44 billion (£921 million) in 2000. In the US, the Salvation Army has 1.6 million dedicated volunteers. Lay members who subscribe to the doctrines of The Salvation Army are called soldiers, and, along with officers, they are known as Salvationists.

BIZARRE BEHAVIOUR

★ FARTHEST DISTANCE TRAVELLED BY "THE WORM" MOVE

James Rubec (Canada) travelled 33.14 m (108 ft 9 in) using "the worm" at the Rogers Centre in Toronto, Canada, on 9 November 2007 as part of Guinness World Records Day 2007. To perform the worm, a breakdance move, you lie flat on the ground and propel yourself forward with a rippling motion of the body.

★ LARGEST UNDERWATER PRESS CONFERENCE

At a press conference organized by Eric J. Pittman (Canada) to promote the release of his new book *Emails from a Nut!!!*, 61 journalists dived to a depth of 10 m (32 ft 9.6 in) at Crystal Pool, Victoria, British Columbia, Canada, on 4 November 2006.

★ LARGEST CUSTARD PIE FIGHT

A total of 105 participants flung flan at a pie fight organized by Camp Toukley in New South Wales, Australia, on 11 July 2007.

LONGEST FULL-BODY BURN

Ted A. Batchelor (USA), a professional stuntman with a lifelong love of fire, endured a full-body burn – without any oxygen supply – for 2 min 38 sec on an island at Ledges Quarry Park, Nelson, Ohio, USA, on 17 July 2004.

★ FASTEST TIME TO PUSH AN ORANGE ONE MILE WITH THE NOSE

Ashrita Furman took 22 min 41 sec to push an orange one mile with his nose at the Green Acres Mall in Valley Stream, New York, USA, on 2 November 2007.

★ LARGEST ROBOT DANCE

On 17 September 2007, 276 students of the University of Kent (UK) dressed as robots and danced for a minimum of five minutes in Canterbury, Kent, UK.

★ LONGEST HUMAN SUCTION SUSPENSION BY THE STOMACH

By pressing a rice bowl on his abdominal muscles, Li Kangle (China) was able to create enough suction to suspend himself from a helicopter on a rope for 7 min 6 sec in Pingyi County, Shandong Province, China. The record was attempted for *Zheng Da Zong Yi – Guinness World Records Special* in Beijing, China, on 6 September 2007.

FARTHEST DISTANCE TRAVELLED UNDER WATER BY POGO STICK

Ashrita Furman (USA) jumped 512.06 m (1,680 ft) under water on a pogo stick at the Nassau County Aquatic Center in East Meadow, New York, USA, on 1 August 2007.

★ NEW RECORD
★ UPDATED RECORD

★ FASTEST MALE PANTOMIME HORSE

Charles Astor and Tristan Williams (both UK) ran 100 m in a time of 13.51 seconds... remaining inside a pantomime horse costume! Charles (front) and Tristan (rear) competed in an event organized by the advertising agency Claydon Heeley Jones Mason at Harrow School in Harrow-on-the-Hill, Middlesex, UK, on 18 August 2005. On the same day, the record was set for the **fastest female pantomime horse** – 18.13 seconds – by Samantha Kavanagh (front) and Melissa Archer (rear).

RACES

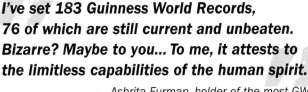

★ MOST TOILET SEAT LIDS BROKEN

Kevin Shelley (USA) broke 46 wooden toilet seat lids with his head on the set of the TV show *Guinness World Records: Die Größten Weltrekorde* in Cologne, Germany, on 1 September 2007.

MOST...

★ CLOTHES PEGS CLIPPED ON A HAND IN ONE MINUTE

Mohammed Ahmed Elkhouly (UAE) pinned 48 clothes pegs to one of his hands at Bab Al Shams Desert Resort & Spa in Dubai, UAE, on 21 April 2007.

★ PEOPLE WEARING GROUCHO MARX GLASSES

A group of 3,459 people donned plastic Groucho Marx glasses (to resemble the famous American comedian) at an event organized by United Way of the Columbia-Willamette in Hillsboro, Oregon, USA, on 4 August 2007.

★ KILTS WORN

While guest-hosting *The New Paul O'Grady Show* on 7 November 2007, Lorraine Kelly (UK) donned three kilts, one at a time, in a minute at the London Studios, UK.

★ PEOPLE DRESSED AS SEA ANIMALS

A total of 5,590 participants dressed as sea animals for an event held in Shenjiamen Fishing Harbor, Zhoushan City, Zhejiang Province, China, on 10 August 2007.

★ UNDERPANTS WORN

Joel Nathan (Australia) was able to pull on 20 pairs of underpants in one minute at the Paramount Nightclub in Perth, Australia, on 27 July 2007.

★ EGGS SMASHED WITH THE HEAD

Osi Anyanwu (UK) smashed 40 eggs against his head in one minute on *The New Paul O'Grady Show* in London, UK, on 7 November 2007.

★ MOST SNAILS ON THE FACE

Alastair Galpin (New Zealand) held eight snails on his face for 10 seconds at The Warehouse shop in Sylvia Park, Auckland, New Zealand, on 27 October 2007. On the same occasion, he set the record for the ★ **most T-shirts torn in one minute** (nine).

Previously, Galpin had achieved the ★ **most gloves worn on one hand** (seven) at The Old Homestead Community House in Auckland on 11 May 2006, and, on 28 April 2007 at the same venue, he set the record for the ★ **most rubber bands stretched over the face** (62).

ACTUAL WIDTH OF DRILL BIT

★ HEAVIEST OBJECT SWORD-SWALLOWED

Thomas Blackthorne (UK) swallowed the 25-mm-thick (1-in) drill bit of a Dewalt D25980 demolition hammer weighing 38 kg (83 lb 12oz), then held the full weight of the hammer and bit for over three seconds, on the set of *Guinness World Records: Die Größten Weltrekorde* in Cologne, Germany, on 23 November 2007.

SOLO PERFORMANCE

★ FARTHEST
INVERTED POLE CLIMB

Nele Bruckmann (Germany) climbed 9.73 m (31 ft 11 in) up a pole, while inverted, in one minute on the set of *Guinness World Records – Die Größten Weltrekorde* in Cologne, Germany, on 1 September 2007.

FASTEST...

★ ESCAPE FROM A STRAITJACKET

Matt the Knife (USA) took just 18.80 seconds to escape from a regulated straitjacket at the Media Center Hotel in Beijing, China, on 17 September 2007.

Matt also holds the record for the **★ fastest time to escape from a straitjacket while submerged under water**, after completing the task in 15.41 seconds for *Zheng Da Zong Yi – Guinness World Records Special* in Beijing, China, on 13 September 2007.

★ MOST WOOD BLOCKS CHOPPED IN HALF

On 23 November 2007, Robert Ebner (Germany) chopped 70 wood blocks in half in one minute on the set of *Guinness World Records – Die Größten Weltrekorde* in Cologne, Germany.

★ FROG JUMP (10 M)

Ashrita Furman (USA) frog jumped (i.e. holding his toes) 10 m (33 ft) in 8.22 seconds in Jamaica, New York, USA, on 7 November 2007.

★ TEXT MESSAGE

On 12 November 2006, Ang Chuang Yang (Singapore) typed a set 160-character text on his mobile phone in 41.52 seconds at the Suntec Convention Centre, Singapore.

★ BALLOON MODELLING BEHIND THE BACK

With his arms behind his back, Daniele Bottalico (Italy), a.k.a. Mago Ciccio, made a balloon poodle in 4.54 seconds in Cassano delle Murge, Bari, Italy, on 10 November 2007.

MOST...

★ HEAD SPINS

Aichi Ono (Japan) performed 101 head spins in one minute on the set of *Zheng Da Zong Yi – Guinness World Records Special* in Beijing, China, on 18 September 2007.

★ KISSES RECEIVED

Adrian Chiles (UK) received 78 kisses in one minute on BBC 1's *The One Show*, London, UK, on 8 November 2007 in celebration of GWR Day.

★ MENTAL CALCULATIONS

Chen Ranran (China) solved eight mental arithmetic problems in one minute on the set of *Zheng Da Zong Yi – Guinness World Records Special* in Beijing, China, on 2 November 2007. Each calculation consisted of 11 numbers with a total of 120 digits. The calculations were supplied in a sealed envelope by the Abacus and Mental Arithmetics Federation.

CHAINSAW JUGGLING: MOST CATCHES

In a dazzling display of bravado (some would say recklessness!), Aaron Gregg (Canada) was able to juggle three running chainsaws, making a total of 86 successful catches, in Portland, Oregon, USA, on 23 September 2005. To those keen to replicate this at home (please don't!), the model used was an Echo CS-301.

★ FASTEST 100 M ON A SPACE HOPPER (FEMALE)

On 26 September 2004, Dee McDougall (UK) covered 100 m (328 ft) in 39.88 seconds while bouncing on a space hopper at the University of St Andrews, Fife, UK.

★ DUCKS AND DRAKES

"Ducks and Drakes", aka stone-skimming, -skipping or -skiffing, involves throwing a smooth stone across a body of water in order to make it bounce across the surface. The record for the most consecutive skips of a stone on water is an incredible 51, held by Russell Byars (USA). The cast was achieved at Riverfront Park, Franklin, Pennsylvania, USA, on 19 July 2007.

X-REF

You'll find a whole universe of space records elsewhere in *GWR 2009*. Lift off with **Space Technology** (p.28), gaze at **Stars** (p.18) and **Galaxies & Nebulae** (p.20), visit **Heavenly Bodies** (p.22) and have a close encounter with **Asteroids, Comets & Meteors** (p.24).

★ **Keyboard playing**: 70 hr 57 min, Patricia Jones (USA), Teresa's Piano Gallery, Jacksonville, Florida, USA, 12–15 November 2007.

★ **Singing**: 75 hr, Marcus LaPratt (USA), Heartland Health Care Center, Allen Park, Michigan, USA, 28–31 August 2007.

★ **Upside-down juggling (three objects)**: 2 min 11 sec, Ashrita Furman (USA), Jamaica, New York, USA, 24 December 2007.

★ **Harp**: 24 hr 30 min, Laurita Pacheco (Peru), Bolivar Hotel, Lima, Peru, 20–21 May 2004.

Dance: 100 hr, Suresh Joachim (Australia), Mississauga, Ontario, Canada, 16–20 February 2005.

★ **Lecture:** 120 hr, Jayasimha Ravirala (India), FAPCCI Hall, Hyderabad, India, 24–29 March 2007.

MARATHONS

★ **Drumming**: 85 hr 30 min, Gery Jallo (Belgium), Pakenhof, Heverlee, Belgium, 22–25 February 2007.

★ **Beatboxing**: 24 hr, Michael Krappel (Austria), Vienna, Austria, 30 September 2007.

★ **Karaoke**: 38 hr 30 min, Thomas Brian Jones (UK), Vienna, Austria, 30 September 2007.

★ FASTEST TIME TO SKIP 5 KM WITHOUT A ROPE

Ashrita Furman (USA) skipped a distance of 5 km (3.1 miles) without using a rope in a time of 35 min 19 sec at Wat Pa Luangta Yannasampanno Forest Monastery in Kanchanaburi, Thailand, on 5 February 2007. Ashrita's performance wasn't entirely solo – for part of his trip, he was joined by a tiger!

★ **NEW RECORD**
★ **UPDATED RECORD**

MOST APPLES CHOPPED IN THE AIR USING A SWORD

Martial arts master Kenneth Lee (USA) cut 23 apples in the air in one minute, using a samurai sword, on the set of *Live with Regis & Kelly* in New York City, USA, on 14 September 2006.

TEAM EFFORTS

★ MOST ICE-CREAM
SCOOPS THROWN AND CAUGHT IN ONE MINUTE BY A TEAM OF TWO

Thrower Gabriele Soravia (left) and catcher Lorenzo Soravia (both Germany) threw and caught 25 ice-cream scoops in a minute on the set of *Guinness World Records – Die Größten Weltrekorde* in Cologne, Germany, on 1 September 2007.

LONGEST...

★ CONCERT (MULTIPLE ARTISTS)

From 4 to 12 November 2006, a 200-hour-long concert by multiple artists took place at Manhattan's Pizza Bistro and Music Club in Gelph, Ontario, Canada.

★ CONGA ON ICE

The record for the longest conga on ice involved 107 participants and was achieved at an event organized by Leeds Metropolitan University (UK) at the "Ice Cube" temporary outdoor ice rink in Millennium Square, Leeds, UK, on 1 February 2008.

★ GRAFFITI SCROLL

A 609.6-m-long (2,000-ft) scroll of paper was covered in graffiti by students and teachers at Bergen County Technical High School (USA) in Paramus, USA, on 2 November 2007.

★ MOST PEOPLE BRUSHING TEETH (MULTIPLE VENUES)

A total of 177,003 people brushed their teeth at 380 locations across India during an event organized by Colgate-Palmolive Ltd., (India) on 9 October 2007.

MOST...

★ DANCERS ON POINTE

A total of 190 ballet dancers gathered at an event organized by Reach for a Dream Foundation and South African Ballet Theatre (both South Africa) in Pretoria, South Africa, to stand *en pointe* – that is, on the tips of their toes – for a minute on 25 February 2006.

★ LITTER COLLECTORS

On 7 August 2005, a litter-collection project in Oita City, Japan, attracted 146,679 volunteers.

★ SMURFS IN ONE VENUE

A total of 451 participants dressed as Smurfs for an exciting event organized by the University of Warwick Students Union in Coventry, UK, on 20 June 2007.

★ PEOPLE INSIDE A SOAP BUBBLE

Fan Yang (Canada) enclosed 42 people in a bubble on the set of *Live with Regis and Kelly* in New York City, USA, on 7 August 2007.

★ LARGEST GUITAR ENSEMBLE

Led by the band Party Blues in Bb, a guitar ensemble comprising 1,802 participants played "Smoke on the Water", by Deep Purple, simultaneously in Leinfelden-Echterdingen, Germany, on 26 June 2007.

LARGEST DALEK GATHERING

Visitors to the Museum of Science and Industry (MOSI) in Manchester, UK, on 26 August 2007 could have been forgiven for thinking that Planet Earth was under attack from an alien race when 70 Daleks – well, people dressed as Daleks from the TV show *Doctor Who* – descended upon the museum.

LARGEST...

EVENT	PARTICIPANTS	LOCATION	DATE
★Ballet class (barres)	551	Pretoria, South Africa	25 Feb 2006
★Bodhran ensemble	980	Sydney, Australia	17 Mar 2006
Bunny hop	3,841	Delta, Utah, USA	4 Jul 2007
Dance by couples	540	Hong Kong, China	7 Jul 2007
Full drum-kit ensemble	533	Seattle, Washington, USA	13 May 2006
★Gathering of pirates	1,140	Soltau, Germany	2 Jun 2007
★Gathering of soft toys	2,304	Washington DC, USA	6 Dec 2006
★Halloween gathering	63	Somerville, Mass, USA	27 Oct 2007
Harmonica ensemble	3,898	Trossingen, Germany	9 Sep 2007
Kazoo ensemble	2,600	Rochester, New York, USA	31 Dec 2006
Mascot gathering	119	Edmonton, Alberta, Canada	30 Aug 2004
★Matouqin ensemble	1,199	Jilin Province, China	1 Sep 2006
Music lesson	1,577	Chicago, Illinois, USA	7 Aug 2007
★Ocarina ensemble	103	Les-Ponts-de-Martel, Switzerland	24 Jun 2006
School reunion	3,299	Tacoma, Washington, USA	16 Sep 2006
★Sirtaki dance	268	Agia Napa, Cyprus	16 Sep 2007
★Speed-dating event	120	Vienna, Austria	30 Sep 2007
★Spoons ensemble	481	Saskatchewan, Canada	2 Jun 2007
★Trumpet ensemble	1,166	Oruro, Bolivia	19 Feb 2006

★BASKETBALLS DRIBBLED

On 17 May 2007, at the BAA Edinburgh Youth Games at Meadowbank Sports Centre in Edinburgh, UK, 1,289 people dribbled basketballs simultaneously.

★PEOPLE WHISTLING

WhiStle Radio's "Whistle Off" at the Strawberry Festival in Whitchurch-Stouffville, Ontario, Canada, attracted 199 people on 30 June 2007.

★SCARECROWS

On 12 October 2003, 3,311 scarecrows were displayed at the Cincinnati Horticultural Society's Flower and Farm Fest on Coney Island, Ohio, USA.

★PEOPLE RAIN DANCING

The Rotary Club of Brisbane Planetarium held a 113-strong aboriginal rain dance at the Royal National Association showground in Brisbane, Australia, on 11 November 2007.

★ MOST PEOPLE KISSING SIMULTANEOUSLY

The largest kiss took place in Weston-super-Mare, UK, on 22 July 2007 when 32,648 people puckered up for a minimum of 20 seconds for the *T4 on the Beach* TV show.

★ NEW RECORD
★ UPDATED RECORD

SPIRIT OF ADVENTURE

CONTENTS

★ HIGHEST
SLACKLINE WALK

Christian Schou (Norway) walked 12 m (39 ft) on a 2.5-cm-wide (1-in) line suspended 1,000 m (3,280 ft) above the ground, at Kjerag Lysefjorden, Norway, on 3 August 2006.

On 7 October 2007, Aleksandar Mork (Norway, inset) achieved the same feat.

AROUND THE WORLD

FIRST...

CIRCUMNAVIGATION

On 20 September 1519, the Spanish ship *Vittoria* set out from Sanlùcar de Barrameda, Andalucía, Spain, as part of a five-vessel expedition led by the Portuguese explorer Ferdinand Magellan.

Under the command of the Spanish navigator Juan Sebastian de Elcano, *Vittoria* rounded Cape Horn, crossed the Pacific via the Philippines and returned to Europe, arriving in Seville, Spain, on 8 September 1522.

The aim of the voyage was to plunder the riches of the Spice Islands and return the spoils to the Spanish king Charles V. As the journey progressed, the fleet suffered huge losses and Magellan himself was killed in a tribal battle in the Phillippines on 27 April 1521.

By the time the expedition left the Spice Islands, two ships remained, but only de Elcano's *Vittoria* made it back to Spain with just 18 of the original 270-man crew returning home.

SOLO CIRCUMNAVIGATION BY AIRCRAFT

Wiley Post (USA) made the first solo flight around the world from 15 to 22 July 1933, in a Lockheed Vega called *Winnie Mae*. Post took off from New York, USA, and landed in Berlin, Germany, 26 hours later (a record at the time). He flew on to Moscow, Russia, where he was forced to stop for repairs, then on to Alaska, where he crash-landed. Finally, 7 days 19 hr – and a total of 11 stops – later, Post landed in New York.

SURFACE CIRCUMNAVIGATION VIA BOTH POLES

Sir Ranulph Fiennes and Charles Burton (both UK) of the British Trans-Globe Expedition travelled south from Greenwich, London, UK, on 2 September 1979, crossed the South Pole on 15 December 1980, the North Pole on 10 April 1982, and returned to Greenwich on 29 August 1982. Their trip covered 56,000 km (35,000 miles).

PIONEERING FIRSTS

First circumnavigation by aircraft Two US Army Douglas DWC seaplanes circled the world in 57 "hops" between 6 April and 28 September 1924, beginning and ending in Seattle, Washington DC, USA. The *Chicago* was piloted by Lieutenant Lowell H. Smith and Lieutenant Leslie P. Arnold, and the *New Orleans* by Lieutenant Erik H. Nelson and Lieutenant John Harding (all USA). The flight time for the 42,398-km (26,345-mile) trip was 371 hr 11 min.

First circumnavigation by aircraft without refuelling Richard G. "Dick" Rutan and Jeana Yeager (both USA) circumnavigated westward from Edwards Air Force Base, California, USA, in nine days from 14 to 23 December 1986 without refuelling.

First circumnavigation via both poles by aircraft Captain Elgen M. Long (USA) achieved the first circumpolar flight in a twin-engined Piper PA-31 Navajo from 5 November to 3 December 1971, covering 62,597 km (38,896 miles) in 215 flying hours.

First woman to sail around the world (solo, non-stop) Kay Cottee (Australia) left Sydney, Australia, on 29 November 1987 in her 11-m-long (36-ft) yacht, *First Lady*, returning there 189 days later on 5 June 1989.

★ **NEW RECORD**
★ **UPDATED RECORD**

★ FASTEST CIRCUMNAVIGATION SAILING SOLO

Francis Joyon (France) sailed solo and non-stop around the world in 57 days 13 hr 34 min 6 sec from 23 November 2007 to 20 January 2008, in the 29.5-m (97-ft) maxi-trimaran *IDEC II*. Joyon began and ended his 38,900-km (24,170-mile) journey in Brest, France, beating the previous record set by Ellen MacArthur (UK) by 14 days.

FASTEST...

CIRCUMNAVIGATION BY POWERED BOAT

Cable & Wireless Adventurer circled the world in 74 days 20 hr 58 min 30 sec between 19 April and 3 July 1998. The 35.05-m-long (115-ft) vessel was captained by Ian Bosworth (UK) and travelled more than 41,841 km (26,000 miles).

★ FIRST CIRCUMNAVIGATION VIA BOTH POLES BY HELICOPTER

The record for the first (and **fastest**) circumnavigation via both poles by helicopter was achieved by Jennifer Murray and Colin Bodill (both UK), from 5 December 2006 to 23 May 2007, in a Bell 407 helicopter. The journey started and finished in Fort Worth, Texas, USA.

★ FARTHEST DRIVE BY CAR USING ALTERNATIVE FUEL

Rainer Zietlow, Florian Hilpert, Falk Gunold and Franz Janusiewicz (all Germany) travelled 38,137 km (23,697 miles) in a Volkswagen Caddy EcoFuel using natural gas as fuel. Their journey started in Cologne, Germany, on 15 October 2006 and finished in Leipzig, Germany, on 13 April 2007.

CIRCUMNAVIGATION SAILING SOLO (FEMALE)

Ellen MacArthur (UK) sailed solo and non-stop around the world in 71 days 14 hr 18 min 33 sec from 28 November 2004 to 7 February 2005 in the trimaran *B&Q*. She started off Ushant, France, rounded the Cape of Good Hope (South Africa), sailed south of Australia and rounded Cape Horn (Argentina) before heading back up the Atlantic to Ushant.

CIRCUMNAVIGATION BY CAR

The record for the first and fastest man and woman to have circumnavigated the Earth by car, covering six continents under the rules applicable in 1989 and 1991 and embracing more than an equator's length of driving (40,075 km; 24,901 road miles), is held by Saloo Choudhury and his wife Neena Choudhury (both India). The journey took 69 days 19 hr 5 min from 9 September to 17 November 1989. The couple drove a 1989 Hindustan "Contessa Classic", starting and finishing in Delhi, India.

CIRCUMNAVIGATION VIA BOTH POLES BY AEROPLANE

A Boeing 747 SP piloted by Captain Walter H. Mullikin (USA) completed an aerial circumnavigation of the Earth via both geographical poles in 54 hr 7 min 12 sec (including refuelling stops) between 28 and 31 October 1977. The journey began and ended in San Francisco, USA, with stops in Cape Town (South Africa) and Auckland (New Zealand).

★ FASTEST ROUND-THE-WORLD CYCLE

Mark Beaumont (UK) cycled the world in 194 days 17 hr, covering a distance of 29,445.81 km (18,296.74 miles). The journey started and finished in Paris, France, from 5 August 2007 to 15 February 2008, and took in Europe, Pakistan, Malaysia, Australia, New Zealand and the USA.

Ocean rowing statistics provided by the Ocean Rowing Society International, www.oceanrowing.com

SPIRIT OF ADVENTURE
EPIC JOURNEYS

WATER BABY

As part of the four-woman crew of *Silver Cloud*, Rachel Flanders (UK, b. 3 September 1990) became the **youngest person to row across an ocean**. She crossed the Atlantic (east to west), leaving La Gomera, the Canary Islands on 2 December 2007, and reaching Antigua on 14 February 2008. Rachel was 17 years 91 days old at the start of the trip.

★ SMALLEST ROWBOAT TO CROSS AN OCEAN

Graham Walters (UK) rowed his boat *Puffin* – 4.65 m (15 ft 6 in) in length and 1.65 m (5 ft 6 in) in beam – across the Atlantic, east to west, from La Gomera, Canary Islands to St-Barthélemy between 3 February and 13 May 2007.

★ FASTEST DOUBLE-CHANNEL SWIM IN RELAY (FEMALE)

The fastest two-way swim of the English Channel by a female team is 18 hr 59 min by the six-woman Altamar 66K (all Mexico) on 10 August 2007.

CHANNEL CHAMPIONS

The **youngest person to swim the English Channel** is Thomas Gregory (UK, b. 6 October 1976), who was aged 11 years 336 days when he achieved the feat in 11 hr 54 min on 6 September 1988.

The **youngest female to swim the English Channel** is Samantha Druce (UK, b. 22 April 1971), who completed the crossing in 15 hr 27 min, aged 12 years 118 days on 18 August 1983.

(NB: current rules state that all Channel swimmers must be at least 16 years old.)

The **oldest person to swim the English Channel** was George Brunstad (USA, b. 25 August 1934), who was aged 70 years 4 days when he swam from Dover, UK, to Sangatte, France, in 15 hr 59 min on 29 August 2004.

Linda Ashmore (UK, b. 21 October 1946) is the ★ **oldest female to swim the English Channel**. She crossed from England to France in 15 hr 11 min, aged 60 years 302 days, on 19 August 2007.

The ★ **most crossings of the English Channel completed by a male swimmer** is 34 by Kevin Murphy (UK) between 1968 and 2006.

The Queen of the English Channel – that is, the ★ **female swimmer who has swum the English Channel the most times** – is Alison Streeter (UK) with 43 crossings from 1982 until 24 July 2004. She also holds the record for the ★ **most crossings of the English Channel by any swimmer**.

FASTEST ROW ACROSS THE ATLANTIC

Led by Leven Brown (UK), the crew of *La Mondiale* crossed the Atlantic in 33 days 7 hr 30 min. The team rowed east to west, leaving Gran Canaria, Spain, on 15 December 2007 and arriving at Barbados on 17 January 2008.

THE WEBB WONDER

The **first person to swim the English Channel** from shore to shore (without a life jacket) was Merchant Navy captain Matthew Webb (UK), who swam an estimated 61 km (38 miles) to make the 33-km (21-mile) crossing from Dover, UK, to Calais Sands, France, in 21 hr 45 min from 12:56 p.m. to 10:41 a.m. on 24–25 August 1875. Strong currents off Cap Gris Nez delayed Webb's arrival in France for five hours.

★ NEW RECORD
☆ UPDATED RECORD

★OLDEST PERSON TO ROW ACROSS ANY OCEAN

Pavel Rezvoy (Ukraine, b. 28 November 1938) rowed the Indian Ocean in his boat *Ukraine*, leaving the Cocos (Keeling) Islands, Australia, on 13 September 2005, aged 66 years 289 days, and arriving on Mahe Island, the Seychelles, on 9 November 2005.

SOLAR-POWERED OCEAN CROSSINGS

The ★**fastest transatlantic crossing made by solar power** is 29 days by *sun21* (Switzerland) and its crew of five from Las Palmas, Gran Canaria, Spain, to Le Marin, Martinique, from 4 January to 2 February 2007.

FASTEST TIMES TO SWIM THE ENGLISH CHANNEL

The ☆**fastest swim of the English Channel**, and the ☆**fastest swim of the England–France route**, is 6 hr 57 min 50 sec by Petar Stoychev (Bulgaria), who crossed from Shakespeare Beach, UK, to Cap Gris Nez, France, on 24 August 2007.

The ☆**fastest one-way swim of the English Channel by a woman** is 7 hr 25 min, achieved by Yvetta Hlavacova (Czech Republic) from England to France on 5 August 2006.

Kenichi Horie (Japan) made the **fastest crossing of the Pacific Ocean by solar power** when he travelled 16,092 km (10,000 miles) from Salinas, Ecuador, to Tokyo, Japan, in 148 days between 20 March and 5 August 1996.

LONGEST ROW ACROSS AN OCEAN

The longest solo ocean row of 312 days 2 hours was completed by Erden Eruç (Turkey) who rowed the Pacific east to west in *Around-n-Over*, leaving Bodega Bay, California, USA on 10 July 2007 and finishing at Papua New Guinea on 17 May 2008. The row was part of Erden's project to travel "around the world by human power."

★FASTEST TIME TO SAIL FROM SAN FRANCISCO TO TOKYO SOLO (MALE)

Peter Hogg (New Zealand) single-handedly sailed from San Francisco, USA, to Tokyo, Japan, in a time of 34 days 6 hr 26 min between 13 April 1992 and 19 May 1992.

★LONGEST JOURNEY NON-STOP IN A FLATS BOAT

The longest non-stop ocean voyage in a flats boat (a flat-bottomed craft with square ends) was 1,245.63 km (774 miles). It was set by Ralph and Robert Brown (both USA), who travelled from St George's, Bermuda, to New York Harbor, USA, from 9 to 11 May 2007.

FIRST CHANNEL CROSSING (FEMALE)

The first woman to successfully swim the English Channel was Gertrude Caroline Ederle (USA, b. 23 October 1906), who swam from Cap Gris Nez, France, to Deal, UK, on 6 August 1926, in a time of 14 hr 39 min.

SPIRIT OF ADVENTURE
EPIC JOURNEYS

ON THE WING

The **longest non-stop flight by any manned aircraft** was achieved by Steve Fossett (USA), who flew 42,469.4 km (26,389.3 miles) in the *Virgin Atlantic GlobalFlyer* airplane. Fossett took off from the Kennedy Space Center, Florida, USA, on 8 February 2006 and landed 76 hr 45 min later in Bournemouth, Dorset, UK, on 11 February 2006. In doing so, he beat the previous record, held by the *Breitling Orbiter 3* balloon, by 165.4 km (102.8 miles).

★ LONGEST AUTORIKSHAW JOURNEY

Susi Bemsel and Daniel Snaider (both Germany) covered 37,410 km (23,245 miles) between Bangkok, Thailand, and Eichstätt, Germany, from 8 February to 17 December 2005. They visited Thailand, Laos, Cambodia, Japan, Russia, Mongolia, Kazakhstan, Kyrgistan, Uzbekistan, Turkmenistan, Iran, Turkey, Syria, Jordan, Egypt, Libya, Tunisia, Italy, France, Spain and Germany.

★ LONGEST ONGOING PILGRIMAGE

The greatest distance claimed for a "round the world" pilgrimage is 60,353 km (37,502 miles) by Arthur Blessitt (USA) since 25 December 1969. He has visited all seven continents, having crossed 310 "nations, island groups and territories" carrying a 3.7-m-tall (12-ft) wooden cross and preaching from the Bible throughout.

LONGEST JOURNEY BY TAXI

The longest taxi journey on record covered 34,908 km (21,691 miles) at a cost of £40,210 ($64,645). Jeremy Levine, Mark Aylett (both UK) and Carlos Arrese (Spain) travelled from London, UK, to Cape Town, South Africa – and back – via taxi from 3 June to 17 October 1994.

LONGEST MOTORCYCLE RIDE (DISTANCE)

Emilio Scotto of Buenos Aires, Argentina, completed the longest ever journey by a motorcycle, covering over 735,000 km (457,000 miles) and 214 countries and territories, from 17 January 1985 to 2 April 1995.

★ LONGEST DRIVEN JOURNEY

Emil and Liliana Schmid (both Switzerland) have covered 617,359 km (383,609 miles) in their Toyota Land Cruiser since 16 October 1984, crossing 156 countries and territories in the process.

★ FIRST OVERLAND CROSSING OF THE DARIEN GAP

Richard E. Bevir (UK) and Terence John Whitfield (Australia) made the first overland crossing of the Darien Gap in their Land Rover *La Cucaracha* during the Trans Darien Expedition. The gap, which consists of dense jungle and numerous rivers, is famous for being the "missing" portion of the pan-American highway that links North and South America. They departed from Chepo, Panama, on 3 June and reached Quibdo, Colombia, on 17 June 1960.

FARTHEST DISTANCE FLOWN IN A BALLOON

The official Fédération Aéronautique Internationale (FAI) distance record for a manned balloon is 40,814 km (25,361 miles). It was set by Bertrand Piccard (Switzerland) and Brian Jones (UK), who piloted the *Breitling Orbiter 3* from 1 to 21 March 1999.

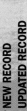

★ NEW RECORD
★ UPDATED RECORD

★ FASTEST JOURNEY ON FOOT ACROSS AUSTRALIA (PERTH TO SYDNEY)

Donnie Maclurcan (Australia) completed the fastest journey on foot across Australia when he ran across the continental mainland from Cottesloe Beach, Perth, Western Australia, to Bondi Beach, Sydney, New South Wales, in 67 days 2 hr 57 min, from 5 January to 13 March 2002.

DID YOU KNOW?

Donnie Maclurcan's epic 3,978-km (2,471-mile) run raised in excess of AUS$30,000 (US$15,660; £11,037) for the international sight-restoring work of The Fred Hollows Foundation.

★ FARTHEST DISTANCE TRAVELLED ON A SKATEBOARD IN 24 HOURS

Skateboarder James Peters (USA) covered 296.12 km (184 miles) in 24 hours in Seattle, Washington, USA, on 11 May 2007.

★ GREATEST DISTANCE ON A MOTORCYCLE IN 24 HOURS (INDIVIDUAL)

Eduardo Vergara Schaffner (Uruguay) covered 1,508.89 km (937.58 miles) by motorcycle in 24 hours on 2–3 November 2002 in Colonia, Uruguay. He travelled at an average speed of 63 km/h (39 mph) on a 125 cc (7.6 cu in) Vince Lifan motorcycle.

LONGEST CARAVAN JOURNEY

Harry B. Coleman and Peggy Larson travelled 231,288 km (143,716 miles) in a Volkswagen Camper between 20 August 1976 and 20 April 1978. Their journey took them through 113 countries.

★ GREATEST DISTANCE ON A HUMAN-POWERED VEHICLE (24 HOURS)

The farthest distance covered on a human-powered vehicle in a 24-hour period is 1,041.24 km (647 miles), achieved by Greg Kolodziejzyk (Canada) at Redwood Acres Raceway in Eureka, Alberta, Canada, on 18 July 2006.

SIR RICHARD BRANSON REMEMBERS STEVE FOSSETT

Multiple world record-holder Steve Fossett (USA) went missing on 3 September 2007 while on a flight over northwestern Nevada, USA. Despite a search of hundreds of square miles, his light aircraft was never found and he was officially declared dead on 26 February 2008. Friend and fellow record-breaker Sir Richard Branson (UK, pictured below left) shares some of his memories of Steve:

I first met Steve Fossett on a freezing January evening at the Busch stadium in St Louis. He was about to attempt a solo circumnavigation of the world by balloon and, although we were rivals, I decided to see him off in the spirit of sportsmanship that still inhabits the world of record-breaking. As I neared his balloon, a TV crew approached and I found myself being filmed chatting with a man I thought was one of his crew. I said one had to be a bit mad to test oneself in this way. The quiet American in front of me looked at me sympathetically and said, "I am Steve Fossett."

That was the beginning of a long and close friendship with one of the most generous, good-natured and kind people I have ever met, but also one of the bravest and most determined adventurers and explorers of all time. Steve held more adventuring world records than any other human being. He began in a modest way, swimming the English Channel in 1985. Over the next 22 years, he amassed over 115 records in aviation, gliding, ballooning, sailing, power boating, mountaineering, skiing, triathlon, even dog sledding. He truly was the adventurer's adventurer.

In no project Steve undertook did he demonstrate greater skill than during his circumnavigation of the globe in the *Virgin Atlantic GlobalFlyer*. He later described this in his autobiography, *Chasing the Wind*, as one of his proudest achievements. The aircraft, now displayed in the Smithsonian Institute, was a unique carbon composite jet that led the way in new, energy-efficient technology now being developed by Boeing and Airbus. Steve proved it was possible to safely fly an ultra-light high-altitude jet burning lean fuel. He did so by sitting in one alone for three days and four nights without rest (apart from a few of his legendary power naps) in difficult weather conditions at altitudes of over 50,000 ft [15,240 m]; outside his tiny Perspex canopy, it was 80 degrees below zero [-112°F].

Steve was a true record-breaker, a man who tested not only himself, but through his record attempts, new green technologies and materials to the limit.

He will be truly missed, not only by all of us who knew him and loved him but by the millions of people around the world who watched in awe a man who believed world records were there to be broken, and break them he did.

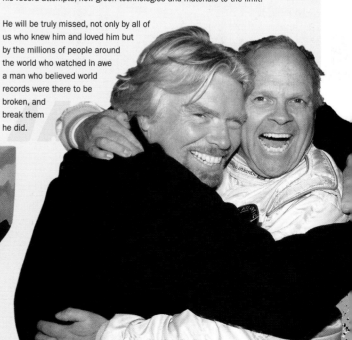

POLAR PIONEERS

★ FASTEST TO THE "THREE POLES"

The shortest time taken to reach the three extreme points of the Earth – Mt Everest, the North Pole and the South Pole (also known as the Three Poles) – is 1 year 217 days by Adrian Hayes (UK). Mr Hayes summitted Mt Everest on 25 May 2006, reached the North Pole on 25 April 2007 (from Ward Hunt Island, Canada) and finally claimed the South Pole, journeying from the Hercules Inlet, on 28 December 2007.

★ OLDEST PERSON TO VISIT THE NORTH POLE

Dorothy Davenhill Hirsch (USA, b. 11 May 1915) reached the North Pole aboard the Russian nuclear icebreaker *Yamal* on 28 August 2004, aged 89 years 109 days.

FASTEST SOLO UNSUPPORTED TREK TO THE NORTH POLE

Børge Ousland (Norway) skied his way to the North Pole from the Severnaya Zemlya archipelago in Russia, without any external assistance, in 52 days from 2 March to 23 April 1994. He was also the **first person to make a solo and unsupported journey to the North Pole from land**.

FIRST SOLO EXPEDITION TO THE SOUTH POLE

Erling Kagge (Norway) became the first person to reach the South Pole after a solo and unsupported surface trek on 7 January 1993, aged 29. His 1,400-km (870-mile) journey from Berkner Island took 50 days.

FASTEST SURFACE JOURNEY TO THE NORTH POLE

An expedition consisting of Hugh Dale-Harris, Matty McNair (both Canada), Andrew Gerber (South Africa), Tom Avery and George Wells (both UK), along with a team of 16 husky dogs, reached the North Pole on 26 April 2005, having travelled for 36 days 22 hr 11 min. The team, which left from Cape Columbia on Ellesmere Island in Arctic Canada, were attempting to re-create as closely as possible the disputed 1909 expedition of American explorer Robert Peary (see next page). Just like Peary, the expedition team had four resupplies along the way.

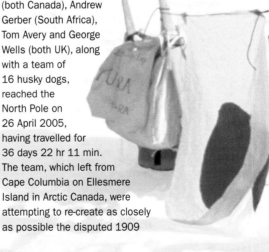

FASTEST SOLO KITE-ASSISTED JOURNEY TO THE SOUTH POLE

Børge Ousland (Norway) travelled to the South Pole on skis, with assistance from a parafoil kite, in 34 days from 15 November to 19 December 1996. The journey was solo and unsupported – in other words, he received no outside assistance.

★ NEW RECORD
★ UPDATED RECORD

> *Many times I have thanked God for a bite of raw dog.*
> Polar explorer Robert Peary (USA, 1856–1920)

FIRST PERSON TO SET FOOT ON BOTH POLES

Dr Albert Paddock Crary (USA, 1911–87), a polar geophysicist and glaciologist, reached the North Pole by Dakota aircraft on 3 May 1952. On 12 February 1961, he arrived at the South Pole by Sno Cat with a scientific traverse party that had set out from McMurdo Station on 10 December 1960.

FIRST SOLO EXPEDITION TO THE NORTH POLE

Naomi Uemura (1941–84), a Japanese explorer and mountaineer, became the first person to reach the North Pole in a solo trek across the Arctic sea ice at 4:45 a.m. GMT on 1 May 1978. He had travelled 725 km (450 miles), setting out on 7 March 1978 from Cape Edward on Ellesmere Island in northern Canada.

FIRST FLIGHT IN AN AEROPLANE OVER ANTARCTICA

The first heavier-than-air flight over the Antarctic continent was made on 16 November 1928 by Sir Hubert Wilkins (Australia) and Carl Ben Eielson (USA) in a Lockheed Vega aircraft.

FIRST FLIGHT OVER THE SOUTH POLE

Pioneering aviator Richard Byrd (USA) made the first flight over the South Pole on 29 November 1929. The round trip to and from the expedition's base on the Ross Ice Shelf took 19 hours.

FIRST PERSON TO REACH THE SOUTH POLE

Leading a Norwegian party of five men, Captain Roald Amundsen (Norway, 1872–1928) reached the South Pole at 11:00 a.m. on 14 December 1911 after a 53-day march with dog sledges from the Bay of Whales.

FIRST TO REACH THE NORTH POLE

The title "first person to reach the North Pole" has long been a matter of debate, with two American explorers staking a claim early in the 20th century. Robert Peary led an expedition (illustrated below) that he claimed reached the North Pole on 6 April 1909; however, Frederick Cook claimed he had done so a year earlier, on 21 April 1908.

THE POLES

Unless specified, the records on these pages refer to the geographic North and South Poles, but did you realize there are, in fact, eight poles?

The **North Pole**, or **Geographic North Pole**, is the northernmost point, aka "True North". This Pole floats on sea ice, so explorers use a GPS (global positioning system) to pinpoint its location. The **South Pole**, or **Geographic South Pole**, is the southernmost point of the Earth's surface.

The Earth has its own magnetic field, created by its iron core and its spinning motion. The northern and southern points of this field are the **Magnetic North Pole** and the **Magnetic South Pole** respectively. These are not fixed, and move continually.

The Earth, which rotates on an axis tilted at 11 degrees, has a geomagnetic field that behaves as if it had a bar magnet inside its core. The **Geomagnetic North Pole** and **Geomagnetic South Pole** are the northernmost and southernmost points of this field respectively.

The **North Pole of Inaccessibility** is the farthest point from any northern coastline; it is purely a geographical reference, not a physical spot. The **South Pole of Inaccessibility** marks the farthest point from any coast on the Antarctic continent.

115

PEAK PERFORMANCE

THE SUMMITS

The mountaineering challenge of the "Seven Summits" means climbing to the very top of the highest mountains on the Earth's seven continents: Africa, Antarctica, Asia, North America, South America, Europe and Oceania. So why are there eight mountains and two lists?

Depending upon how a continent is defined geographically, there are two possible contenders for the highest mountain in continental Australia.

Carstensz Pyramid (a.k.a. Puncak Jaya) is the tallest mountain in Oceania, a region that includes Australia, New Zealand and New Guinea.

If Australia is considered to be the only continental country in the region (with no land borders to other countries), then Mt Kosciuszko, near Sydney, is the tallest.

It is a great achievement for climbers to summit either list, but often they choose to do both to avoid any doubt!

★ FASTEST CLIMB OF THE SEVEN SUMMITS (CARSTENSZ LIST)

Daniel Griffith (Canada) climbed the highest peak on each continent in 187 days between 24 May 2006 – when he ascended Mt Everest in Nepal – and 27 November 2006 – when he conquered Vinson Massif, Antarctica.

★ HIGHEST ALTITUDE CONCERT ON LAND

A concert was performed at a height of 6,069 m (19,911 ft) by Musikkapelle Roggenzell – 10 musicians from Germany and Bolivia – on Mt Acotango, Bolivia, on 6 August 2007.

★ YOUNGEST PERSON TO CLIMB THE SEVEN SUMMITS

Samantha Larson (USA, b. 7 October 1988) became the youngest climber of the seven summits (Kosciuszko list) when she reached the seventh peak – Mt Everest – on 17 May 2007, aged 18 years 222 days. Samantha then went on to climb Carstensz Pyramid on 4 August 2007, aged 18 years 301 days, making her the ★ youngest person to summit the Carstensz version of the seven summits challenge.

★ FASTEST CLIMB OF THE SEVEN SUMMITS (KOSCIUSZKO LIST)

Mastan Babu Malli (India) climbed the highest peak on each continent in 172 days between 19 January 2006, when he summited Vinson Massif (Antarctica), and 10 July 2006, when he topped Mt Denali (USA).

★ BUSIEST YEAR FOR EVEREST ASCENTS

There were a record 526 ascents of Everest in the calendar year 2007.

FASTEST ASCENT OF MT EVEREST (NORTH SIDE)

Hans Kammerlander (Italy) completed the fastest ascent of Mt Everest on the northern side, making the climb from Base Camp to the summit in 16 hr 45 min on 23 and 24 May 1996.

KOSCIUSZKO

Named after a Polish military general, Australia's highest peak is 2,228 m (7,310 ft), and located in the Great Dividing Range.

EL CAPITAN

Located in Yosemite National Park, California, USA, El Capitan is a giant granite rock 2,307 m (7,569 ft) tall.

CARSTENSZ PYRAMID

The continent of Oceania's highest mountain, at 4,884 m (16,023 ft), is on the Indonesian island of New Guinea. The peak is also called Puncak Jaya.

VINSON MASSIF

The summit of Antarctica is 4,892 m (16,049 ft) and sits in the Sentinel mountain range, 1,200 km (750 miles) from the South Pole.

ELBRUS

Europe's tallest mountain has a peak height of 5,642 m (18,510 ft) and sits in the Caucasus range of Russia.

★ OLDEST FEMALE TO CLIMB THE SEVEN SUMMITS (KOSCIUSZKO LIST)

Jeanne Stawiecki (USA, b. 24 June 1950) became the oldest woman to climb the Seven Summits, including Mt Kosciuszko, when she completed her last climb (Mt Everest, Nepal) on 22 May 2007, aged 57 years 36 days.

★ HIGHEST ALTITUDE REACHED BY CAR

Gonzalo Bravo and Eduardo Canales (both Chile) drove to an altitude of 6,688 m (21,942 ft) in their modified 1986 Suzuki Samurai, on the slopes of the Ojos Del Salado volcano, near the Atacama desert, Chile, on 21 April 2007.

FACT
The "Death Zone" in climbing refers to the altitude above 8,000 m (26,245 ft) at which the human body can no longer adapt to the climatic conditions. In other words, you start to die!

FASTEST ASCENT OF MT EVEREST (SOUTH SIDE)

Pemba Dorje Sherpa (Nepal) climbed from Base Camp to the summit of Mt Everest in a time of 8 hr 10 min on 21 May 2004. This is the fastest ever ascent of the world's tallest mountain.

MOST ASCENTS OF MT EVEREST BY A WOMAN

Lakpa Sherpa (Nepal) successfully reached the summit of Mt Everest for the fifth time on 2 June 2005. She made the climb with her husband, George Demarescu (USA), who was himself completing his seventh ascent of the world's tallest mountain.

★ FIRST ASCENT OF K2 (WEST FACE)

Russia's Andrew Mariev and Vadim Popovich completed the first successful ascent of the notoriously vicious west face of K2. The expedition – led by Viktor Kozlov (Russia) – reached the 8,500-m-high (28,251-ft) peak on 21 August 2007, after a gruelling 10-week climb.

★ HIGHEST UNCLIMBED PEAK

At 7,570 m (24,835 ft), Gangkar Punsum in Bhutan is the world's 40th highest peak, and the highest mountain yet to be climbed. Unsuccessful attempts were made to summit the peak in the 1980s, then in 1994 a partial of ban of mountaineering in the country was declared. Since 2003, all climbing in Bhutan has been outlawed – for religious reasons – so it could remain unclimbed for many years to come.

The **highest unclimbed peak where climbing is not prohibited** is the demanding east face of Saser Kangri II in Indian Kashmir, which reaches 7,518 m (24,665 ft).

★ OLDEST PERSON TO CLIMB MT EVEREST

Katsusuke Yanagisawa (Japan, b. 20 March 1936), a former school teacher, reached the summit from the north side with team Himex on 22 May 2007, aged 71 years 63 days.

★ NEW RECORD
★ UPDATED RECORD

KILIMANJARO
Reaching high above the African plains of Tanzania, "Kili" stands 5,895 m (19,340 ft) tall. It is classified as an inactive stratovolcano, although Kili has never actually recorded an eruption.

DENALI
North America's highest peak is also known as Mt McKinley. This Alaskan mountain is 6,194 m (20,321 ft) tall.

ACONCAGUA
The highest point of South America is in the Andes mountain range of Argentina, and measures 6,962 m (22,841 ft). It was first summited on 14 January 1897.

K2
At 8,611 m (28,251 ft), K2 – in the Karakoram range on the Pakistan–China border – is the world's second highest mountain. It was first climbed on 31 July 1954.

EVEREST
The highest mountain in the world, at 8,848 m (29,029 ft), is in Asia's Himalayan region. Its other names are Sagarmatha and Chomolungma.

MODERN LIFE

CONTENTS

LONGEST LIVING DOG

With a nose-to-tail-tip length of 232 cm (91.3 in), Mon Ami von der Oelmühle is the longest dog alive today. The Irish Wolfhound was bred by Jürgen Rösner (pictured) and owned by Joachim and Elke Müller of Wegberg-Arsbeck, Germany.

COLLECTIONS

★ PHONES

As of 20 April 2007, Zhang Dafang (China) had collected 600 telephones from all eras and from all over the world, including a phone in the shape of a whisky bottle. He found his oldest piece, dating from 1900, in a Russian flea market.

★ BELLS

Myrtle B. Eldridge (USA) has 9,638 bells that she has collected since the 1980s.

BOARD GAMES

As of 21 February 2007, Brian Arnett (USA) had collected 1,345 different board games. Brian started his collection in 1996.

★ CANDLES

Kathrin Koch (Germany) had amassed 1,820 different candles by 3 May 2007. She began her collection in 1993.

FOUR-LEAFED CLOVERS

Edward Martin Sr (USA) has been collecting four-leafed clovers since 1999 and had amassed 111,060 of them by May 2007.

★ LADYBIRDS

Sheri Gartner (USA) had put together a collection of 2,050 ladybird-related items as of November 2007.

MODEL CARS

Michael Zarnock (USA) had collected 8,128 different Hot Wheels model cars as of 14 February 2007. He began his collection in 1968.

X-REF

In January 2001, teachers and students at St Joseph School in Cairo, Illinois, USA, made the **largest rosary**, which measured 52.9 m (173 ft 9 in) long. For more outsize records, turn to **Big Stuff** on p.148.

MOST ROSARIES

Mohammed Yahya Al-Aseeri (Saudi Arabia) had collected 3,220 rosaries as of 31 August 2007. Closely associated with Roman Catholicism, rosaries – strings of beads used in prayer – are also common to other faiths.

LARGEST MASK COLLECTION

Gerold Weschenmoser (Germany) had acquired 5,121 different masks by 22 January 2008 (he even has one of his own face!). He began collecting in 1957.

We wanted to share the angels with more people than we could accommodate at home...
Joyce Berg (USA), co-owner of the largest collection of angels and co-founder of the Angel Museum, Beloit, Wisconsin, USA

TOP 20 ODDEST GWR COLLECTIONS

COLLECTION	NUMBER	HOLDER (NATIONALITY)
★ Angels	13,165	Joyce & Lowell Berg (USA)
★ Artificial apples	2,300	Erika & Kurt Werth (Italy)
Armoured vehicles	229	Jacques Littlefield (USA)
★ Bus tickets	21,000	G. Vasanthakumar (India)
★ Casino chips	374	Bruce & Sue Wunder (USA)
★ Commemorative church plates	1,206	Tom & Barbara Southwell (USA)
★ "Do Not Disturb" signs	7,806	Jean-François Vernetti (Switzerland)
Hair from historical figures	115	John Reznikoff (USA)
Lipstick prints	39,537	Breakthrough Breast Cancer and Avon Cosmetics (UK)
Matchbox labels	743,512	Teiichi Yoshizawa (Japan)
Nail clippers	505	Andrè Ludwick (South Africa)
★ Nativity sets	874	Sue Koenig (USA)
★ Parking meters	292	Lotta Sjölin (Sweden)
★ "Robin" Christmas Cards	11,010	Joan Gordon (UK)
★ Sick bags	5,180	Niek Vermeulen (Netherlands)
Spoon-rests	635	Frank Cassa (USA)
★ Stamps featuring ships	6,459	Celso Fernandes (Canada)
★ Tea-bag labels	8,661	Felix Rotter (Germany)
★ Trolls	490	Sophie Marie Cross (UK)
Vintage lawn mowers	790	Andrew Hall & Michael Duck (UK)

MODEL COACHES AND BUSES
By 4 December 2007, Geoff Price (UK) had collected 10,017 model buses and coaches, having begun in 1959.

★ NUMBER PLATES
Mohammed Yahya Al-Aseeri (Saudi Arabia) had a collection of 80 different car licence plates as of 31 August 2007.

★ PAPER DOLLS
Malin Fritzell (Sweden) has been collecting paper dolls since the 1960s. As of 23 March 2006, his collection numbered 4,720.

★ PENCIL SHARPENERS
Demetra Koutsouridou (Greece) has collected 8,514 different pencil sharpeners since 1997.

★ SANTA CLAUS MEMORABILIA
Since 1988, Jean-Guy Laquerre (Canada) has built up a collection of 13,014 items of Father Christmas memorabilia.

★ SIMPSONS MEMORABILIA
Cameron Gibbs (Australia) had a collection of 951 different Simpsons items as of 23 April 2007. He has been collecting for five years.

★ SNOWMEN
As of 23 March 2007, Kathleen G. Sauk (USA) had collected 1,693 different snowman-related items. Her collection is nine years old.

★ SPORTS MASCOTS
Soeren Christian Hesse (Germany) presented his record-breaking collection of 161 sports mascots in the AOL Arena, Hamburg, Germany, on 28 March 2007.

TEAPOTS
The largest collection of teapots belongs to Tang Yu (China), who has amassed 30,000 different teapots dating from the Song Dynasty to modern times. He began his collection in 1955.

BACK SCRATCHERS
Manfred S. Rothstein (USA) has 518 back scratchers housed in his dermatology clinic in Fayetteville, North Carolina, USA. He started his collection in the 1970s.

★ NEW RECORD
UPDATED RECORD

EXTREME CUISINE

★ MOST MENTOS-AND-SODA FOUNTAINS

A total of 973 Mentos-and-soda fountains were made by residents of southeast Missouri at Arena Park, Cape Girardeau, Missouri, USA, on 3 October 2007. Each eruption had an average height of 4 m (13 ft 1 in).

AGAINST THE CLOCK

★ MOST EXPENSIVE COCKTAIL

The Skyview Bar in the Burj Al Arab Hotel in Dubai, UAE, offers a cocktail named "27321" that costs 27,321 Dirham (£3,766.52, $7,439). The cocktail, an ultra-luxurious version of a traditional Old Fashioned, consists of 55 year-old Macallan whisky, ice made from the water used at their distillery, a drop or so of exclusive dried fruit bitters and passionfruit-scented sugar. It is stirred using a rod made from a Macallan cask and served in a glass produced in the French town of Baccarat.

MOST APPLES PICKED IN EIGHT HOURS

The greatest recorded weight of apples collected is 7,180.3 kg (15,830 lb), picked in eight hours by George Adrian of Indianapolis, Indiana, USA, on 23 September 1980.

★ FASTEST TIME TO EAT A RAW ONION

Samuel Grazette (Barbados) ate a raw onion in 48 seconds at the 2007 Barbados World Records Festival held at the National Stadium, Barbados, on 31 March 2007.

★ FASTEST TIME TO OPEN 2,000 BEER BOTTLES

Krunoslav Budiselic (Croatia) opened 2,000 beer bottles in 37 min 39 sec. The record was achieved in Karlovac, Croatia, on 25 August 2007.

★ MOST PANCAKES MADE IN EIGHT HOURS (TEAM)

Members of the Fargo Kiwanis Club in Fargo, North Dakota, USA, made 34,818 pancakes in eight hours at the 50th Annual Pancake Karnival at the Fargo Civic Auditorium on 9 February 2008. All the pancakes counted were actually served to and eaten by visitors to the Karnival.

★ FASTEST TIME TO PEEL AND EAT A LEMON

Serial record-breaker Ashrita Furman (USA) peeled and ate a lemon in just 10.97 seconds at the Panorama Cafe in Jamaica, New York, USA, on 24 August 2007.

★ MOST COCONUTS SMASHED IN ONE MINUTE

Using just one hand, Muhamed Kahrimanovic (Germany) successfully smashed a total of 81 coconuts in one minute in Hamburg, Germany, on 6 December 2007.

★ MOST ICE-CREAM CONES PREPARED IN ONE MINUTE

The greatest number of ice-cream cones prepared in one minute is 19, achieved by Mitch Cohen (USA) of Baskin-Robbins. He broke the record on the Food Network TV show *Paula's Party* on 28 June 2007.

★ MOST RICE GRAINS EATEN IN THREE MINUTES

Rob Beaton (USA) ate 78 grains of rice, one by one, using only a pair of chopsticks, in three minutes in Ocean Gate, New Jersey, USA, on 9 November 2007.

★ MALTESER CATCHING

The record for the most Maltesers (chocolate covered honeycomb malt balls) thrown 2 m (6 ft 6 in) and then caught in the mouth in a minute is 19, by thrower Ranald Mackechnie (pictured left) and catcher Stuart Hendry (both UK) at the Guinness World Record Offices in London, UK, on 28 September 2007.

TALLEST...

★ COOKIE TOWER
Members of the Girl Scouts – Seal of Ohio Council, Inc., managed to construct a tower of cookies 1.57 m (5 ft 2 in) tall in Columbus, Ohio, USA, on 15 September 2007.

★ STACK OF DOUGHNUTS
Members of Twentieth Century Fox and Capital Radio (both UK) created a stack of doughnuts measuring 110.5 cm (43.5 in) tall to celebrate the premiere of *The Simpsons Movie* (USA, 2007) in London, UK, on 25 July 2007.

★ CHAMPAGNE FOUNTAIN
Luuk Broos (Netherlands) and his team made a champagne pyramid fountain consisting of 41,664 glasses, forming 62 storeys, in Zeelandhallen, Goes, the Netherlands, on 12 September 2007.

MISC.

★ MOST DANGEROUS CHEESE
The most dangerous cheese to human health is casu marzu ("rotten cheese"), made from sheep's milk and considered a delicacy in Sardinia, Italy – even though it is illegal to buy. Casu marzu is essentially a Pecorino cheese left to rot. Flies can then lay their eggs in it, resulting in thousands of maggots. The enzymes produced by these maggots assist the fermentation process of the cheese, which supposedly adds to the desired taste. If the maggots survive the digestive juices in the human stomach, however, they can provoke vomiting, abdominal pain and bloody diarrhoea.

★ FASTEST TIME TO OPEN 100 MUSSELS
Kannha Keo (New Zealand) managed to open 100 mussels in a record-breaking time of 2 min 11 sec at the Havelock Mussel Festival, Havelock, New Zealand, on 17 March 2007.

★ MOST PEOPLE TOSSING EGGS
The Wrangell Chamber of Commerce (USA) managed to amass 338 people to toss eggs in Wrangell, Alaska, USA, on 3 July 2007.

★ MOST WINE GLASSES HELD IN ONE HAND
The most wine glasses held in one hand (without using equipment of any kind) is 39 by Reymond Adina (Philippines) at the Quatre-Cats restaurant in Barcelona, Spain, on 24 October 2007. There is strong competition between waiters in Barcelona to hold this smashing record.

★ MOST CHICKENS SPIT-ROASTED SIMULTANEOUSLY

Using a 20-m-long (65-ft 7-in), 5-m-high (16-ft 5-in) rotisserie wall, chef Jiang Bing (China) managed to spit-roast 2,008 chickens at the same time in Nanning, Guangxi, China, on 24 October 2007.

INCREDIBLE EDIBLES

★ MOST EXPENSIVE SANDWICH

Comprising 24-hour fermented sour-dough bread, Iberico ham, poulet de Bresse, white truffles, quail eggs and semi-dried Italian tomatoes, the most expensive commercially available sandwich is the von Essen Platinum Club Sandwich, created by Daniel Galmiche (UK) for the menu at Cliveden, Buckinghamshire, UK. Costing £100 ($200), the sandwich was added to the menu in March 2007.

★ MOST LAYERS IN A LAYER CAKE

Jayn Parenti (USA) baked a layer cake containing 230 layers on 4 July 2006. Jayn's patriotic red, white and blue creation was prepared and displayed at the Springdale Country Club, Springdale, Arkansas, USA.

HIGHEST PANCAKE TOSS

Bill Weir (USA), one of the hosts of the television show *Good Morning America!* (ABC, USA), tossed a pancake 4.2 m (14 ft) outside the ABC television studios in Times Square, New York City, USA, on 7 August 2006.

★ LONGEST NOUGAT

A nougat measuring 408.61 m (1,340 ft 6 in) in length was made by chef Paolo Attili (Italy) in collaboration with the Associazione Turistica Pro Camerino to celebrate the Day of Torrone (nougat) in Camerino, Italy, on 7 January 2007.

★ LONGEST ONION STRING

The longest string of onions measured 4.518 km (2.8 miles) and was made by 48 people from Pericei, Salaj County, Romania, as part of the Pericei Onion Fest on 8 September 2007.

★ LONGEST ICE-CREAM DESSERT

To celebrate the 25th birthday of its much-loved Viennetta ice-cream dessert, maker Unilever–Wall's prepared a Viennetta measuring 22.75 m (74 ft 7 in) in length at the company's Barnwood Factory in Gloucester, UK, on 11 July 2007.

★ LARGEST BOWL OF CEREAL

The world's largest bowl of cereal contained 1,000 kg (2,204 lb 10 oz) of Kellogg's cornflakes and was made by Kellogg's South Africa, Sync Communications and Automatic in Johannesburg, South Africa, on 2 July 2007. The bowl itself measured 2.6 m (8 ft 6 in) in diameter and 1.5 m (4 ft 11 in) in height.

LONGEST GARLIC STRING

A string of garlic measuring 255 m (836 ft 7 in) was made for the annual Garlic Festival in Mako, Hungary, on 8 September 2006.

LONGEST SALAMI

A salami with a length of 718.9 m (2,358 ft 7 in) was created in San Donà di Piave, Venice, Italy, on 4 December 2005. The successful attempt was organized by Giuseppe Vidotto (Italy).

BIG FOOD

FOOD	SIZE	NAME (NAT.)	YEAR
★ Chocolate bar	3,580 kg (7,892 lb 8 oz)	Elah Dufour - Novi (Italy)	2007
★ Cup of coffee	3,613 litres (795 gal)	Vinacafe Bien Hoa (Vietnam)	2007
★ Dulce de leche	1,419.65 kg (3,129 lb 12.6 oz)	Rosario Olvera (Mexico)	2007
★ Fishcake	106.59 kg (235 lb)	Dover Downs Hotel & Casino and Handy International (USA)	2006
★ Fudge (slab)	2.29 tonnes (5,050 lb)	Chantelle Gorham of Northwest Fudge Factory (Canada)	2007
Gingerbread man	593.53 kg (1,308 lb 8 oz)	Smithville Chamber of Commerce (USA)	2006
★ Goulash soup (bowl)	7,200 litres (1,583.78 gal)	Orizont TV (Romania)	2007
Guacamole serving	1,819.7 kg (4,011 lb 12 oz)	APEAM, A.C. (Mexican Avocado Industry) and the FECADEMI (Michoacan Community Federation in California)	2007
★ Hotpot	208.904 kg (460 lb 8 oz)	Garstang and District Partnership (UK)	2007
★ Nougat	1,300 kg (2,866 lb)	Jerome Guigon and Bernard Morin (both France)	2005
★ Okonomiyaki	1.6 tonnes (3,527 lb)	Kamigata Okonomiyaki Takoyaki Cooperative Association (Japan)	2002
★ Pupusa	3.09 m (10 ft 2 in)	Chamber of Commerce El Salvador-California and Liborio Markets, Inc. (both USA)	2007
★ Ravioli	16 kg (35 lb 4 oz)	16 cooks in Saas-Fee (Switzerland)	2007
★ Salad	10,260 kg (22,619 lb 6 oz)	Sde Warburg Agricultural Association (Israel)	2007
★ Scotch egg	5.435 kg (11 lb 15 oz)	*Loaded* magazine (UK)	2007
Soup (bowl)	15,000 litres (3,962 gal)	Ministerio del Poder Popular para la Alimentación (Venezuela)	2007
★ Tiramisu	305.95 kg (674 lb 8 oz)	Alpini Group of Caronno Pertusella and Bariola (Italy)	2007

MOST EXPENSIVE ICE-CREAM SUNDAE

The Frrrozen Haute Chocolate, costing $25,000 (£12,000), was added to the menu of the Serendipity 3 restaurant, New York City, USA, on 7 November 2007. Made in partnership with luxury jeweller Euphoria of New York, the sundae uses a fine blend of 28 cocoas, including 14 of the world's most expensive. It is decorated with 5 g (0.17 oz) of edible 23-carat gold and is served in a goblet lined with edible gold. The base of the goblet is an 18-carat gold bracelet with 1 carat of white diamonds. The dessert is eaten with a gold and diamond spoon, which can also be taken home.

TALLEST POPPADOM STACK

Richard Bradbury, Kristopher Growcott, Marley Bradbury and Millie Bradbury (all UK) created a free-standing stack of poppadoms 1.42 m (4 ft 7.9 in) tall in aid of the Indian Flood Relief charity at La Porte Des Indes Restaurant, London, UK, on 8 November 2007.

MOST EXPENSIVE PIZZA

The most expensive commercially available pizza is a thin-crust, wood fire-baked pizza topped with onion puree, white truffle paste, fontina cheese, baby mozzarella, pancetta, cep mushrooms and freshly picked wild mizuna lettuce, garnished with fresh shavings of a rare Italian white truffle, itself worth £1,400 ($2,800) per 1 kg (2 lb 3 oz).

Depending upon the amount of truffles available each season, the pizza is regularly sold at £100 ($200) each to customers of Gordon Ramsay's Maze restaurant in London, UK.

LONGEST TAMALE

Measuring 15.78 m (51 ft 9 in), the longest tamale (steam-cooked corn dough) was made at El Chico in Jackson, Tennessee, USA, on 5 May 2006.

LONGEST STRAND OF PASTA

Gewerbe-Verein Siblingen (Siblingen trade association, Switzerland) created a strand of pasta measuring 3,333 m (10,935 ft) in length in Siblingen, Switzerland, on 12 September 2004.

LARGEST BURGER

A hamburger tipping the scales in at 60.78 kg (134 lb) is commercially available on the menu at Mallie's Sports Grill & Bar in Southgate, Michigan, USA, for $350 (£176). It takes three people to flip the "Absolutely Ridiculous Burger", which takes 12 hours to prepare. It is topped with cheese, bacon, tomatoes, onions and lettuce, and weighs the same as an average adult male!

LARGEST SALAD

The record for the largest salad is 10,260 kg (22,619 lb) and was achieved by the Sde Warburg Agricultural Association in Sde Warburg, Israel on 10 November 2007. It contained 9,000 kg (19,841 lb) of Lettuce, 1,500 kg (3,307 lb) of Carrots, 500 kg (112 lb) of Cherry Tomatoes and 800 litres (211 gal) of Salad Dressing.

GARDEN GREATS

★ HEAVIEST KALE

Scott Robb (USA) exhibited a kale weighing a record 48.04 kg (105 lb 14.5 oz) at the Alaska State Fair, Palmer, Alaska, USA, on 29 August 2007.

★ LARGEST CUCUMBER PLANT

Covering an area of 56.7 m² (610 ft²), the largest cucumber plant can be found at the Epcot Science project at Walt Disney World Resort in Lake Buena Vista, Florida, USA. The plant was measured in July 2006.

The Epcot Science project is home to the world's ★ largest tomato plant too, which also covered an area of 56.7 m² (610 ft²) when measured on 27 March 2007. Both the tomato plant and the cucumber plant are grown on a rectangular trellis measuring 6.1 x 9.3 m (20 ft x 30 ft 6 in).

HEAVIEST FRUIT & VEGETABLES

FRUIT/VEG	WEIGHT	NAME/NATIONALITY	YEAR
Apple	1.84 kg (4 lb 1 oz)	Chisato Iwasaki (Japan)	2005
Avocado	1.99 kg (4 lb 6 oz)	Anthony Llanos (Australia)	1992
Beetroot	71.05 kg (156 lb 10 oz)	Piet de Goede (Netherlands)	2005
Blueberry	7 g (0.24 oz)	Brian Carlick (UK)	2005
Broccoli	15.87 kg (35 lb)	John & Mary Evans (both USA)	1993
Brussels sprout	8.3 kg (18 lb 3 oz)	Bernard Lavery (UK)	1992
Cabbage	56.24 kg (124 lb)	Bernard Lavery (UK)	1989
Cabbage (red)	19.05 kg (42 lb)	R. Straw (UK)	1925
Cantaloupe	29.4 kg (64 lb 13 oz)	Scott & Mardie Robb (both USA)	2004
Carrot	8.61 kg (18 lb 13 oz)	John Evans (USA)	1998
Cauliflower	24.6 kg (54 lb 3 oz)	Alan Hattersley (UK)	1999
Celery	28.7 kg (63 lb 4 oz)	Scott & Mardie Robb (both USA)	2003
Cherry	21.69 g (0.76 oz)	Gerardo Maggipinto (Italy)	2003
Cucumber	12.4 kg (27 lb 5 oz)	Alfred J. Cobb (UK)	2003
Garlic head	1.19 kg (2 lb 10 oz)	Robert Kirkpatrick (USA)	1985
Gooseberry	61.04 g (2 oz)	Kelvin Archer (UK)	1993
Gourd	42.8 kg (94 lb 5 oz)	Robert Weber (Australia)	2001
★ Grapefruit	3.21 kg (7 lb 12 oz)	Cloy Dias Dutra (Brazil)	2006
Jackfruit	34.6 kg (76 lb 4 oz)	George & Margaret Schattauer (both USA)	2003
★ Kale	48.04 kg (105 lb 14.5 oz)	Scott Robb (USA)	2007
Kohlrabi	43.98 kg (96 lb 15 oz)	Scott Robb (USA)	2006
Leek	8.1 kg (17 lb 13 oz)	Fred Charlton (UK)	2002
Lemon	5.26 kg (11 lb 9 oz)	Aharon Shemoel (Israel)	2003
Mango	3.1 kg (6 lb 13 oz)	Tai Mok Lim (Malaysia)	2006
Marrow	62 kg (136 lb 9 oz)	Mark Baggs (UK)	2005
Nectarine	360 g (12 oz)	Tony Slattery (New Zealand)	1998
Onion	7.49 kg (16 lb 8 oz)	John Sifford (UK)	2005
★ Parsnip	4.95 kg (10 lb 14 oz)	Joe Atherton (UK)	2007
Peach	725 g (25 oz)	Paul Friday (USA)	2002
Pear	2.1 kg (4 lb 8 oz)	Warren Yeoman (Australia)	1999
Pineapple	8.06 kg (17 lb 12 oz)	E. Kamuk (Papua New Guinea)	1994
Pomegranate	1.04 kg (2 lb 3 oz)	Katherine Murphy (USA)	2001
Potato	3.5 kg (7 lb 11 oz)	K. Sloane (UK)	1994
Potato (sweet)	37 kg (81 lb 9 oz)	Manuel Pérez Pérez (Spain)	2004
Pummelo	4.86 kg (10 lb 10 oz)	Seiji Sonoda (Japan)	2005
★ Pumpkin	766.12 kg (1,689 lb)	Joseph Jutras (USA)	2007
Quince	2.34 kg (5 lb 2 oz)	Edward Harold McKinney (USA)	2002
Radish	31.1 kg (68 lb 9 oz)	Manabu Oono (Japan)	2003
Courgette (Zucchini)	29.25 kg (64 lb 8 oz)	Bernard Lavery (UK)	1990

★ MOST CUCUMBERS HARVESTED FROM ONE PLANT IN ONE YEAR

The cucumber plant at the Epcot Science project (see previous record) produced a crop weighing 943 kg (2,078 lb). The harvest started on 24 March 2006 and ended on 5 July 2006.

★ LONGEST CARROT

A carrot grown by Joe Atherton (UK) measured 5.841 m (19 ft 1.96 in) at the UK National Giant Vegetable Championship in Somerset, UK, on 2 September 2007. Joe grew his champion carrot in a special tube tilted at 45 degrees.

★ HEAVIEST PUMPKIN

Weighing in at a whopping 766.12 kg (1,689 lb), the heaviest pumpkin was presented by Joseph Jutras (USA) at the New England Giant Pumpkin Weigh-off at Topsfield Fair in Topsfield, Massachusetts, USA, on 29 September 2007. Joseph's gigantic vegetable beat the previous record for the heaviest pumpkin by a massive 84.8 kg (186.9 lb).

★ NEW RECORD
☆ UPDATED RECORD

☆ LONGEST GOURD

A gourd grown at the Beidaihe Jifa Agriculture Sightseeing Garden in Beidaihe, China, measured 4.05 m (13 ft 3 in) in length on 12 October 2006.

★ MOST BLOOMS ON A HELLEBORE PLANT

On 4 May 2006, Anna Maclean (UK) counted a record 66 blooms on a hellebore (*Helleborus*) plant growing in her garden in Richmond, Surrey, UK.

★ MOST PLANT SPECIES GRAFTED ON TO THE SAME PLANT

A single host chrysanthemum plant had a record 513 varieties of chrysanthemum grafted on to it as part

TALLEST TOPIARY

Since 1983, Moirangthem Okendra Kumbi of Manipur, India, has been shaping the shoots of a Sky Flower bush (*Duranta repens variegata*) in his "Hedge to Heaven" garden, which has grown to a height of 18.59 m (60 ft 11.9 in). Overall, with the help of a specially constructed ladder, he has cut 41 structural shapes repeating a design of a rounded umbrella followed by two discs. Moirangthem was originally informed that his plant would be unlikely to grow higher than 6 m (20 ft), but with his twice-daily pruning, it's now a record holder!

of the celebrations for the 9th China (Xiaolan, Zhongshan) Chrysanthemum Exhibition in Xiaolan Town, China, on 23 November 2007.

LARGEST GINSENG ROOT

A ginseng root weighing 0.92 kg (2 lb 0.5 oz) on 1 July 1999 was grown by Don and Joy Hoogesteger (both USA) of Ridgefield, Washington, USA.

★ TALLEST COLLARD

A collard plant (a green-leafed member of the cabbage family) was found to be 4.06 m (13 ft 4 in) tall when it was measured on 24 May 2007 in Leesburg, Florida, USA. It was grown by Woodrow Wilson Granger (USA).

★ LARGEST SEED COLLECTION

The Millennium Seed Bank Project, housed at the Wellcome Trust Millennium Building, Wakehurst Place, West Sussex, UK, had 20,495 species collected as of 10 January 2008. The seeds are stored in underground frozen vaults and are part of an international conservation project, managed by the Royal Botanical Gardens of Kew (UK), with the aim of insuring thousands of species against possible extinction. The project banked its billionth seed, a type of African bamboo called *Oxytenanthera abyssinica,* in April 2007.

HEAVIEST EDIBLE FUNGI

An edible "chicken of the woods" mushroom (*Laetiporus sulphureus*) weighing 45.35 kg (100 lb) was found in the New Forest, Hampshire, UK, by Giovanni Paba of Broadstone, Dorset, UK, on 15 October 1990.

★ CLOVER WITH THE MOST LEAVES

An 18-leaf clover was discovered by Shigeo Obara of Hanamaki City, Iwate, Japan, on 25 May 2002. This luckiest of clovers beat the previous record holder by four leaves.

TALLEST PLANTS

PLANT	HEIGHT	NAME/NATIONALITY	YEAR
☆ Amaranthus	7.06 m (23 ft 2 in)	Brian Moore (USA)	2007
Bean plant	14.1 m (46 ft 3 in)	Staton Rorie (USA)	2003
Brussels sprout	2.8 m (9 ft 3 in)	Patrice & Steve Allison (both USA)	2001
Cactus (homegrown)	21.3 m (70 ft)	Pandit S. Munji (India)	2004
Celery	2.74 m (9 ft)	Joan Priednieks (UK)	1998
Chrysanthemum	4.34 m (14 ft 3 in)	Bernard Lavery (UK)	1995
Coleus	2.5 m (8 ft 4 in)	Nancy Lee Spilove (USA)	2004
☆ Collard	4.06 m (13 ft 4 in)	Woodrow Wilson Granger (USA)	2007
Cosmos	3.75 m (12 ft 3 in)	Cosmos Executive Committee, Okayama, Japan	2003
☆ Cotton	9.04 m (29 ft 8 in)	D. M. Williams (USA)	2007
Daffodil	1.55 m (5 ft 1 in)	M. Lowe (UK)	1979
☆ Dandelion	1.28 m (4 ft 2.4 in)	Jeppe, Elise & Simon Hvelplund (all Denmark)	1991
Aubergine (Eggplant)	5.5 m (18 ft)	Abdul Masfoor (India)	1998
Fuchsia (climbing)	11.40 m (37 ft 5 in)	Reinhard Biehler (Germany)	2005
Herba cistanches	1.95 m (6 ft 4 in)	Yongmao Chen (China)	2006
Papaya tree	13.4 m (44 ft)	Prasanta Mal (India)	2003
☆ Parsley	1.82 m (5 ft 12 in)	Herbert Jonas (Germany)	2007
Pepper	4.87 m (16 ft)	Laura Liang (USA)	1999
Periwinkle	2.19 m (7 ft 2 in)	Arvind, Rekha, Ashish & Rashmi Nema (all India)	2003
Petunia	5.8 m (19 ft 1 in)	Bernard Lavery (UK)	1994
Rosebush (self-supported)	4.03 m (13 ft 3 in)	Paul & Sharon Palumbo (both USA)	2005
Rose (climbing)	27.7 m (91 ft)	Anne & Charles Grant (both USA)	2004
Sugarcane	9.5 m (31 ft)	M. Venkatesh Gowda (India)	2005
Sunflower	7.76 m (25 ft 5 in)	Martien Heijms (Netherlands)	1986
Sweet corn (maize)	9.4 m (31 ft)	D. Radda (USA)	1946
Texas Bluebonnet	1.64 m (5 ft 5 in)	Margaret Lipscomb & Arthur Cash (both USA)	2005
Tomato	19.8 m (65 ft)	Nutriculture Ltd, Lancashire, UK	2000
Umbrella	8.22 m (27 ft)	Konstantinos Xytakis & Sara Guterbock (both USA)	2002
Zinnia	3.81 m (12 ft 6 in)	Everett Wallace Jr & Melody Wagner (both USA)	2004

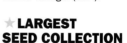

TALLEST AND SHORTEST DOGS

The **tallest living dog** is Gibson, a harlequin Great Dane, who measured 107 cm (42.2 in) tall on 31 August 2004 and is owned by Sandy Hall of California, USA.

The **shortest living dog** is a long-haired female Chihuahua called Boo Boo, who measured 10.16 cm (4 in) tall on 12 May 2007 and is owned by Lana Elswick of Kentucky, USA.

★ MOST SKIPS BY A DOG IN ONE MINUTE

Sweet Pea, an Australian shepherd/border collie cross, completed 75 jump-rope skips in one minute, aided by her owner Alex Rothaker (USA), on the set of *Live with Regis and Kelly* in New York City, USA, on 8 August 2007.

★ MOST KEYS REMOVED FROM A KEYRING BY A PARROT IN TWO MINUTES

Smudge, a parrot owned by Mark Steiger (Switzerland), removed 20 keys from a keyring in two minutes on the set of the *Circo Massimo Show*, in Rome, Italy, on 23 May 2007.

★ MOST QUARANTINED DOMESTIC ANIMAL

Smarty, a ginger cat, was quarantined for the 40th time in Larnaca, Cyprus, after her 79th flight from Cairo, Egypt, on 28 June 2005. Smarty – owned by Peter and Carole Godfrey (UK), who live in Cairo, Egypt – also holds the record for the **most flights by a cat**.

★ OLDEST HORSE TWINS

Taff and Griff, identical male twins of the Cremello breed, were born in 1982. They measure 11.2 hands (1.16 m; 3 ft 10 in) and are owned by the Veteran Horse Society in Wales, UK. They have spent their entire lives together, giving rides to children at London Zoo before retiring to Wales.

FACT

Both the Netherland and Polish dwarf rabbits have a weight range of just 0.9–1.13 kg (2–2 lb 7 oz). The two breeds tie for the record of the **smallest breed of rabbit**.

★ LONGEST RABBIT

Amy, a Flemish giant rabbit belonging to Annette Edwards (UK), measured 81.5 cm (2 ft 8 in) – from the tip of her nose to the tip of her tail – when measured on 23 March 2008. The Flemish giant is the **largest rabbit breed**, weighing up to 8 kg (17 lb 10 oz). *NB: Animal weight records are not monitored by GWR.*

★ OLDEST DOCUMENTED CAGED PARROT

Sandra LaFollette of Chariton, Iowa, USA, bought her pet parrot Fred in 1968 when he was six months old. Fred was still going strong in 2007, aged 39 years.

★ NEW RECORD
UPDATED RECORD

SMALLEST DOMESTIC HAMSTER BREED

The domesticated Roborovski hamster (*Phodopus roborovskii*) typically grows to a length of 4.5 cm (1.52 in). Roborovski hamsters originate from Mongolia and northern China.

★CHICKEN

As of 2007, the oldest living chicken was Blacky, a black bantam, who was born in 1986 and belongs to Veronika and Ladislav Seljak from Geelong, Australia.

DOMESTIC BIRD

Excluding the ostrich, which has been known to live up to 68 years, the longest-lived domesticated bird is the goose (*Anser a. domesticus*), which has an average life span of about 25 years. On 16 December 1976, a gander named George, owned by Florence Hull of Thornton, Lancashire, UK, died aged 49 years 8 months. He was hatched in April 1927.

★PIG

A pig named Cedric was born in 1988 and lived with his owner, Faye Fyfe, in Nimbin, Australia, until he died on 5 October 2006, aged 18 years.

LONGEST TONGUE ON A DOG

The longest canine tongue belonged to a boxer dog named Brandy and measured 43 cm (17 in). She lived with her owner John Scheid in St Clair Shores, Michigan, USA, until her death in September 2002.

OLDEST CAGED CANARY

A caged canary named Joey lived to the venerable age of 34 years under the care of his owner, Mrs K. Ross of Hull, UK. Joey was purchased in Calabar, Nigeria, in 1941 and died on 8 April 1975.

HEAVIEST DOG BREED

The Old English mastiff and the St Bernard share the record for the heaviest breed of domestic dog (*Canis familiaris*), with males of both species regularly weighing 78 kg (170 lb).

LONGEST TAIL ON A DOMESTIC CAT

Furball, a domestic cat who lives with her owner, Jan Acker (USA), in Battle Creek, Michigan, USA, had a tail length of 40.6 cm (16 in) when measured on 21 March 2001.

LARGEST PIGEON

A Canadian Giant Runt Cock pigeon called Doc Yeck, owned by Leonard Yeck of Brantford, Ontario, Canada, weighed an unprecedented 1.8 kg (4 lb) and had a chest width of 12.7 cm (5 in) when measured on 6 March 1999.

★LARGEST PET SPIDER

Rosi, a 12-year-old female Goliath bird-eating spider (*Theraphosa blondi*), weighed 175 g (6.17 oz), had a body length of 12 cm (4.7 in), a leg-span of 26 cm (10.2 in) and a mandible measuring 2.5 cm (0.9 in) on 27 July 2007. She belongs to Walter Baumgartner of Andorf, Austria.

★ NEW RECORD
★ UPDATED RECORD

MOST EXPENSIVE PERFUME

A 30-ml (1-fl-oz) bottle of "Clive Christian No.1 for Men" or "No.1 for Women" typically costs £1,317 ($2,355). In November 2005, Clive Christian created "No.1 Imperial Majesty", a 10-bottle, limited edition of the Clive Christian No.1 Collection, priced at £115,000 ($205,000) per 500 ml (17 fl oz). The price included delivery in a Bentley.

LARGEST KIMONO

On 23 March 2001, the largest kimono in the world was created as part of the National Kimono Festival in Cho Kagoshima City, Japan. The giant kimono was 11.72 m (35 ft 4 in) wide, 12.8 m (41 ft 10 in) high and weighed 100 kg (220 lb 6 oz).

★ LARGEST PHOTO SHOOT OF PEOPLE WEARING BIKINIS

A total of 1,010 participants took part in a bikini photo shoot organized by *Cosmopolitan* magazine and Venus Breeze (both Australia) on Bondi Beach, Sydney, Australia, on 26 September 2007.

★ LARGEST DRESS

Created by the Association de la Femme Artisane Agadir and displayed at the Kaftan show in Agadir, Morocco, from 7 to 11 July 2006, the largest dress measured 11.2 m (36 ft 8.9 in) in length.

LARGEST T-SHIRT

OMO Safe Detergent created a T-shirt that measured 57.19 m (187 ft 7 in) long and 40.88 m (134 ft 1 in) wide in Ho Chi Minh City, Vietnam. It was displayed on 9 March 2006.

FIRST DESIGNER LABEL

Charles Frederick Worth, who died in 1895, was the first designer to sign his work with a label and to show garments on live models. Born in Lincolnshire, UK, he moved to Paris, France, in 1845, where his designs were worn by the ladies of the court of Napoleon III. He started his own business and by 1871 was making £14,981 ($80,000) a year.

DID YOU KNOW?

The world's **most expensive bra** is the $10-million (£6.3-million) "Millennium Bra" produced by Victoria's Secret and first unveiled on *The Tonight Show* by model Heidi Klum on 11 November 1999. The bra has 3,024 stones – including diamonds and 1,988 sapphires.

★ LARGEST UNDERPANTS

On 15 November 2007, swimwear and underwear company aussieBum made a pair of underpants measuring 15.9 m (52 ft 1 in) across the waist and 10.5 m (34 ft 7 in) from crotch to waistband. It was displayed in Sydney's Royal Botanic Gardens, New South Wales, Australia.

As the first designer who employed real models to wear his designs for clients, he is also seen as the **first haute couturier**.

YOUNGEST HAUTE COUTURIER

Yves (-Mathieu) Saint-Laurent (France, b. 1936), who became Christian Dior's assistant aged 17, was named head of the House of Dior on Dior's death in 1957. In 1962, he opened his own fashion house and in the 1970s created ready-to-wear lines, household linens and fragrances.

I've never been to the gym. I do nothing.
Adriana Lima (Brazil), the youngest model on the Forbes Celebrity 100 List, discussing her fitness regime

GUINNESS WORLD RECORDS

★ YOUNGEST MODEL ON THE FORBES CELEBRITY 100 LIST

Adriana Lima (Brazil, b. 12 June 1981) was aged 26 years 2 days when she first featured in Forbes' Celebrity 100 list, on forbes.com, on 14 June 2007. Best known for her modelling contracts with Maybelline and Victoria's Secret (both USA), Lima was listed at no.99, with a wealth estimated at $4 million (£2 million).

★ OLDEST MODEL ON THE FORBES CELEBRITY 100 LIST

Heidi Klum (Germany, b. 1 June 1973) was aged 34 years 13 days when Forbes' Celebrity 100 list was published on 14 June 2007. Klum was listed no.84 on the list, with a wealth estimated at $8 million (£4 million).

HIGHEST ANNUAL EARNINGS BY A MODEL

Brazilian beauty Gisele Bündchen earned $35 million (£16.9 million) in 2007, according to Forbes. The model, famously discovered at the age of 14 while eating in a McDonald's restaurant, has worked for such famous brands as Ralph Lauren, Dolce & Gabbana, Versace, Valentino, Celine and Gianfranco Ferré.

RICHEST WOMAN

Liliane Bettencourt (France), the 85-year-old heiress to the L'Oréal cosmetics fortune, is estimated to be worth $22.9 billion (£11.3 billion).

★ MOST EXPENSIVE SARI

A silk sari manufactured by Chennai Silks, India, and featuring reproductions of 11 paintings by the celebrated Indian artist Raja Ravi Varma, took 4,760 work-hours to produce and was sold for a record 3,931,627 rupees ($100,021; £50,679) on 5 January 2008.

LONGEST CATWALK

A group of 111 fashion models walked the entire length of a 1.111-km (3,645-ft) catwalk built in the parking lot of Seacon Square shopping centre, Sri Nakarin Road, Thailand, between 27 and 30 May 1998.

LONGEST CATWALK MARATHON

A 10-hour catwalk marathon took place as part of the *More* magazine fashion awards 2005 (UK) at the Commonwealth Club, London, UK, on 4 February 2005. The show included exhibits from 24 high-street retailers with over 530 summer outfits, shoes and accessories.

WEALTH & POVERTY

★ NEW RECORD
★ UPDATED RECORD

BANKNOTE VALUES

HIGHEST

The **highest-value banknotes in circulation** are those for $10,000 released by the US Federal Reserve between 1865 and 1945. High-denomination bills were discontinued in the USA in 1969, but the 200 $10,000 bills that remain in circulation are still legal tender.

LOWEST

The one-sen (or 1/100th of a rupiah) Indonesian banknote had an exchange value of 358,624 to the UK£ in July 1996, making it the **lowest-value legal tender banknote ever**.

★ HIGHEST BUDGET EXPENDITURE

It has been estimated that the US government spent $2.731 trillion (£1.392 trillion) – including capital expenditures – in 2007, the greatest governmental expenditure of any country.

★ HIGHEST GNI PER CAPITA

According to the World Bank figures for September 2007, the country with the highest Gross National Income (GNI) per capita for 2006 was Luxembourg, with $76,040 (£37,494). Gross National Income is the total value of goods and services produced by a country in one year, divided by its population. GNI per capita shows how much of a country's GNI each person would have if GNI were divided equally.

HIGHEST AND LOWEST EDUCATION BUDGETS

The country with the ★ **highest percentage of Gross Domestic Product (GDP) spent on education** is Cuba (above left) with 9.8%, according to the latest annual figures available for 2000–2005. Meanwhile, Equatorial Guinea (above right) has the ★ **lowest percentage of Gross Domestic Product (GDP) spent on education**, with just 0.6% over the same period.

★ LOWEST GNI PER CAPITA

According to the World Bank figures from September 2007, the country with the lowest Gross National Income (GNI) per capita in 2006 was Burundi, with $100 (£49).

★ LOWEST BUDGET EXPENDITURE

The Pitcairn Islands in the Pacific Ocean had a budget expenditure of $878,119 (£455,503) – including capital expenditures – as of December 2003.

★ LOWEST BUDGET REVENUE

As of December 2003, Tokelau in the south Pacific had a budget revenue of $430,830 (£223,483).

★ FASTEST TIME TO EARN A BIG MAC

The banking giant UBS (Switzerland) has created the Big Mac Index to estimate how long the average person from 70 countries worldwide would have to work to earn enough money to buy a Big Mac. The worldwide average is 35 minutes, but in Japan the average time required is just 10 minutes. The index measures purchasing power by eliminating variables such as exchange rates. In Bogota, Colombia, workers must work an average of 97 minutes in order to buy a Big Mac, illustrating that the purchase power in Central and South America is a third of that of a typical North American city.

LARGEST NATIONAL DEBT

By 22 April 2008, the US national debt stood at $9,372,485,723,263.83 (£4,716,285,558,172.72), making it the largest debtor nation in history. You can watch the progress of the debt live online at the US Treasury Office website: www.treasurydirect.gov/NP/BPDLogin?application=np.

HIGHEST RATE OF UNEMPLOYMENT

Macedonia is the country with the highest rate of unemployment – 37.2 per cent of the labour force is without a job, despite being available for work.

HIGHEST PERCENTAGE OF GDP TAXED (COUNTRY)

When viewed as a percentage of a country's Gross Domestic Product (GDP), the country that taxed the highest amount (of national income) in 2006 was Sweden, with 50%.

HIGHEST COST OF LIVING

According to the Economist Intelligence Unit's Worldwide Cost of Living Survey, the world's most expensive city is Oslo, Norway, as of March 2007.

HIGHEST AND LOWEST INFLATION RATES

The country with the world's ★ **highest annual rate of consumer price inflation** is Zimbabwe (above left), with a rate of 349.8% between 2001 and 2006.
Between 2001 and 2005, the country with the world's ★ **lowest annual rate of consumer price inflation** was Libya (above right) with a rate of -3.1%.

★ MOST EXPENSIVE CITY TO EAT IN RESTAURANTS

According to Zagat restaurant guides, London (UK) is the world's most expensive city for dining out. In 2007, the average cost of a three-course meal plus one glass of wine was £39.09 ($79.66) – practically double that of New York City, USA, where the equivalent meal cost £19.30 ($39.33).

★ MOST SUCCESSFUL
CHIMPANZEE ON WALL STREET

Raven, a six-year-old chimpanzee, became the 22nd most successful money manager in the USA after choosing her stocks by throwing darts at a list of 133 internet companies. The chimp created her own index, dubbed MonkeyDex, and in 1999 delivered a 213% gain – outperforming more than 6,000 professional brokers on Wall Street. "She quadrupled the performance of the Dow and doubled the performance of the Nasdaq composite," said Roland Perry, editor of the *Internet Stock Review*.

★ RICHEST FOOTBALL CLUB

According to Deloitte's annual Football Money League for the 2006/2007 season, Real Madrid (Spain) is the world's richest football club. The Spanish champions had a total income of €318.2 million (£236.2 million; $465.1 million) for the year.

LARGEST ANIMAL LEGACY

A standard poodle called Toby was the beneficiary of the largest legacy ever devoted to an animal. On her death in 1931, Ella Wendel of New York City, USA, left $15 million (£10.5 million) to her favourite pet. Using the Retail Price Index as an indicator, Toby's inheritance would be worth $220 million (£111 million) today.

CRIME & PUNISHMENT

★ LARGEST OPIUM PRODUCER

Afghanistan is the world's leading producer of opium, having cultivated 193,000 ha (476,910 acres) of opium poppies in 2007 – a 17% increase over 2006. The war-torn country produced an extraordinary 8,200 tonnes (18 million lb) of opium in 2007, which amounts to 93% of the global opiates market.

★ FIRST RECORDED MURDER BY RADIATION

On 23 November 2006, Alexander Litvinenko (Russia) died from radiation poisoning in London, UK, becoming the first known victim of Polonium 210-induced acute radiation syndrome. The case is unsolved.

★ FIRST HIJACK OF A COMMERCIAL AIRLINER

The first hijack of a commercial airliner occurred on 17 July 1948, when terrorists attempted to gain control of a Cathay Pacific Airways seaplane en route from Macau to Hong Kong, ultimately causing it to crash into the sea off the coast of Macau. Only one out of 26 passengers and crew survived.

★ GREATEST PAYOUT FOR SEXUAL ABUSE

The largest amount of compensation awarded to victims of sexual abuse is $660 million (£342 million). On 15 July 2007, the Roman Catholic Archdiocese of Los Angeles, USA, agreed to share this amount out to 508 people who had suffered from abuse by members of the clergy over a period of 50 years.

DID YOU KNOW?

Helmand Province in the south of Afghanistan, where much of the current fighting between NATO forces and the Taliban is taking place, provides 50% of the country's opium crop.

★ HIGHEST INCIDENCE OF SHIP PIRACY (REGION)

The area that experiences the highest incidence of ship piracy is that round south-east Asia, particularly in Indonesian waters. There were 43 attacks here in 2007 out of an annual worldwide total of 263.

★ FIRST
HIJACK OF
AN AIRCRAFT

The first recorded aircraft hijack took place on 21 February 1931 in Peru, when Byron Rickards (USA) was flying a Ford Tri-motor from Lima to Arequipa. Once he had landed the plane, he was surrounded by soldiers and told he had become the prisoner of a revolutionary organization. He was released on 2 March of the same year.

★ LONGEST CAREER AS A POLICE OFFICER

Detective Lieutenant Andrew F. Anewenter (USA, b. 12 January 1916) worked continuously as a police officer for 61 years for the Milwaukee (Wisconsin) Police Department from 1 June 1942 until his retirement on 15 May 2003.

★ MOST MURDERS PER YEAR (COUNTRY)

According to the United Nations, the country with the highest number of murders for the latest year available is the Philippines, with 3,515 homicides in 2004.

★ FIRST USE OF "FORENSIC GAIT ANALYSIS" EVIDENCE IN COURT

Forensic gait analysis is the study of a person's style of walking (gait) as a method of identification. The first time that this form of evidence became admissible in criminal law occurred in the case of R versus Saunders at The Old Bailey, London, UK, on 12 July 2000. Consultant podiatrist Haydn Kelly (UK) was able to identify jewellery thief John Saunders (UK) as the person attempting to rob a shop from earlier police surveillance footage. Despite Saunders wearing two pairs of trousers, a mask and gloves, Mr Kelly was able to confirm that less than 5% of the UK population had walking mechanics that were similar to those of the suspected thief, evidence that helped end Saunders' lucrative criminal career.

★ HIGHEST MURDER RATE PER CAPITA (COUNTRY)

According to the 9th United Nations Survey of Crime Trends and Operations of Criminal Justice Systems, the country with the highest murder rate – as of 2004 – is Ecuador, with 18.87 per 100,000 people.

★ HIGHEST POPULATION OF PRISONERS (FEMALE)

According to the World Female Imprisonment List of the International Centre for Prison Studies at King's College, London, UK, the country with the largest population of female prisoners is the USA, with 183,400 as of April 2006. This figure represents 8.6% of the total US prison population.

★ HIGHEST POPULATION OF PRISONERS DOCUMENTED

According to figures released by the US Bureau of Justice Statistics, the USA incarcerates more people than any other country. At the end of 2006, a total of 2,258,983 people were inmates in US Federal or State prisons or in local jails, a rate of 751 per 100,000 US residents.

★ NEW RECORD
★ UPDATED RECORD

★ LARGEST FRAUD BY A ROGUE TRADER

On 24 January 2008, major French bank Société Générale declared that it had uncovered a fraud that had resulted in losses totalling €4.9 billion ($7.16 billion; £3.6 billion), following rogue trading by a member of its staff. On 26 January 2008, bank trader Jerome Kerviel (France) was taken into police custody and was later said to have admitted hiding his activities from his superiors.

WORLD AT WAR

★ YOUNGEST AGE TO JOIN THE ARMED FORCES

In the East Asian country of Laos, the minimum age for military service is 15 years.

★ LARGEST EXPORTER OF ARMS

According to the Stockholm International Peace Research Institute (SIPIRI) Arms Transfers Database, the USA exported an annual average of $7,964,100,000 (£4,000,271,235) worth of arms – that is to say, major conventional weapons or systems – in the 10 years between 1998 and 2007.

★ LARGEST ALL-FEMALE PEACEKEEPING UNIT

For the first time, the United Nations has deployed an all-female police peacekeeping unit to help rebuild the Liberian police force, which had acquired a bad reputation for corruption. The force of 103 women has been provided by the Indian government.

★ HIGHEST PERCENTAGE OF MILITARY PERSONNEL (COUNTRY)

In 2007, 4.75% of North Korea's total population of 23,301,725 was actively engaged in military duty.

★ LARGEST IMPORTER OF ARMS

From 1998 to 2007, China topped the list of the largest arms importers, averaging an annual spend of $2,318,200,000 (£1,164,403,860).

★ LARGEST ARMS MANUFACTURER

Excluding Chinese companies, for which data are limited, the top manufacturer of arms (not just the manufacture but also the research and development, maintenance, servicing and repair of equipment used by the military) is Boeing (USA). In 2005, it sold $54,845,000,000 (£31,881,393,500) worth of mainly aircraft, electronics, missiles and space hardware.

★ LARGEST NAVY BY ARMED SUBMARINES

The US Navy has 71 armed submarines (14 strategic ballistic missile craft and 57 tactical craft). The USA's entire submarine fleet is nuclear powered.

★ MOST DANGEROUS COUNTRY FOR THE MEDIA

According to Reporters Without Borders, 210 journalists and media assistants have been killed in Iraq since the start of fighting in March 2003. This is more than in the 1955–75 Vietnam War.

★ NEW RECORD
★ UPDATED RECORD

Women police are seen to be much less threatening, although they can be just as tough as men.

Seema Dhundiya, commander of the United Nations' first women-only unit

The former Indian state has been fought over since the end of British rule of India and partition in 1947. India also refuses to recognize Pakistan's ceding of Kashmir lands to China in 1964, and recently claimed that China transferred nuclear weapons to Pakistan.

At any one time, up to 1 million troops confront each other across the Line of Control that separates Indian- and Pakistani-controlled Kashmir.

TARGET: BIN LADEN

★ LARGEST LANDLOCKED NAVY

In 2007, Bolivia's landlocked navy had 4,800 personnel, of which marines comprise 1,700 (including 1,000 Naval Military Police) to patrol the country's river systems and Lake Titicaca. The navy's headquarters is at Puerto Guayaramerín.

X-REF

Mad about the military? Shoot forwards to our **Weapons** section on p.158. Plane crazy about **Aircraft**? Check in at pp.156–57

between $200 million and $300 million (£100 million–£150 million), according to the US Council on Foreign Relations.

★ LARGEST MILITARIZED TERRITORIAL DISPUTE

According to the CIA World Factbook, the dispute between China, India and Pakistan for the Kashmir region is the largest and most militarized territorial dispute currently taking place on the planet – despite the massive earthquake that devastated the area in 2005, killing 80,000 people.

★ COUNTRY WITH MOST TROOPS DEPLOYED OVERSEAS

As of May 2005, the country with the highest number of military personnel serving their country, but overseas, is the USA with approximately 350,000 personnel on active duty. This figure includes those forces normally present in Germany, Italy, the United Kingdom and Japan, unless bases at those locations are actively supporting a combat operation.

MOST WANTED TERRORIST

Osama bin Laden (Saudi Arabia), figurehead of the terrorist organization Al-Qaeda is sought by many nations for his alleged terrorist activities and is the only terrorist on the US Federal Bureau of Investigation (FBI) "Ten Most Wanted" list.

★ RICHEST INSURGENCY GROUP

The Revolutionary Armed Forces of Colombia (FARC) is considered to be the richest insurgent group in the world, thanks mostly to profits made from drug trafficking topped up with extortion and kidnap ransoms.

Estimates place their funds at up to $1 billion (£500,000,000), with annual profits from the drugs trade

★ LARGEST PEACEKEEPING OPERATION

On 31 July 2007, the United Nations (UN) authorized the deployment of a hybrid UN/African Union force to support the Darfur Peace Agreement in Sudan, Africa. At full strength, it will be the largest peacekeeping mission in the world deployed on one operation, with nearly 26,000 personnel involved.

LARGEST LAND VEHICLE

The largest machine capable of moving on land under its own power is the RB293 bucket wheel excavator, an earth-moving machine manufactured by TAKRAF GmbH of Leipzig, Germany. It is currently employed in an open-cast mine owned by RWE Rheinbraun in Hambach, Germany.

The vehicle's 18 bucket scoops are fitted to the outside of a massive wheel at the front of the machine. As the wheel revolves, the buckets scoop up earth and then dump it on to a conveyor belt to be carried away.

- **WEIGHT**: 14,196 tonnes (31.3 million lb) – three times heavier than the Space Shuttle
- **LENGTH**: 220 m (722 ft) – roughly as long as two football pitches
- **HEIGHT**: 94.5 m (310 ft) – just taller than the Statue of Liberty and her pedestal
- **BUCKET-WHEEL HEIGHT**: 21.6 m (71 ft) – as tall as a four-storey building!
- **BUCKET VOLUME**: 6,600 litres (1,452 gal) – each bucket can hold the same as 80 bathtubs
- **EARTH MOVED PER DAY**: 240,000 m³ (8.475 million ft³) – enough to fill the *Hindenburg*, the largest ever airship!

CONTENTS

SCIENCE FRONTIERS

★ LONGEST-LASTING AA BATTERY CELLS

Panasonic's EVOLTA alkaline battery cells – produced by Matsushita Battery Industrial Co., Ltd, and Matsushita Electric Industrial Co., Ltd (both Japan) – are the longest-lasting AA battery cells available, keeping gadgets running 20% longer than current batteries. To assess the cells, discharge tests were conducted in accordance with guidelines set by the International Electrotechnical Commission (IEC).

★ MOST POWERFUL TESLA COIL

The Tesla coil at the Mid-America Science Museum in Hot Springs, Arkansas, USA, can produce 1,500,000 volts of electricity (by comparison, a bug zapper operates at 1,500 volts). It is enclosed in a steel Faraday cage to protect visitors from the "lightning" (corona discharges).

★ DARKEST SUBSTANCE

The darkest man-made substance is a low-density carbon nanotube array created by researchers from US colleges Rensselaer Polytechnic Institute (Zu-Po Yang, James A. Bur, Prof. Shawn-Yu Lin) and Rice University (Dr Lijie Ci, Prof. P. M. Ajayan). Regular black paint reflects between 5% and 10% of light (it absorbs the rest), but this new coating is so dark that it only reflected 0.045% of light when tested at Rensselaer Polytechnic Institute on 24 August 2007.

★ LONGEST DOCUMENT SCANNED

A document measuring 1,181 m (3,875 ft) was scanned on a Trüper 3600 scanner by Böwe Bell + Howell (USA) at the Healthcare Information and Management Systems Society's Annual Conference, Orlando, Florida, USA, on 25 February 2008.

★ LARGEST KNOWN PRIME NUMBER

The largest known prime number is $2^{32,582,657}-1$. It was discovered by a team at Central Missouri State University in September 2006. With a staggering 9,808,358 digits, this latest Mersenne Prime is close to claiming the $100,000 (£50,000) reward for finding the first 10-million-digit prime number.

★ LARGEST MAN-MADE AIR VORTEX

The Mercedes-Benz museum in Stuttgart, Germany, boasts a unique smoke-elimination system. On detecting a fire, air is injected into the interior courtyard of the museum in such a way that it generates a 34.4-m-high (112-ft) artificial tornado; this collects smoke, which is then discharged into the outside air via a smoke-elimination ventilator located in the upper part of the building.

★ MOST POWERFUL ELECTRO-ACOUSTIC SPEAKER

The Hyperspike HS-60, invented by Curt Graber of Wattre Corporation, USA, is an Acoustic Hailing Device (AHD) capable of producing a coherent beam of sound – like a laser beam in the human voice range. In certified field tests conducted in March 2007, its beam remained coherent for 264 m (866 ft), and output was measured at 140.2 decibels (dB) at a 128-m (420-ft) range using less than 3 kW of electricity. Its output is equivalent to 182 dB from a distance of 1 m (3 ft) and, under optimal conditions, it can transmit audible voice communications to a target across a distance of over 3 km (2 miles).

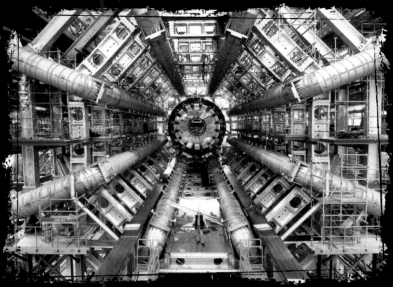

★ SMALLEST ROBOT HUMANOID

Be-Robot, which measures 153 mm (6 in) high, is able to walk, kick and perform push-ups. The robot was manufactured by GeStream (Taiwan) and demonstrated at the Global SMEs Convention 2007 on 6 September 2007 in Kuala Lumpur, Malaysia.

ACTUAL SIZE

★ NEW RECORD
★ UPDATED RECORD

★ LARGEST PARTICLE DETECTOR

The ATLAS Detector, part of the Large Hadron Collider (LHC) at CERN – located on the border between France and Switzerland – measures 46 m (150 ft) long, 25 m (82 ft) wide and high. It weighs 7,000 tonnes (15.4 million lb) and contains 100 million sensors that measure particles produced in proton–proton collisions in the Compact Muon Solenoid, seen above. The last piece of ATLAS, part of the instrument's muon spectrometer, was installed in March 2008.

DID YOU KNOW?

Built at a cost of over $6 billion (£3 billion) and with a 27-km (16-mile) circumference, the LHC is designed to smash particles together at close to the speed of light. Scientists hope that by studying the results of these collisions they will be able to discover more about the way that matter works.

★ SMALLEST OBJECT FILMED IN MOTION

In February 2008, Swedish scientists announced they had footage of an electron riding a wave of light just after being pulled away from an atom.

★ QUANTUM COMMUNICATION DISTANCE RECORD

In March 2008, scientists announced they had detected and identified single photons of light bounced off an orbiting satellite some 1,485 km (922 miles) above the Earth. This achievement is a critical step towards establishing a space-based quantum communications channel – the holy grail of secure and uninterceptable digital communications researchers.

★ MOST POWERFUL PULSED SPALLATION NEUTRON SOURCE

The Spallation Neutron Source at the Oak Ridge National Laboratory (USA) is the most powerful of its kind in the world. By using a proton beam to pound a target with more than 300 kW of energy, it is able to produce 4.8×10^{16} neutrons per second. Eventually, these neutrons will be focused into beams that will allow the molecular analysis of advanced materials.

★ MOST POWERFUL LASER (OUTPUT)

In terms of output in wattage, the Texas Petawatt Laser at the University of Texas, USA, is the most powerful laser in the world. On 31 March 2008, it achieved an output of 1 petawatt, or 1,000,000,000,000,000 watts, when it was fired for a tenth of a trillionth of a second (0.0000000000001 seconds).

MOST POWERFUL HAND-HELD LASER

Tested three times in five-minute durations using two separate photon-measuring devices, the Hercules 500 outputted a 1 W peak and 940 mW (+/- 20 mW) average of brilliant-green (532 nm) laser light. Made by Laserglow Technologies of Ontario, Canada, the Class IV hand-held battery-powered device features five independent safety devices to make it legal to use around the world. Its long-range applications include construction and antenna alignment, but at close range it is capable of starting fires.

GENETICS

★ FASTEST-EVOLVING ANIMAL

Sphenodon punctatus, a reptile known as a tuatara, is evolving almost 10 times faster than the average for all animals. In March 2008, a report revealed that this species is making about 1.37 substitutions per base pair every million years, compared to the average of just 0.2.

★ STRONGEST GENETICALLY MODIFIED MOUSE

In November 2007, US scientists announced the creation of a genetically modified mouse with extraordinary physical abilities. In tests, the mouse astonished scientists by running non-stop at 20 m (65 ft) per minute for five hours. It also lives longer than normal mice and is described as being 10 times more active.

LARGEST CAT HYBRID

The largest hybrid of the cat family (Felidae) is the liger (no scientific name), which is the offspring of a male lion and a tigress. Ligers typically grow larger than either parent, reaching lengths of 3–3.6 m (10–12 ft). The size and appearance of the liger can vary, depending upon which subspecies of lion or tiger is involved. Although these hybrids could occur in the wild, wherever lions and tigers inhabit the same territory – for example, the Gir forest in India – such cross-breeding usually happens in zoos or private menageries.

FIRST CLONED DOG

The first cloned dog to survive birth is Snuppy, an Afghan hound puppy created by Hwang Woo-Suk (South Korea) and his team at Seoul National University (SNU) in South Korea, after which the dog was named. Snuppy's growth was stimulated when a donor egg cell fused with deoxyribonucleic acid (DNA) from the ear of a three-year-old male Afghan hound named Tie, before being transferred to a surrogate female for 60 days of pregnancy. Snuppy was born on 25 April 2005.

MOST GENETICALLY DIVERSE PEOPLE

Pygmies and the bushmen of Africa are the most genetically diverse people on Earth. For some genetic traits they have as many as 17 variations, whereas most people have only two or three. A possible explanation is that our oldest ancestors came from these regions, perhaps 200,000 years ago, and that not all of them left to spread around the world.

FIRST GENE THERAPY RECIPIENT

The first attempt to fix a genetic disorder in a human being was made in September 1990. Four-year-old Ashanthi DeSilva (USA) suffered from a deficiency of adenosine deaminase (ADA). As a result of her weak immune system caused by the condition, she had been chronically ill for her whole life. Her pioneering doctors gave her healthy copies of the gene that produces ADA by placing the gene in a modified virus that was then allowed to infect her blood cells. She now lives a healthy life.

★ LARGEST PRODUCER OF GENETICALLY MODIFIED SEEDS

Food biotechnology giant Monsanto (USA) currently dominates the global market for genetically modified seeds. In 2006, the company saw a global revenue of $7.344 billion (£3.75 billion).

sent another man's blood sample during the testing of 5,000 local men, was finally caught after his deception was discovered. Pitchfork's DNA matched that of the killer and he was sentenced to life imprisonment in 1988.

FARTHEST TRACED DESCENDANT BY DNA

Adrian Targett, a teacher from Cheddar, Somerset, UK, can trace his family tree back some 300 generations. He is a direct descendant, on his mother's side, of Cheddar Man, a 9,000-year-old skeleton and one of the oldest complete skeletons found in the UK.

☆ OLDEST DNA

In July 2007, scientists announced they had discovered DNA dating back as far as 800,000 years from ice cores taken from Greenland's ice sheet. The DNA reveals that moths and butterflies were abundant in the spruce and pine forests that existed in Greenland during this much warmer period of its history.

★ FIRST PUBLICATION OF A HUMAN GENOME

In September 2007, scientist and entrepreneur Dr Craig Venter (USA) published his own genome (genetic code) in its entirety. This complete record of his genetic make-up contained some 6 billion letters and was retrieved at an estimated cost of $35 million (£17.5 million).

FACT

Dr Venter's genome confirms the blue colour of his eyes and reveals he has a genetic degree of protection against tobacco addiction. Some of the sequences in his genome are associated with increased risk of antisocial behaviour, Alzheimer's and cardiovascular diseases.

FIRST USE OF DNA PROFILING IN A CONVICTION

The first person to be convicted of a crime using DNA evidence was Robert Melias (UK), who was found guilty of rape and convicted by a British court on 13 November 1988. Soon after in the USA, Tommy Lee Andres (USA) became the first American to be convicted based on DNA evidence.

FIRST USE OF DNA PROFILING TO OVERTURN A CONVICTION

The first person to have a conviction overturned due to DNA profiling was Gary Dotson (USA), who was wrongly accused of raping Cathleen Crowell (UK). In July 1979, he was sentenced to 25–50 years for the rape and the same again for aggravated kidnapping. In 1988, DNA tests (not available earlier) were conducted proving that Dotson was innocent. This led to Dotson being exonerated on 14 August 1989, having served eight years of his sentence.

FIRST USE OF DNA PROFILING TO CLEAR A SUSPECT

The world's first DNA-based manhunt took place between 1986 and 1988 in Enderby, Leicestershire, UK, during the investigation of a double rape-murder. The prime suspect, a local boy named Richard Buckland (UK), confessed to the second killing, but DNA profiling of the victims revealed that his DNA did not match that of the killer. Buckland thus became the first suspect cleared using DNA profiling. The actual killer, Colin Pitchfork (UK), who

SCIENCE & ENGINEERING
INTERNET

★ NEW RECORD
UPDATED RECORD

★ HIGHEST PERCENTAGE OF ILLEGALLY DOWNLOADED MUSIC (COUNTRY)

According to a report in January 2008 by the International Federation of the Phonographic Industry (IFPI), 99% of all digital music files distributed in China had been pirated from the Internet. Described as "potentially the largest online music-buying population", the Chinese only spent $76 million (£38 million) in 2007 on legal online music downloads.

★ FIRST TRUE VIRTUAL EMBASSY

On 30 May 2007, Sweden opened a virtual copy of its Washington DC, USA, embassy in *Second Life*. The avatar of Minister for Foreign Affairs Carl Bildt (Sweden) performed the "cutting of the ribbon" for the virtual embassy, which is intended to provide information to *Second Life* players about Sweden.

★ MOST POPULAR MMORPG GAME

In terms of the number of online subscribers, *World of Warcraft* is the most popular Massively Multiplayer Online Role-Playing Game (MMORPG), with 10 million subscribers as of January 2008. According to its developers, Blizzard Entertainment, *World of Warcraft* hosts over 2 million subscribers in Europe, more than 2.5 million in North America and around 5.5 million in Asia.

★ MOST SEARCHED-FOR PERSON ON THE INTERNET

In 2007, the most searched-for person on the Internet was Britney Spears (USA). The record-breaking singer spent the year in and out of drug and alcohol rehabilitation centres, fought and lost a custody battle for her children, had her hair shaved off with electric clippers, was charged with a hit-and-run incident and driving without a licence and made a critically panned (but commercially successful) comeback at the MTV Video Music Awards performing "Gimme More".

★ LARGEST SOURCE OF SPAM

Research by spam and virus experts Sophos reveals that during the third quarter of 2007, 28.4% of all unsolicited emails worldwide originated in the USA. South Korea came second with 5.2% of global spam.

★ LARGEST DATA WAREHOUSE

Sybase, Inc. and Sun Microsystems (both USA) operate a data warehouse containing 1 petabyte (1,000 terabytes) of raw data. Its data capacity is such that it could track every credit and debit card transaction that has taken place worldwide in the past seven years.

★ FIRST ROYAL CHRISTMAS PODCAST

In December 2006, the Christmas message delivered by Her Majesty Queen Elizabeth II was made available as a podcast for the first time. The Queen owns a 6 GB silver iPod mini; she also has her own channel on YouTube, launched 50 years after her first televised Christmas message in 1957. A Buckingham Palace spokesperson said that the Queen "always keeps abreast with new ways of communicating with people".

★ WORST INTERNET BLACKOUT

In just one week during January 2008, four undersea Internet cables were severed, causing loss of connection for millions of users in Asia, the Middle East and North Africa. Some experts have blamed ships dragging their anchors across the sea floor, while others suspect sabotage by unknown agents.

★ FIRST GOOGLE BOMB

Google bombing is a technique where Internet users manipulate Google search results by using specific terms to link to another page. The first significant Google bomb occurred in 1999 when search results for the term "more evil than satan himself" brought up the home page for Microsoft. In 2005, Google bombing forced searches for "miserable failure" to bring up the official biography of US President George W. Bush.

★ MOST DOWNLOADED FILM

In 2007, the movie downloaded most often using the BitTorrent peer-to-peer (P2P) protocol was *Transformers* (USA, 2007), which was accessed 569,259 times on Mininova alone. Globally, considering the vast number of P2P websites, the actual figure will be much higher.

★ FASTEST RESIDENTIAL INTERNET CONNECTION

Sigbritt Lothberg (Sweden) has a home broadband connection of 40 Gbps – thousands of times greater than the average domestic broadband. Her connection is a demonstration arranged by her son, the Swedish Internet guru Peter Lothberg, and it allows Sigbritt to download a full high-definition DVD in around two seconds.

★ MOST PEOPLE TO DELIBERATELY DOWNLOAD A COMPUTER VIRUS

In an experiment by Belgian IT expert Didier Stevens in 2007, 409 people willingly and deliberately downloaded a virus on to their computer. Stevens had been running a Google Adwords campaign for six months that offered users a free virus via the slogan "Is your PC virus-free? Get it infected here!"

★ FIRST SPEEDCABLING COMPETITION

The world's first speedcabling competition was held in Los Angeles, California, USA, in January 2008. The aim of this new "sport", invented by IT developer Steven Schkolne (USA), is to untangle a mass of cables and wires in the fastest time and in such a way that the wires can still carry a network signal. The winner of the final – in which contestants were required to unknot 12 ethernet cords up to 7.5 m (25 ft) long, then hold them above their heads – was web designer Matthew Howell (USA).

2007 TOP 10 MOVIE DOWNLOADS

MOVIE (NAT., YEAR)	DIRECTOR	NUMBER
1. *Transformers* (USA, 2007)	Michael Bay	569,259
2. *Knocked Up* (USA, 2007)	Judd Apatow	509,314
3. *Shooter* (USA, 2007)	Antoine Fuqua	399,960
4. *Pirates of the Caribbean: At World's End* (USA, 2007)	Gore Verbinski	379,749
5. *Ratatouille* (USA, 2006)	Brad Bird & Jan Pinkava	359,904
6. *300* (USA, 2006)	Zack Snyder	358,226
7. *Next* (USA, 2007)	Lee Tamahori	354,044
8. *Hot Fuzz* (UK, 2007)	Edgar Wright	352,905
9. *The Bourne Ultimatum* (USA, 2007)	Paul Greengrass	336,326
10. *Zodiac* (USA, 2007)	David Fincher	334,699

Source: www.mininova.org

MOBILE TECHNOLOGY

FAMOUS FIRST WORDS

● The telephone was invented by Alexander Graham Bell (UK), who filed his patent on 14 February 1876. The **first intelligible phone call** occurred in March 1876 in Boston, Massachusetts, USA, when Bell phoned his assistant in a nearby room and said: "Mr Watson – come here – I need you."

● The concept of a portable telephone first appeared in 1947 at Lucent Technologies' Bell Labs in New Jersey, USA, but the **first portable telephone handset** was invented by Martin Cooper (USA) of Motorola. He made the **first mobile phone call** on 3 April 1973 to his rival, Joel Engel, head of research at Bell Labs. The **first commercial mobile phone network** was launched in Japan in 1979.

● On 28 April 1999, at 10:30 a.m. (GMT), the **first pole-to-pole phone call** was made between NASA employees Mike Comberiate and Andre Fortin (both USA).

★ FASTEST RADIO-CONTROLLED MODEL CAR

The top speed ever reached by a battery-powered radio-controlled model car is 216.29 km/h (134.4 mph), set by the 1:10 scale Associated Nitro TC3 car, driven and built by Nic Case (USA) at the Auto Club Dragway, Fontana, California, USA, on 20 July 2007.

MOBILE PHONES

★ FASTEST NATIONAL MOBILE BROADBAND NETWORK

Next G, announced by Telstra (Australia) in February 2007, can achieve peak network download speeds of 14.4 Mbps – in other words, up to 250 times faster than a standard dial-up connection.

★ LARGEST MOBILE PHONE

A scaled-up version of Sony Ericsson's W810i measured 2.5 x 1.14 x 0.49 m (8 ft 2.4 in x 3 ft 8.8 in x 1 ft 7.2 in) when examined at the MTN ScienCenter in Cape Town, South Africa, on 20 September 2007. The phone is fully functional and made from the same materials as the normal-sized version.

★ THINNEST MOBILE PHONE

As of February 2008, the world's slimmest mobile phone is the Samsung Ultra Edition II, at just 5.9 mm (0.2 in) thick. The handset has a three-megapixel camera and 11 hours of music play time. Samsung's Ultra Edition 8.4 is the **world's thinnest 3G mobile phone**, with a 2-megapixel camera in a body just 8.4 mm (0.3 in) thick.

HIGHEST RESOLUTION MOBILE PHONE CAMERA

In March 2006, Samsung unveiled the SCH-B600, a mobile phone with the world's highest-resolution camera at 10 megapixels – higher than many digital cameras. The LCD can reproduce 16 million colours, and users can also watch live TV through a satellite DMB (digital multimedia broadcasting) function.

★ MOST DURABLE MOBILE PHONE NUMBER

David Contorno of Lemont, Illinois, USA, has owned and used the same mobile telephone number since 2 August 1985. His first mobile phone was an Ameritech AC140 and his carrier has been Ameritech Mobile Communications, the first company in the United States to provide a cellular mobile phone service to the general public, ever since.

MOST EXPENSIVE MOBILE PHONE

A mobile phone designed by GoldVish of Geneva, Switzerland, was sold for €1 million ($1,287,200; £675,123) at the Millionaire Fair in Cannes, France, on 2 September 2006.

★ SMALLEST GPS CHIP

In February 2008, NXP Semiconductors (Netherlands) announced the launch of its GNS7560 GPS receiver chip. Designed to be incorporated into mobile phones and PDAs, it measures just 3.6 x 2.4 x 0.6 mm (0.1 x 0.09 x 0.02 in) and consumes less than 15 mW of power.

★ LARGEST SCREEN ON A MOBILE PHONE

The Readius, by Dutch company Polymer Vision, is due to go on sale in late 2008. As well as being a mobile phone, it can browse the internet and read e-books. Its revolutionary flexible screen measures 13 cm (5.1 in) diagonally and can fold up into the body of the Readius when not in use.

ACTUAL SIZE

17-12-2007 - 18:02

READIUS

★ MOST EXPENSIVE PSP COVER

A PlayStation Portable jacket made from 14-carat gold with 8-carat black and yellow diamonds on the front can be bought for $35,000 (£18,000). It was made by Simmons Jewelry Co. (USA) and made its debut at the Pacific Design Center, West Hollywood, California, USA, on 14 March 2005.

FACT
The PSP case, backed with real alligator skin, was designed by Kimora Lee Simmons as part of a gamer-chic catwalk event thrown for a variety of designers and celebrities, including Marc Jacobs, Nicole Richie and Jennifer Lopez.

★ LIGHTEST MOBILE PHONE

Made by modu Ltd (Israel) and launched on 11 February 2008, the modu weighs just 40.1 g (1.41 oz) and measures 72.1 x 37.6 x 7.8 mm (2.8 x 1.4 x 0.3 in). It has a full-colour screen and 1 Gb of internal memory.

ACTUAL SIZE

PORTABLE MEDIA

★ MOST VERSATILE WIRE-FREE GADGET CHARGER

The WildCharger, by USA company, WildCharge, is a pad that allows portable gadgets to recharge without wires. Any gadget that is fitted with a special adaptor can be recharged by resting it on the conductive WildCharger pad. Up to five gadgets can recharge on the pad at any one time. So far adaptors are available for Motorola RAZR V3, iPod nano 2G, iPhone, Blackberry Pearl, Blackberry 8800 and iPod.

★ CHEAPEST LAPTOP

Founded by Nicholas Negroponte (USA), the One Laptop Per Child Programme is a project to deliver very cheap laptops for educational use in the developing world. As of February 2008, the programme had a production rate of 110,000 laptops every month, each priced at just $187 (£94).

HIGHEST DEFINITION SCREEN ON A TV WRISTWATCH

The sharpest picture achieved on a wearable television screen is on the NHJ TV Wristwatch, with 130,338 pixels. The 1.5-in (3.8-cm) colour TV screen relies on TFT (Thin Film Transistor) technology to deliver a high-resolution picture.

★ MOST POPULAR FORMAT FOR MUSIC

The compact disc (CD) remains the most popular format for listening to music, with a global sales revenue of over $17 billion (£8.6 billion) in 2005, although this represents a drop of 6% on the previous year.

★ BEST-SELLING SMARTPHONE

According to analyst firm iSuppli, Apple's iPhone outsold all other smartphones in the USA in July 2007, its first full month on sale. In the last four months of 2007, the company sold 2,315,000 iPhones, helping to push their net quarterly profits to $1.58 billion (£805,326,016) – Apple's most profitable quarter ever – and making the iPhone the fastest-selling smartphone ever.

★ NEW RECORD
★ UPDATED RECORD

★ THINNEST MAC

The MacBook Air, which was launched by Apple Inc. (USA) in January 2008, is the thinnest Mac currently in production. At its thickest point, the laptop measures 1.94 cm (0.76 in), and at its thinnest 0.4 cm (0.16 in). The MacBook Air's screen measures 33.7 cm (13.3 in), and it weighs 1.63 kg (3 lb). Apple say the thinness of the MacBook Air is the result of numerous innovations, including a slimmer hard drive and a lower-profile battery than other laptops.

ACTUAL SIZE

SCIENCE & ENGINEERING
BIG STUFF

LARGEST...

COLOSSAL CHRISTMAS

- The ★ **largest Christmas stocking** measured 32.56 m (106 ft 9 in) long and 14.97 m (49 ft 1 in) wide, heel to toe. It was made by the Children's Society (UK) in London, UK, on 14 December 2007.

- The ★ **largest floating Christmas tree** is 85 m (278 ft 10 in) tall. Erected in Rio de Janeiro, Brazil, for Christmas 2007, it was sponsored by Bradesco Seguros e Previdência.

★ ADVENT CALENDAR
To mark the refurbishment of St Pancras station, London, UK, in December 2007, an outsize advent calendar was created, measuring 71 m (232 ft 11 in) high and 23 m (75 ft 5 in) wide.

★ BONFIRE
The largest bonfire had a volume of 1,715.7 m³ (60,589 ft³). It was constructed by ŠKD mladi Boštanj and lit on 30 April 2007 in Boštanj, Slovenia, to celebrate Labour Day.

Its 43.44-m (142-ft 6.2-in) height also qualifies the conflagration as the ★ **tallest bonfire**.

★ CARDBOARD BOX
On 30 October 2007, students of Aarhus Business College in Aarhus, Denmark, designed and manufactured a cardboard box measuring 11.53 x 4.61 x 2.31 m (37 ft 10 in x 15 ft 1.5 in x 7 ft 7 in).

★ LARGEST PAIR OF SCISSORS
A pair of functional scissors 1.78 m (5 ft 10 in) from tip to handle, made by Michael Fish (Canada) and his team from Keir Surgical Ltd., was displayed at the Operating Room Nurses Association of Canada's (ORNAC) 20th National Conference in Victoria, Canada, on 24 April 2007.

★ DISCO BALL
Raf Frateur (Belgium) of Frateur Events created a mirrored disco ball with a 7.35-m (24-ft 1.3-in) diameter. It was displayed at a party in the club Studio 54 in Antwerp, Belgium, on 20 July 2007.

★ FOOTBALL
MTN Sudan made a football measuring 10.54 m (34 ft 7 in) in diameter in Khartoum, Sudan, on 23 August 2007.

★ GINGERBREAD HOUSE
Roger A. Pelcher (USA) built a gingerbread house with an internal volume of 1,036 m³ (36,600 ft³) at Mall of America, Bloomington, Minnesota, USA, on 22 November 2006. The house was 13.86 m (45 ft 6 in) long, 10.81 m (35 ft 6 in) wide and around 18.28 m (60 ft) tall at its highest point.

★ GOLD COIN
The largest gold coin weighs 100 kg (220 lb 7 oz), measures 50 cm (19.6 in) in diameter, 3 cm (1.1 in) in thickness and is made from bullion with a purity of 99.999%.

The legal-tender coin was introduced on 3 May 2007 by the Royal Canadian Mint with a face value of CAN$1 million ($900,375; £451,585).

★ TALLEST SANDCASTLE
Camp Sunshine created a sandcastle 9.6 m (31 ft 6 in) tall at the Point Sebago Resort in Casco, Maine, USA, on 1 September 2007.

★ LONGEST BALLPOINT PEN
The largest ballpoint pen measures 3.33 m (10 ft 11 in) long and weighs 8 kg (17 lb 10 oz). The prodigious pen was manufactured by Olaf Fügner (Germany) in Sachsen, Germany, during 2005.

We made him like a parade float.
Maria Reidelbach (USA), on creating the largest garden gnome

★ LARGEST PLASTIC DUCK

As part of the Loire Estuary Project 2007, which involved a series of art installations along the riverbank from June to September 2007, the port of Saint-Nazaire, France, hosted a 25-m-tall (82-ft) plastic duck.

★ PAPERCLIP

On 12 July 2007, a solid steel paperclip measuring 4.62 m (15 ft 2 in) in height – and created by the Town of Kipling, Saskatchewan, Canada – was put on display.

★ PHOTO ALBUM

Dodge Brand (USA) created a photo album measuring 3.6 x 2.7 m (12 x 9 ft) in Orlando, Florida, USA, on 6 September 2007. It held 21 double-sided pages; all photos were to scale.

★ LARGEST SKATEBOARD

On 17 August 2007, students in Jerry Havill's Team Problem Solving course at Bay de Noc Community College (all USA) designed and produced a skateboard 9.4 m (31 ft 0.5 in) long, 2.4 m (8 ft) wide and 1.19 m (47 in) high. It was made in Escanaba, Michigan, USA.

DID YOU KNOW?

The **largest collection of rubber ducks** belongs to Charlotte Lee (USA). Charlotte started her collection in 1996 when she bought a pack of rubber ducks for her bathroom. Friends soon began to give her ducks as gifts. As of 3 April 2006, Charlotte has amassed 2,583 ducks, all displayed in glass showcases throughout her home.

★ POM-POM

A pom-pom measuring 90 cm (2 ft 11.43 in) in diameter and 2.56 m (8 ft 4.8 in) in circumference was manufactured and displayed by the children, parents and staff of the Ribby with Wrea Endowed Church of England Primary School in Preston, UK, on 16 March 2007.

★ PRINTED MAP

In December 2006, Stiefel Eurocart (Germany) produced a printed map that measured 4.35 x 3.09 m (14 ft 3 in x 10 ft 1 in) in Lenting, Germany.

☆ PUPPET

A 15.21-m (49-ft 11-in) marionette named Zozobra was presented by the Kiwanis Club in Santa Fe, New Mexico, USA, at the Fiestas de Santa Fe on 7 September 2007.

★ SPECIAL STAMP

Measuring 600 mm x 493 mm (1 ft 11 in x 1 ft 7 in), the largest special stamp was made by Koninklijke Joh. Enschedé and issued by TNT Post for Team Nationaal Schoolontbijt (Team National School Breakfast) in the Netherlands on 6 November 2007. The stamp was used to send a giant Thank You card to Dutch Bakeries for delivering breakfasts to schools.

★ SWEATER

Dalang Woollen Trade Center (China) created a sweater with a chest measurement of 8.6 m (28 ft 2 in), body length of 5 m (16 ft 4 in) and sleeve length of 4.3 m (14 ft 1 in) in Dongguan City, Guangdong Province, China, on 18 October 2007.

★ TROUSERS

On 27 December 2006, Value Planning Co., Ltd, created a pair of trousers 10.83 m (35 ft 6.4 in) long with a 6.48-m (21-ft 3.2-in) waist. They were displayed at Kobe City Central Gymnasium in Kobe City, Japan.

The World's Largest Garden Gnome
Kelder's Farm, Route 209, Kerhonkson, NY

LARGEST GARDEN GNOME

Created by Maria Reidelbach, with the help of Ken Brown and John Hutchison (all USA), the largest garden gnome is 4.11 m (13 ft 6 in) tall. It resides at the Gnome on the Grange Mini Golf Range at Kedler's Farm, Kerhonkson, New York, USA.

EPIC ENGINEERING

CARD CASTLE

On 12 December 2004, Bryan Berg (USA) constructed a replica of the Walt Disney castle using only playing cards. Measuring 4.22 m (13 ft 10.5 in) tall, 3.6 m (11 ft 10 in) wide and 2.61 m (8 ft 7.25 in) deep, the castle, built at Walt Disney World in Orlando, Florida, USA, needed 162,000 cards to complete.

★ NEW RECORD
★ UPDATED RECORD

★ TALLEST HOUSE OF CARDS

Bryan Berg (USA) constructed a free-standing house of cards that measured 7.86 m (25 ft 9.44 in) tall. It was completed on 15 October 2007 as part of the State Fair of Texas, in Dallas, Texas, USA.

★ LONGEST DIKE

The Saemangeum Seawall is located on the south-west coast of South Korea. Measuring 33 km (20.5 miles) in length, it links two headlands near the industrial port of Gunsan and has created 400 km² (154 miles²) of new farmland, as well as a freshwater reservoir in the former Saemangeum Estuary. It was completed in April 2006.

MOST EXTENSIVE UNDERGROUND RAIL SYSTEM

The New York City subway system in the USA has a total track mileage of 1,355 km (842 miles), including 299 km (186 miles) of track in yards, shops and storage.

LARGEST MANMADE ARCHIPELAGO

The World Islands, 4 km (2.5 miles) off the Dubai coast, is a project to construct more than 300 islands that collectively resemble the shape of Earth's continents. When complete, it will cover an area of 9 x 6 km (5.5 x 3.7 miles), with each island measuring between 23,000 m² (247,570 ft²) and 86,000 m² (925,696 ft²). As of December 2006, more than 90% of the land reclamation on which each island will be developed was complete.

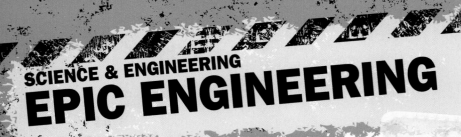

LONGEST PLASTIC BRIDGE

The longest span reinforced-plastic bridge is at the Aberfeldy Golf Club at Aberfeldy, Perth and Kinross, UK. The main span is 63 m (206 ft 8 in) and the overall bridge length 113 m (370 ft 9 in).

LONGEST ROAD TUNNEL

The two-lane Lærdal tunnel on the main road between Bergen and Oslo, Norway, measures 24.5 km (15.2 miles) in length. The tunnel was opened to the public in 2001, having cost a reported $113.1 million (£57.4 million) to build.

LARGEST RAILWAY NETWORK

The USA is the country with the largest railway network, with 227,236 km (141,198 miles) of railway lines.

WIDEST BRIDGE

The widest long-span bridge is the 503 m (1,650 ft) Sydney Harbour Bridge, Australia, which is 48.8 m (160 ft) wide. It carries two electric overhead railway tracks, eight lanes of roadway and a cycle track and footway. It was officially opened on 19 March 1932.

★ LARGEST WIND GENERATOR

The largest wind turbine is the Enercon E-126, which has a hub height of 135 m (443 ft) and a rotor diameter of 127 m (416 ft). Its capacity is rated at 6 MW (or 20 million kilowatt hours each year) – enough to fuel 5,000 four-person households! The wind generator was manufactured by Enercon GmbH (Germany), installed on the Rysumer Nacken in Emden, Germany, and began operation in November 2007.

A little more than 2,200 years after the Seven Wonders of the Ancient World were declared in 200 BC, the New 7 Wonders campaign was launched in 2000 by film-maker and aviator Bernard Weber (Canada). Its aim was to select seven new Wonders of the World as a celebration of human achievement in the last two millennia. The selection process was billed as "the world's first global election campaign" and was open to anyone who had access to the internet or a mobile phone.

After seven years of campaigning and 100 million votes

received, the results of the global ballot were announced on 7 July 2007 in Lisbon, Portugal. During a spectacular gala show in the "Estadio da Luz", in the presence of 50,000 spectators and watched by millions of TV viewers worldwide, the New 7 Wonders were revealed: The Pyramid at Chichén Itzá (pre-AD 800), Yucatan Peninsula, Mexico; Cristo Redentor (1931), Rio de Janeiro, Brazil; The Colosseum (AD 70–82), Rome, Italy; The Great Wall of China (220 BC and AD 1368–1644), China; Machu Picchu (1460–70), Peru; Petra (9 BC–AD 40), Jordan; and The Taj Mahal (AD 1630), Agra, India.

Of these incredible monuments, three are officially acknowledged as Guinness World

Record holders. The Great Wall of China is the **longest wall in the world** and has a main-line length of 3,460 km (2,150 miles) plus 3,530 km (2,195 miles) of branches and spurs; Machu Picchu is recognized as the **largest Inca discovery**, having been "found" in 1911 by a Yale University expedition led by US historian Hiram Bingham; finally, GWR lists Cristo Redentor, in Brazil, as the **largest statue of Jesus** (see right).

★ LARGEST STATUE OF CHRIST

The concrete statue Cristo Redentor (Christ the Redeemer) in Rio de Janeiro, Brazil, is 39.6 m (130 ft) tall and weighs over 700 tonnes (1.5 million lb). It was completed in 1931.

LARGEST IRRIGATION PROJECT

The Great Manmade River Project was begun in 1984. Its aim is to transport water from vast underground natural aquifers to the coastal cities of Libya. As of 2007, over 5,000 km (3,100 miles) of pipelines had been completed, capable of carrying 6.5 million m³ (229.5 million ft³) water per day from around 1,000 wells in Libya's desert.

LARGEST HIGH-SPEED RAIL NETWORK

According to the International Union of Railways (UIC), Japan has the largest high-speed rail network in the world, with 2,700 km (1,678 miles) of high-speed lines in operation or under construction. The country opened the world's first dedicated high-speed line between Tokyo and Osaka in 1964.

★ LONGEST POWERLINE

The Inga-Shaba Electrical Transmission Project is a powerline that stretches from the Inga hydroelectric dam in the mouth of the Congo River to distant copper-mining regions in the Democratic Republic of the Congo, 1,700 km (1,056 miles) away. It took 10 years to construct and was completed in 1982.

★ MOST POWERFUL WATER PUMP

The most powerful water pump operates at a rate of 60,000 litres (13,200 gal) per second and was made by Nijhuis Pumps in Winterswijk, the Netherlands, in 2004.

LONGEST RAIL TUNNEL

The Seikan rail tunnel is 53.85 km (33.46 miles) long and links Tappi Saki on the main Japanese island of Honshu with Fukushima, on the northern island of Hokkaido. The first test run through the tunnel took place on 13 March 1988.

LONGEST RUBBER DAM

The Xiaobudong rubber dam is situated on the Yihe River, Shandong Province, China. Completed on 1 July 1997, it measures 1,135 m (3,723 ft) long and consists of 16 sections, each of which is 70 m (229 ft) long.

LONGEST CANTILEVER BRIDGE

The Quebec Bridge (Pont de Quebec) over the St Lawrence River in Canada has a cantilever truss span measuring 549 m (1,800 ft) between the piers and 987 m (3,239 ft) overall. The bridge carries a railway and two carriageways. Work started in 1899 and it was finally opened to traffic on 3 December 1917.

HOTELS

TALLEST

The all-suite Burj Al Arab (The Arabian Tower), situated 15 km (9 miles) south of Dubai, United Arab Emirates, is the tallest hotel in the world, standing at 320.94 m (1,052 ft) high from ground level to the top of its mast, when measured on 26 October 1999. Built on a man-made island, the hotel, shaped like a sail, has 202 suites, 28 "double-height" storeys and covers a total floor area of 111,480 m^2 (1.2 million ft^2).

★ LARGEST GROUP

InterContinental Hotels is the world's largest hotel operator by number of bedrooms, with 537,500 rooms divided between 3,606 hotels. In the year to 31 December 2005, the group reported a turnover of £1.239 billion ($2.425 billion) from nearly 100 countries.

LARGEST

The First World Hotel has 6,118 rooms. It is part of the Genting Highlands Resort in Pahang Darul Makmur, Malaysia, and was completed in 2005.

HIGHEST ALTITUDE

The Hotel Everest View above Namche, Nepal – the village closest to Everest base camp – is at a record height of 3,962 m (13,000 ft).

HEAVIEST RELOCATED

The three-storey brick Hotel Fairmount (built 1906) in San Antonio, Texas, USA, which weighed 1,451 tonnes (3,198,907 lb), was moved on 36 dollies with pneumatic tyres over city streets – approximately five blocks – and over a bridge, which had to be reinforced. The move took six days, from 30 March to 4 April 1985.

★ MOST EXPENSIVE ROOM

As of July 2006, the most expensive hotel room is the presidential suite at the Hotel Martinez, Cannes, France, which costs $37,200 (£20,485; €29,600) for one night's stay. This sound-proofed suite on the seventh floor has four bedrooms and a private terrace with a jacuzzi.

★ MOST RESTAURANTS

The Venetian Resort Hotel Casino, opened in May 1999 in Las Vegas, Nevada, USA, has 17 different restaurants.

FACT

The Peninsula Group operates eight hotels in Hong Kong, New York, Chicago, Beverly Hills, Tokyo, Bangkok, Beijing and Manila. The Peninsula Shanghai (China) opens in 2009.

LARGEST HOTEL ROLLS-ROYCE FLEET

The Peninsula Group has purchased a total of 50 Rolls-Royces since its first order of seven Brewster Green Silver Shadows in 1970.

★ HIGHEST LIBRARY

The library on the 60th floor of the J. W. Marriott Hotel at Tomorrow Square in Shanghai, China, is situated at 230.9 m (757 ft 6 in) above street level. Membership is available to the public, and the 103 shelves in the library contain an ever-expanding collection of Chinese and English books.

MOST FOUNTAINS

The Bellagio hotel in Las Vegas, USA, features an artificial lake covering 4.8 ha (12 acre) – equivalent to the area of nearly 70 tennis courts – containing more than 1,000 fountains.

GUINNESS WORLD RECORDS

OLDEST

The Hoshi Ryokan at the village of Awazu in Japan is the world's oldest hotel, dating back to AD 717, when Taicho Daishi built an inn near a hot-water spring that was said to have miraculous healing powers. The waters are still celebrated for their recuperative effects and the Ryokan now has 100 bedrooms.

MOST NORTHERLY

The most northerly full-service hotel is the Radisson SAS Polar Hotel in Longyearbyen, Svalbard, Norway. Svalbard consists of several islands from Bjornoya in the south to Rossoya in the north, Europe's northernmost point. About 60% of the archipelago is covered by ice.

MOST REMOTE CONCIERGE

Anna Morris (USA) works 130 km (80 miles) from the hotel where she is employed as a concierge. Guests at the Westin Hotel in Santa Clara, California, USA, can talk to her via an interactive webcam, while Anna can see the guests via a camera in the hotel.

LARGEST DEMOLITION

On 26 May 1972, the 21-storey Traymore Hotel, Atlantic City, New Jersey, USA, was demolished. This 600-room hotel had a cubic capacity of 181,340 m^3 (6,403,926 ft^3).

HIGHEST DENSITY OF HOTEL ROOMS

Las Vegas, Nevada, USA, boasts an incredible 120,000 hotel and motel rooms – that's nearly one for every four of its 456,000 inhabitants. The city single-handedly accounts for roughly one-thirtieth of all hotel rooms in the US.

LARGEST FLOOR AREA OF POLISHED MARBLE TILES

The Venetian Resort-Hotel-Casino in Las Vegas, USA, which opened to the public on 3 May 1999, has a total floor area of 139,354 m^2 (1.5 million ft^2) covered in cream, brown and black marble tiles imported from Italy and Spain. This space is equivalent to the area of 535 tennis courts.

★ LARGEST CASINO

The largest casino is the 51,100-m^2 (550,000-ft^2) gambling area in the Venetian Macau, a casino-hotel resort owned by the Las Vegas Sands Corporation, USA, which opened in Macau, China, on 27 August 2007. Guests can play on 3,400 slot machines or at 870 gaming tables, while staying in one of 3,000 suites.

★ TALLEST REVOLVING DOOR

The tallest revolving door measures 4.8 m (15 ft 9 in) and is located in the Novotel Citygate Hong Kong hotel in Tung Chung, Hong Kong. The door was measured during the hotel's official opening on 12 June 2006.

LARGEST PRESIDENTIAL SUITE

The largest hotel presidential suite is the Villa Salaambo attached to the Hasdrubal Thalassa Hotel in Yasmine Hammamet, Tunisia. It covers a total area of 1,542 m^2 (16,597 ft^2).

LARGEST ICE HOTEL

The Ice Hotel in Jukkasjärvi, Sweden, has a total floor area of between 4,000 m^2 and 5,000 m^2 (43,000–54,000 ft^2), and in the winter of 2004–05 featured 85 rooms, as well as an ice bar and an ice church. Lying 200 km (120 miles) north of the Arctic circle, the hotel has been re-created (and enlarged) every December since 1990.

MEGA MOTORS

CAR CLASSICS

● The **largest car produced for private use** is the Bugatti "Royale" Type 41, known in the UK as the "Golden Bugatti". First built in 1927, it measures over 6.7 m (22 ft) in length.

● The **greatest confirmed price paid for a car** is $15 million (£9,135,200) for the 1931 Bugatti Type 41 "Royale" Sports Coupe by Kellner, sold by Nicholas Harley (UK) to the Meitec Corp. (Japan) on 12 April 1990.

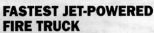

● The world's **most expensive production car** is the Mercedes Benz CLK/LM, which cost $1,547,620 (£957,100) when launched in 1997. It has a top speed of 320 km/h (200 mph) and can travel from 0 to 100 km/h (62 mph) in 3.8 seconds.

● The MTT Turbine Superbike, powered by a Rolls-Royce Allison gas turbine engine, cost $185,000 (£101,000) in 2004, making it the **most expensive production motorcycle**. The bike's turbine engine produces 213 kW (286 hp) of power at the rear wheel.

● On 15 October 1997, Andy Green (UK) achieved a speed of 1,227.985 km/h (763.035 mph; Mach 1.020) over a distance of one mile in his car *Thrust SSC*. This feat, which took place in the Black Rock Desert, Nevada, USA, made *Thrust SSC* the **fastest car** and established a new **official land-speed record**.

★ FIRST FULLY SUBMERSIBLE SPORTS CAR

The Rinspeed sQuba car, manufactured by Rinspeed (Switzerland), can be driven on land, float on the surface of water and can also be steered to underwater depths of 10 m (33 ft) by a driver wearing breathing apparatus.

★ FASTEST CAR POWERED BY DRY CELL BATTERIES

The Oxyride Racer is the fastest car to be powered by dry cell batteries. It achieved an average speed of 105.95 km/h (65.83 mph) on 4 August 2007 using a power pack of 194 "AA" batteries. It was set by the Oxyride Speed Challenge Team consisting of Matsushita Electric Industrial Co., Ltd, and Osaka Sangyo University (both Japan) in Ibaraki, Japan. The frame of the lightweight Oxyride Racer is made of carbon-fibre-reinforced plastic and weighs just 38 kg (84 lb).

FASTEST JET-POWERED FIRE TRUCK

The world's fastest fire truck is the jet-powered *Hawaiian Eagle*, owned by Shannen Seydel of Navarre, Florida, USA, which attained a speed of 655 km/h (407 mph) in Ontario, Canada, on 11 July 1998.

The truck is a red 1940 Ford, powered by two Rolls-Royce Bristol Viper engines boasting 4,470 kW (6,000 hp) per engine, which generate 5,443 kg (12,000 lb) of thrust.

FASTEST CAR IN PRODUCTION

The Ultimate Aero TT Super Car, built by Shelby Supercars (USA), is the fastest car currently in production. It achieved two-way timed speeds in excess of 412 km/h (256.14 mph) on Highway 221, Washington, USA, on 13 September 2007.

★ FASTEST PRODUCTION PICKUP TRUCK

A standard VZ HSV Maloo R8 pickup truck ("ute"), driven by 39-year-old HSV race car driver Mark Skaife (Australia), reached 271.44 km/h (168.7 mph) on a road in the Woomera Prohibited Area, Australia, on 25 May 2006.

★ LARGEST PRODUCTION CAR ENGINE

The largest standard engine installed in any car currently in series production is the 8.275 litre (505 cu in) V10 engine of the Dodge Viper SRT-10. It produces 373 kW (500 hp) of power and 712 Nm (525 lb-ft) of torque, enough to power the Viper to 96.5 km/h (60 mph) in under four seconds.

★ VEHICLE ENGINE WITH THE MOST CYLINDERS

Simon Whitelock (UK) has built a motorcycle with a two-stroke engine that has 48 cylinders and a capacity of 4,200 cc (256 cu in). It consists of 16 Kawasaki KH250 three-cylinder engines arranged in six banks of eight, and is road-legal.

FACT

The SSC Ultimate Aero TT retails at around $585,000 (£290,075) and was originally planned to have a limited-edition production of around 25 vehicles. It houses a 1,183 bhp twin-turbo Chevrolet V8 engine, can go from 0–60 mph in just 2.78 seconds and in tests covered 0.4 km (0.25 miles) in 9.9 seconds, at a speed of 89.4 km/h (144 mph).

MOST POWERFUL MOTORCYCLE

The $185,000 (£101,000) MTT Turbine Superbike's Rolls-Royce Allison gas turbine engine is claimed by its manufacturer to supply 213 kW (286 hp) of power at the rear wheel, with 577 Nm (425 lb-ft) of torque at 2,000 rpm, making the Superbike the most powerful motorcycle to enter into series production.

★ OLDEST CAR

La Marquise, a steam-powered, four-wheeled, four-seater vehicle, was manufactured by De Dion, Bouton et Trépardoux (France) in 1884; three years later it won the world's first automobile race, powering along the 30.5-km (19-mile) track at an average speed of 42 km/h (26 mph) from Paris to Neuilly, France. It was sold at auction for $3,520,000 (£1,767,000) on 19 August 2007.

★ HEAVIEST MOTORBIKE

The heaviest motorcycle is the Harzer Bike Schmiede, created by Tilo Niebel of Zilly, Germany, which weighed 4.749 tonnes (10,470 lb) on 23 November 2007. The massive machine, which is 5.28 m (17 ft 4 in) long, 2.29 m (7 ft 6 in) tall and powered by a Russian tank engine, took a team of welders and mechanics nearly a year to build.

★ LARGEST CONVOY OF TRUCKS

A total of 416 trucks, all driven by women, took part in a convoy at Dronten, Netherlands, on 6 November 2004 at an event organized by VTL.

AIRCRAFT

★ LARGEST CONTRACT TO PRODUCE MILITARY ENGINES

The Eurojet EJ200 production programme is contracted to produce more than 1,400 engines for the Eurofighter Typhoon fighter aircraft – the world's ★ **most advanced multi-swing-role aircraft** – which is the ★ **largest military engine production programme under contract**. Each engine provides 90 kilonewtons (20,000 lb-force) of power with afterburner and 60kN (13,500 lbf) without.

ACTUAL SIZE

TRANSATLANTIC FLIGHTS

FIRST

Lt Cdr Albert Cushing Read (1887–1967) and his crew flew the US Navy/Curtiss flying-boat NC-4 from Newfoundland (now Canada), via the Azores, to Lisbon, Portugal, from 16 to 27 May 1919.

FIRST NON-STOP

John William Alcock and Arthur Whitten Brown (both UK) flew a Vickers Vimy biplane from St John's, Newfoundland (now Canada), to Clifden, Ireland, on 14 June 1919.

FASTEST

On 1 September 1974, USAF Major James V. Sullivan and Major Noel F. Widdifield flew a Lockheed SR-71A Blackbird eastwards across the Atlantic in 1 hr 54 min 56.4 sec.

★ FIRST MONOPLANE FLIGHT

The first monoplane to achieve successful flight was *Traian Vuia 1*, built by Trajan Vuia, a Romanian inventor who lived in Paris, France. Vuia flew his monoplane at a height of 1 m (3 ft) for 12 m (40 ft) in Montesson, Paris, France, on 18 March 1906.

★ FASTEST-SELLING AIRLINER

The new Boeing 787 Dreamliner is the fastest-selling airliner in history, with a total of 857 orders from 56 customers worldwide, following an initial order for 16 Boeing 787s from Gulf Air at the beginning of 2008.

The company launched the aircraft in April 2004, and it was originally scheduled to enter service in May 2008. The Dreamliner will seat between 210 and 250 passengers (although later models will carry more) and fly at speeds of Mach 0.85.

★ LARGEST PRIVATE JET

In November 2007, it was announced that HRH Prince Waleed Bin Talai of Saudi Arabia had ordered the first private Airbus A-380 for around $300 million (£150 million). With a wing-span of 79.8 m (261 ft 8 in) and a maximum designed take-off weight of 560 tonnes (1,235,000 lb), it is the largest private jet in the world.

★ FASTEST BUSINESS JET

On 13 June 2005, the Bombardier Global 5000 set a new transcontinental speed record for a business jet. It flew 3,510 nautical miles (6,500 km; 4,040 miles) from Chicago (Palwaukee Airport), USA, to Paris (Le Bourget), France, in 7 hr 15 min, flying at Mach 0.88. The aircraft first entered service on 18 April 2005.

★ SMALLEST AUTOPILOT

Weighing only 16.65 g (0.58 oz) and measuring 5 x 3.4 x 1.2 cm (2 x 1.37 x 0.47 in), the Kestrel Autopilot is the smallest and lightest full-featured autopilot currently on the market. Manufactured by Procerus Technologies (USA), the Kestrel Autopilot is designed for use in Unmanned Aerial Vehicles (UAVs) with surveillance and reconnaissance applications.

★ LONGEST CARGO LOADER

In order to transport large components of the Boeing 787 Dreamliner aircraft from production centres around the world for assembly at the company's facility at Everett, USA, Boeing unveiled the world's longest cargo loader on 12 June 2006. Designed by TLD of Quebec, Canada, it measures 35.96 m (118 ft 1 in) long and will be used in conjunction with the modified Boeing 747-400 "Dreamlifter" freighters.

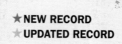

★ NEW RECORD
★ UPDATED RECORD

★ LARGEST CAPACITY FOR A JET AIRLINER

The double-decker Airbus 380 (manufactured by EADS [Airbus S.A.S.]), which had its maiden flight in Toulouse, France, on 27 April 2005, has a nominal capacity of 555 seats but has a potential maximum seating capacity of 853, depending on the interior configuration.

X-REF

The Airbus 380 has a wing-span of 79.8 m (261 ft 8 in), a range of 8,000 nautical miles (15,000 km; 9,320 miles) and a cruising speed of Mach 0.85 (1,049 km/h; 652 mph). You can find out about more incredible feats of construction by turnng to **Epic Engineering** on pp.150–51.

★ FARTHEST FLIGHT BY AN UNMANNED AIRCRAFT (NON-FAI APPROVED)

During trials at the US military White Sands Missile Range in New Mexico on 10 September 2007, the Zephyr High Altitude Long Endurance UAV (Unmanned Aerial Vehicle) from the British defence technology company QinetiQ, powered by new solar array technology, achieved a flight time of 54 hours to an altitude of 17,786 m (58,355 ft). However, as no

★ LONGEST FLIGHT FOR A MICRO UNMANNED AERIAL VEHICLE

The "Pterosoar", a joint micro Unmanned Aerial Vehicle (UAV) project between Oklahoma State University and California State University (both USA) flew 120 km (74.5 miles) in Lancaster, California,

Fédération Aéronautique Internationale (FAI) official was present during the trial, this is not currently the official FAI-approved world record.

The **longest FAI-approved flight ever completed by a full-scale unmanned conventional aircraft** is 13,840 km (8,600 miles), by the USAF Northrop Grumman Global Hawk *Southern Cross II*, which took off from Edwards Air Force Base in California, USA, on 22 April 2001 and landed at RAAF Base Edinburgh, South Australia, Australia, 23 hr 23 min later on 23 April 2001.

USA, consuming only 16 g of the 64 g (0.5 oz of the 2.5 oz) of hydrogen carried on board in a pressurized hydrogen tank. The distance achieved was itself a record – however, potentially the UAV could increase this distance significantly to nearly 500 km (310 miles) based on its fuel capacity.

FARTHEST FLIGHT BY A COMMERCIAL AIRCRAFT

A Boeing 777-200LR Worldliner flew 11,664 nautical miles (21,601.7 km; 13,422.7 miles) non-stop and without refuelling from Hong Kong, China, to London, UK, from 9 to 10 November 2005, in 22 hr 42 min – the longest flight ever by an unmodified commercial aircraft. The 777-200LR is powered by two General Electric GE90-115Bs, the world's **most powerful jet engines**. The first aircraft were delivered to customer airlines in the early part of 2006.

ECO FUEL FIRSTS

ELECTRICITY

On 23 December 2006, a wood and fabric single-seat aircraft (the Electra F-WMDJ, above) powered by an electric, 25-hp (18-kW) British-made motor (often used to power golf carts), flew for 48 minutes for 50 km (30 miles) around the southern Alps in France, making it the ★ **first electric-powered aircraft**.

NATURAL GAS

On 1 February 2008, an Airbus A-380 MSN004 completed the ★ **first flight by a commercial aircraft using a liquid fuel processed from gas** (gas to liquid [GTL] fuel). The flight from Filton, UK, to Toulouse, France, took three hours.

BIODIESEL

On 2 October 2007, a Czech Delfin L-29 Albatross (below) achieved the ★ **first flight of a jet fighter powered only with 100% biodiesel fuel** at Reno, Nevada, USA.

WEAPONS

★ NEW RECORD
★ UPDATED RECORD

★ NEWEST CLASS OF NUCLEAR SUBMARINE

The newest class of Sub Surface Nuclear Submarine was introduced with the launch of HMS *Astute* by the British Royal Navy on 8 June 2007. With four on order, this new class will be armed with Spearfish torpedoes and Tomahawk cruise missiles and will represent the largest and most powerful attack submarines operated by the Royal Navy.

★ MOST MAIN BATTLE TANKS IN ONE ARMY

In 2006, the Russian Federation was credited with at least 22,831 Main Battle Tanks (MBT), making it the army with the most tanks in the world. It is estimated that China has about 7,580 MBTs, while the USA possesses approximately 7,620.

★ FIRST NUCLEAR-POWERED AIRCRAFT CARRIER

The USS *Enterprise,* which was launched in 1960 and commissioned by the US Navy in 1961, was the first nuclear-powered aircraft carrier. The ship has taken part in numerous missions, including the Cuba crisis of 1962 and operations during the war in Vietnam (1959–75); it was the first nuclear ship to transit the Suez Canal and has supported operations in Afghanistan and Iraq. It is currently due to remain in commission until 2015.

★ FASTEST ANTI-TANK MISSILE

Lockheed Martin's LOSAT (Line of Sight Anti-Tank) missile can achieve speeds of over 154 m/s (500 ft/s). With a range of 8 km (5 miles), it does not require explosives, but instead relies on the power of its kinetic energy to drive a penetrator rod into an enemy tank. Its guided missile test flight occurred at the White Sands Missile Range, New Mexico, USA, in June 2003.

FIRST NUCLEAR SUBMARINE

The US Navy's USS *Nautilus,* the world's first nuclear-powered submarine, was launched at Groton, Connecticut, USA, on 21 January 1954. Built by General Dynamics Electric Boat, *Nautilus* was 98.7 m (324 ft) long and had a beam of 26.8 m (88 ft). *Nautilus* was also the ★ **first submarine to travel under the ice cap to the North Pole**, arriving there at 11:15 a.m. on 3 August 1958.

FACT

The 7,800-tonne (17,200,000-lb) HMS *Astute* uses a Rolls-Royce PWR 2, pressurized water reactor, for propulsion and will be capable of speeds of over 20 knots (23 mph; 37 km/h). The craft is designed to complete a service-life of over 25 years without refuelling.

★ MOST POWERFUL ELECTROMAGNETIC RAILGUN

Electromagnetic (EM) railguns use an extremely high current flow to create an electromagnetic force that can propel projectiles at speeds greater than Mach 7.0, and destroy targets through sheer force of impact (i.e., without explosives being used) at ranges in excess of 200 nautical miles (370 km; 230 miles).

On 16 January 2007, a test shot was fired at the US Naval Warfare Center Dahlgren Division, with a muzzle energy of 7.4 megajoules and an achieved velocity of 2,146 m/s (7,040 ft/s).

★ LARGEST NON-NUCLEAR CONVENTIONAL WEAPON

The largest non-nuclear conventional weapon was reportedly successfully tested by Russia on 11 September 2007. With destruction achieved by an ultrasonic shockwave and extremely high temperatures, this weapon is said to be four times more powerful than the previous record holder, the US Massive Ordnance Air Blast Bomb (MOAB) – or more commonly the "Mother Of All Bombs" (a precision-guided weapon weighing 9,752 kg; 21,500 lb).

★ MOST ADVANCED WARSHIP

Due to enter service in 2009, the Royal Navy's HMS *Daring* is the world's most capable air defence ship. It is equipped with the Principal Anti-Air Missile System (PAAMS) – a surface-to-air missile system that enables the ship to defend itself (and others) from enemy aircraft or missiles approaching at subsonic or supersonic speed.

★ FIRST LASER GUNSHIP

The first laser gunship was built at Kirkland Air Force Base, New Mexico, USA, on 4 December 2007, when the Boeing Company installed a high-energy chemical laser on a Hercules C-130H aircraft. It is seen as a further step in the development of the Advanced Tactical Laser, which will be able to destroy ground targets more accurately and with less collateral damage than conventional guns or missiles.

LARGEST CREW ON A WARSHIP

The US Navy Nimitz class nuclear-powered aircraft carriers each carry at least 5,680 personnel when battle-ready, of which around 3,200 are ship's company and at least 2,280 belong to the Air Wing. Five Nimitz class aircraft carriers, including the USS *Ronald Reagan*, have a displacement of 102,000 tonnes (224.8 million lb) fully loaded, a length of 317 m (1,040 ft) and beam of 40.8 m (133 ft 10 in), making them the **largest warships** afloat.

★ FIRST SUCCESSFUL TEST OF UAVs IN COOPERATIVE FLIGHT

The first successful demonstration of Unmanned Aerial Vehicles (UAVs) flying fully autonomously in cooperative flight was achieved by the United States Air Force (USAF), under the operational control of the USAF UAV Battle Lab at Creech Air Force Base, Nevada, USA, between 1 and 11 July 2007. SkyWatcher and SkyRaider UAVs were flown in these cooperative test flights, each guided by its own onboard virtual pilot but controlled by SkyForce Distributed Management System (DMS), which enabled one operator to manage four aircraft.

WEAPONRY FIRSTS

CANNON
The **oldest dated cannon** in existence is the Dardanelles Gun, cast in 1464 for Sultan Mehmet II in Turkey. It is made from bronze, weighs 16.8 tonnes (37,037 lb) and measures 5.2 m (17 ft) long.

TANK
The No. 1 Lincoln was built by William Foster Co., Ltd, of Lincoln, Lincolnshire, UK, and, after modification, became known as "Little Willie". It first ran on 6 September 1915 and although it never saw active service, it is recognized as the **first real tank**.

ROCKETS
The **first use of true rockets** was reported in 1232 when the Chinese and Mongols were at war with each other. During the battle of Kai-Keng, the Chinese repelled the Mongol invaders by a barrage of "arrows of flying fire".

GUN
Documentary evidence of guns dates from 1326. However, the **first known example of a gun** was found in the ruins of the castle of Monte Varino in Italy. The castle was destroyed in 1341.

ENTERTAINMENT

★ MOST SUCCESSFUL ENTERTAINMENT LAUNCH

On 29 April 2008, the release of Rockstar's controversial video game *Grand Theft Auto IV* generated $310 million (£159 million) worth of first-day sales worldwide. This is five times the $60 million (£30 million) revenue generated by the most successful 24 hours for a movie, held by *Spider-Man 3* (USA, 2007). The "Midnight Madness" launch at thousands of stores worldwide made *GTA IV* the **most successful entertainment product launch** in history.

CONTENTS

BEST-SELLING VIDEO GAMES 2007

RANK	GAME	SALES
01	Call of Duty 4 (All)	7.13 million
02	Wii play with Remote (Wii)	6.90 million
03	Halo 3 (Xbox 360)	6.79 million
04	More Brain Training (DS)	5.29 million
05	World of Warcraft: Burning Crusade (PC/Mac)	4.81 million
06	Super Mario Galaxy (Wii)	4.66 million
07	Pokemon Diamond/Pearl (DS)	4.27 million
08	Wii Sports (Wii)	3.2 million
09	Assassin's Creed (PS3)	2.83 million
10	Guitar Hero 3 (All)	2.82 million

Charts compiled using data sourced from The NPD group, Famitsu, Chart Track, The GFK Group and VG Chartz.

ART & SCULPTURE

MOSAIC MASTERPIECES

PICTURES

The world's ★ **largest picture mosaic** was created as part of a competition by Liberty Life that asked children aged between three and 12 to draw pictures of their dreams. The resulting 8,064 colourful drawings were organized into a mosaic measuring 1,005 m² (10,817 ft²), depicting the South African flag. It was unveiled at Sharonlea Primary School, Johannesburg, South Africa on 12 March 2007.

FRUIT

On 25–26 September 2007, 341,969 apples were used to make the ★ **largest fruit mosaic**, measuring 1,500 m² (16,145 ft²). It was created for an event organized by the People's Government of Zhaoyang, Zhaotong City, Yunnan Province, China.

TOOTHPICKS

The ★ **largest toothpick mosaic** was made by Saimir Strati (Albania) and measured 8 m² (86 ft²). It was displayed in Tirana, Albania, on 4 September 2007.

LARGEST...

★ SCULPTURE OF AN ANIMAL

Milka (Germany) created the largest animal sculpture in the shape of a cow. It had a height of 14.18 m (46 ft 6 in), a width of 11.77 m (38 ft 7 in) and a total length of 21.24 m (69 ft 8 in), when measured in Berlin, Germany, on 11 November 2007.

★ MURAL BY ONE ARTIST

Pontus Andersson (Sweden) painted a mural measuring 696.3 m² (7,494 ft²) on a concrete wall in Gothenburg, Sweden. It depicts Gothenburg's harbour and coast, and took 250 working days (stretched across a period of six years) to complete.

POPCORN SCULPTURE

Using popcorn, 50 members of the Sri Chinmoy Center in Jamaica, New York, USA, created a sculpture of a five-tiered cake measuring 6.35 m (20 ft 10 in) tall, 3.88 m (12 ft 9 in) wide and weighing 5,301.59 kg (11,688 lb), when displayed on 27 August 2006.

★ PICTURE MADE OF LITE-BRITE PEGS

Mark Beekman (USA) used 124,418 Lite-Brite pegs to depict Leonardo da Vinci's *The Last Supper*. It was unveiled in Malvern, Pennsylvania, USA, on 6 November 2006.

★ LARGEST PLASTIC BAG SCULPTURE

On 16 February 2007, a dinosaur sculpture – 4 m (13.1 ft) tall and 15 m (49.2 ft) long, and made of 16,651 recycled plastic shopping bags – was exhibited at Thinktank in Millennium Point, Birmingham, UK.

★ MOST EXPENSIVE RAW MATERIALS USED IN AN ARTWORK

For the Love of God by Damien Hirst (UK) was created from materials worth £12 million ($23.7 million) in 2007. The human skull (of a European male living between 1720 and 1810) was cast in 2,156 g (76 oz) of platinum and set with 8,601 ethically sourced flawless diamonds (weighing 1,106.18 carats), including a 52.4-carat, pear-shaped pink diamond surrounded by 14 white brilliant-cut pear-shaped diamonds (weighing 37.81 carats) on the forehead. The skull's original teeth were also set in the jaws of the skull. The work was unveiled at The White Cube gallery, London, UK, on 1 June 2007.

LARGEST SNOW SCULPTURE

A team of 600 sculptors from 40 countries used 3,398 m³ (120,000 ft³) of snow to create an French-themed landscape, including a cathedral and an ice maiden, entitled *Romantic Feelings*. It measured 35 m (115 ft) tall and 200 m (656 ft) long and was part of the annual Harbin International Ice and Snow Sculpture Festival, which opened in Heilongjiang Province, China, on 20 December 2007.

> **Liz showed what a terrific medium Blu-Tack can be for modelling anything you can imagine.** *Bostik, Blu-Tack creators*

★ NEW RECORD
★ UPDATED RECORD

★ LARGEST BLU-TACK SCULPTURE

Spiderus Biggus is a giant model of a common house spider made by Elizabeth Thompson (UK, seen here posing next to her creation). It went on display as part of the BUGS! exhibition at London Zoo, UK, in October 2007 to launch a *Spider-Man 3* competition. The artist used 4,000 packs of Blu-Tack to make the sculpture, also known as "Blu-ey". It weighs 200 kg (440 lb) and has a span of 1.2 m (4 ft).

LONGEST...

★ DRAWING

A drawing titled *The Longest Train* was created by 3,573 participants from Kinokawa City and Iwade City, Japan. The work of art was begun on 6 May and finished on 5 August 2007 when it measured 4,662.6 m (15,297 ft 2 in).

★ PAINTING BY NUMBERS

On 17 July 2007, Knights Templar School in Baldock, UK, finished a 144-m-long (472-ft 5-in) painting by numbers.

★ PAINTING

Círculo Artístico e Cultural Artur Bual and the City of Amadora in Portugal produced a 4,001.8-m-long (13,129-ft) painting on 15 September 2007.

DID YOU KNOW?

To support the weight of the Blu-Tack (roughly equivalent to the weight of three grown men) Liz first had to make a thin steel frame. She then used a pasta maker to form strips of Blu-Tack that she wrapped around the frame.

★ PHOTO NEGATIVE

Using a handmade panoramic camera, Shinichi Yamamoto (Japan) printed a photograph 145 m (475 ft 8 in) long and 35.6 cm (14 in) wide, after producing a single photographic negative 30.5 m (100 ft) long and 7 cm (2 in) wide on 18 December 2000.

★ WOODBLOCK PRINT

Christopher Brady (USA) exhibited a 85.87-m-long (281-ft 9-in) woodblock print at Vaught-Hemingway Stadium, Mississippi, USA, on 29 March 2007. The work of art formed part of Brady's master's thesis project and took about four months to complete.

★ LARGEST COAT HANGER INSTALLATION

Silver Back is an installation by David Mach (UK) made entirely from coat hangers. David created a 2.1-m-tall (7-ft), 2.7-m-long (9-ft), 1.5-m-wide (5-ft) sculpture of a male gorilla using 7,500 metal coat hangers. *Silver Back* took 2,705 working hours to create and first went on display at the FIAC art fair in Paris, France, in October 2007.

LARGEST NUDE PHOTO SHOOT

On 6 May 2007, a total of 18,000 naked people volunteered to pose together in Zócalo Square, Mexico City, Mexico. Photographer Spencer Tunick (USA) wanted the world to see how the naked body could be treated as art, not pornography.

MOVIE MILESTONES

★ 2007: FIRST PIRATED HD DOWNLOAD

The sci-fi action movie *Serenity* (USA, 2005) was the first full-resolution rip of an HD DVD movie. The 19.6 GB file was made available on BitTorrent as an .evo file, confirming the suspicion that the copyright protection on HD DVDs had been bypassed.

1893: FIRST FILM STUDIO

Thomas Edison's (USA) "Black Maria", a frame building covered in black roofing-paper, was built at the Edison Laboratories in West Orange, New Jersey, USA, and completed at a cost of $637.67 (then £132.15) on 1 February 1893.

★ 2007: LARGEST 3D OPENING

Robert Zemeckis' *Beowulf* (USA, 2007) opened on 16 November 2007 in 1,000 3D-equipped cinemas, beating Zemeckis' previous record-holder, *The Polar Express* (USA, 2004). Between the release of the two movies, the number of 3D-ready cinemas had increased greatly to over 1,100, not including the 120 IMAX screens and 80 Dolby 3D Digital cinemas.

1925: FIRST IN-FLIGHT MOVIE

The first movie shown on an aircraft was First National's *The Lost World* (USA, 1925), screened during an Imperial Airways flight in a converted Handley-Page bomber travelling from London to Paris in April 1925.

2007: HIGHEST GROSSING MOVIE (OPENING DAY)

Spider-Man 3 (USA, 2007), starring Tobey Maguire (USA), took a record $59.8 million (£29.98 million) on its opening day in the USA on 4 May 2007.

1935: FIRST USE OF TECHNICOLOR

Rouben Mamoulian's (Russia) *Becky Sharp* (USA, 1935), an adaptation of William Thackeray's 1847 novel *Vanity Fair* starring Cedric Hardwicke and Miriam Hopkins, is historically important as being the first full-length feature filmed in Technicolor – a colour film process that gave movies of the time a distinctive "saturated" look.

GUINNESS WORLD RECORDS AGAINST MOVIE PIRACY

Manufacturing, selling or distributing motion pictures or television programmes without the consent of the copyright owner is illegal. If you want to download movies, please use sites that offer legal downloads. Report piracy at http://www.mpaa.org/

FROM THE CREATORS OF 'BUFFY' & 'ANGEL'

They aim to misbehave

SERENITY

1954: FIRST MOVIE BASED ON A TV SHOW

Dragnet (USA, 1954) starred Jack Webb (USA) as Sergeant Joe Friday, a role he had created in the NBC TV series (1951–59) of the same name.

1971: FIRST MOVIE WITH DOLBY SOUND

Dolby – a noise reduction system that removes hiss from recorded sound – was first used on the masters of Stanley Kubrick's *A Clockwork Orange* (UK, 1971).

1975: FIRST BLOCKBUSTER

Steven Spielberg's (USA) *Jaws* (USA, 1975) is considered the first summer blockbuster. People queued up around the block to see the movie, which also became the **first film to earn $100 million** at the box office.

1985: FIRST CG CHARACTER

A stained-glass knight that comes alive in *Young Sherlock Holmes* (USA/UK, 1985) was the first character to be entirely computer-generated in a full-length feature. It was designed by *Toy Story* (USA, 1995) creator John Lassiter (USA).

1994: FIRST MOVIE BUDGET TO EXCEED $100 MILLION

True Lies (USA, 1994), starring Arnold Schwarzenegger (Austria) and Jamie Lee Curtis (USA), was the first movie that cost over $100 million (then £64.1 million) to make. It ended up grossing $365 million.

★ NEW RECORD
☆ UPDATED RECORD

OSCAR TIMELINE

1929: First Oscar ceremony The first Academy Awards were held at the Hollywood Roosevelt on 16 May 1929.

1936: First person to refuse an Oscar Dudley Nichols (USA), screenwriter of *The Informer* (USA, 1935), refused his award because of a union boycott of the ceremony that year.

1949: First person to direct themselves to a Best Actor win The first actor to direct himself in an Oscar-winning performance was Laurence Olivier (UK), who directed himself in the lead role of *Hamlet* (UK, 1948) and went on to win Best Actor and Best Picture (making it the **first non-American director to win Best Picture**).

1953: Most Oscars won in a single year Walter (Walt) Elias Disney (USA) won four Academy Awards in 1953.

1959: Most Oscars won *Ben-Hur* (USA, 1959) won 11 of its 12 nominations; the only other movies to win 11 statues are *Titanic* (USA, 1997), from 14 nominations, and *The Lord of the Rings: The Return of the King* (USA/NZ, 2003), from 11 nominations.

1977: First posthumous Best Actor winner Peter Finch (UK) died on 14 January 1977 while promoting the film *Network* (USA, 1976). His performance in the film later won him the Best Actor Oscar.

1999: Longest Oscar ceremony The 71st Academy Awards, hosted by Whoopie Goldberg (USA) on 21 March 1999 and broadcast by ABC, lasted 4 hr 2 min.

2003: First anime to win an Oscar *Sen to Chihiro no kamikakushi*, a.k.a. *Spirited Away* (Japan, 2001), won the Oscar for Best Animated Feature on 23 March 2003.

2006: HIGHEST GROSSING MOVIE FRANCHISE

The 21 Bond movies, from *Dr No* (UK, 1962) to *Casino Royale* (UK/USA, 2006), have grossed over $4.49 billion (£2.28 billion) worldwide. The 22nd movie, *Quantum of Solace* (2008, pictured below), is due for release in November 2008.

2004: FIRST MOVIE PRODUCED WITH ENTIRELY COMPUTER-GENERATED SETS

The first publically released film in which the background footage was wholly created using computer-generated imagery (CGI) was *Able Edwards* (USA, 2004). The film combined real actors shot against a green screen.

1997: HIGHEST GROSSING MOVIE OF ALL TIME

Love it or hate it, the film with the highest earnings is *Titanic* (USA, 1997), which took $1,834,165,466 (then £1,249,388,962) at the international box office. It also became the **first film to gross $1 billion**.

1895: FIRST CINEMA

The Cinématographe Lumière at the Salon Indien – a former billiard hall in the Grand Café, 14 Boulevard de Capucines, Paris, France – first admitted the public on 28 December 1895. The opening performance, to an audience of 35, included *L'Arrivée d'un train en gare* (France, 1895) by the Lumière brothers.

2003: FASTEST TIME TO GROSS $1 BILLION

The Lord of the Rings: The Return of the King (USA/NZ, 2003) grossed $1 billion (£536.7 million) in just 9 weeks 4 days! It went on win a record-equalling 11 American Academy Awards (Oscars) – see right.

POP DIVAS

★ BEST START
TO AN ALBUM CAREER (US)

New York recording star Alicia Keys (USA, born Alicia Cook) has released four albums since 2001 and every one has topped the Billboard 200 – the **best start on the US Album chart by a female artist**.

★ FIRST DOWNLOAD-ONLY NO.1 UK SINGLE BY A UK ACT

On 6 October 2007, the Sugababes' (UK) single "About You Now" became the first track by a British pop act to top the singles chart solely on the strength of download sales. The song was also the ★ **biggest chart mover to the No.1 position in the UK**, leaping from No.35 to the top spot.

★ SLOWEST CLIMBER ON THE US HOT 100

On 2 June 2007, "Before He Cheats", by *American Idol* winner Carrie Underwood (USA), finally reached the US Top 10 in its 38th week on the Hot 100 chart.

★ YOUNGEST PERSON TO ENTER THE UK ALBUM CHART

Connie Talbot (UK, b. 20 November 2000), who was runner-up in the first *Britain's Got Talent* (ITV, UK) TV series, became the youngest artist to reach the UK album chart when her debut record *Over The Rainbow* entered at No.35 on 8 December 2007, just 18 days after her seventh birthday.

★ BEST START ON THE US DANCE CLUB PLAY CHART

On 8 December 2007, vocalist Rihanna (Barbados, born Robyn Rihanna Fenty) topped the US Dance Club Play chart with her seventh release, "Shut Up And Drive". It was a feat also accomplished by all of her previous six singles across her first two albums.

★ BEST-SELLING DEBUT ALBUM ON THE UK CHART BY A FEMALE ARTIST

Dido (UK) had sold 3 million copies of her debut album *No Angel* (2000) in the UK by November 2006.

★ LONGEST SPAN ON THE UK SINGLES CHART BY A FEMALE ARTIST

Shirley Bassey (UK) reached the Top 50 on 4 August 2007 with "Get The Party Started" at the age of 70 years 208 days, more than 50 years after her first hit in February 1957, "The Banana Boat Song".

★ NEW RECORD
★ UPDATED RECORD

★ FIRST US FEMALE TO WRITE A MILLION-SELLING DEBUT ALBUM

In 2007, 17-year-old Pennsylvania-born country music singer/songwriter Taylor Swift (USA) became the first US female to write or co-write every track on a million-selling debut album (*Taylor Swift*).

★ OLDEST ARTIST TO REACH NO.1 ON THE US DANCE CLUB PLAY CHART

At the age of 73 years 321 days, Yoko Ono (Japan), the wife of late Beatle John Lennon (UK), became the oldest person to top the US Dance Club Play chart when "No, No, No" reached the peak on 12 January 2008.

★ BEST-SELLING DOWNLOAD ALBUM IN THE UK

As of January 2008, Amy Winehouse's (UK) album *Back To Black* was the most downloaded album in the UK, with sales of over 80,000.

GRAMMY WINEHOUSE

The ★ most Grammy Awards won by a British female act in a single year is five by Amy Winehouse (UK) at the 50th Annual Grammy Awards in Los Angeles, California, USA, on 10 February 2008. She took home the prizes for: Record of the Year, Best New Artist, Song of the Year, Best Pop Vocal Album and Best Female Pop Vocal Performance.

★ MOST WEEKS ON THE US ADULT CONTEMPORARY CHART

UK singer Natasha Bedingfield's recording of "Unwritten" – from her 2004 debut album of the same name – topped the US Adult Contemporary chart on 3 March 2007 – its 51st week on that chart.

★ MOST HITS ON THE US COUNTRY SONGS CHART BY A FEMALE ARTIST

On 29 September 2007, veteran country star Dolly Parton (USA) had her record 105th US Country Songs chart entry with "Better Get To Livin'", taken from her *Backwoods Barbie* album. Two dozen of her 105 hits have reached No.1 on the Country Songs chart.

DID YOU KNOW?

In 1978, Kate Bush (UK) released her entirely self-penned debut album *The Kick Inside*, which sold over 1 million copies in the UK alone, making her the **first female in pop history to write a million-selling debut album**.

★ MOST CONSECUTIVE TOP 10 HITS BY A FEMALE GROUP (UK)

Girls Aloud (UK), the winners of the 2002 TV show *Popstars: The Rivals* (ITV, UK) became the first female group to achieve 17 successive UK Top 10 singles when "Call The Shots" achieved that feat on 1 December 2007.

★ HIGHEST-GROSSING MOVIE OF A MUSIC TOUR

The most commercially successful film of a music tour is *Hannah Montana/ Miley Cyrus: Best Of Both Worlds Concert Tour* starring Miley Cyrus (USA, aka Hannah Montana), which grossed an unprecedented $53.4 million (£26.9 million) in just two weeks in February 2008.

AN ALBUM WITH THE X FACTOR

Leona Lewis (UK) won the talent show *The X Factor* (ITV, UK) in 2006 and has been breaking records ever since. Leona's debut album, *Spirit*, sold 375,872 copies in its first week on sale in November 2007, making it the ★ **best-selling debut album in the UK in one week by a female**. The album continued to sell in huge numbers, with sales reaching 1 million copies in the UK in just 29 days, becoming the ★ **fastest-selling album to reach 1 million copies in the UK by a female artist**.

ROCK JOCKS

★ MOST WEEKS AT NO.1 ON US MODERN ROCK CHART

On 29 December 2007, Seattle, USA, rock group the Foo Fighters' track "The Pretender" completed a record 18 weeks at the top of the US Modern Rock chart.

★ HIGHEST DEMAND FOR TICKETS FOR ONE MUSIC CONCERT

There were over 20 million requests for tickets for rock band Led Zeppelin's (UK) one-off reunion show at the 02 Arena, London, UK, on 10 December 2007. Such was the demand that tickets were selling at a record £914 ($1,783) – over seven times their original price of £125 ($244) – in the secondary market.

DOWNLOADS

★ MOST DOWNLOAD SALES IN ONE WEEK IN THE USA

In the week ending 29 December 2007, almost 43 million tracks were legally downloaded in the USA – a figure 42.5% higher than the record set on the same week in the previous year. In total, a record 844.1 million tracks were downloaded in 2007 (45% up on the previous record-breaking year) and this figure included an unprecedented 50 million complete album downloads, beating 2006's total by 53.5%.

★ BEST-SELLING DOWNLOAD ALBUM IN THE USA

Singer/songwriter Jack Johnson's (USA) fifth album *Sleep Through The Static* debuted at No.1 on the US album chart on 23 February 2008 with 139,000 downloads.

FACT

The White Stripes (Jack and Meg White, both USA) performed the ★ shortest music concert ever when, on 16 July 2007, they played just one note at St John's in Newfoundland, Canada. This short gig was the culmination of a tour that took the duo to every province and territory in Canada.

CHART LONGEVITY

★ MOST SUCCESSFUL SONGWRITER

In terms of the number of songs that have charted in the UK singles chart since its launch in November 1952, the most successful songwriter is Sir Paul McCartney (UK), who has written/co-written 188 charted records, of which 129 are different songs. Of these records, 91 reached the Top 10 and 33 made it to No.1. In total, the songs have spent 1,662 weeks on the chart (up to the end of 2007).

★ BEST-SELLING DOWNLOAD SINGLE IN THE USA IN ONE WEEK

US rapper Flo Rida (born Tramar Dillard) sold 467,000 downloads of the track "Low" during the week ending 29 December 2007. In the same week, a record 27 tracks sold over 100,000 downloads.

★ NEW RECORD
★ UPDATED RECORD

BEST-SELLERS

BEST-SELLING ALBUM

The year 2007 marked the 25th anniversary of the first release of Michael Jackson's 1982 album *Thriller*. At that time, estimations from Sony and the Recording Industry Association of America (RIAA) put sales at over 55 million copies, although Jackson's management claim that international sales have pushed the total worldwide figure to over 100 million. While it is impossible to verify the final global sales, there is no doubt that it remains the biggest-selling album of all time.

BEST–SELLING SINGLE SINCE CHARTS BEGAN

Elton John's (UK) "Candle In The Wind 1997/Something About The Way You Look Tonight" is the biggest-selling single since UK and US charts began in the 1950s, having accumulated worldwide sales of 33 million copies. As of 20 October 1997, the single had also reached No.1 in 22 countries. *(The **best-selling single of all time** was released before the first pop charts – see pp.14–15.)*

★ BEST-SELLING DOWNLOAD SINGLE IN THE USA IN ONE YEAR

"Crank That (Soulja Boy)" by 17-year-old Chicago, USA, rapper Soulja Boy Tellem (born DeAndre Cortez Way) sold an unprecedented 2.7 million downloads in 2007.

THE DARK SIDE OF THE MOON

On 12 April 2008, Pink Floyd's (UK) album *The Dark Side Of The Moon* spent its 1,600th week on the US best-sellers charts, over 35 years after making its debut at No.95 on 17 March 1973, making it the album with the **longest stay on the US album charts**. The album's success straddles two charts: The Billboard 200 and the Top Pop Catalogue chart, to which albums move when they are more than 18 months old and have fallen below position 100 on The Billboard 200. It is estimated that the album has sold over 40 million copies worldwide.

★ MOST UK CHART ENTRIES IN ONE YEAR BY THE SAME ARTIST

In 2006, Michael Jackson (USA) notched up 19 UK chart hits, more than any other act in one year. The singles, re-issued as part of Jackson's *Visionary – The Video Singles* box set, were released from 25 February to 1 July 2006. All 19 tracks made the Top 40.

★ LONGEST TIME-SPAN BETWEEN UK NO.1 SINGLES

A re-issue of Elvis Presley's (USA) "It's Now Or Never" hit No.1 in the UK singles chart in 2005, 48 years after "All Shook Up" took the top spot in 1957.

BIGGEST-SELLING BOY-BAND ALBUM

The Backstreet Boys' (USA) *Millennium* album, released in 1999, had sales of 13 million by March 2001. The record entered the US Billboard 200 album chart at No.1 in June 1999. It sold 1,134,000 copies in its first week, shattering Garth Brooks's one-week sales world record.

THE PRINTED WORD

PAULO COELHO

★ LARGEST MAGAZINE

Bayard Revistas S.A. (Spain) published a 36-page, scaled-up issue of *Caracola* measuring 90.5 x 102.1 cm (2 ft 11.6 in x 3 ft 4.2 in). It was unveiled in the Palacio de Congresos in Madrid, Spain, on 19 May 2007.

★ LARGEST PUBLISHED BOOK

Eidouro Publicacoes S.A. (Brazil) have created a 128-page edition of Antoine de Saint Exupéry's (France) *The Little Prince* measuring 2.01 m (6 ft 7 in) high and 3.08 m (10 ft 1 in) wide when open. It was shown at the XIII Biannual Book Fair of Rio de Janeiro, Brazil, on 13 September 2007.

ACTUAL SIZE

★ SMALLEST NEWSPAPER

The most diminutive newspaper measures just 32 x 22 mm (1.25 x 0.86 in). It was created by First News newspapers in West Horsley, Surrey, UK, and published on 8 November 2007 in celebration of Guinness World Records Day.

The Alchemist, by Paulo Coelho (Brazil), had been translated into 67 different languages as of March 2008, giving Coelho the record for the ★ **most translated a living author**. The success of *The Alchemist* took the author himself by surprise. He told GWR that he had no idea why this book in particular – which he sees as "my own journey" – became so popular.

Coelho admires a number of writers, from visionary English poet William Blake ("because he privileges inspiration, not memories") to controversial 20th-century US author Henry Miller ("because there is blood, sweat and tears in his words") and fellow Brazilian Jorge Amado ("because he understands the Brazilian soul").

And how does this best-selling author feel about having a Guinness World Record? "It is a benchmark – the most respected one – for everyone who wants to exceed his or her limits."

★ SMALLEST PUBLISHED BOOK

Measuring just 0.9 x 0.9 mm, the smallest printed book is an edition of *Chameleon* by the Russian author Anton Chekhov. The book was made and published by Anatoliy Konenko, of Omsk, Siberia, Russia, in 1996. Each book consists of 30 pages.

DID YOU KNOW?

The **youngest commercially published author** is Dorothy Straight (USA, b. 25 May 1958), who wrote *How the World Began* in 1962, aged four. It was published in August 1964 by Pantheon Books.

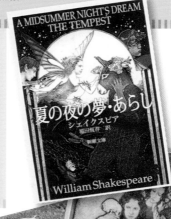

★ LARGEST PHOTO ALBUM

The record for the largest photo album measures 4 m x 3 m (9 ft 10 in x 13 ft 1 in). It is entitled "Women of Vietnam" and was created by Canon Singapore displaying photographs by Hitomi Toyama (Japan). It was presented in Hanoi, Vietnam, on 7 April 2008.

★ MOST TRANSLATED AUTHOR

The works of William Shakespeare (England, 1564–1616) had been translated into at least 116 languages as of October 2005.

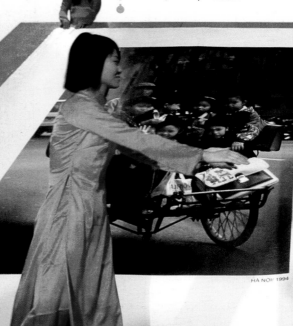

MOST LETTERS PUBLISHED

Subhash Chandra Agrawal (India) has had 3,699 letters published by editors of various national newspapers in India, the ★**most letters published in newspapers in a lifetime**. His wife, Madhu Agrawal (India), also pictured here, had a total of 447 letters published during 2004 in 30 prominent Indian papers with circulations of over 50,000 – the ★**most letters published in newspapers in one year**.

★ NEW RECORD
★ UPDATED RECORD

BEST-SELLING COPYRIGHT BOOK

Excluding non-copyright works such as the Bible – the **best-selling non-fiction book of all time** (with an estimated 6 billion copies sold) – and the Koran, the world's best-selling book is *Guinness World Records* (formerly *The Guinness Book of Records*). First published in October 1955, global sales, in some 37 languages, exceeded 100 million copies as of October 2003.

★LARGEST ONLINE BOOKSHOP

Amazon.com, founded in 1994 by Jeff Bezos (USA), opened its virtual doors in July 1995. Twelve years on, it has over 69 million active customer accounts.

In 2006, the company shipped products to over 200 countries. Its catalogue of more than 40 million items also makes it the **largest online shop**.

NOVEL

Greek author Chariton wrote *Chaireas & Callirhoe*, subtitled "Love Story in Syracuse", in the first century AD. Apuleius' *The Golden Ass,* or *Metamorphoses,* reportedly written in AD 123, is the only Latin novel that survives whole.

DAILY NEWSPAPER

Wiener Zeitung, the Austrian government's official gazette, was first published in 1703.

★HIGHEST DAILY NEWSPAPER CIRCULATION

Founded in 1874 and published in Tokyo, Japan, the *Yomiuri Shimbun* had a combined morning and evening circulation of 14,532,694 in 2005.

MALE AUTHOR

In February 2003, Constantine Kallias (Greece, b. 26 June 1901) published a first-edition, 169-page paperback entitled *A Glance of My Life*.

TOWERING TOMES

Michele assembled a 3.78-m-high (12-ft 4-in) tower of the books he has typed, with the largest, a copy of the Egyptian Book of the Dead, at the bottom of the stack. That book weighed 78.8 kg (173.7 lb) and had 610 huge pages 104.5 x 66 cm (41.14 x 25.98 in).

★MOST COMICS PUBLISHED BY ONE AUTHOR

Shotaro Ishinomori (Japan) created 770 published comic titles and is today known as "The King of Manga".

OLDEST...

MECHANICALLY PRINTED BOOK

It is widely accepted that the first mechanically printed, full-length book was the Gutenberg Bible, printed in Mainz, Germany, *ca.* 1455 by Johann Henne zum Gensfleisch zur Laden, who was known as zu Gutenberg.

FEMALE AUTHOR

Louise Delany's (USA) second book, *The Delany Sisters' Book of Everyday Wisdom* – co-written with her sister A. Elizabeth Delany – was published by Kodansha America in October 1994, when she was 105.

★LONGEST-RUNNING MONTHLY COMIC

Since Issue #1 in March 1937, *Detective Comics* has been printed every month by DC Comics in the USA. The comic introduced the character of Batman in Issue #27, which was published in May 1939.

No. 27 · 64 PAGES OF ACTION! · MAY, 1939 · Detective COMICS · STARTING THIS ISSUE: THE AMAZING AND UNIQUE ADVENTURES OF THE BATMAN!

MOST BOOKS TYPED BACKWARDS

Using a computer and four blank keyboards, and without looking at the screen, Michele Santelia (Italy, pictured right) has typed 64 books (3,361,851 words – 19,549,382 characters) backwards in their original languages, including *The Odyssey* and *Macbeth*. He completed reverse-typing the volumes of the Dead Sea Scrolls in Ancient Hebrew on 26 July 2007.

TV HEAVEN

GREATEST EVER TV AUDIENCES

COMEDY
The final episode of *M*A*S*H* (CBS, USA) – *Goodbye, Farewell and Amen* – had an estimated audience of 125 million people when it aired on 28 February 1983.

LIVE BROADCAST
An estimated 2.5 billion people watched the funeral of Diana, Princess of Wales (UK, 1961–97), broadcast live from Westminster Abbey, London, UK, on 6 September 1997.

SERIES
At its peak of popularity, *Baywatch* (NBC, then syndicated, USA) had an estimated weekly audience of more than 1.1 billion people in 142 countries in 1996.

FOOTBALL
An estimated 300 million viewers watched Italy beat France in the 2006 FIFA World Cup football final in Germany on 9 July.

AMERICAN FOOTBALL
138.5 million viewers watched the NBC transmission of Super Bowl XXX on 28 January 1996.

HIGHEST ANNUAL EARNINGS BY A TV ACTOR
Jerry Seinfeld earned an estimated $267 million (£159.5 million) in 1998 according to the 1999 Forbes Celebrity 100 list, the highest annual earnings ever by a television or film actor.

HIGHEST ANNUAL EARNINGS FOR A TELEVISION ACTRESS
Helen Hunt, the star of *Mad About You* (1992–99), became the world's wealthiest TV actress with annual earnings estimated at $31 million (£18.7 million) in 1999, according to the Forbes 2000 list.

HIGHEST PAID TV PRODUCER
Ally McBeal creator David E. Kelley (USA) became the highest paid TV producer ever after a $300 million (£185 million) six-year deal with Twentieth Century Fox Television (USA) in January 2000.

HIGHEST PAID TELEVISION CAST
According to Forbes' Celebrity 100, the cast of *The Sopranos* (HBO, USA) earned a combined salary of $52 million (£26 million) for the seventh series of the New Jersey-based Mob drama. James Gandolfini (USA), who plays Mob boss Tony Soprano, reportedly secured himself a $1 million (£505,000) fee for each of the last eight episodes.

HIGHEST ANNUAL EARNINGS BY A TV CHAT SHOW HOST
Oprah Winfrey (USA) continually tops the list of the world's top-earning television chat show hosts; according to Forbes, Oprah earned $225 million (£130 million) in 2005.

MOST EXPENSIVE TV PILOT
The production budget for the two-hour pilot of *Lost* (ABC, USA), which first aired on 22 September 2004, was

DID YOU KNOW?
The **largest TV telephone vote** was for the Season 6 finale of *American Idol*, when 74,030,147 votes were cast by telephone and text messaging from viewers selecting the winner of the singing contest. The results were announced on 22 May 2007 with Jordin Sparks (USA) declared the winner.

★ MOST WATCHED CURRENT TV SHOW (USA)
The Wednesday night episodes of *American Idol* broadcast in 2007 were watched by 17.3% of homes in the USA. This made the programme the most popular regularly scheduled TV show in the United States up to that time (as opposed to the most popular show voted for by the public).

$12 million (then £6.9 million) – far greater than the cost of most television shows. This led to Disney firing ABC Entertainment Chairman Lloyd Braun (USA) for green-lighting the show, which went on to become one of the channel's most successful ever.

LONGEST-RUNNING SHOW
US news programme *Meet the Press* (NBC, USA) was first transmitted on 6 November 1947 and subsequently each week since 12 September 1948.

★ MOST DOWNLOADED TELEVISION SHOW
According to data from the peer-to-peer (P2P) media site Mininova, the TV show most frequently downloaded in 2007 using BitTorrent protocol is *Heroes* (NBC), which was downloaded 2,439,154 times. Considering that Mininova is just one of many P2P sites, the actual number of downloads will be much higher.

Wacky Races ™ and © Hanna-Barbera

> *You can have it all. You just can't have it all at once.*
>
> Oprah Winfrey, highest paid TV personality

★ MOST WINS OF THE WACKY RACES

Four of the regular entrants to the Wacky Races – as seen in Hannah–Barbera's eponymous cartoon TV series, broadcast from 1968 to 1970 – share the record for the most wins, with four first-place victories each: Penelope Pitstop (driving the *Compact Pussycat*), the Ant Hill Mob (*Bullet Proof Bomb*), Lazy Luke and Blubber Bear (*Arkansas Chug-a-bug*) and Peter Perfect (*Turbo Terrific*). The fewest wins, of course, was zero by Dick Dastardly and Mutley (*Mean Machine*), who always came to a sticky end at the conclusion of each race.

★ MOST POPULAR CURRENT TV SHOW

According to TV.com, a CNET Networks Entertainment website, the most popular TV show as of February 2008 – with a review score of 9.4 out of 10 – is the hospital drama *House* (Fox, USA), starring Hugh Laurie (UK) as the unconventional, maverick doctor Gregory House.

LONGEST TV COMMERCIAL

A television commercial advertising Lipton Ice Tea Green (Unilver Bestfoods, Netherlands) lasted for 24 minutes and was broadcast by the Yorin TV channel, the Netherlands, on 27 March 2005.

MOST CHARACTERS VOICED BY ONE ARTIST IN A TV CARTOON SERIES

Kara Tritton (UK) voiced 198 different cartoon characters in the same TV show, the most by a single artist. The characters appeared in *Blues Clues* (Nick Jr., UK), which ran for 75 episodes over six series, with episode 75 first broadcast on the Nickelodeon Channel on 15 March 2003.

MOST SUCCESSFUL TV SOAP (EVER)

Dallas (CBS, USA) began in 1978 as a mini-series and went on to become the most successful soap opera of all time. By 1980, it was watched by an estimated 83 million people in the USA – giving it a record 76% share of the TV audience – and had been seen in more than 90 countries. The last episode aired in the USA on 3 May 1991.

★ LONGEST TV TALK SHOW MARATHON

Kristijan Petrovic (Croatia) continuously interviewed and presented on live television for 36 hr 15 min on 27–8 August 2007. The marathon talk show took place on VTV Television in Varazdin, Croatia.

★ MOST WATCHED TV SHOW ONLINE

Market research analyst Hitwise names *Deal or No Deal* (NBC, pictured) as the TV show most commonly watched online, taking 15.46% of the total online television viewership.

MOST HOURS LIVE ON TV IN ONE WEEK

Mino Monta (Japan) regularly hosts 11 live-broadcast programmes each week. He appears on TV for a total of 21 hours and 42 minutes weekly and has earned the sobriquet "host among hosts".

www.

CIRCUS SKILLS

MOST...

★ CANDLES EXTINGUISHED BY A WHIP IN ONE MINUTE

Jai Wancong (China) extinguished 22 candles by cracking a whip, without touching the wax, in one minute on the set of *Zheng Da Zong Yi – Guinness World Records Special* in Beijing, China, on 2 November 2007.

★ DIABOLO CATCHES IN ONE MINUTE

Wang Yueqiu (China) threw and caught a diabolo a minimum of 6 m (19 ft 8 in) high 16 times in one minute in Beijing, China, on 20 September 2007.

★ HULA HOOPS CAUGHT AND SPUN IN ONE MINUTE

The greatest number of hula hoops caught and spun in one minute is 236, achieved by Liu Rongrong (China) on the set of *Zheng Da Zong Yi – Guinness World Records Special* in Beijing, China, on 17 September 2007.

★ KNIVES THROWN IN ONE MINUTE

The record for the most knives thrown around a human target in one minute is 102 and was achieved by David Adamovich (USA) in Freeport, New York, USA, on 26 December 2007. Adamovich, who uses the name the Great Throwdini, threw his knives at Dick Haines during the attempt.

DID YOU KNOW?

Contortionists Daniel Smith, Bonnie Morgan and Leslie Tipton (all USA) together climbed into a box with an interior measuring 66.04 x 68.58 x 55.88 cm (26 x 27 x 22 in) and were able to stay inside for 2 min 55 sec in Madrid, Spain, on 5 December 2001.

★ FASTEST ESCAPE FROM A SUITCASE

Leslie Tipton (USA) escaped from a zipped suitcase in 13.31 seconds at the offices of Guinness World Records, London, UK, on 27 September 2007.

★ PEOPLE ON UNICYCLES

On 12 June 2005, 1,142 people rode unicycles simultaneously at an event organized by Andrea Hardy (Germany) at the Dultplatz in Regensburg, Germany.

★ SPEARS CAUGHT FROM A SPEAR GUN UNDER WATER IN ONE MINUTE

Anthony Kelly (Australia) successfully caught five spears fired from a gun under water in the swimming pool of the University of New England (UNE) at Armidale, New South Wales, Australia, on 16 September 2007.

★ NEW RECORD
★ UPDATED RECORD

HIGHEST SHALLOW DIVE

The loftiest shallow dive took place from an altitude of 10.7 m (35 ft 2 in) and was achieved by Darren Taylor (USA) on the set of the TV show *Kiteretsu Superman Award 2007* in Tokyo, Japan, on 25 July 2007.

Mostly what contortionists do is...
we sit on our own heads!

Leslie Tipton (USA), professional contortionist
and circus performer

★ TIGHTROPE WALKING – STEEPEST GRADIENT

Abulaiti Maijun (China) completed a 58.24-m (191-ft 0.9-in) tightrope walk, with an average slope of 34.15 degrees, in Xinjiang, China, on 24 August 2007. The record attempt took place on *Zheng Da Zong Yi – Guinness World Records Special* in Beijing, China.

FIRST...

DOUBLE-BACK SOMERSAULT

Eddie Silbon (UK) achieved the first double-back somersault on the flying-return trapeze at the Paris Hippodrome, Paris, France, in 1879.

HUMAN ARROW

Tony Zedoras (USA), billed as "Alar", performed the first human arrow trick at the Barnum & Bailey Circus in the USA in 1896.

HUMAN CANNONBALL

The first human cannonball was "Zazel", who was shot a distance of about 6.1 m (20 ft) at Westminster Aquarium, London, UK, in 1877.

FLYING-RETURN TRAPEZE ACT

The first flying-return trapeze act was performed by Jules Léotard (France) at Cirque Napoleon, Paris, France, on 12 November 1859.

The **highest trapeze act** was carried out by Mike Howard (UK), hanging from a hot-air balloon above Glastonbury and Street, Somerset, UK, between altitudes of 6,000 m and 6,200 m (19,600 ft and 20,300 ft), on 10 August 1995.

TRIPLE SOMERSAULT ON THE TRAPEZE

The first public performance of this trick took place at the Chicago Coliseum, USA, in 1920.

THREE-RING CIRCUS

The world's first three-ring circus was presented by "Lord" George Sanger (UK) in 1860.

★ FASTEST TIME TO BURST THREE BALLOONS WITH THE BACK

Julia Gunthel, aka "Zlata" (Germany), burst three balloons in 12 seconds, using just her back, on the set of *Guinness World Records: Die Größten Weltrekorde* in Cologne, Germany, on 23 November 2007.

★ SWORDS SWALLOWED SIMULTANEOUSLY

Nine members of the Sword Swallowers Association International (eight men and one woman, all from the USA) simultaneously swallowed 52 swords at Wilkes-Barre, Pennsylvania, USA, on 2 September 2005. Matt Henshaw (USA) holds the solo record, with 14 swords swallowed on 6 April 2000 at Fremantle, Perth, Australia.

★ YOUNGEST LION TAMER

Jorge Elich (Spain), the world's youngest lion tamer, has been learning his trade since the age of five. He most recently performed in this capacity for the Circus Paris in El Ejido, near Almeria, Spain, in January 2008, aged eight.

★ LONGEST TIME TO MAINTAIN A HUMAN FLAG

Dominic Lacasse (Canada) maintained the pose of a human flag for 39 seconds on the set of *Guinness World Records: Die Größten Weltrekorde* in Cologne, Germany, on 23 November 2007.

SPORTS

CONTENTS

BRETT FAVRE

Despite an inauspicious debut season in the National Football League (NFL) with the Atlanta Falcons (USA) in 1991, Brett Favre (USA) became one of the most celebrated American Football players of all time. That first season saw Favre attempt just four passes in regular play, none of which was completed. However, Favre was traded to the Green Bay Packers (USA) in 1992 and, following an injury to the regular quarterback, started the fourth game of the season on 27 September 1992. From that game until he announced his retirement on 4 March 2008, Favre started 275 consecutive games (including playoffs), the ★ **most by an NFL quarterback**. During his career with the Packers, Favre amassed a host of records, among them: the ★ **most touchdown passes** (442); the ★ **most pass attempts** (8,758); the ★ **most completed passes** (5,377); the ★ **most passing yards** (61,655 yd); and the ★ **most victories as a starting quarterback** (160).

ACTION SPORTS

MOST PARACHUTE DESCENTS

By 2007, Cheryl Stearns (USA) had done the ★ **most parachute descents by a woman**, with a total of 16,000.

Between 1961 and 2003, Don Kellner (USA) did 34,000 freefall skydives – the **most descents by a man**.

★ FASTEST 15-M SPEED CLIMBS

The fastest International Federation of Sport Climbing 15-m climb by a man is 8.76 seconds by Qixin Zhong (China) in Aviles, Spain, on 21 September 2007.

The **fastest 15-m climb by a woman** is 12.90 seconds by Li Chun-Ha (China) in Macau, China, on 30 October 2007.

★ FASTEST SPEED IN A MICROLIGHT OVER A STRAIGHT 15/25 KM COURSE BY A TEAM OF TWO

On 19 October 2005, Jiri Unzeitag and Vera Vavrinova (both Czech Republic) achieved an average speed of 274.78 km/h (170.74 mph) in a microlight over a straight 15/25 km course at Horovice, Czech Republic.

★ FASTEST PARACHUTING FREEFALL STYLE

The fastest men's parachuting Freefall Style is 5.18 seconds by Marco Pflueger (Germany) over Eisenach, Germany, on 15 September 2007. In the freefall style discipline, skydivers must complete a pre-determined set of manoeuvres in the quickest possible time.

The **fastest women's parachuting Freefall Style** is 6.10 seconds by Tatiana Osipova (Russia) over Bekescsaba, Hungary, on 19 September 1996.

★ FARTHEST FLIGHT BY A PARAGLIDER

Three pilots – Frank Brown, Marcelo Prieto and Rafael Monteiro Saladini (all Brazil) – each flew a distance of 461.6 km (286.8 miles) in a paraglider between Quixada and Duque, Brazil, on 14 November 2007.

★ FASTEST GLIDER

The highest speed achieved in a glider while setting an official FAI (Fédération Aéronautique Internationale) record is 306.8 km/h (190.6 mph) over an out-and-return course of 500 km (310 miles) by Klaus Ohlmann (Germany) on 22 December 2006 at Zapala, Argentina. He flew a Schempp-Hirth Nimbus 4 DM.

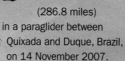

YOUNGEST KITE-SURFING CHAMPION

Gisela Pulido (Spain, above and left) won her first Kiteboard Pro World Tour (KPWT) World Championship on 4 November 2004, at the age of 10 years 294 days. She won her first professional championship on 26 August 2007, at 13 years 224 days.

★ HIGHEST SKATEBOARD RAMP JUMP INTO WATER

On 17 September 2007 in Los Angeles, California, USA, pro-skateboarder Rob Dyrdek (USA) achieved a skateboard ramp jump measuring 3.29 m (10 ft 8 in) high. It was broadcast on MTV's *The Rob & Big Show*.

★ LONGEST RAMP JUMP ON A SNOWMOBILE

The world record for the longest ramp jump on a snowmobile is 80.31 m (263 ft 6 in) and was set by Ross Mercer (Canada) in Steamboat Springs, Colorado, USA, on 10 March 2007.

★ LARGEST PARACHUTE HEAD-DOWN FORMATION

On 3 August 2007, 69 parachutists from across the globe jumped in a freeflying head-down formation over Chicago, Illinois, USA.

★ MOST WINS OF THE CLASS 1 WORLD POWERBOAT CHAMPIONSHIP BY A TEAM

Bjorn Rune Gjelsten (Norway) and Steve Curtis (UK) won the Class 1 World Powerboat Championships five times (in 1998, 2002–04 and 2006).

★ MOST WINS OF THE CLASS 1 WORLD POWERBOAT CHAMPIONSHIP BY AN INDIVIDUAL

Steve Curtis (UK) won the Class 1 World Powerboat Championships six times, in 1998 and 2002–06. Curtis competed with Bjorn Rune Gjelsten (Norway) in 1998, 2002–04 and 2006, and with Bard Eker (Norway) in 2005.

★ LONGEST INDOOR FREEFALL

The longest indoor freefall is 1 hr 18 min 22 sec and was achieved by Andy Scott (UK) at the Airkix Windtunnel, Xscape Centre, Milton Keynes, UK, on 8 March 2007.

★ FASTEST STREET LUGE

Streetluger Joel "Gravity" King (UK) reached a speed of 181.37 km/h (112.7 mph) on his jet engine-powered street luge at Bentwaters Airfield, UK, on 28 August 2007. King shattered the previous record of 157 km/h (98 mph), which had been held by Billy Copeland (USA) since May 2001.

AMERICAN FOOTBALL

★ MOST CONSECUTIVE NFL GAME WINS

The New England Patriots (USA) won 19 consecutive games from 17 December 2006 to 29 December 2007. This included a 16-0 record in 2007, which saw them become the ★**first team in the National Football League (NFL) to achieve an undefeated regular season** since the league went to a 16-game schedule in 1978.

★ MOST YARDS PASSING IN AN NFL GAME BY A ROOKIE QUARTERBACK

Playing for the Arizona Cardinals (USA), rookie quarterback Matt Leinart (USA) passed for 370 m (405 yd) against the Minnesota Vikings (USA) at the Metrodome in Minneapolis, Minnesota, USA, on 26 November 2006.

★ FASTEST NFL PLAYER TO REACH 400 CATCHES

Anquan Boldin (USA) needed just 67 games to reach 400 catches in his career, which he achieved on 24 December 2007.

★ MOST CONSECUTIVE NFL GAMES PLAYED

Punter Jeff Feagles (USA) has played a record 320 consecutive NFL games. His long career has taken in stints at the New England Patriots (1988–89), Philadelphia Eagles (1990–93),

★ OLDEST PAIR OF STARTING QUARTERBACKS

The oldest starting quarterback match-up in NFL history was formed by 44-year-old Vinny Testaverde (above right) of the Carolina Panthers and 38-year-old Brett Favre of the Green Bay Packers (all USA), on 18 November 2007.

Arizona Cardinals (1994–97), Seattle Seahawks (1998–2002) and New York Giants (2002–07). When Feagles appeared for the New York Giants in Super Bowl XLII on 3 February 2008, aged 41 years 333 days, he became the ★**oldest player in Super Bowl history**.

FACT

Aged 44 years 19 days, Vinny Testaverde (USA) became the **oldest starting quarterback to win a game**, when he led the Carolina Panthers to a 31-14 win over the San Francisco 49ers (USA) at the Bank of America Stadium, Charlotte, North Carolina, USA, on 2 December 2007.

★ HIGHEST SCORE IN AN NFL EUROPA WORLD BOWL

When the Hamburg Sea Devils defeated the Frankfurt Galaxy (both Germany) 37-28 in World Bowl XV at the Commerzbank-Arena in Frankfurt, Germany, on 23 June 2007, their combined score of 65 made the game the highest scoring in World Bowl history.

★ NEW RECORD
★ UPDATED RECORD

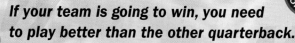

If your team is going to win, you need to play better than the other quarterback.

Peyton Manning, record-breaking quarterback

★ MOST TOUCHDOWN CATCHES IN AN NFL SEASON

Randy Moss (USA) made 23 touchdown catches for the New England Patriots during the 2007 NFL season. The previous record of 22 was established by Jerry Rice (USA) of the San Francisco 49ers in 1987.

★ MOST TOUCHDOWN PASSES IN AN NFL CAREER

Brett Favre (USA) completed 442 touchdown passes in a career that lasted from 1992 to 2008.

★ MOST YARDS GAINED RUSHING IN AN NFL SEASON

Eric Dickerson (USA) recorded the most yards gained rushing in an NFL season with 1,924 m (2,105 yd) when playing for the Los Angeles Rams (USA) in the 1984 season.

★ MOST NFL GAMES PLAYED BY AN INDIVIDUAL

Morten Andersen (Denmark) has played in 382 games during his NFL career as a place kicker with the New Orleans Saints, Atlanta Falcons, New York Giants, Kansas Chiefs and Minnesota Vikings (all USA) since 1982.

★ HIGHEST NET PUNTING AVERAGE (SEASON)

Shane Lechler (USA) had a net punting average of 37.58 m (41 yd 3 in) playing for the Oakland Raiders (USA) in 2007.

★ MOST TIMES SACKED IN AN NFL CAREER

John Elway (USA) was sacked 516 times during his career with the Denver Broncos (USA) from 1983 to 1998.

★ MOST SEASONS PASSING 4,000 YARDS IN AN NFL CAREER

Peyton Manning (USA) of the Indianapolis Colts (USA) set an NFL record in 2007 by reaching 4,000 passing yards in a season for the eighth time in his illustrious career.

★ MOST CONSECUTIVE EXTRA POINTS BY AN INDIVIDUAL IN THE NFL

Jeff Wilkins (USA) has kicked 371 consecutive extra points since 1999, equalling the record set by Jason Elam (USA) from 1993 to 2002.

★ MOST TOUCHDOWN PASSES IN AN NFL SEASON

Tom Brady (USA) threw 50 touchdown passes playing for the New England Patriots during the 2007 season, surpassing the previous score of 49 by Peyton Manning (USA) in 2004.

★ FIRST NFL REGULAR-SEASON GAME PLAYED IN EUROPE

On 28 October 2007, the Miami Dolphins (USA) played the New York Giants at Wembley Stadium in London, UK, in what was the first NFL regular-season game to be played in Europe. The New York Giants ran out 13-10 winners in a game played in front of 81,176 fans.

MOST FIELD GOALS BY AN INDIVIDUAL IN AN NFL GAME

Rob Bironas (USA) scored eight field goals for the Tennessee Titans in an NFL game against the Houston Texans (both USA) on 21 October 2007.

SUPER BOWL STATS

ATTENDANCE

The **largest attendance at a Super Bowl** is 103,985 for Super Bowl XIV between the Pittsburgh Steelers (USA) and the LA Rams at the Rose Bowl, Pasadena, California, USA, on 20 January 1980.

WINS

The **most Super Bowl wins by a player** is five by Charles Hayley (USA), who played for the San Francisco 49ers in 1989–90 and the Dallas Cowboys (USA) in 1993–94 and 1996.

MVP AWARDS

The **person with the most Most Valuable Player (MVP) awards** is San Francisco 49ers quarterback Joe Montana (USA), who was voted MVP in three Super Bowls: 1982, 1985 and 1990.

ATHLETICS

SPRINT SPEED

When Usain Bolt (Jamaica) ran 100 m in 9.72 seconds in 2008 (see below), his average speed was 37.03 km/h (23.01 mph). When Michael Johnson (USA) ran 200 m in 19.32 seconds in 1996, he averaged 37.26 km/h (23.15 mph). This makes Johnson – in theory, at least – the **fastest man in history**.

★ **NEW RECORD**
⋆ **UPDATED RECORD**

★ FASTEST 100 M (MALE)

Jamaica's Usain Bolt ran the 100 m in 9.72 seconds at the Reebok Grand Prix in Icahn Stadium, New York City, USA, on 31 May 2008. He broke the previous record, held by fellow Jamaican Asafa Powell, by 0.02 seconds to become the "world's fastest man".

TRACK & FIELD

FASTEST INDOOR 4 X 800 M RELAY (WOMEN)

Moskovskaya Region (Anna Balakshina, Natalya Pantelyeva, Anna Emashova, Olesya Chumakova; all Russia) ran the 4 x 800 m relay in 8 min 18.54 sec at an indoor event in Volgograd, Russia, on 11 February 2007.

⋆ FASTEST INDOOR 1,500 M (FEMALE)

Yelena Soboleva (Russia) ran 1,500 m in 3 min 57.71 sec at an indoor event held in Valencia, Spain, on 9 March 2008, cutting over one quarter of a second off the previous record of 3 min 58.05 sec, which she had set just 28 days earlier.

⋆ FASTEST INDOOR 3,000 M (FEMALE)

Meseret Defar (Ethiopia) ran 3,000 m, indoors, in 8 min 23.72 sec at the Sparkassen Cup in Stuttgart, Germany, on 3 February 2007.

⋆ FASTEST 5,000 M (FEMALE)

Meseret Defar (Ethiopia) ran 5,000 m in 14 min 16.63 sec in Oslo, Norway, on 15 June 2007, knocking nearly eight seconds off the previous record, which she had set a year earlier.

LONGEST HAMMER THROW (FEMALE)

Tatyana Lysenko (Russia) recorded a hammer throw of 77.8 m (255 ft 3 in) at an event in Tallinn, Estonia, on 15 August 2006.

★ FARTHEST DISTANCE RUN IN ONE HOUR (MALE)

Haile Gebrselassie (Ethiopia) ran 21,285 m in one hour in Ostrava, Czech Republic, on 27 June 2007. On his way to the one hour record, Gebrselassie broke the record for the ★ **fastest 20,000 m**, which he achieved in a time of 56 min 26 sec.

⋆ HIGHEST INDOOR POLE VAULT (FEMALE)

Yelena Isinbayeva (Russia) completed a 4.95-m pole vault at an indoor event in Donetsk, Ukraine, on 16 February 2008.

ROAD

⋆ FASTEST 20 KM ROAD WALK (MALE)

Vladimir Kanaykin (Russia) walked 20 km in 1 hr 17 min 16 sec in the final of the IAAF Race Walking Challenge in Saransk, Russia, on 29 September 2007.

★ MOST WORLD CROSS COUNTRY CHAMPIONSHIP WINS (MALE)

Kenenisa Bekele (Ethiopia) has won the World Cross Country Championship, long course, on six occasions: in 2002–06 and 2008. Bekele has also won the short course title a record five times: 2002–06.

★ FASTEST INDOOR 5,000 M (FEMALE)

Tirunesh Dibaba (Ethiopia) ran the fastest indoor 5,000 m when she recorded a time of 14 min 27.42 sec at the Boston Indoor Games in Boston, USA, on 27 January 2007.

★ MOST HALF MARATHON WORLD CHAMPIONSHIPS TEAM WINS (WOMEN)

Romania has won the women's IAAF Half Marathon World Championships team event on seven occasions: in 1993–97, 2000 and 2005.

★ MOST WINS OF THE WORLD ROAD RUNNING CHAMPIONSHIPS BY A TEAM

Kenya won both the men's and women's team events at the World Road Running Championships in 2006 and 2007.

FASTEST 20 KM ROAD WALK (FEMALE)

Olimpiada Ivanova (Russia) completed a 20 km road walk in 1 hr 25 min 41 sec in Helsinki, Finland, on 7 August 2005.

★ MOST 50 KM WORLD RACE WALKING CUP WINS (MALE)

Since the inaugural competition was held in 1961, two male walkers have

X-REF

Are you inspired by the commitment and dedication it takes to become a world-record-breaking athlete? Why not check out **pp.98–99** for a host of very different **Inspirational Acts**?

★ MOST EUROPEAN CUP WINS (WOMEN)

Russia has won the women's European Cup on 13 occasions: in 1993, 1995, and each year from 1997 to 2007.

each won the 50 km event at the World Race Walking Cup on three occasions: Christoph Hohne (East Germany) was victorious in 1965, 1967 and 1970; and Raul Gonzalez (Mexico) was champion in 1977, 1981 and 1983.

★ FASTEST 20 KM ROAD RUN (FEMALE)

Lornah Kiplagat (Netherlands) ran 20 km in 1 hr 2 min 57 sec in Udine, Italy, on 14 October 2007.

★ MOST EUROPEAN CUP WINS (MEN)

Germany has won the men's European Cup on seven occasions: in 1994–96, 1999, 2002 and 2004–05.

CROSS COUNTRY

MOST WORLD CROSS COUNTRY CHAMPIONSHIP WINS (FEMALE)

Grete Waitz (Norway) has won the World Cross Country Championship, long course, on five occasions: in 1978–81 and 1983.

OUTDOOR HURDLES

WOMEN

Yordanka Donkova (Bulgaria) ran the 100 m hurdles in 12.21 seconds on 20 August 1988.

MEN

Xiang Liu (China) ran the 110 m hurdles in 12.88 seconds on 11 July 2006.

★ FASTEST INDOOR 60 M HURDLES (FEMALE)

Susanna Kallur (Sweden) ran the 60 m hurdles, indoors, in 7.68 sec in Karlsruhe, Germany, on 10 February 2008.

MARATHONS

★ FASTEST TIME TO COMPLETE A MARATHON IN ORBIT

NASA astronaut Sunita Williams (USA) achieved the fastest time to complete a marathon in orbit above Earth on board the *International Space Station*. Ms Williams, who ran the 42 km (26.2 miles) strapped to a treadmill with bungy cord, competed as an official entrant of the 111th Boston Marathon (USA) on 16 April 2007, finishing in a time of 4 hr 24 min.

★ TALLEST COSTUME WORN

The tallest costume worn while running a marathon measured 4.27 m (14 ft) high and was worn by Tim Rogers (UK) in aid of WellChild at the Flora London Marathon, London, UK, on 22 April 2007.

★ MOST TRIATHLONS COMPLETED

The most triathlons completed by one athlete is 250 by James "Flip" Lyle (USA) up to 18 March 2006.

FASTEST MARATHON BY A WOMAN

Paula Radcliffe (UK) ran the London Marathon in 2 hr 15 min 25 sec on 13 April 2003 in London, UK.

★ FASTEST HALF MARATHONS

Lornah Kiplagat (Netherlands) ran the ladies' half marathon in 1 hr 6 min 25 sec in Udine, Italy, on 14 October 2007.

The **men's half marathon record** is held by Samuel Wanjiru Kamau (Kenya), who clocked 58 min 35 sec in The Hague, the Netherlands, on 17 March 2007.

MARATHONS ON EACH OF THE SEVEN CONTINENTS

The ★ **shortest time to finish a marathon on each of the seven continents by a man** is 29 days 16 hr 17 min by Richard Takata (Canada), between 4 February and 6 March 2007.

The ★ **shortest time to finish a marathon on each continent by a woman** Is 48 days 15 hr 49 min 38 sec by Dawn Hamlin (USA) between between 18 January and 5 March 2008.

The **fastest aggregate time for a man to run a marathon on each continent** is 34 hr 23 min 8 sec by Tim Rogers (UK) from 13 February to 23 May 1999.

The ★ **fastest aggregate time for a woman** is 28 hr 41 min 24 sec by Jeanne Stawiecki (USA), between 8 October 2006 and 26 February 2007.

1. Platz

★ FASTEST MARATHON

Haile Gebrselassie and Gete Wami (both Ethiopia) celebrate their victories as winners of the 34th Berlin Marathon on 30 September 2007 in Berlin, Germany. Gebrselassie became the world's **fastest male marathon runner** after he finished in a time of 2 hr 4 min 26 sec at this event.

Inaugurated in 2006, the **World Marathon Majors** is a competition encompassing the five annual marathon races in Berlin (Germany), London (UK), New York City, Boston and Chicago (all USA), with athletes scoring points for top five finishes over two calendar years. The World Championship and Olympic marathons are also included in the years that they are run. The winner of the first women's championship in 2006–07 was Gete Wami, with 80 points.

★ **NEW RECORD**
★ **UPDATED RECORD**

FLORA
LONDON MARATHON
2008

★ DRESSED AS A CLOWN

Jason Westmoreland (UK) ran the Flora London Marathon 2008 in London, UK, on 13 April 2008. He did so dressed as a clown and finished in 3 hr 24 min 4 sec.

FLORA LONDON MARATHON

Other Guinness World Records broken:

Fastest marathon...

★ **by a linked team:** Oliver Holland, James Kennedy, James Wrighton, Eoghan Murray and Nathan Jones: 3 hr 38 min 24 sec

★ **as a film character:** James McComish (Darth Maul): 3 hr 55 min 22 sec

★ **dressed as Santa:** Ian Sharman: 3 hr 12 min 27 sec

★ **dressed as a superheroine:** Christina Tomlinson (Supergirl): 3 hr 13 min 33 sec

★ **in a fireman's uniform:** Mark Rogers and Paul Bartlett: 5 hr 36 min 12 sec

★ **by a group of Maasai warriors:** 5 hr 24 min 47 sec

★ FASTEST MARATHON ON STILTS

Michelle Frost (UK) ran the entire Flora London Marathon 2008 on stilts. She finished in a time of 8 hr 25 min on 13 April 2008 in London, UK.

★ IN MILITARY UNIFORM

The record for the fastest marathon in a military uniform is 5 hr 11 min 42 sec and was achieved by Myles Morson (UK) at the Flora London Marathon 2008, in London, UK.

★ DRIBBLING A BASKETBALL

Jean-Yves Kanyamibwa (UK) ran the Flora London Marathon 2008 dribbling a basketball in 4 hr 30 min 29 sec.

★ MOST LINKED RUNNERS

A group of 24 Metropolitan Police Officers ran the Flora London Marathon 2008 while being linked with plastic chains that had been taped in place. They remained linked for the entire race in London, UK, on 13 April 2008.

★ KNITTING A SCARF

The longest scarf knitted by a marathon runner while running a marathon is 1.62 m (5 ft 2 in) and was achieved by Susie Hewer (UK) at the Flora London Marathon on 13 April 2008.

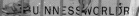

AUTOSPORTS

Who would have thought I'd be ranked number two in my first year of Formula One?

Lewis Hamilton

LEWIS HAMILTON

The 2007 season saw rookie driver Lewis Hamilton (UK) take Formula One by storm.

Although he missed out on the F1 title, Hamilton still set a number of F1 records.

In securing six pole positions, Hamilton set a new mark for ★ **most pole positions in a rookie season**; and in winning four races, he claimed a share of the F1 record for **most wins in a season by a rookie**, also held by Jacques Villeneuve (Canada), who achieved the feat in 1996.

★ MOST CONSECUTIVE SEASONS WINNING MULTIPLE RACES TO START A NASCAR CAREER

Tony Stewart (USA) has won multiple races in nine consecutive seasons from 1999 to 2007, the longest such streak at the start of a driver's career in National Association for Stock Car Auto Racing (NASCAR).

NASCAR

HIGHEST CAREER EARNINGS

The highest career earnings in NASCAR is $89,397,060 (£44,778,987) by Jeff Gordon (USA) up to and including the 2007 season.

★ MOST RESTRICTOR PLATE VICTORIES (CAREER)

The most career victories at restrictor plate tracks is 12 by Jeff Gordon (USA) up to the 2007 season. Gordon surpassed the previous mark held by Dale Earnhardt (USA) of 11 plate victories by winning at the Talladega Superspeedway in Talladega, Alabama, USA, on 7 October 2007. Restrictor plates are devices installed on cars at certain tracks to increase safety by reducing engine power.

★ MOST TOP TEN FINISHES IN ONE YEAR

The NASCAR record for most top ten finishes in one year in the modern era (1972 to present) is 30 by Jeff Gordon (USA) in 2007. The all-time record is 43 by Richard Petty (USA) in 1964.

FACT

The **largest margin of victory by a Busch Series champion** is 824 points by Kevin Harvick (USA) in 2006. That season, Harvick clinched the title with four races remaining, setting a record for **earliest clinch of the championship** on 13 October 2006.

★ HIGHEST CAREER EARNINGS (TRUCK SERIES)

Jack Sprague (USA) holds the NASCAR Truck Series record for most career earnings with $6,762,094 (£3,387,132) up to and including the 2007 season.

★ MOST POLES WON IN A CAREER (TRUCK SERIES)

Mike Skinner (USA) has had more NASCAR Truck Series pole positions in his career than any other driver, with 43 up to and including the 2007 season.

MOST WINS IN A CAREER (TRUCK SERIES)

Ron Hornaday Jr (USA) has had 33 wins in his NASCAR Truck Series career up to and including the 2007 season.

★ NEW RECORD
★ UPDATED RECORD

INDYCAR

★ MOST RACE STARTS

Scott Sharp (USA) started 146 IndyCar Series races in a career stretching from 1996 to 2007.

★ MOST RACES WON IN AN INDYCAR SERIES CAREER

Sam Hornish Jr (USA) has had 19 IndyCar Series wins in a career that began in 2000.

MOST CONSECUTIVE NASCAR WINS

Eight drivers have recorded four consecutive victories in the modern NASCAR era (since 1972); the most recent of these is Jimmie Johnson (USA, above) in 2007. Richard Petty (USA) holds the all-time record for consecutive wins, with 10 victories in a row in 1967.

★ MOST POLES WON IN A CAREER

The IndyCar Series record for most poles won in a career is 23 by Helio Castroneves (Brazil) from 2001 to 2007.

★ MOST LAPS LED IN A SINGLE RACE BY THE RACE WINNER

The most laps led in a single race by the race winner is 242 by Dario Franchitti (Scotland) at Richmond International Raceway in Richmond, Virginia, USA, on 30 June 2007.

DRAG RACING

★ MOST WINS IN A NATIONAL HOT ROD ASSOCIATION (NHRA) DRAG RACING CAREER

John Force (USA) has had more career wins than any drag racer, with 125 victories up to and including 2007.

★ FASTEST SPEED IN PRO STOCK (CAR), NHRA DRAG RACING

For a petrol-driven, piston-engined car (Pro Stock), the highest terminal velocity is 340.61 km/h (211.69 mph) by Jason Line (USA) at Gainesville, Florida, USA, on 18 March 2007.

★ FASTEST SPEED IN FUNNY CAR, NHRA DRAG RACING

Mike Ashley (USA) reached a terminal velocity of 537.02 km/h (334.32 mph) in a Dodge Charger at Las Vegas, Nevada, USA, on 13 April 2007.

MOST CONSECUTIVE INDYCAR SERIES WINS

Three drivers have won three consecutive IndyCar Series races: Scott Dixon (New Zealand, above) in 2007, Dan Wheldon (UK) in 2005 and Kenny Brack (Sweden) in 1998.

BALL SPORTS

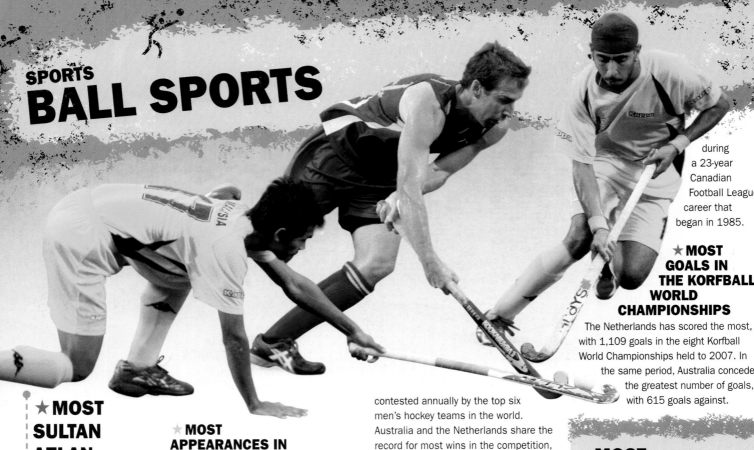

during a 23-year Canadian Football League career that began in 1985.

★ MOST GOALS IN THE KORFBALL WORLD CHAMPIONSHIPS

The Netherlands has scored the most, with 1,109 goals in the eight Korfball World Championships held to 2007. In the same period, Australia conceded the greatest number of goals, with 615 goals against.

★ MOST SULTAN AZLAN SHAH CUPS

The Sultan Azlan Shah Cup is an annual international field hockey tournament held in Malaysia. Australia has lifted the cup more times than any other nation, winning in 1983, 1998, 2004, 2005 and 2007.

HANDBALL CHAMPIONS

The ★ most African Handball Championships won by a men's team is seven, by Tunisia.

The ★ most Asian Handball Championships won by a men's team is also seven, by South Korea.

★ MOST APPEARANCES IN INTERNATIONAL HOCKEY MATCHES (MALE)

Jeroen Delmee (Netherlands) made a record 373 international appearances for the Netherlands from 1994 to 2008.

★ MOST MEN'S CHAMPIONS TROPHY WINS

The Champions Trophy was first held in 1978 and since 1980 has been contested annually by the top six men's hockey teams in the world. Australia and the Netherlands share the record for most wins in the competition, with eight victories each to date.

★ LARGEST STREET HOCKEY TOURNAMENT

A total of 2,010 players in 192 teams took part in a street hockey tournament in Ladysmith, British Columbia, Canada, on 3 June 2007.

★ MOST WOMEN'S HANDBALL WORLD CHAMPIONSHIPS

Three women's titles have been won by three teams: East Germany in 1971, 1975 and 1978; the USSR in 1982, 1986 and 1990; and Russia in 2001, 2005 and 2007. Pictured is Russia's Irina Bliznova.

★ MOST PASS COMPLETIONS BY A QUARTERBACK IN CANADIAN FOOTBALL

Quarterback Damon Allen (USA) set a new professional football record for the most career pass completions with 5,158 up to the 2007 season. Allen has played for seven teams

★ MOST TOUCHDOWNS IN A CANADIAN FOOTBALL CAREER

By 2007, Milt Stegall (USA) had scored 144 touchdowns for Canadian Football League team the Winnipeg Blue Bombers. His career began in 1995.

★MOST CONSECUTIVE MATCHES PLAYED IN THE AFL FROM DEBUT

Jared Crouch (Australia) played 194 consecutive Australian Football League (AFL) matches for the Sydney Swans from his debut on 10 May 1998 until he was forced out of the team through injury in July 2006.

★MOST WINS OF ALL-IRELAND HURLING FINALS

Two teams have won 30 All-Ireland Hurling Championships: Cork between 1890 and 2005; and Kilkenny between 1904 and 2007.

★OLDEST NETBALL CLUB

Poly Netball Club, London, UK, is the oldest netball club in continuous existence. The club was founded in 1907 and celebrated its centenary in 2007.

★MOST NATIONAL BANK CUP WINS

The National Bank Cup is the elite national tournament in New Zealand netball. Melbourne Southern Sting (New Zealand) has won the cup on seven occasions: every season from 1999 to 2004 and again in 2007.

MOST NETBALL WORLD TITLES

Australia has won the Netball World Championships a record nine times: 1963, 1971, 1975, 1979 (shared), 1983, 1991, 1995, 1999 and 2007. The only other teams to have won the title are New Zealand in 1967, 1979 (shared), 1987 and 2003; and Trinidad & Tobago, who shared the title in 1979. Pictured is Australia's Mo'onia Gerrard.

★GREATEST PRIZE MONEY FOR A BEACH VOLLEYBALL WORLD TOUR

A record $7.37 million (£3.66 million) prize money fund was available for the Federation Internationale de Volleyball beach volleyball world tour in 2007.

★HIGHEST CAREER EARNINGS, AVP TOUR, BEACH VOLLEYBALL

Holly McPeak (USA) has won $1,466,396 (£728,498) in official AVP Tour earnings through to the end of the 2007 season, the **highest career earnings by an AVP**

★MOST AVP BEST DEFENSIVE PLAYER AWARDS

Two players have won the Association of Volleyball Professionals (AVP) Pro Beach Tour defensive player of the year award for a male player on four occasions: Mike Dodd (USA) in 1994–97; and Todd Rogers (USA, pictured) in 2004–2007.

X-REF

If you are interested in all things Australian, take a look a the **Australia** page in our **Gazetteer** section on **p.276**. If it's more ball sports that you're lookng for, then why not check out our four fabulous pages of **Football**, which begin on **p.200**?

Tour female player.

Karch Kiraly (USA) has won $3,198,748 (£1,602,330) in official AVP Tour earnings through to the end of the 2007 season, the **highest career earnings by an AVP Tour male player**.

MOST BROWNLOW MEDAL WINS

The most wins of the Brownlow Medal in the Australian Football League is three, held jointly by Haydn Bunton in 1931, 1932 and 1935; Dick Reynolds in 1934, 1937 and 1938; Bob Skilton in 1959, 1963 and 1968; and Ian Stewart in 1965, 1966 and 1971 (all Australia).

★MOST GAELIC FOOTBALL ALL-IRELAND FINAL WINS

The greatest number of All-Ireland Championships won by one team is 35, by Kerry between 1903 and 2007.

★ NEW RECORD
UPDATED RECORD

SPORTS
BASEBALL

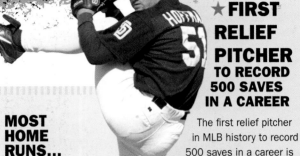

★ FIRST RELIEF PITCHER TO RECORD 500 SAVES IN A CAREER

The first relief pitcher in MLB history to record 500 saves in a career is Trevor Hoffman (USA) playing for the Florida Marlins and San Diego Padres from 1993 to 2007.

MOST HOME RUNS...

★ In a career
Barry Bonds (USA) clocked up 762 home runs playing for the Pittsburgh Pirates and San Francisco Giants from 1986 to 2007.

In a match by one player
Robert Lincoln "Bobby" Lowe (USA) achieved four home runs for Boston v. Cincinnati on 30 May 1894. The same feat has been achieved many times since then.

★ By a designated hitter
Frank Thomas (USA) has recorded 261 playing for the Chicago White Sox, Oakland Athletics and Toronto Blue Jays (Canada) from 1990 to 2007.

★ In a post-season career
Manny Ramirez (Dominican Republic) has slugged 24 playing for the Cleveland Indians and Boston Red Sox since 1995.

From start of career under one manager
Chipper Jones (USA) recorded 386 playing for manager Bobby Cox (USA) of the Atlanta Braves from 1993 to 2007.

★ MOST VALUABLE BASEBALL FRANCHISE

The New York Yankees are valued at $1.026 billion (£525 million), according to a *Forbes* magazine report in 2007, making them the first US Major League Baseball (MLB) team – and the first baseball franchise – to pass the $1 billion (£512 million) mark.

★ FIRST PROFESSIONAL FRANCHISE TO LOSE 10,000 MATCHES

The Philadelphia Phillies became the first professional sports franchise ever to lose 10,000 games, dropping a 10–2 decision to the St Louis Cardinals on 15 July 2007. The franchise has a long history of losing, having played – and lost – its first game in May 1883. The Phillies have won only one World Series (1980) in 125 years.

★ MOST STRIKEOUTS IN A GAME BY A BATTER

The MLB record for most times striking out in a game is five by many players, most recently Craig Monroe (USA) of the Detroit Tigers on 14 June 2007.

★ MOST SAVES IN A CAREER

The MLB record for most career saves is 524, recorded by Trevor Hoffman (USA) playing for the Florida Marlins and San Diego Padres from 1993 to 2007.

★ MOST GOLD GLOVE AWARDS IN A CAREER

The Gold Glove is an MLB award for fielding excellence. The most Gold Gloves won in a career is 17 by Greg Maddux (USA) between 1990 and 2007, while playing for the Chicago Cubs, Atlanta Braves, Los Angeles Dodgers and San Diego Padres.

★ YOUNGEST PERSON TO HIT 500 HOME RUNS (CAREER)

At 32 years 8 days old, Alex Rodriguez (USA, b. 27 July 1975) became the youngest player in baseball history to reach 500 career home runs. He homered off Kyle Davies (USA), pitching for the Kansas City Royals, at Yankee Stadium in Bronx, New York, USA, on 4 August 2007.

★ MOST EJECTIONS IN A CAREER

Bobby Cox (USA) has been ejected 132 times from a game while managing the Toronto Blue Jays and the Atlanta Braves from 1978 to 2007.

★ HIGHEST SLUGGING PERCENTAGE BY A ROOKIE

Ryan Braun (USA) hit a percentage of .634 while playing for the Milwaukee Brewers in 2007.

★ MOST PLATE APPEARANCES IN A SEASON

Jimmy Rollins (USA) made 778 plate appearances for the Philadelphia Phillies in 2007.

★ MOST STOLEN BASES IN A POST-SEASON CAREER

The record for most career stolen bases in the post-season is 34 by Kenny Lofton (USA), playing for several teams. Lofton surpassed the previous mark of 33 by Rickey Henderson (USA). See Awards panel below right for more of Lofton's incredible achievements.

★ YOUNGEST PERSON TO HIT 50 HOME RUNS IN A SEASON

At 23 years 139 days, Prince Fielder (USA, b. 9 May 1984) became the youngest major league player ever to hit 50 home runs in a season when he homered while playing for the Milwaukee Brewers against the St Louis Cardinals at Miller Park in Milwaukee, Wisconsin, USA, on 25 September 2007.

★ OLDEST PLAYER TO HIT A HOME RUN

At the age of 48 years 254 days, Julio Franco (Dominican Republic, b. 23 August 1958) became the oldest player in MLB history to hit a home run when he connected off Randy Johnson (USA) to help the New York Mets to a 5–3 win over the Arizona Diamondbacks at Chase Field in Phoenix, Arizona, USA, on 4 May 2007.

★ MOST BATTERS CONSECUTIVELY RETIRED BY A PITCHER

The MLB record for most consecutive batters retired is 41 by Bobby Jenks (USA) while pitching for the Chicago White Sox in several games from 17 July 2007 to 12 August 2007. He shares this record with Jim Barr (USA), who pitched two straight shutouts for the San Francisco Giants against the Pittsburgh Pirates on 23 August 1972 and against the St Louis Cardinals on 29 August 1972. Barr retired the last 21 Pirates he faced and the first 20 Cardinals.

★ MOST TIMES HIT BY A PITCH IN A CAREER

Craig Biggio (USA) was hit 285 times playing for the Houston Astros from 1988 to 2007 – the most times in a career.

★ MOST BASE ON BALLS IN A MAJOR LEAGUE BASEBALL CAREER

The record for most bases on balls in a career is 2,558 by Barry Bonds (USA), playing for the Pittsburgh Pirates and San Francisco Giants from 1986 to 2007.

★ MOST EXPENSIVE BASEBALL CARD SOLD

A baseball card known as T206 Honus Wagner issued by the American Tobacco Company in 1909 was sold in a deal brokered by SCP Auctions (USA) to an anonymous collector for $2.8 million (£1.37 million) in September 2007.

★ OLDEST FIELD DIAMOND

The oldest baseball diamond is Labatt Park in London, Ontario, Canada, which was established in 1877 and hosts baseball games to the present day.

KENNY LOFTON'S AWARDS

Kenny (pictured above) is a free agent MLB outfielder who has won recognition numerous times for his baseball talents:
- Six-time All-Star (1994–99)
- Four-time Gold Glove Award (1993–96)
- Five-time stolen bases league leader (1992–96)

LONGEST BASEBALL MARATHON

A baseball marathon lasting 32 hr 29 min 25 sec was played by the St Louis Chapter of the Men's Senior Baseball League at TR Hughes Ballpark, home to the River City Rascals, O'Fallon, Missouri, USA, on 13–14 October 2007. After a gruelling 92 innings, the St Louis Browns beat the St Louis Stars 119–81.

BASKETBALL

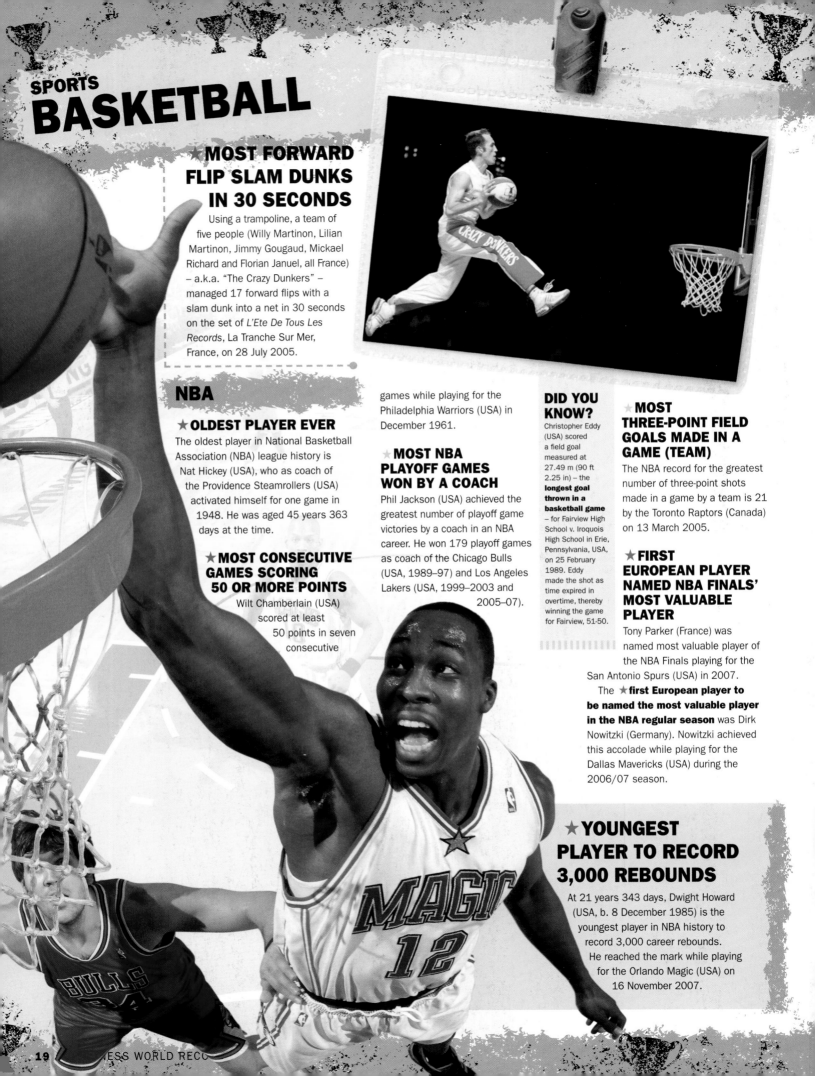

★ MOST FORWARD FLIP SLAM DUNKS IN 30 SECONDS

Using a trampoline, a team of five people (Willy Martinon, Lilian Martinon, Jimmy Gougaud, Mickael Richard and Florian Januel, all France) – a.k.a. "The Crazy Dunkers" – managed 17 forward flips with a slam dunk into a net in 30 seconds on the set of *L'Ete De Tous Les Records*, La Tranche Sur Mer, France, on 28 July 2005.

NBA

★ OLDEST PLAYER EVER

The oldest player in National Basketball Association (NBA) league history is Nat Hickey (USA), who as coach of the Providence Steamrollers (USA) activated himself for one game in 1948. He was aged 45 years 363 days at the time.

★ MOST CONSECUTIVE GAMES SCORING 50 OR MORE POINTS

Wilt Chamberlain (USA) scored at least 50 points in seven consecutive games while playing for the Philadelphia Warriors (USA) in December 1961.

★ MOST NBA PLAYOFF GAMES WON BY A COACH

Phil Jackson (USA) achieved the greatest number of playoff game victories by a coach in an NBA career. He won 179 playoff games as coach of the Chicago Bulls (USA, 1989–97) and Los Angeles Lakers (USA, 1999–2003 and 2005–07).

DID YOU KNOW?

Christopher Eddy (USA) scored a field goal measured at 27.49 m (90 ft 2.25 in) – the **longest goal thrown in a basketball game** – for Fairview High School v. Iroquois High School in Erie, Pennsylvania, USA, on 25 February 1989. Eddy made the shot as time expired in overtime, thereby winning the game for Fairview, 51-50.

★ MOST THREE-POINT FIELD GOALS MADE IN A GAME (TEAM)

The NBA record for the greatest number of three-point shots made in a game by a team is 21 by the Toronto Raptors (Canada) on 13 March 2005.

★ FIRST EUROPEAN PLAYER NAMED NBA FINALS' MOST VALUABLE PLAYER

Tony Parker (France) was named most valuable player of the NBA Finals playing for the San Antonio Spurs (USA) in 2007.

The ★ **first European player to be named the most valuable player in the NBA regular season** was Dirk Nowitzki (Germany). Nowitzki achieved this accolade while playing for the Dallas Mavericks (USA) during the 2006/07 season.

★ YOUNGEST PLAYER TO RECORD 3,000 REBOUNDS

At 21 years 343 days, Dwight Howard (USA, b. 8 December 1985) is the youngest player in NBA history to record 3,000 career rebounds. He reached the mark while playing for the Orlando Magic (USA) on 16 November 2007.

★ YOUNGEST PLAYER TO REACH 20,000 POINTS (CAREER)

While playing for the Los Angeles Lakers on 23 December 2007, Kobe Bryant (USA, b. 23 August 1978) reached 20,000 career points, aged 29 years 122 days.

WNBA

★ BIGGEST COMEBACK

The greatest comeback in Women's National Basketball Association (WNBA) playoff history is 22 points by the Indiana Fever (USA). They overcame a 39-17 second-quarter deficit to defeat the Connecticut Sun (USA) 93-88 in overtime in an Eastern Conference playoff game on 27 August 2007.

MOST...

• ★ **Games played (career)**. Vickie Johnson (USA) has played in 346 games during her career with the New York Liberty (USA) between 1997 and 2005 and the San Antonio Silver Stars (USA) in 2006 and 2007.

• ★ **Minutes played (career)**. Johnson has also played a record 10,805 minutes in her WNBA career.

• ★ **Minutes played per game (career)**. Katie Smith (USA) averaged 34.9 minutes per game over the course of her career for the Minnesota Lynx (USA) from 1995 to 2005 and the Detroit Shock (USA) from 2005 to 2007.

• **Points scored (career)**. Lisa Leslie (USA) scored 5,412 points for the Los Angeles Sparks (USA), 1997 to 2006.

• **Field goals scored (career)**. During her career with the Los Angeles Sparks, Leslie scored 2,000 field goals.

• ★ **Three-point field goals**. Katie Smith scored 598 three-point field goals playing for the Minnesota Lynx from 1995 to 2005 and the Detroit Shock from 2005 to 2007.

• ★ **Rebounds**. Lisa Leslie recorded 2,863 rebounds while playing for the Los Angeles Sparks.

★ YOUNGEST PLAYER TO SCORE 9,000 POINTS

At 22 years 252 days, LeBron James (USA, b. 30 December 1984) is the youngest player in NBA history to score 9,000 career points. He reached the mark while playing for the Cleveland Cavaliers (USA) on 18 December 2007.

• ★ **Assists**. Ticha Penicheiro (Portugal) provided 1,851 assists in 306 games for the Sacramento Monarchs (USA) between 1998 and 2007.

• ★ **Steals (career)**. The greatest number of steals in a WNBA career is 589 in 262 games by Sheryl Swoopes (USA) playing for the Houston Comets (USA) between 1998 and 2007.

• ★ **Blocks (career)**. Margo Dydek (Poland) achieved 877 blocks in 321 games playing for the Utah Starzz (1998–2002), the San Antonio Silver Stars (2003–04) and the Connecticut Sun (2005–07).

★ FIRST COACH TO WIN TITLES IN NBA AND WNBA

Paul Westhead (USA) is the first and, to date, only coach to win championships in both the NBA and WNBA. Westhead guided the Los Angeles Lakers to the NBA title in 1980 and the Phoenix Mercury (USA) to the WNBA title in 2007.

NBA ALL-STAR JAM SESSION

NBA All-Star Jam Session
provides fans the once-in-a-lifetime experience of participating in the NBA All-Star excitement, where the chance to meet, and collect free autographs from, NBA players and legends is just the beginning. Jam Sessions are non-stop basketball action, as fans can shoot, slam, dribble and drive all day, compete against their friends in skills challenges or get tips from NBA players and legends. NBA All-Star Jam Sessions allow fans to gain access to the NBA like never before!

★ MOST BOUNCES OF A BASKETBALL IN ONE MINUTE

Jordan Farmar (USA) of the Los Angeles Lakers (USA) dribbled his way to a record by bouncing a basketball 228 times in one minute at the NBA All-Star Jam Session, New Orleans, Louisiana, USA, on 16 February 2008.

★ HIGHEST FORWARD FLIP TRAMPOLINE SLAM DUNK

High Impact Squad member Jerry Burrell (USA) achieved the highest forward flip trampoline slam dunk when he reached 3.22 m (10 ft 9 in) at the NBA All-Star Jam Session, New Orleans, Louisiana, USA, on 17 February 2008.

★ LONGEST TIME SPINNING A BASKETBALL ON ONE FINGER (USING ONE HAND)

Joseph Odhiambo (USA) span a basketball on one finger using one hand for 37.46 seconds at the NBA All-Star Jam Session, New Orleans, Louisiana, USA, on 13 February 2008.

★ LONGEST TIME SPINNING A BASKETBALL ON ONE TOE

Jack Ryan (USA) span a basketball on his toe for 9.53 seconds at the NBA All-Star Jam Session, New Orleans, Louisiana, USA, on 13 February 2008.

★ LONGEST TIME SPINNING A BASKETBALL ON THE NOSE

Jack Ryan (USA) span a basketball on his nose for 4 seconds at the NBA All-Star Jam Session, New Orleans, Louisiana, USA, on 13 February 2008.

★ MOST BACKWARD FREE THROWS MADE IN ONE MINUTE

Two people have achieved three backward free throws in one minute:

Melvin Banks, wearing the NBA mascot costume Harry the Hawk, and Nicole Joseph Dumas, an NBA Jam Session spectator (both USA). Both achieved the feat at the NBA All-Star Jam Session, New Orleans, Louisiana, USA, on 17 February 2008.

★ MOST HALF-COURT SHOTS MADE IN ONE MINUTE

Chris Paul (USA) of the New Orleans Hornets (USA) made four half-court shots in one minute at the NBA All-Star Jam Session, New Orleans, Louisiana, USA, on 16 February 2008.

★ MOST SLAM DUNK BOUNCE PASSES IN 30 SECONDS

The Milwaukee Bucks Rim Rockers' (USA, main image) Kevin Vanderkolk, John Schwartz, Torie Gamez, Marcus Tyler and Matt Marzo (all USA) completed 21 slam dunk bounce passes in 30 seconds at the NBA All-Star Jam Session, New Orleans, Louisiana, USA, on 14 February 2008. Each player bounces off the trampoline and passes the ball back to the next person, who repeats the move, ending the cycle with a slam dunk.

★ MOST FREE THROWS IN ONE MINUTE FROM A WHEELCHAIR

National Wheelchair Basketball Association (NWBA) players Trooper Johnson of the Golden State Warriors and Jeff Griffin of the Utah Wheelin' Jazz (both USA) each made 25 free throws in one minute at the NBA All-Star Jam Session on 14 February 2008.

★ MOST FREE THROWS MADE IN ONE MINUTE (FEMALE)

Becky Hammon (USA) of the San Antonio Silver Stars (USA) made 38 free throws in one minute at the NBA All-Star Jam Session, New Orleans, Louisiana, USA, on 16 February 2008.

★ FARTHEST FORWARD FLIP TRAMPOLINE SLAM DUNK

Milwaukee Bucks Rim Rockers member Kevin Vanderkolk (USA) achieved a forward flip trampoline slam dunk with a distance of 5.84 m (19 ft 2 in) at the NBA All-Star Jam Session, New Orleans, Louisiana, USA, on 14 February 2008.

★ MOST UNDERHANDED HALF-COURT SHOTS MADE IN ONE MINUTE

Jason Kidd (USA) of the Dallas Mavericks (USA) made two underhanded half-court shots in one minute at the NBA All-Star Jam Session, New Orleans, Louisiana, USA, on 16 February 2008.

★ MOST BLINDFOLDED FREE THROWS MADE IN ONE MINUTE

Jack Ryan (USA) achieved five blindfolded free throws in one minute at the NBA All-Star Jam Session, New Orleans, Louisiana, USA, on 17 February 2008.

★ MOST UNDERHANDED FREE THROWS MADE IN ONE MINUTE

NBA Hall of Famer Rick Barry (USA) made 24 underhanded free throws in one minute at the NBA All-Star Jam Session, New Orleans, Louisiana, USA, on 13 February 2008.

★ MOST THREE-POINTERS MADE IN TWO MINUTES

Jason Kapono (USA) of the Toronto Raptors (Canada) scored 43 basketball three-pointers in two minutes at the NBA All-Star Jam Session, New Orleans, Louisiana, USA, on 17 February 2008.

★ NEW RECORD
★ UPDATED RECORD

CRICKET

★ MOST SIXES IN A TEST MATCH CAREER

Australian wicket-keeper/batsman Adam Gilchrist hit 100 sixes in a Test cricket career encompassing 96 matches between 1999 and 2008, the most scored by an individual batsman.

HIT FOR SIX

INTERNATIONAL
Herschelle Gibbs (South Africa) became the **first person to score six sixes in one over in an international match** against the Netherlands at Basseterre, St Kitts, on 16 March 2007.

YOUNGEST
Anthony McMahon (UK) became the **youngest player to hit six sixes in an over** playing for Chester-le-Street against Eppleton at Eppleton Cricket Club, Durham, UK, on 24 May 2003, when aged 13 years and 261 days.

TEST MATCHES

★ MOST WICKETS TAKEN IN TESTS
Muttiah Muralitharan (Sri Lanka) is the leading Test match wicket-taker, with 723 wickets (average 21.77 runs per wicket) in 118 matches from August 1992 to 22 December 2007.

★ MOST TEST CENTURIES
Sachin Tendulkar (India) has scored 39 Test match centuries between 1989 and January 2008.

HIGHEST BATTING AVERAGE IN TESTS
Sir Donald Bradman (Australia) scored an average of 99.94 runs per innings playing for Australia in 52 Tests between 1928 and 1948. (Bradman scored a total of 6,996 runs in 80 Test innings.)

★ MOST CONSECUTIVE TEST INNINGS WITHOUT SCORING A DUCK
David Gower (UK) batted for 119 consecutive Test match innings without being dismissed for a duck (zero runs) between 1982 and 1990.

★ MOST CATCHES BY A WICKET-KEEPER IN TESTS
Mark Boucher (South Africa) has taken 394 catches in 109 Tests playing for South Africa as wicket-keeper between 1997 and 2008.

★ MOST TIMES TO UMPIRE IN TESTS
Steve Bucknor (Jamaica) has officiated at a total of 122 Test matches between 1989 and February 2008.

★ MOST MAN OF THE MATCH AWARDS IN TESTS
Jacques Kallis (South Africa) has won 20 Man of the Match awards in Test cricket between 1995 and 2008.

★ MOST EXTRAS IN A TEST INNINGS
India conceded 76 extras in Pakistan's 1st innings at Bangalore, India, from 8 to 12 December 2007. The figure consisted of 35 byes, 26 leg byes and 15 no-balls.

★ MOST CATCHES BY A FIELDER IN TWENTY20 INTERNATIONALS
The most catches taken in a Twenty20 International cricket career is 11 by Ross Taylor (New Zealand) for New Zealand in 12 matches between 2006 and 2008.

★ NEW RECORD
★ UPDATED RECORD

★ MOST WICKETS IN TWENTY20 INTERNATIONALS
The most wickets taken in a Twenty20 International cricket career is 15 by three players: Nathan Bracken (Australia) for Australia in 12 matches between 2006 and 2008; Shahid Afridi (Pakistan) for Pakistan between 2005 and 2008; and Shaun Pollock (South Africa) for South Africa, also between 2005 and 2008.

I was never told how to hold a bat.

Sir Donald Bradman, the
greatest ever Test batsman

★ MOST RUNS IN TWENTY20 INTERNATIONALS

Graeme Smith (South Africa) has scored more runs in a Twenty20 International cricket career than any other player. He has totalled 364 for South Africa in 12 matches between 2005 and 2008.

★ HIGHEST LIMITED OVERS INNINGS BY A TEAM

Surrey County Cricket Club (UK) scored 496-4 from 50 overs in their match against Gloucestershire County Cricket Club (UK) at the Brit Oval, London, UK, on 29 April 2007.

★ MOST RUNS SCORED IN WORLD CUP MATCHES (FEMALE)

Debbie Hockley (New Zealand) scored 1,501 runs across 45 games between 1982 and 2000 – the most runs scored by an individual in women's cricket World Cup matches.

DID YOU KNOW?

Debbie Hockley also holds the world record for the **most international appearances in women's cricket**: 126 (19 Tests and 107 one-day internationals) between 1979 and 2000.

LIMITED OVERS

★ LOWEST WORLD CUP INNINGS BY A TEAM

The lowest score (that is, the fewest runs) by a team in a World Cup match is 36 by Canada against Sri lanka at Boland Park in Paarl, South Africa, on 19 February 2003.

★ FASTEST WORLD CUP CENTURY

Matthew Hayden (Australia) hit 101 runs from 68 balls during his team's World Cup 2007 match against South Africa at Warner Park, Basseterre, St Kitts, on 24 March 2007.

MOST CRICKET WORLD CUP WINS (WOMEN)

The greatest number of women's cricket World Cup wins by a national side is five, by Australia: 1978, 1982, 1988, 1997 and 2005.

CYCLING

★ MOST TOUR OF ITALY STAGE WINS

Between 1989 and 2003, Mario Cipollini (Italy) won 42 stages of the Giro d'Italia (Tour of Italy), the most stage wins by an individual rider.

ROAD CYCLING

★ MOST TOUR OF SPAIN WINS

Two riders have won the Tour of Spain on three occasions: Tony Rominger (Switzerland), who won from 1992 to 1994; and Roberto Heras Hernandez (Spain), who won in 2000, 2003 and 2004. Hernandez also won the race in 2005, but he tested positive for the banned substance erythropoietin (EPO) and his win was handed to Denis Menchov (Russia).

★ MOST TOUR OF SPAIN STAGE WINS

Delio Rodriguez (Spain) won 39 stages of the Tour of Spain in races between 1941 and 1947.

★ LONGEST TIME BETWEEN VICTORIES IN THE TOUR DE FRANCE

Gino Bartali (Italy) won his first Tour de France in 1938, aged 24 years old, and his second in 1948. The gap of 10 years between wins is the longest time between victories in the history of the race, which began in 1903.

FASTEST AVERAGE SPEED IN THE TOUR DE FRANCE

Lance Armstrong (USA) finished first in the 2005 Tour de France – his last ever Tour – with an average speed of 41.654 km/h (25.882 mph). He finished the 3,607-km-long (2,241-mile) Tour in 86 hr 15 min 2 sec.

★ MOST TOUR OF BRITAIN WINS

Malcolm Elliot (UK) has won the Tour of Britain on three occasions: in 1987 (pro-am), 1988 and 1990.

★ FASTEST WOMEN'S 500 M UNPACED STANDING START

Anna Meares (Australia) cycled 500 m from a standing start and without a pacemaker in 33.588 seconds at the Palma Arena, Palma de Mallorca, Spain, on 31 March 2007.

MOST CYCLO-CROSS WORLD TITLES (FEMALE)

Instituted in 2000, the women's cyclo-cross World Championships have been won on four occasions by Hanka Kupfernagel (Germany), in 2000, 2001, 2005 and 2008.

★ MOST MOUNTAIN-BIKE CROSS-COUNTRY WORLD CUPS (MALE)

Two men have each won the cross-country World Cup title on three occasions: Thomas Frischknecht (Switzerland) in 1992, 1993 and 1995; and Julien Absalon (France, below) in 2003, 2006 and 2007.

BMX

★ MOST WORLD CHAMPIONSHIPS (FEMALE)

Two female riders have each won the Union Cycliste Internationale BMX World Championships on two occasions: Gabriela Diaz (Argentina) in 2001 and 2002; and Willy Kanis (Netherlands) in 2005 and 2006.

★ MOST WORLD CHAMPIONSHIPS (MALE)

Kyle Bennett (USA) has won the Union Cycliste Internationale BMX World Championships on three occasions: in 2002, 2003 and 2007.

MOST COMPETITORS IN THE BMX WORLD CHAMPIONSHIPS

The 2005 UCI BMX World Championships in Paris, France, drew 2,560 competitors from 39 countries between 29 and 31 July of that year.

MOST TRIALS CYCLING WORLD TITLES (MALE)

Benito Ros Charral (Spain) has won the elite men's trials cycling World Championships in the 20-in (50.8-cm) wheel category four times: from 2003 to 2005 and in 2007.

★ MOST MOUNTAIN-BIKE DOWNHILL WORLD TITLES (WOMEN)

Anne-Caroline Chausson (France) has won 12 mountain-bike downhill world titles – three in the junior championship from 1993 to 1995 and nine in the senior class from 1996 to 2005.

X-REF

The **oldest winner of the Tour de France** was Firmin Lambot (Belgium), aged 36 years 4 months in 1922. For more records by golden oldies, check out our **Oldest...** pages in the Human Achievement section on **pp.90–91**.

MOUNTAIN-BIKING

★ MOST FOUR-CROSS WORLD CUPS (MALE)

Brian Lopes (USA) has won three four-cross mountain-biking World Cups: in 2002, 2005 and 2007.

★ MOST TEAM RELAY WORLD TITLES

Spain has won three team relay mountain-biking World Championships: in 1999, 2000 and 2005.

★ MOST CROSS-COUNTRY WORLD TITLES (FEMALE)

Gunn-Rita Dahle Flesjaa (Norway) has won the Cross-Country World Championships on four occasions: in 2002 and from 2004 to 2006.

★ FASTEST MEN'S 500 M UNPACED FLYING START

Chris Hoy (UK) set a record time of 24.758 seconds for the men's 500 m cycle, riding unpaced and from a flying start, in La Paz, Bolivia, on 13 May 2007.

FOOTBALL

★ HIGHEST PAID MANAGER

England national team manager Fabio Capello (Italy) signed a four-and-a-half-year deal with the English Football Association reportedly worth £6 million ($12 million) a year. Capello took up the role on 7 January 2008.

INTERNATIONAL WINNERS

MOST GOALS IN EUROPE

The ★ **most goals scored in European club competitions** is 63 by Filippo Inzaghi (Italy), playing for AC Milan to 4 December 2007.

MOST WINS OF THE AFRICA CUP OF NATIONS

Egypt has won the Africa Cup of Nations six times – in 1957, 1959, 1986, 1998, 2006 and 2008.

MOST WOMEN'S WORLD CUP WINS

The female German national team won its second Fédération Internationale de Football Association (FIFA) Women's World Cup in Shanghai, China, in 2007, having also won in 2003. This equalled the record held by the USA, which won the tournament in 1991 and 1999.

★ MOST CLEAN SHEETS BY A PREMIER LEAGUE GOALKEEPER

David James (UK) has kept 159 clean sheets (conceding no goals in a game) playing for Liverpool, Aston Villa, West Ham, Manchester City and Portsmouth (all UK) between 1992 and 20 April 2008 – more than any other keeper in the English Premier League.

★ MOST WINS OF THE CONCACAF CHAMPIONSHIPS (FEMALE)

The most wins of the women's CONCACAF (the Confederation of North, Central American and Caribbean Association Football) Championship is six by the USA in 1991, 1993, 1994, 2000, 2002 and 2006.

MOST WINS OF THE CONCACAF GOLD CUP (MALE)

Two sides have won the CONCACAF Gold Cup a record four times: Mexico in 1993, 1996, 1998 and 2003; and USA in 1991, 2002, 2005 and 2007.

TOP SCORERS

★ AFRICA CUP OF NATIONS

The greatest number of goals scored in Africa Cup of Nations tournaments is 16, by Samuel Eto'o (Cameroon) playing for Cameroon between 1996 and 2008.

★ COPA AMERICA

The highest goal tally in Copa America tournaments is 17, by two footballers: Zizinho (Brazil) between 1941 and 1953; and Norberto Mendez (Argentina) between 1945 and 1956.

★ MOST CLUBS SCORED FOR IN THE UEFA CHAMPIONS LEAGUE

Hernan Crespo (Argentina, pictured left in blue) scored goals in UEFA Champions League matches for a record five different clubs between 1997 and 2008. The clubs were: Parma, Lazio, Inter Milan (all Italy), Chelsea (UK) and AC Milan (Italy).

★ FASTEST GOAL BY A SUBSTITUTE IN THE ENGLISH PREMIER LEAGUE

Playing for Arsenal, Nicklas Bendtner (Denmark) scored six seconds after coming on as a substitute against Tottenham Hotspur in an English Premier League match at the Emirates Stadium, London, UK, on 22 December 2007.

★ MOST EXPENSIVE PLAYER (CAREER)

The highest combined transfer fees for a footballer is £84.8 million ($169 million) for Nicolas Anelka (France). Anelka has played for Paris St Germain (France) twice, Arsenal (UK), Real Madrid (Spain), Liverpool, Manchester City (both UK), Fenerbahçe (Turkey), Bolton Wanderers and Chelsea (both UK) between 1997 and 2008.

★ FIFA WOMEN'S WORLD CUP

Brigit Prinz (Germany) has scored a total of 14 goals during the course of FIFA Women's World Cup matches. This record-breaking total includes her goal in the FIFA Women's World Cup final, staged at the Hongkou Stadium in Shanghai, China, on 30 September 2007.

★ MAJOR LEAGUE SOCCER

The Major League Soccer (MLS) record for most career goals is 115 by Jaime Moreno (Bolivia), up to May 2008.

MISC.

HIGHEST TRANSFER FEE

Zinedine Zidane (France) moved from Juventus to Real Madrid for a reported 13,033,000,000 Spanish pesetas (£47 million; $66.36 million) on 9 July 2001.

MOST CAPPED FOOTBALLER

Kristine Lilly (USA) has played 340 international matches for the US women's national team.

MOST CHAMPIONS LEAGUE APPEARANCES

Raúl González Blanco (Spain) has made 118 Champions League appearances between 1994 and 2008, playing for Real Madrid. Raúl also holds the record for the **most goals in the UEFA (Union of European Football Associations) Champions League matches**, with 61.

UEFA CHAMPIONS LEAGUE MOST...

VICTORIES

The **most UEFA Champions League matches won by a team** is 73 by Real Madrid (Spain) between 1992 and December 11, 2007, scoring a record 263 goals.

★ CLEAN SHEETS

The **most consecutive clean sheets by a team in Champions League matches** is 10, by Arsenal (UK) in 2006.

GAMES MANAGED

Sir Alex Ferguson (UK) has **managed the most Champions League games**. He took charge of his 140th game as manager of Manchester United in the 2008 final in Moscow on 21 May.

www

FOOTBALL

SKILLS FROM HEAD TO TOE

The **most football rolls across the forehead** is 50 and was achieved by Victor Rubilar (Argentina) as part of the Guinness World Records Tour 2007, at the ICA Maxi, in Haninge, Sweden, on 2 November 2007.

The record for the **longest time controlling a football with the soles** is 6 min 1 sec and was achieved by Tomas Lundman (Sweden) at the Nordstan Shopping Mall in Gothenburg, Sweden, on 24 November 2007.

LONGEST TIME TO CONTROL A FOOTBALL

Martinho Eduardo Orige (Brazil) juggled a regulation football for 19 hr 30 min non-stop with feet, legs and head without the ball ever touching the ground at Padre Ezio Julli Gym in Araranguá, Brazil, on 2–3 August 2003.

MOST GOALS SCORED DIRECT FROM CORNERS

The greatest number of goals scored direct from corner kicks in one match by an individual is three by Steve Cromey (UK) for Ashgreen United against Dunlop FC on 24 February 2002 at Bedworth, Warwickshire, UK, and by Daniel White (UK) for Street and Glastonbury under-11s against Westfield Boys on 7 April 2002.

MOST FOOTBALLS JUGGLED

Victor Rubilar (Argentina) juggled five regulation-size footballs for the required minimum of 10 seconds at the Gallerian Shopping Centre, Stockholm, Sweden, on 4 November 2006.

LARGEST FOOTBALL COMPLEX (PITCHES)

The National Sports Center at Blaine, Minnesota, USA, has 57 pitches.

LONGEST FA CUP TIE

The FA Cup tie between Alvechurch and Oxford City (both UK) in the fourth qualifying round in November 1971 lasted for six games and 11 hours. The match results sequence was 2–2, 1–1, 1–1, 0–0, 0–0, with Alvechurch eventually winning 1–0.

MOST TERRITORIES VISITED ON A FOOTBALL TOUR

Lenton Griffins FC (UK) visited a total of 12 territories from 3 July to 3 August 2004: Wales, Belgium, Luxembourg, Germany, Austria, Liechtenstein, Italy, Switzerland, France, Andorra, Spain and Morocco.

★ LARGEST FOOTBALL TOURNAMENT

The Copa Telmex, held in Mexico between February and October 2007, was contested by 8,600 teams totalling 148,714 players. The tournament was organized with the aim of improving the quality of life of Mexican youth.

★ MOST "AROUND THE WORLD" BALL-CONTROL TRICKS IN ONE MINUTE

John Farnworth (UK) achieved 83 "Around the World" football tricks in one minute on the set of *Zheng Da Zong Yi – Guinness World Records Special* in Beijing, China, on 2 November 2007.

★ NEW RECORD
★ UPDATED RECORD

I knew I could do it. It was just a matter of not being too nervous. Chloe Hegland, record-breaking footballer

⭐ LONGEST TIME CONTROLLING A FOOTBALL LYING DOWN

Tomas Lundman (Sweden) controlled a football without using his hands while lying down for 10 min 4 sec at the Nordstan Shopping Mall in Gothenburg, Sweden, on 24 November 2007.

⭐ LONGEST FIVE-A-SIDE MARATHON

The Rossendale Mavericks and the Fearns Community Sports College (both UK) played five-a-side football for 24 hr 30 min at Fearns Community Sports College Hall in Waterfoot Rossendale, Lancashire, UK, on 23–24 November 2007.

MOST BOOKINGS IN A FOOTBALL MATCH

In the local cup match between Tongham Youth Club, Surrey, and Hawley, Hants (both UK), on 3 November 1969, the referee booked all 22 players, including one who went to hospital and one of the linesmen. The match, which was won by Tongham 2–0, was described by a player as "A good, hard game".

It was reported on 1 June 1993 that in a league match between Sportivo Ameliano and General Caballero in Paraguay, referee William Weiler sent off 20 players. Trouble flared after two Sportivo players were sent off; a 10-minute fight ensued and Weiler then dismissed a further 18 players, including the rest of the Sportivo team. Not surprisingly, the match was abandoned.

SILKY SKILLS

⭐ MOST PEOPLE DOING "KEEPIE UPPIES" (SINGLE VENUE)

The greatest number of people to keep a football in the air at the same time is 627. The record, organized by the Stadt Wien, was set during the event Vienna Recordia in Vienna, Austria, on 30 September 2007.

⭐ MOST TOUCHES OF A BALL WITH THE HEAD IN A MINUTE

The most touches of a football in a minute, using only the head, while keeping the ball in the air, is 341 by Gao Chong (China) in Beijing, China, on 3 November 2007.

LONGEST THROW-IN

Michael Lochner (USA) performed the longest throw-in of a football when projecting a ball a distance of 48.17 m (158 ft 0.5 in) at Bexley High School, Ohio, USA, on 4 June 1998.

LONGEST TIME CONTROLLING A FOOTBALL WITH THE HEAD WHILE SEATED

The longest time to keep a football in the air by using just the head while seated on the floor is 4 hr 9 min 26 sec, and was achieved by Tomas Lundman (Sweden) in Märsta, Stockholm, Sweden, on 20 April 2007.

MOST TOUCHES OF A BALL

The ⭐ **most touches of a football in 30 seconds while keeping the ball in the air by a female** is 163, by Chloe Hegland (Canada) on the set of *Lo Show dei Record* in Madrid, Spain, on 23 February 2008. She also holds the record for the **most touches of a football in one minute**, having recorded 339 touches without the ball hitting the ground on the set of *Zheng Da Zong Yi – Guinness World Records Special* in Beijing, China, on 3 November 2007.

⭐ MOST "KEEPIE UPPIES" (MULTIPLE VENUES)

The greatest number of people to keep a football airborne without using their hands – simultaneously, at multiple locations – is 634 and was achieved by The Likeaballs and students from 21 UK schools in support of Sport Relief 2008 on 4 March 2008.

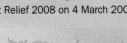

GOLF

LARGEST UNDERWATER GOLF TOURNAMENT

Five players, all following regular golfing rules, took part in a golf tournament in a 15-m-deep (50-ft) water tank at Zuohai Aquarium in Fuzhou, Fujian Province, China, on 28 May 2007.

HIGHEST GOLF COURSE

The golf course situated at the highest altitude is the Yak golf course at 3,970 m (13,025 ft) above sea level in Kupup, East Sikkim, India. It was measured on 10 October 2006.

MOST HOLES PLAYED IN A YEAR

Leo Fritz of Youngstown, Ohio, USA, played 10,550 holes of golf in 1998, averaging 28.9 holes per day.

FASTEST ROUND OF GOLF BY AN INDIVIDUAL

The fastest 18-hole round played (allowing the golf ball to come to rest before each new stroke) is 27 min 9 sec by James Carvill (UK) at Warrenpoint Golf Course (18 holes; 5,628 m; 6,154 yd) in Co. Down, Ireland, on 18 June 1987.

LARGEST GOLF RANGE

The SKY72 Golf Club Dream Golf Range has 300 individual bays, making it the largest golf range in the world. The facility opened in Joong-Ku, Incheon, Korea, on 9 September 2005.

PRO GOLF

LARGEST MARGIN OF VICTORY IN A MAJOR

Tiger Woods (USA) won the 2000 US Open by 15 shots. He finished with a round of 67 to add to rounds of 65, 69 and 71 for a 12 under par total of 272, the biggest margin of victory in any of the four major golf tournaments (Masters, Open Championship, US Open and US PGA).

EXTREME GOLF

YOUNGEST...

SCORER OF A HOLE-IN-ONE

Christian Carpenter (USA), aged 4 years 195 days, at the Mountain View Golf Club, Hickory, North Carolina, USA, on 18 December 1999.

★ CURTIS CUP PLAYER

Michelle Wie (USA), aged 14 years 244 days, at the Formby Golf Club, Merseyside, UK, on 11 June 2004.

FASTEST TIME TO PLAY A ROUND OF GOLF ON SIX CONTINENTS

Heinrich du Preez (South Africa) played an 18-hole round of golf on six of the seven continents (excluding Antarctica) in 119 hr 48 min between 22 and 27 May 2007.

LARGEST GOLF FACILITY

Mission Hills Golf Club, China, had 12 fully operational 18-hole courses in December 2006.

★ MOST 18-HOLE GOLF COURSES PLAYED IN ONE YEAR

Glenn Turner (UK) played 381 different 18-hole golf courses in one year between 1 April 2006 and 31 March 2007. All of the courses he played were in the UK and Spain.

Oaks Course

Woodbury Park

8

207 YARDS
PAR 3   S.I. 16

149 YARDS
PAR 3   S.I. 16

129 YARDS
PAR 3   S.I. 16

111 YARDS

HIGHEST EARNINGS...

CAREER – PGA EUROPEAN TOUR

Colin Montgomerie (UK) won €22,912,717 (£17,334,158; $34,455,227) on the PGA European Tour between 1986 and 2008.

CAREER – US LPGA TOUR

Annika Sorenstam (Sweden) amassed total winnings of $21,069,392 (£10,600,312) on the US LPGA Tour between 1993 and 2008.

SEASON – PGA EUROPEAN TOUR

Ernie Els (South Africa) won €4,061,905, (£3,053,739; $6,011,002) on the PGA European Tour in 2004.

SEASON – LADIES EUROPEAN TOUR

Laura Davies (UK) won €471,727 (£354,644; $698,084) on the Ladies European Tour in 2006.

HIGHEST SEASON'S EARNINGS (US PGA)

Vijay Singh (Fiji) won $10,905,166 (£5,888,789) in prize money on the US PGA tour in 2004.

★ LARGEST ONE-DAY GOLF TOURNAMENT

A record 614 golfers took part in the largest one-day golf tournament at the La Cala Resort in Mijas, Malaga, Spain, on 22 July 2007.

MOST WORLD MATCH PLAY CHAMPIONSHIPS

Ernie Els (South Africa) has won more World Match Play Championships than any other golfer, triumphing in 1994–96, 2002–04 and 2007 to win seven titles.

MOST MAJOR TOURNAMENT TITLES BY A MAN

Jack Nicklaus (USA) triumphed in 18 major tournaments between 1962 and 1986. Nicklaus won the Masters six times, the Open Championship three times, the US Open four times and the US PGA championship five times.

MOST WOMEN'S BRITISH OPEN WINS

Karrie Webb (Australia), in 1995, 1997 and 2002, and Sherri Steinhauer (USA), in 1998, 1999 and 2006, have both won the British Open golf tournament on three occasions. The British Open only became an LPGA major in 2006.

THE MASTERS

Nick Price (Zimbabwe), in 1986, and Greg Norman (Australia), in 1996, both shot 63, the **lowest single-round score at the Masters**, at the Augusta National Golf Course, Georgia, USA.

The **lowest aggregate score for the four rounds of the Masters** is 270 (70, 66, 65, 69) by Tiger Woods (USA) in 1997.

HIGHEST-EARNING GOLFER

Tiger Woods (USA) amassed $78,865,376 (£39,678,297) in prize money on the US PGA Tour between 1996 and 2008, the **highest career earnings of any golfer**.

In the year to June 2007, Tiger earned *ca.* $100 million (£50 million) according to Forbes, the **highest earnings, including endorsements, by a golfer in one year**.

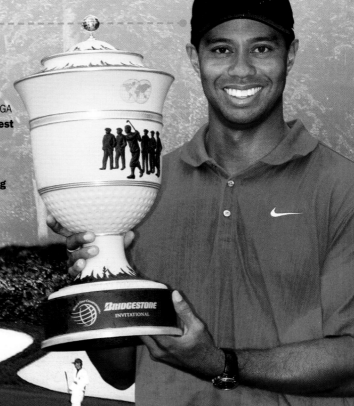

ICE HOCKEY

★ MOST CAREER POINTS – US ICE HOCKEY (FEMALE)

Cammi Granato (USA) is the leading career scorer among USA Women's team members with 343 points (186 goals, 157 assists) through January 2006. Granato captained the Americans to the first Olympic women's hockey gold medal in 1998 and to silver in 2002.

★ OLDEST NHL PLAYER

Gordie Howe (Canada, b. 31 March 1928) was the oldest player in NHL history when he retired in 1980, aged 52 years old. In 1997, Howe was signed to a one-game contract by the Detroit Vipers (USA) of the International Hockey League, aged nearly 70.

FASTEST GOAL SCORED IN ICE HOCKEY

Per Olsen (Denmark) scored two seconds after the start of the match for Rungsted v. Odense in the Danish First Division on 14 January 1990.

Jorgen Palmgren Erichsen (Norway) scored three goals in 10 seconds for Frisk v. Holmen in a Norway junior league match on 17 March 1991.

FASTEST NHL HAT-TRICK

Bill Mosienko (Canada) scored a hat-trick in 21 seconds playing for the Chicago Blackhawks against the New York Rangers (both USA) on 23 March 1952.

★ BEST START IN AN NHL SEASON

The best start by a team in National Hockey League (NHL) history is 26 points in the first 14 games of the 2007–08 season by the Ottawa Senators (Canada). The Senators started the season with a 13–1 win–loss record.

★ FIRST PERSON TO SCORE ON A PENALTY SHOT IN STANLEY CUP FINALS

Chris Pronger (Canada) of the Edmonton Oilers (Canada) was the first player to score on a penalty shot in the Stanley Cup finals, beating goaltender Cam Ward (Canada) of the Carolina Hurricanes (USA) in Game 1 of the Stanley Cup finals on 5 June 2006. It was the ninth penalty shot attempt in Stanley Cup finals history.

★ LARGEST ATTENDANCE AT AN NHL MATCH

The largest crowd to attend an NHL game is 71,217 people for a game between the Pittsburgh Penguins and Buffalo Sabres (both USA) at Ralph Wilson Stadium in Orchard Park, New York, USA, on 1 January 2008.

★ LONGEST SUSPENSION FOR AN INFRACTION DURING A GAME

The National Hockey League record for longest suspension is 30 games, given to Chris Simon (Canada) of the New York Islanders (USA) as punishment for stepping on the leg of Pittsburgh's Jarkko Ruutu (Finland) with his skate on 15 December 2007.

★ HIGHEST SAVE PERCENTAGE IN STANLEY CUP FINALS

Terry Sawchuk (Canada), playing for the Detroit Red Wings (USA) in 1952, achieved the best save percentage in a Stanley Cup final series. Sawchuk recorded a percentage of .981, saving 104 of the 106 shots he faced.

★ OLDEST PERSON TO LEAD AN NHL SEASON IN GOALS SCORED

Bill Cook (Canada, b. 9 October 1896) was 37 years old when he was the league's top goal scorer while playing for the New York Rangers in the 1932–33 season. Cook tallied 50 points with 28 goals and 22 assists.

AstraZeneca

All hockey players are bi-lingual.
They know English and profanity.

Gordie Howe, NHL legend

★ NEW RECORD
UPDATED RECORD

★ MOST SEASONS IN THE STANLEY CUP PLAYOFFS BY A PLAYER

Chris Chelios (USA), playing for the Montreal Canadiens (Canada), Chicago Blackhawks and Detroit Red Wings, has played in the Stanley Cup playoffs on 22 occasions since 1984, missing out in only two seasons as an NHL player.

SIDNEY CROSBY

Ice hockey sensation Sidney Crosby (Canada, b. 7 August 1987) has been breaking records with ease since his first professional NHL game for the Pittsburgh Penguins (USA) on 5 October 2005. Aged 18 years 253 days, Crosby scored his 100th point of the season in a game against the New York Islanders in Pittsburgh on 17 April 2006, becoming the **youngest player in NHL history to produce 100 points in a season**. Crosby finished the 2005/06 season with 102 points.

At 19 years 245 days old, Crosby became the **★ youngest player in NHL history to win a league scoring title** when the final game of the 2006/07 season was played on 9 April 2007. And just 52 days later, aged 19 years 297 days, Crosby became the ★ **youngest player in NHL history to be named team captain**.

MOST POINTS SCORED BY AN INDIVIDUAL IN A PRO ICE HOCKEY GAME

Two Canadians share the record for the most points scored in a game, with 10 points each: Jim Harrison (three goals, seven assists) for Alberta, later Edmonton Oilers (Canada), in a World Hockey Association game in Edmonton, Canada, on 30 January 1973; and Darryl Sittler (six goals, four assists) for the Toronto Maple Leafs (Canada) vs. Boston Bruins (USA) in an NHL game in Toronto, Canada, on 7 February 1976.

★ MOST PLAYOFF GAMES CONSECUTIVELY STARTED BY A GOALTENDER

The New Jersey Devils (USA) netminder Martin Brodeur (Canada) started in a record 137 straight playoff games through the 2007 Stanley Cup playoffs.

LARGEST ICE HOCKEY TOURNAMENT BY PLAYERS

With 510 teams taking part from eight countries – and a total of 8,145 players – the largest ice hockey tournament ever was the Bell Capital Cup held in Ottawa, Ontario, Canada, from 28 December 2006 to 1 January 2007. Over 1,000 games were played during this festival of ice hockey.

★ MOST MATCHES PLAYED IN AN NHL CAREER

Gordie Howe (Canada) played 1,767 games for the Detroit Red Wings and Hartford Whalers (USA) between 1946 and 1980, an all-time NHL record. *See box on left for more on the record-breaking Gordie Howe.*

★ FIRST NHL REGULAR SEASON MATCH PLAYED IN EUROPE

The first National Hockey League (NHL) regular season games played in Europe were contested between the Los Angeles Kings and the Anaheim Ducks (both USA) at the O$_2$ Arena in London, UK, on 29 and 30 September 2007. The Kings won the first game 4–1 and the Ducks won the second by the same score. The NHL has opened its season outside North America three other times: in Japan in 1997, 1998 and 2000, but this was the first league game played in Europe.

MARTIAL ARTS

★ MOST WORLD JUDO TITLES (WOMEN)

Japanese martial artist Ryoko Tani (nee Tamura) has won seven women's World Judo Championship titles in the 48 kg (106 lb) category from 1993 to 2007.

HEAVIEST LIVING ATHLETE

Sumo wrestler Emmanuel "Manny" Yarborough, of Rahway, New Jersey, USA, stands 2.03 m (6ft 8 in) tall and weighs a colossal 319.3 kg (704 lb). He was introduced to Sumo by his judo coach and went on to become ranked No.1 in the Open Sumo Wrestling Category for Amateurs.

★ HEAVIEST UFC FIGHTER

The record for the heaviest Ultimate Fighting Championship contestant is shared by five fighters: Sean Gannon, Gan McGee, Tim Sylvia, Scott Junk and Brock Lesnar (all USA), all weighing in at 120 kg (265 lb).

The ★ **lightest Ultimate Fighting Championship contestants** are Thiago Alves (Brazil), Jeff Curran and Jens Pulver (both USA), all of whom weigh in at 63.5 kg (145 lb).

TEAM KATA WORLD CHAMPIONSHIPS

The ★**most women's Team Kata Karate World Championships won by a national team** is seven, by Japan, between 1988 and 2004.

The ★**most men's Team Kata Karate World Championships won by a national team** is eight, again by Japan, between 1986 and 2002.

★ MOST WINS OF THE UFC LIGHT HEAVYWEIGHT CHAMPIONSHIPS

Tito Ortiz (USA, left) won six Ultimate Fighting Championship (UFC) light heavyweight championship bouts between 2000 and 2002.

★ MOST SUMO MATCHES WON IN A CAREER

Yokozuna Mitsugu Akimoto (Japan), alias Chiyonofuji Mitsugu, holds the record for the most wins throughout his professional career, with 1,045 between September 1970 and May 1991. He has also won the most *Makunouchi* (top division) matches, with 807 victories.

WWE CHAMPIONSHIP

Bruno Sammartino (Italy) was World Wrestling Entertainment (WWE) Champion for 2,803 days between 17 May 1963 and 18 January 1971, the ★**longest WWE Championship reign**.

André the Giant (France) was the WWE Champion with the ★**shortest WWE Championship reign** – just 45 seconds on 5 February 1988. He defeated Hulk Hogan in controversial circumstances, but immediately sold the title to fellow wrestler Ted Dibiase. World Wrestling Federation (WWF) president Jack Tunney promptly nullified the transaction and the title was vacated.

19 September 2007. The record-breaking feat took place on the set of *The Best House 123* in Tokyo, Japan.

HIGHEST MARTIAL ARTS KICK

Jessie Frankson (USA) performed a 2.94-m-high (9-ft 8-in) kick on the set of *Guinness World Records Primetime* in Los Angeles, USA, on 21 December 2000.

MOST MARTIAL ARTS KICKS IN ONE MINUTE (USING BOTH LEGS)

In 1989, on the set of *Record Breakers* in London, UK, 14-year-old Scott Reave (UK) completed 218 kicks successfully in one minute. He alternated legs during the attempt, starting and finishing on his right side.

DID YOU KNOW?

In 2001, the World Wildlife Fund sued the World Wrestling Federation over the use of the initials WWF. The trial led to the wrestling organization rebranding itself to WWE (World Wrestling Entertainment) in 2002.

★ MOST PEOPLE IN A WWE ROYAL RUMBLE COMPETITION

On two occasions, 30 wrestlers have been entered into a World Wrestling Entertainment Royal Rumble competition. The first occasion was on 28 January 2007, in San Antonio, Texas, USA, in a contest won by The Undertaker (USA). The second time, on 27 January 2008 in New York City, USA, the contest was won by John Cena (USA).

★ WORLD JUDO CHAMPIONSHIPS

Four *judoka* have won four World Judo Championship titles: Naoya Ogawa (Japan), between 1987 and 1991; Shozo Fujii (Japan), between 1971 and 1979; Yasuhiro Yamashita (Japan), between 1979 and 1983; and David Douillet (France, below), between 1993 and 1997.

MOST MARTIAL ARTS THROWS IN ONE HOUR

Dale Moore and Nigel Townsend (both UK) completed 3,786 judo throws in one hour at Esporta Health Club, Chiswick Park, London, UK, on 23 February 2002.

★ FASTEST 1,000 MARTIAL ARTS SWORD CUTS

Isao Machii (Japan) completed a total of 1,000 cuts of rolled straw mats with a sword in 36 min 4 sec on

MOST UFC HEAVYWEIGHT CHAMPIONSHIPS

Randy Couture (USA, right) won six UFC heavyweight championship bouts between 1997 and 2007 – the most by an individual fighter.

★ **NEW RECORD**
★ **UPDATED RECORD**

RUGBY

★ MOST TRIES IN A RUGBY WORLD CUP TOURNAMENT

In the history of the Rugby World Cup, two players have scored a record eight tries in the finals stage of the tournament. Jonah Lomu (New Zealand) achieved the feat in 1999 and Bryan Habana (South Africa, right) equalled Jonah's achievement during the 2007 competition.

RUGBY UNION

★ MOST APPEARANCES IN THE FIVE NATIONS CHAMPIONSHIP BY A PLAYER

Mike Gibson (Ireland) played 56 times for Ireland in the Five Nations Championship between 1964 and 1979. (The Five Nations became the Six Nations in 2000.)

MOST APPEARANCES IN ENGLISH PREMIERSHIP MATCHES BY A PLAYER

Neal Hatley (UK) played 193 times in English Premiership matches between 1998 and 2007 for his club London Irish. The Premiership (currently known as the Guinness Premiership) is the top division of the English rugby union system.

★ MOST INTERNATIONAL RUGBY UNION TESTS REFEREED

Derek Bevan (UK) refereed 44 international rugby union matches in a career that lasted from 1985 to 2000.

★ MOST POINTS IN A TRI-NATIONS CAREER

Andrew Mehrtens (New Zealand) scored 328 points playing for the All Blacks (the New Zealand national team) in the Tri-Nations championships between 1995 and 2004.

DID YOU KNOW?

With two titles each, Australia (in 1991 and 1999) and South Africa (in 1995 and 2007) share the record for **most Rugby Union World Cup final victories**.

MOST IRB SEVENS WORLD SERIES TITLES

The IRB Sevens World Series, which began in 1999, has been won seven times by New Zealand, in 1999–2000, 2000–01, 2001–02, 2002–03, 2003–04, 2004–05 and 2006–07. Fiji broke New Zealand's dominance to claim its first title in 2005–06.

★ MOST TRIES IN A SUPER RUGBY CAREER

Doug Howlett (New Zealand, above) scored a total of 58 tries in Super Rugby playing for the Auckland Blues between 1998 and 2007.

Playing for the Canterbury Crusaders from 1996 to 2005, Andrew Mehrtens (New Zealand) scored 981 points – the **most points scored by an individual player in a Super Rugby career**.

MOST RUGBY LEAGUE STATE OF ORIGIN SERIES WINS

Queensland have won Australia's rugby league State of Origin series 16 times between 1980 and 2007. Pictured is Greg Inglis of the Maroons scoring against the New South Wales Blues.

RUGBY RECORD MACHINE

England fly-half Jonny Wilkinson (UK, left) has scored 1,099 points in 75 matches for England (1,032 points in 69 matches) and the British and Irish Lions (67 points in 6 matches) from 4 April 1998 to 8 March 2008 – the **greatest number of points scored in a Rugby Union international career**.

Wilkinson has scored 249 points in 15 World Cup matches between 1999 and 2007, making him the **leading scorer in World Cup matches**, and he is the ★ **only person to score in two World Cup Final matches** (2003 and 2007). His glittering career has also seen him score the **most points in a Five/Six Nations Championship career**, with 443 in matches between 1998 and 2008. And when he kicked a drop goal against France in the 2008 Six Nations Championship on 23 February 2008, he had kicked 29 drop goals in Test rugby – the ★ **most Test drop goals ever**.

MOST TRI-NATIONS TITLES

The Tri-Nations – an international rugby union competition inaugurated in 1996 and played annually between Australia, New Zealand and South Africa – has been won a record eight times by New Zealand, in 1996–97, 1999, 2002–03 and 2005–07.

★ MOST NRL TITLES

The Brisbane Broncos have won the National Rugby League (NRL) title three times, in 1998, 2000 and 2006. The NRL, which is Australia's premier rugby league competition, was instituted in 1998.

RUGBY LEAGUE

MOST WORLD CLUB TROPHY WINS

Two teams have won the World Club Challenge Trophy on three occasions: Wigan (UK) in 1987, 1991 and 1994; and Bradford Bulls (UK) in 2002, 2004 and 2006. The World Club Challenge trophy is contested each year by the winners of the Super League (Europe) and National Rugby League (Australia).

★ MOST TRIES SCORED IN A NATIONAL RUGBY LEAGUE CAREER

Ken Irvine (Australia) scored 212 tries between 1958 and 1973, playing for the North Sydney Bears and the Manly-Warringah Sea Eagles – the most tries scored by an individual player in the National Rugby League.

★ MOST INTERNATIONAL APPEARANCES IN RUGBY UNION

George Gregan (Australia, b. Zambia) has made 139 appearances for the Australian national rugby union team between 1994 and 2007, more international appearances than any other player.

MOST POINTS SCORED IN A NATIONAL RUGBY LEAGUE CAREER

Andrew Johns (Australia) scored 2,176 points in the National Rugby League between 1993 and 2007, playing for the Newcastle Knights.

FASTEST TRY

Lee Jackson (UK) scored after nine seconds for Hull against Sheffield Eagles in a Yorkshire Cup semi-final at Don Valley Stadium, Sheffield, UK, on 6 October 1992.

★ NEW RECORD
UPDATED RECORD

TENNIS & RACKET SPORTS

TENNIS

★ MOST WINS OF THE WHEELCHAIR TENNIS WORLD CHAMPIONSHIPS BY AN INDIVIDUAL (FEMALE)

Esther Vergeer (Netherlands) won the International Tennis Federation (ITF) Wheelchair Tennis World Championships eight-times between 2000 and 2007.

★ OLDEST SEEDED WIMBLEDON PLAYERS

The ★ **oldest seeded Wimbledon male competitor** is Ricardo Gonzalez (USA, b. 9 May 1928), who was 41 years 45 days old when he played at the championships in 1969.

The ★ **oldest seeded Wimbledon female competitor** is Billie Jean King (USA, b. 22 November 1943), who was aged 39 years 210 days when she played at the championships in 1983.

TABLE TENNIS

MOST WORLD CHAMPIONSHIP WINS BY A TEAM (MEN)

China has won the Swaythling Cup 16 times, in 1961, 1963, 1965, 1971, 1975, 1977, 1981, 1983, 1985, 1987, 1995, 1997, 2001, 2004 and 2006–07.

MOST TABLE TENNIS OLYMPIC GOLDS (WOMEN)

Deng Yaping (China) won four Olympic golds: the women's singles in 1992 and 1996, and the women's doubles (both with Qiao Hang) in 1992 and 1996.

FACT

The ★ **shortest tennis player to play at the Wimbledon Championships** is Gem Hoahing (UK), who was 1.46 m (4 ft 9.5 in) tall when she took part in the 1937 competition.

★ TALLEST PLAYER AT WIMBLEDON

Ivo Karlovic (Croatia) measured 2.08 m (6 ft 10 in) at the 2003 Wimbledon Championships.

SQUASH

MOST WORLD OPEN TITLES

Jansher Khan (Pakistan) won eight World Open titles: in 1987, 1989 and 1990; and from 1992 to 1996.

The **most women's World Open titles** is five, by Sarah Fitzgerald (Australia) in 1996–98 and 2001–02.

★ HIGHEST EARNINGS IN A TENNIS SEASON

Tennis star Roger Federer (Switzerland) won an unprecedented $10,130,620 (£5,202,866) in prize money during the 2007 season.

MOST WINS OF THE THOMAS CUP

Indonesia has won the men's World Team Badminton Championships (for the Thomas Cup, instituted 1948) 13 times, in 1958, 1961, 1964, 1970, 1973, 1976, 1979, 1984, 1994, 1996, 1998, 2000 and 2002).

The ★**most consecutive wins of the Sudirman Cup**, for the World Mixed Team Badminton Championships, is four, again by China, from 1995 to 2001.

MOST WINS OF THE UBER CUP (WOMEN)

China has won the women's World Team Badminton Championships for the Uber Cup (instituted 1956) 10 times, in 1984, 1986, 1988, 1990, 1992, 1998, 2000, 2002, 2004 and 2006.

★MOST MIXED DOUBLES WORLD CHAMPIONSHIPS

Rachael Grinham (Australia) has won two Mixed Doubles World Squash Championships, playing with David Palmer (Australia) in 2004 and Joe Kneipp (Australia) in 2006. The Mixed Doubles World Squash Championships have been held on three occasions, in 1997, 2004 and 2006.

★MOST PRO SQUASH ASSOCIATION SUPER SERIES TITLES

Peter Nicol (UK) won three Professional Squash Association Super Series titles consecutively, in 1999–2001.

BADMINTON

MOST WINS OF THE SUDIRMAN CUP

China has won the mixed World Team Badminton Championships (for the Sudirman Cup (instituted in 1989) on six occasions, in 1995, 1997, 1999, 2001, 2005 and 2007.

★LONGEST GRAND SLAM DOUBLES MATCH

The Wimbledon quarter-final match between Daniel Nestor (Canada) and Mark Knowles (Bahamas) and Simon Aspelin (Sweden) and Todd Perry (Australia), on 4–5 July 2006, lasted 6 hr 9 min. Knowles and Nestor won 5-7, 6-3, 6-7, 6-3, 23-21.

★LATEST FINISH TO A GRAND SLAM SINGLES MATCH

An Australian Open match between Lleyton Hewitt (Australia, pictured right) and Marcos Baghdatis (Cyprus), played in Melbourne, Australia, on 19–20 January 2008, finished at 4:33 a.m. Hewitt finally won 4-6, 7-5, 7-5, 6-7 (4-7), 6-3.

TITANS OF TENNIS

Most Wimbledon men's singles titles: seven, by W. C. Renshaw (UK) in 1881–86 and 1889, and Pete Sampras (USA) in 1993–95 and 1997–2000.

Most Wimbledon ladies' singles titles: nine, by Martina Navratilova (USA) in 1978–79, 1982–87 and 1990.

Grand Slam pioneers: The **first man to achieve the tennis grand slam** (winning all four of the world's major tennis singles championships – Wimbledon, the US Open, the Australian Open and the French Open) was Fred Perry (UK), after he won the French title in 1935.
Maureen Connolly (USA) was the **first woman to achieve the tennis grand slam**, in 1953. She went on to win six successive grand slam tournaments.

★ **NEW RECORD**
★ **UPDATED RECORD**

WATERSPORTS

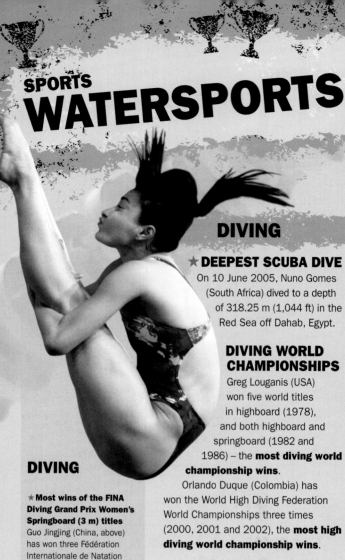

DIVING

★ DEEPEST SCUBA DIVE
On 10 June 2005, Nuno Gomes (South Africa) dived to a depth of 318.25 m (1,044 ft) in the Red Sea off Dahab, Egypt.

DIVING WORLD CHAMPIONSHIPS
Greg Louganis (USA) won five world titles in highboard (1978), and both highboard and springboard (1982 and 1986) – the **most diving world championship wins**.

Orlando Duque (Colombia) has won the World High Diving Federation World Championships three times (2000, 2001 and 2002), the **most high diving world championship wins**.

DIVING

★ Most wins of the FINA Diving Grand Prix Women's Springboard (3 m) titles
Guo Jingjing (China, above) has won three Fédération Internationale de Natation (FINA) Diving Grand Prix Springboard titles, in 1999–2000 and 2006.

★ Most wins of the FINA Diving Grand Prix Men's Springboard titles
Dmitri Sautin (Russia, below) has won seven FINA Diving Grand Prix Springboard titles, in 1995–2001.

ROWING

★ FASTEST 2,000 M BY AN EIGHT (MEN)
On 15 August 2004, a US team rowed 2,000 m in 5 min 19.85 sec at the World Championships in Athens, Greece.

MOST OLYMPIC WATER POLO TITLES (WOMEN)

Since women's water polo was introduced at the 2000 Olympic Games, two countries have won the title: Australia in 2000 and Italy in 2004. Pictured right are Alexandra Araujo of Italy and Georgia Lara of Greece during the Olympic gold medal match in Athens, Greece, in 2004.

★ FASTEST 2,000 M, SINGLE SCULLS (FEMALE)
Rumyana Neykova (Bulgaria) rowed 2,000 m in a time of 7 min 7.71 sec at Seville, Spain, on 21 September 2002.

★ FASTEST DOUBLE SCULLS, LIGHTWEIGHT CLASS (MEN)
Mads Rasmussen and Rasmus Quist (both Denmark) recorded a time of 6 min 10.02 sec in Amsterdam, the Netherlands, on 23 June 2007.

★ MOST UNIVERSITY BOAT RACE WINS
The first boat race between Oxford and Cambridge universities (both UK), which Oxford won, was staged

HIGHEST SURFING CAREER EARNINGS
At the end of the 2007 season, Kelly Slater (USA) had earned $1,587,805 (£806,931.11).

Layne Beachley (Australia, above) had earned $605,035 (£307,501.55) by the end of the same season, the **highest career earnings for a female surfer**.

on 10 June 1829. In the 154 races to 2008, Cambridge had won 79 times, Oxford 74 times and there was a dead heat on 24 March 1877.

I would have a tough time saying anyone has a better job than I have. I get a salary to go surf around the world! Kelly Slater, surfing's top earner

★ FASTEST SWIM SHORT COURSE 800 M FREESTYLE (FEMALE)

Kate Ziegler (USA) swam the women's short course 800 m freestyle in 8 min 8 sec in Essen, Germany, on 14 October 2007.

SWIMMING

MOST INDIVIDUAL OLYMPIC GOLD MEDALS

Krisztina Egerszegi (Hungary) has won five swimming gold medals, in 100 m backstroke (1992), 200 m backstroke (1988, 1992 and 1996) and 400 m medley (1992).

Six swimmers share the record for the **most Olympic swimming gold medals won by a man**, with four each: Charles Meldrum Daniels (USA) in 100 m freestyle (1906 and 1908), 220 yd freestyle (1904) and 440 yd freestyle (1904); Roland Matthes (GDR) in 100 m and 200 m backstroke (1968 and 1972); Mark Spitz (USA) in 100 m and 200 m freestyle, 100 m and 200 m butterfly (1972); Tamás Daryni

(Hungary) in 200 m and 400 m medley (1988 and 1992); Aleksandr Popov (Russia) in 50 m and 100 m freestyle (1992 and 1996); and Michael Phelps (USA) in 100 m and 200 m butterfly and 200 m and 400 m medley (2004).

MOST OLYMPIC MEDALS

Jenny Thompson (USA) won 12 Olympic medals in 1992–2004: eight golds, three silvers and a bronze.

MOST WORLD RECORDS

Ragnhild Hveger (Denmark) set 42 swimming world records from 1936 to 1942.

WATER POLO

MOST INTERNATIONAL GOALS

Debbie Handley scored 13 goals for Australia (16) v. Canada (10) at the World Championship in Guayaquil, Ecuador, in 1982.

OLYMPIC WATER POLO

The record for the **most Olympic gold medals in water polo** is shared by five players, each of whom have won three golds: George Wilkinson (UK) in 1900, 1908 and 1912; Paulo "Paul" Radmilovic and Charles Sidney Smith (both UK) in 1908, 1912 and 1920;

and Desz Gyarmati and Gyorgy Karpati (both Hungary), both of whom won gold medals in 1952, 1956 and 1964.

Hungary holds the record for the **most Olympic water polo titles (men)**, with eight victories, in 1932, 1936, 1952, 1956, 1964, 1976, 2000 and 2004.

SURFING

NAME/NATIONALITY	RECORD	NUMBER OF WINS
Nat Young (Australia)	★Most wins of ASP* Tour Longboard World Championship	Four (1986, 1988–90)
Layne Beachley (Australia)	Most wins of ASP Tour World Championship for surfing (female)	Seven (1998–2003, 2006)
Kelly Slater (USA)	Most wins of Pro Surfing World Championships (male)	Eight (1992, 1994–98, 2005–06)
Michael Novakov (Australia)	Most World Amateur Surfing Championships	Three (1982, 1984, 1986)

*Association for Surfing Professionals

WATER-SKIING

FASTEST SPEED

Christopher Michael Massey (Australia) water-skied at a speed of 230.26 km/h (143.08 mph) on the Hawkesbury River, Windsor, New South Wales, Australia, on 6 March 1983.

Dawna Patterson Brice (USA) water-skied at 178.8 km/h (111.11 mph) at Long Beach, California, USA, on 21 August 1977, the **fastest speed by a female water-skier.**

★ FASTEST SPEED (BAREFOOT)

Scott Michael Pellaton (USA) reached 218.44 km/h (135.74 mph) over a course at Chandler, Arizona, California, USA, in November 1989.

★ FARTHEST WATER-SKI JUMP

Freddy Krueger (USA, below) performed a water-ski jump measuring 74.2 m (243 ft 5 in) in Seffner, Florida, USA, on 5 November 2005.

Elena Milakova (Russia) set the record for the **farthest water-ski jump by a woman**, with a leap of 56.6 m (186 ft) in Rio Linda, California, USA, on 21 July 2002.

WHEEL SKILLS

LONGEST JUMP ON A UNICYCLE

David Weichenberger (Austria) jumped 2.95 m (9 ft 8 in) on his unicycle during the Vienna Recordia event in Vienna, Austria, on 16 September 2006.

SKATEBOARD

★ LONGEST ONE-WHEELED WHEELIE

Brent Kronmueller (USA) covered 40.84 m (134 ft) while performing a one-wheeled wheelie on MTV's *The Rob & Big Show* in Los Angeles, California, USA, on 17 September 2007.

LONGEST DISTANCE SIDE-WHEEL DRIVING IN A CAR

Sven-Eric Söderman (Sweden) covered 345.6 km (214.7 miles) on the side wheels of his car at Mora Siljan Airport, Dalarna, Sweden, on 25 September 1999. In an event lasting 10 hr 38 min, he covered 108 laps of a circuit 3.2 km (1.9 miles) long.

★ LONGEST NO-HANDS MOTORCYCLE WHEELIE

AC Farias (Netherlands) performed an 89-m (292-ft) wheelie without using his hands in Amsterdam, the Netherlands, on 22 October 2004. Farias propels the bike on to its back wheel in the usual manner and, once it is balanced, he then lets go of the handlebars and continues to ride.

★ MOST 360 KICKFLIPS (ONE MINUTE)

The greatest number of 360 degree kickflips performed in a minute is 23, by Kristos Andrews (USA) at the X Games in Los Angeles, California, USA, on 4 August 2007.

★ MOST SKATEBOARD TRICKS INVENTED

Widely regarded as the most influential skater of all time, Rodney Mullen (USA) invented 30 skateboard tricks between 1997 and 2008.

FACT
David Weichenberger was born in 1985 and has been unicycling since 1995. His competitive successes include 2006 Downhill World Champion, 2006 Street World Bronze Medallist, 2004 World Long Jump Champion, 2004 World Silver Medallist in Downhill and Bronze in Trials.

UNICYCLE

★ MOST SKIPS (ONE MINUTE)

Daiki Izumida (Japan), a.k.a. Shiojyari, jumped over a skipping rope on his unicycle 214 times in one minute at New Town Plaza in Hong Kong, China, on 12 August 2007.

★ MOST STAIRS CLIMBED (30 SECONDS)

The most stairs climbed on a unicycle in 30 seconds is 56, achieved by Peter Rosendahl (Sweden) at the Millennium Monument in Beijing, China, on 1 November 2007.

★ KARTING – GREATEST DISTANCE IN 24 HOURS (OUTDOOR)

Team Equipe Vitesse covered 2,056.7 km (1,277.97 miles) in 24 hours at Teesside Karting's track at Redcar & Cleveland Offroad Centre, Middlesbrough, UK, on 20–21 September 2007.

LONGEST WHEELIE

Yasuyuki Kudo (Japan) covered 331 km (205 miles) non-stop on the rear wheel of his Honda TLM220R at the Japan Automobile Research Institute proving ground, Tsukuba, Japan, on 5 May 1991.

★ MOST STAIRS CLIMBED

Benjamin Guiraud (France), a.k.a. Yoggi, climbed 670 stairs on a unicycle without his feet or any part of his body touching the ground, in 22 min 32 sec at the Eiffel Tower in Paris, France, on 20 November 2006.

★ LARGEST SIMULTANEOUS BURN-OUT

The record for the largest motorcycle burn-out is 213, set by the team Harleystunts and Smokey Mountain Harley-Davidson in Maryville, Tennessee, USA, on 26 August 2006.

MOTORBIKE

★ MOST DONUTS (ONE MINUTE)

Axel Winterhoff (Germany) achieved 21 donuts in one minute in Cologne, Germany, on 23 November 2007. A donut is performed by locking the front wheel with the brake and accelerating the rear so that the bike spins around in a tight circle at speed.

BICYCLE

★ MOST PINKY SQUEAKS (ONE MINUTE)

Andreas Lindqvist (Sweden) achieved 57 pinky squeaks in one minute on his BMX in Gothenburg, Sweden, on 24 November 2007.

★ LONGEST 50-50 RAIL GRIND

Rob Dyrdek (USA) achieved a 30.62-m (100-ft 5.75-in) 50-50 skateboard rail grind on MTV's *The Rob & Big Show* in Los Angeles, California, USA, on 17 September 2007. This also represents the ★ **longest board slide**.

★ LONGEST DISTANCE FRONT-WHEEL WHEELIE (FEET OFF PEDALS)

The longest distance covered in a front-wheel wheelie without the feet touching the bike's pedals is 154.5 m (506 ft 10 in), set by Andreas Lindqvist (Sweden) in Stockholm, Sweden, on 2 November 2007.

★ NEW RECORD
★ UPDATED RECORD

HOW HE DOES IT...

To raise the car as he drives, Terry Grant deploys a jack that passes through the car floor and anchors it to the ground. The car spins round the jack, similar to a motorcycle performing a donut, when the car is raised. With the car in motion, Terry balances on the running board to get access to the wheel nuts. He also jumps off the car, leaving it spinning, to pick up tools. When the wheel is changed, Terry retracts the jack and drives off.

★ FASTEST TIME TO CHANGE A WHEEL ON A SPINNING CAR

The record for the fastest time to change a wheel on a spinning car is 3 min 47 sec, achieved by Terry Grant (UK) at Santa Pod Raceway, Wellingborough, Northamptonshire, UK, on 3 October 2007.

WORLD'S STRONGEST MAN

STRONG STUFF

The first World's Strongest Man (WSM) championships took place in 1977. It is an annual contest, and since 2001 the World's Strongest Woman has been held alongside the men's competition.

Among the events featured in these competitions of strength are the following:
- Farmer's Walk
- Yoke Walk/Fridge Carry
- Husafell Stone
- Truck Pulling
- Overhead Press
- Log Throw/Caber Toss
- Decapitation Punch
  - Carry and Drag
  - Fingal's Fingers
  - Hercules Hold
  - Power Stairs
  - Tug of War
  - Duck Walk
  - Crucifix

- Dead Lift
- Loading
- Car Carry
- Keg Toss
- Pole Pushing
- Squat Lift
- Plane Pulling
- Atlas Stones

★ HEAVIEST OBJECT PULLED AT THE WSM COMPETITION

An aircraft weighing approximately 70 tonnes (154,323 lb), plus 300 kg (661 lb) of anchors and chains, is the heaviest single challenge facing competitors in the World's Strongest Man competition. Athletes have just 75 seconds to pull the plane 30 m (98 ft 5 in), the winner being the fastest to complete the course or he who covers the greatest distance in 30 seconds. Pictured is 1997 and 1999 champion Jouko Ahola (Finland).

★ MOST REPS OF AN OVERHEAD SAFE LIFT

In the overhead safe lift, competitors strive to lift two safes that have been clamped together, weighing 125 kg (275 lb) in total. On the third day of the 2007 World's Strongest Man competition in Anaheim, California, USA, Sebastian Wenta (Poland) achieved an incredible 19 repetitions (reps) in this event.

★ FASTEST TIME TO COMPLETE FINGAL'S FINGERS

On the last day of the 2007 World's Strongest Man event in Anaheim, California, USA, Sebastian Wenta (Poland, left) became the first person to complete the Fingal's Fingers event in under 31 seconds, with a time of 30.92 seconds. Fingal's Fingers are an ever-lengthening series of five wooden poles weighing from 200 to 300 kg (441 to 661 lb) hinged at ground level; the aim is to flip over each finger 180 degrees in as fast a time as possible.

★ COUNTRY WITH THE MOST WINS

The competition has travelled to many locations – Zambia, Iceland, Mauritius, Malaysia, Morocco and China, to name a few – and entrants also represent a wide range of countries. Since the competition started, Iceland has provided the winner for a record eight times (1984, 1986, 1988, 1990, 1991, 1994, 1995, 1996). The last Icelandic winner, more than a decade ago, was four-times winner Magnús Ver Magnússon.

★ MOST FINALS REACHED

Magnus Samuelsson (Norway) reached the final round of a record 10 World's Strongest Man competitions in the 13 years between 1995 and 2007. He won the title once, in 1998.

★ OLDEST ENTRANT

Odd Haugen (Norway, b.16 January 1960) was 46 years and 241 days old at the championship in Sanya, China, in September 2006.

★ YOUNGEST ENTRANT

Kevin Nee (USA, b. 21 August 1985) was just 20 years 1 month and 6 days old at the start of the WSM event held in Chengdu, China, on 27 September 2005. Although he failed to qualify in his first two years of competing, in 2007 in Anaheim, California, USA, he was placed a credible 6th in the final ranking.

"*The World's Strongest Man competition is pure jaw-dropping entertainment... Last man standing, no-way-I-can-do-that, primitive stuff.*"

Jay Weiner, MinnPost

★ LARGEST MARGIN OF VICTORY

In the 1980 World's Strongest Man championship, Bill Kazmaier (USA) finished a record 23.5 points ahead of his nearest rival, Lars Hedlund (Sweden). Kazmaier won the WSM title three times, in 1980, 1981 and 1982. His final WSM appearance was in 1989.

★ **NEW RECORD**
★ **UPDATED RECORD**

★ MOST WINS OF THE WORLD'S STRONGEST MAN TITLE

Three competitors share the record for the most overall wins of this championship. Mariusz Pudzianowski (Poland, pictured) won in 2002, 2003, 2005 and 2007. Sharing the record with him is Jón Páll Sigmarsson (Iceland, 1984, 1986, 1988, 1990) and Magnús Ver Magnússon (Iceland, 1991, 1994, 1995, 1996).

★ MOST CONSECUTIVE WINS

Two heavyweights have won the prestigious WSM title three years in a row: Bill Kazmaier (USA) won from 1980 to 1982 and Magnús Ver Magnússon (Iceland, pictured at the 1995 event) held the title from 1994 to 1996.

★ SHORTEST WINNER OF THE CHAMPIONSHIP

Welsh weightlifter and bodybuilder Gary Taylor (UK) was named the World's Strongest Man in 1993. His height at the time was 1.82 m (5 ft 11.5 in). Taylor's career came to a premature end in 1997 when his legs were crushed during a tractor tyre flipping event.

★ TALLEST WINNER OF THE CHAMPIONSHIP

Ted van der Parre (Netherlands) was 2.13 m (7 ft) tall when he won the World's Strongest Man championship in 1992. He was also the **heaviest ever winner**, at 159 kg (350 lb) and the only winner from the Netherlands. The Dutch champion had the lowest WSM body mass index (BMI) of 35. (BMI is a statistical measure of weight in relation to height, to give the approximate total body fat.)

★ SMALLEST MARGIN OF VICTORY

In the 1990 World's Strongest Man championship, only a half point separated the winner, Jón Páll Sigmarsson (Iceland), from the runner-up, O.D. Wilson (USA). Pictured is Sigmarsson in the truck-pulling event in 1984.

X GAMES

SUMMER

HIGHEST ATTENDANCE FOR AN ACTION SPORTS EVENT

The ESPN X Games Five, held in San Francisco, California, USA, was attended by 268,390 visitors over its 10-day duration in 1999.

MOST GOLD MEDALS WON

The individual with the most ESPN X Games gold medals is Dave Mirra (USA) with 14 wins as of 2007.

FIRST "900" ON A SKATEBOARD

Skateboard legend Tony Hawk (USA) became the first person to achieve a "900" in competition at the ESPN X Games Five in San Francisco, California, USA, on 27 June 1999. The "900" (named after the fact that the skater spins two and a half rotations, or 900°) is regarded as one of the most difficult tricks in vert skateboarding.

LONGEST BMX 360 RAMP JUMP

Mike Escamilla (USA, a.k.a. "Rooftop") completed a 15.39 m (50 ft 6 in) BMX 360-degree ramp jump on the Mega Ramp at X Games 11 in Los Angeles, California, USA, on 3 August 2005.

YOUNGEST GOLD MEDAL HOLDER

Ryan Sheckler (USA, b. 30 December 1989) was 13 years 230 days old when he won the Skateboard Park gold medal at ESPN X Games Nine in Los Angeles, California, USA, on 17 August 2003.

MOST MOTO X MEDALS WON

Travis Pastrana (USA) has won the most medals for Moto X at the X Games, with 11 as of ESPN X Games 12 – held in Los Angeles, California, USA, from 3 to 6 August 2006.

Pastrana won gold for Freestyle every year from 1999 to 2005; silver for Step Up in 2001; and for Best Trick he won bronze in 2004, silver in 2005 and gold in 2006.

X-REF

Danny Way won his third X Games Big Air gold medal at the 2006 X Games. For more incredible skateboard records, including kickflips and rail grinds as well as other exploits on four, two and one wheels, take a look at **Wheel Skills** on pp.216–17.

★ LONGEST SKATEBOARD RAMP JUMP

Professional skateboarder Danny Way (USA) achieved a 24-m (79-ft) 360 degree air on his Mega Ramp at X Games 10 in Los Angeles, California, USA, on 8 August 2004.

WINTER

MOST GOLD MEDALS

Shaun Palmer and Shaun White (both USA) have each won six gold medals at the Winter X Games. Palmer earned gold in Skier X Men's in 2000, Snowboarder X Men's from 1997 to 1999, Snow Mountain Biking in 1997 and UltraCross in 2001. White won his golds in Snowboard Superpipe Men's in 2003 and 2006 and Slopestyle Men's from 2003 to 2006.

MOST SKATEBOARD MEDALS WON

Both Tony Hawk (USA) and Andy Macdonald (USA, pictured) have earned 16 Summer X Games Skateboard medals.

FIRST MOTORCYCLE DOUBLE BACK FLIP

Travis Pastrana (USA) completed the first successful double back flip on a motorcycle at X Games 12 in Los Angeles, California, USA, on 4 August 2006.

MOST WAKEBOARDING MEDALS WON

Darin Shapiro (pictured), Dallas Friday and Tara Hamilton (all USA) have each earned six X Games medals in the sport of wakeboarding.

★ **NEW RECORD**
★ **UPDATED RECORD**

They're so much faster and so much less under control.
Shaun White on why skateboards are tougher than snowboards

MOST SNOWBOARDING MEDALS WON

Barrett Christy and Shaun White (both USA) have each won 10 individual Winter X Games medals for Snowboarding. Christy won gold in 1997, silver in 1998 and 1999 and bronze in 2000 and 2002 for Slopestyle Women's; in Big Air, she won gold in 1997 and 1999, silver in 1998 and 2001 and she earned a silver for SuperPipe Women's in 2000.

In the Slopestyle Men's event, White won silver in 2002, golds from 2003 to 2006 and bronze in 2007. In the SuperPipe Men's, he won silver in 2002 and 2007 and gold in 2003 and 2006.

MOST SKIING SLOPESTYLE MEDALS

Tanner Hall (USA) and Jon Olsson (Sweden) have each earned four medals for Skiing Slopestyle. Hall took gold from 2002 to 2004 and silver in 2005. Olsson took bronze from 2002 to 2005.

MOST SKIING SUPERPIPE MEN'S MEDALS

The most medals won in ESPN Winter X Games competitions in the Skiing SuperPipe Men's discipline is four by Jon Olsson (Sweden), Tanner Hall and Simon Dumont (both USA). Olsson took gold in 2002, silver in 2004 and bronze in 2003 and 2005; Hall won golds in 2006 and 2007 and silvers in 2003 and 2005; and Dumont earned two golds in 2004 and 2005, bronze in 2006 and silver in 2007.

MOST SNOCROSS MEDALS

Blair Morgan (Canada) has won eight SnoCross medals: gold from 2001 to 2003, 2005 and 2006, silver in 1999 and 2000 and bronze in 2004. SnoCross has featured at the Winter X Games since 1998.

and Janna Meyen (both USA). Christy won gold in 1997, silver in 1998 and 1999 and bronze in 2000 and 2002; Meyen earned four golds from 2003 to 2006 and silver in 2002.

MOST SNOWBOARD SUPERPIPE MEN'S MEDALS

Danny Kass and Shaun White (both USA) have each won four medals in the Snowboard SuperPipe Men's discipline of the ESPN Winter X Games. Kass won gold in 2001, silver in 2003 and 2004 and bronze in 2005; White won gold in 2003 and 2006 and silver in 2002 and 2007.

MOST SNOWBOARD SUPERPIPE WOMEN'S MEDALS WON

Kelly Clark (USA) has earned four Snowboard SuperPipe Women's medals: gold in 2002 and 2006 as well as silver in 2003 and 2004.

MOST SNOWBOARD SLOPESTYLE WOMEN'S MEDALS

Two women have each won the five medals for Snowboard Slopestyle Women's in ESPN Winter X Games competitions – Barrett Christy

MOST SNOWBOARDER X WOMEN'S MEDALS WON

Lindsey Jacobellis (USA) has won four medals for Snowboarder X Women's at ESPN Winter X Games competitions. Jacobellis won gold from 2003 to 2005 and silver at ESPN Winter X Games 10 in Aspen/Snowmass, Colorado, USA, in January 2007.

MOST AGGRESSIVE IN-LINE SKATE MEDALS

Fabiola da Silva (Brazil) has won eight medals for Aggressive In-line Skating at the X Games, seven of which are gold.

MOST MEDALS WON BY AN INDIVIDUAL

Dave Mirra (USA), who competes in BMX Freestyle, has won 21 medals in the ESPN X Games.

SPORTS REFERENCE

MEN'S 2,000 M

Morocco's Hicham El Guerrouj wins the 2,000 m in Berlin, Germany, in 4 min 44.79 sec (see right).

★ WOMEN'S 5,000 M

On 15 June 2007, at the IAAF Golden League Bislett Games in Oslo, Norway, Meseret Defar (Ethiopia) ran the outdoor 5,000 m in 14 min 16.63 sec.

ATHLETICS – OUTDOOR TRACK EVENTS

MEN	TIME/DISTANCE	NAME & NATIONALITY	PLACE	DATE
★100 m	9.72	Usain Bolt (Jamaica)	New York, USA	31 May 2008
200 m	19.32	Michael Johnson (USA)	Atlanta, USA	1 Aug 1996
400 m	43.18	Michael Johnson (USA)	Seville, Spain	26 Aug 1999
800 m	1:41.11	Wilson Kipketer (Denmark)	Cologne, Germany	24 Aug 1997
1,000 m	2:11.96	Noah Ngeny (Kenya)	Rieti, Italy	5 Sep 1999
1,500 m	3:26.00	Hicham El Guerrouj (Morocco)	Rome, Italy	14 Jul 1998
1 mile	3:43.13	Hicham El Guerrouj (Morocco)	Rome, Italy	7 Jul 1999
2,000 m	4:44.79	Hicham El Guerrouj (Morocco)	Berlin, Germany	7 Sep 1999
3,000 m	7:20.67	Daniel Komen (Kenya)	Rieti, Italy	1 Sep 1996
5,000 m	12:37.35	Kenenisa Bekele (Ethiopia)	Hengelo, Netherlands	31 May 2004
10,000 m	26:17.53	Kenenisa Bekele (Ethiopia)	Brussels, Belgium	26 Aug 2005
★20,000 m	56:26.00	Haile Gebrselassie (Ethiopia)	Ostrava, Czech Republic	26 Jun 2007
★1 hour	21,285 m	Haile Gebrselassie (Ethiopia)	Ostrava, Czech Republic	27 Jun 2007
25,000 m	1:13:55.80	Toshihiko Seko (Japan)	Christchurch, New Zealand	22 Mar 1981
30,000 m	1:29:18.80	Toshihiko Seko (Japan)	Christchurch, New Zealand	22 Mar 1981
3,000 m steeplechase	7:53.63	Saif Saaeed Shaheen (Qatar)	Brussels, Belgium	3 Sep 2004
110 m hurdles	12.88	Xiang Liu (China)	Lausanne, Switzerland	11 Jul 2006
400 m hurdles	46.78	Kevin Young (USA)	Barcelona, Spain	6 Aug 1992
4 x 100 m relay	37.40	USA (Michael Marsh, Leroy Burrell, Dennis Mitchell, Carl Lewis)	Barcelona, Spain	8 Aug 1992
	37.40	USA (John Drummond Jr, Andre Cason, Dennis Mitchell, Leroy Burrell)	Stuttgart, Germany	21 Aug 1993
4 x 200 m relay	1:18.68	Santa Monica Track Club, USA (Michael Marsh, Leroy Burrell, Floyd Heard, Carl Lewis)	Walnut, USA	17 Apr 1994
4 x 400 m relay	2:54.20	USA (Jerome Young, Antonio Pettigrew, Tyree Washington, Michael Johnson)	Uniondale, USA	22 Jul 1998
4 x 800 m relay	7:02.43	Kenya (Joseph Mutua, William Yiampoy, Ismael Kombich, Wilfred Bungei)	Brussels, Belgium	25 Aug 2006
4 x 1,500 m relay	14:38.80	West Germany (Thomas Wessinghage, Harald Hudak, Michael Lederer, Karl Fleschen)	Cologne, Germany	17 Aug 1977

WOMEN	TIME/DISTANCE	NAME & NATIONALITY	PLACE	DATE
100 m	10.49	Florence Griffith-Joyner (USA)	Indianapolis, USA	16 Jul 1988
200 m	21.34	Florence Griffith-Joyner (USA)	Seoul, South Korea	29 Sep 1988
400 m	47.60	Marita Koch (GDR)	Canberra, Australia	6 Oct 1985
800 m	1:53.28	Jarmila Kratochvílová (Czechoslovakia)	Munich, Germany	26 Jul 1983
1,000 m	2:28.98	Svetlana Masterkova (Russia)	Brussels, Belgium	23 Aug 1996
1,500 m	3:50.46	Qu Yunxia (China)	Beijing, China	11 Sep 1993
1 mile	4:12.56	Svetlana Masterkova (Russia)	Zürich, Switzerland	14 Aug 1996
2,000 m	5:25.36	Sonia O'Sullivan (Ireland)	Edinburgh, UK	8 Jul 1994
3,000 m	8:06.11	Wang Junxia (China)	Beijing, China	13 Sep 1993
★5,000 m	14:16.63	Meseret Defar (Ethiopia)	Oslo, Norway	15 Jun 2007
10,000 m	29:31.78	Wang Junxia (China)	Beijing, China	8 Sep 1993
20,000 m	1:05:26.60	Tegla Loroupe (Kenya)	Borgholzhausen, Germany	3 Sep 2000
1 hour	18,340 m	Tegla Loroupe (Kenya)	Borgholzhausen, Germany	7 Aug 1998
25,000 m	1:27:05.90	Tegla Loroupe (Kenya)	Mengerskirchen, Germany	21 Sep 2002
30,000 m	1:45:50.00	Tegla Loroupe (Kenya)	Warstein, Germany	6 Jun 2003
3,000 m steeplechase	9:01.59	Gulnara Samitova-Galkina (Russia)	Iráklio, Greece	4 Jul 2004
100 m hurdles	12.21	Yordanka Donkova (Bulgaria)	Stara Zagora, Bulgaria	20 Aug 1988
400 m hurdles	52.34	Yuliya Pechonkina (Russia)	Tula, Russia	8 Aug 2003
4 x 100 m relay	41.37	GDR (Silke Gladisch, Sabine Rieger, Ingrid Auerswald, Marlies Göhr)	Canberra, Australia	6 Oct 1985
4 x 200 m relay	1:27.46	United States "Blue" (LaTasha Jenkins, LaTasha Colander-Richardson, Nanceen Perry, Marion Jones)	Philadelphia, USA	29 Apr 2000
4 x 400 m relay	3:15.17	USSR (Tatyana Ledovskaya, Olga Nazarova, Maria Pinigina, Olga Bryzgina)	Seoul, South Korea	1 Oct 1988
4 x 800 m relay	7:50.17	USSR (Nadezhda Olizarenko, Lyubov Gurina, Lyudmila Borisova, Irina Podyalovskaya)	Moscow, Russia	5 Aug 1984

ATHLETICS – INDOOR TRACK EVENTS

MEN	TIME	NAME & NATIONALITY	PLACE	DATE
50 m	5.56	Donovan Bailey (Canada)	Reno, USA	9 Feb 1996
	5.56	Maurice Greene (USA)	Los Angeles, USA	13 Feb 1999
60 m	6.39	Maurice Greene (USA)	Madrid, Spain	3 Feb 1998
	6.39	Maurice Greene (USA)	Atlanta, USA	3 Mar 2001
200 m	19.92	Frankie Fredericks (Namibia)	Liévin, France	18 Feb 1996
400 m	44.57	Kerron Clement (USA)	Fayetteville, USA	12 Mar 2005
800 m	1:42.67	Wilson Kipketer (Denmark)	Paris, France	9 Mar 1997
1,000 m	2:14.96	Wilson Kipketer (Denmark)	Birmingham, UK	20 Feb 2000
1,500 m	3:31.18	Hicham El Guerrouj (Morocco)	Stuttgart, Germany	2 Feb 1997
1 mile	3:48.45	Hicham El Guerrouj (Morocco)	Ghent, Belgium	12 Feb 1997
3,000 m	7:24.90	Daniel Komen (Kenya)	Budapest, Hungary	6 Feb 1998
5,000 m	12:49.60	Kenenisa Bekele (Ethiopia)	Birmingham, UK	20 Feb 2004
50 m hurdles	6.25	Mark McKoy (Canada)	Kobe, Japan	5 Mar 1986
60 m hurdles	7.30	Colin Jackson (GB)	Sindelfingen, Germany	6 Mar 1994
4 x 200 m relay	1:22.11	Great Britain & N. Ireland (Linford Christie, Darren Braithwaite, Ade Mafe, John Regis)	Glasgow, UK	3 Mar 1991
4 x 400 m relay	3:02.83	USA (A. Morris, D. Johnson, D. Minor, M. Campbell)	Maebashi, Japan	7 Mar 1999
4 x 800 m relay	7:13.94	Global Athletics & Marketing, USA (Joey Woody, Karl Paranya, Rich Kenah, David Krummenacker)	Boston, USA	6 Feb 2000
5,000 m walk	18:07.08	Mikhail Shchennikov (Russia)	Moscow, Russia	14 Feb 1995

WOMEN	TIME	NAME & NATIONALITY	PLACE	DATE
50 m	5.96	Irina Privalova (Russia)	Madrid, Spain	9 Feb 1995
60 m	6.92	Irina Privalova (Russia)	Madrid, Spain	11 Feb 1993
	6.92	Irina Privalova (Russia)	Madrid, Spain	9 Feb 1995
200 m	21.87	Merlene Ottey (Jamaica)	Liévin, France	13 Feb 1993
400 m	49.59	Jarmila Kratochvílová (Czechoslovakia)	Milan, Italy	7 Mar 1982
800 m	1:55.82	Jolanda Ceplak (Slovenia)	Vienna, Austria	3 Mar 2002
1,000 m	2:30.94	Maria de Lurdes Mutola (Mozambique)	Stockholm, Sweden	25 Feb 1999
★ 1,500 m	3:57.71	Yelena Soboleva (Russia)	Valencia, Spain	9 Mar 2008
1 mile	4:17.14	Doina Melinte (Romania)	East Rutherford, USA	9 Feb 1990
3,000 m	8:23.72	Meseret Defar (Ethiopia)	Stuttgart, Germany	3 Feb 2007
5,000 m	14:27.42	Tirunesh Dibaba (Ethiopia)	Boston, USA	27 Jan 2007
50 m hurdles	6.58	Cornelia Oschkenat (GDR)	Berlin, Germany	20 Feb 1988
★ 60 m hurdles	7.68	Susanna Kallur (Sweden)	Karlsruhe, Germany	10 Feb 2008
4 x 200 m relay	1:32.41	Russia (Yekaterina Kondratyeva, Irina Khabarova, Yuliva Pechonkina, Yulia Gushchina)	Glasgow, UK	29 Jan 2005
4 x 400 m relay	3:23.37	Russia (Yulia Gushchina, Olga Kotlyarova, Olga Zaytseva, Olesya Krasnomovets)	Glasgow, UK	28 Jan 2006
4 x 800 m relay	8:18.54	Moskovskaya Region (Anna Balakshina, Natalya Pantelyeva, Anna Emashova, Olesya Chumakova)	Volgograd, Russia	11 Feb 2007
3,000 m walk	11:40.33	Claudia Stef (Romania)	Bucharest, Romania	30 Jan 1999

ATHLETICS – ULTRA-LONG DISTANCE (TRACK)

MEN	TIME/DISTANCE	NAME & NATIONALITY	PLACE	DATE
50 km	2:48:06	Jeff Norman (GB)	Timperley, UK	7 Jun 1980
100 km	6:10:20	Donald Ritchie (GB)	London, UK	28 Oct 1978
100 miles	11:28:03	Oleg Kharitonov (Russia)	London, UK	2 Oct 2002
1,000 miles	11 days 13:54:58	Peter Silkinas (Lithuania)	Nanango, Australia	11–23 Mar 1998
24 hours	303.306 km (188.46 miles)	Yiannis Kouros (Greece)	Adelaide, Australia	4–5 Oct 1997
48 hours	473.495 km (294.21 miles)	Yiannis Kouros (Greece)	Surgères, France	3–5 May 1996
6 days	1,023.2 km (635.78 miles)	Yiannis Kouros (Greece)	Colac, Australia	26 Nov–2 Dec 1984

WOMEN	TIME/DISTANCE	NAME & NATIONALITY	PLACE	DATE
50 km	3:18:52	Carolyn Hunter-Rowe (GB)	Barry, South Wales, UK	3 Mar 1996
100 km	7:14:06	Norimi Sakurai (Japan)	Verona, Italy	27 Sep 2003
100 miles	14:25:45	Edit Berces (Hungary)	Verona, Italy	21–22 Sep 2002
1,000 miles	13 days 1:54:02	Eleanor Robinson (GB)	Nanango, Australia	11–23 Mar 1998
24 hours	250.106 km (155.40 miles)	Edit Berces (Hungary)	Verona, Italy	21–22 Sep 2002
48 hours	377.892 km (234.81 miles)	Sue Ellen Trapp (USA)	Surgères, France	2–4 May 1997
6 days	883.631 km (549.06 miles)	Sandra Barwick (New Zealand)	Campbelltown, Australia	18–24 Nov 1990

WOMEN'S 1,500 M

Yelena Soboleva (Russia) celebrates winning gold in the women's indoor 1,500 m. She competed at the 12th IAAF World Indoor Championships in Valencia, Spain, on 9 March 2008, achieving a new world record time of 3 min 57.71 sec.

★ NEW RECORD
★ UPDATED RECORD

OFFICIAL WEBSITES

ATHLETICS:
www.iaaf.org

ULTRARUNNING:
www.iau.org.tw

MEN'S 800 M

Two indoor world records belong to Wilson Kipketer (Denmark): 800 m and 1,000 m. Pictured is Kipketer after running the outdoor 800 m in a record 1 min 41.11 sec at the International Track and Field meeting in Cologne, Germany, on 24 August 1997.

SPORTS REFERENCE

ATHLETICS – ROAD RACE

MEN	TIME	NAME & NATIONALITY	PLACE	DATE
10 km	27:02	Haile Gebrselassie (Ethiopia)	Doha, Qatar	11 Dec 2002
15 km	41:29	Felix Limo (Kenya)	Nijmegen, the Netherlands	11 Nov 2001
★ 20 km	55:48	Haile Gebrselassie (Ethiopia)	Phoenix, USA	15 Jan 2006
★ Half marathon	58:33	Samuel Wanjiru (Kenya)	The Hague, the Netherlands	17 Mar 2007
25 km	1:12:45	Paul Malakwen Kosgei (Kenya)	Berlin, Germany	9 May 2004
30 km	1:28:00	Takayuki Matsumiya (Japan)	Kumamoto, Japan	27 Feb 2005
★ Marathon	2:04:26	Haile Gebrselassie (Ethiopia)	Berlin, Germany	30 Sep 2007
100 km	6:13:33	Takahiro Sunada (Japan)	Tokoro, Japan	21 Jun 1998
Road relay	1:57:06	Kenya (Josephat Ndambiri, Martin Mathathi, Daniel Mwangi, Mekubo Mogusu, Onesmus Nyerere, John Kariuki)	Chiba, Japan	23 Nov 2005

WOMEN	TIME	NAME & NATIONALITY	PLACE	DATE
10 km	30:21	Paula Radcliffe (GB)	San Juan, Puerto Rico	23 Feb 2003
15 km	46:55	Kayoko Fukushi (Japan)	Marugame, Japan	5 Feb 2006
★ 20 km	1:02:57	Lornah Kiplagat (Netherlands)	Udine, Italy	14 Oct 2007
★ Half marathon	1:06:25	Lornah Kiplagat (Netherlands)	Udine, Italy	14 Oct 2007
25 km	1:22:13	Mizuki Noguchi (Japan)	Berlin, Germany	25 Sep 2005
30 km	1:38:49	Mizuki Noguchi (Japan)	Berlin, Germany	25 Sep 2005
Marathon	2:15:25	Paula Radcliffe (GB)	London, UK	13 Apr 2003
100 km	6:33:11	Tomoe Abe (Japan)	Tokoro, Japan	25 Jun 2000
Road relay	2:11:41	China (Jiang Bo, Dong Yanmei, Zhao Fengdi, Ma Zaijie, Lan Lixin, Li Na)	Beijing, China	28 Feb 1998

ATHLETICS – RACE WALKING

MEN	TIME	NAME & NATIONALITY	PLACE	DATE
20,000 m	1:17:25.6	Bernardo Segura (Mexico)	Bergen, Norway	7 May 1994
20 km (road)	1:17:16	Vladimir Kanaykin (Russia)	Saransk, Russia	29 Sep 2007
30,000 m	2:01:44.1	Maurizio Damilano (Italy)	Cuneo, Italy	3 Oct 1992
50,000 m	3:40:57.9	Thierry Toutain (France)	Héricourt, France	29 Sep 1996
50 km (road)	3:35:47	Nathan Deakes (Australia)	Geelong, Australia	2 Dec 2006

WOMEN	TIME	NAME & NATIONALITY	PLACE	DATE
10,000 m	41:56.23	Nadezhda Ryashkina (USSR)	Seattle, USA	24 Jul 1990
20,000 m	1:26:52.3	Olimpiada Ivanova (Russia)	Brisbane, Australia	6 Sep 2001
20 km (road)	1:25:41	Olimpiada Ivanova (Russia)	Helsinki, Finland	7 Aug 2005

★ MEN'S HALF MARATHON

Samuel Wanjiru (Kenya) competes at the Great North Run in Newcastle-Upon-Tyne, UK, on 30 September 2007. Earlier the same year, he broke the half marathon world record with a time of 58 min 33 sec.

★ MEN'S 20 KM RACE WALK (ROAD)

Vladimir Kanaykin (Russia) celebrates after crossing the finishing line as the winner of the men's 10 km race walk at the IAAF Junior Athletics World Championships at the National Stadium in Kingston, Jamaica, in July 2002. Kanaykin broke the 20 km men's record on 29 September 2007 in Saransk, Russia, when he achieved a time of 1 hr 17 min 16 sec.

OFFICIAL WEBSITES

ATHLETICS & RACEWALKING:
www.iaaf.org

CYCLING:
www.uci.ch

★ NEW RECORD
★ UPDATED RECORD

ATHLETICS – OUTDOOR FIELD EVENTS

MEN	RECORD	NAME & NATIONALITY	PLACE	DATE
High jump	2.45 m (8 ft 0.45 in)	Javier Sotomayor (Cuba)	Salamanca, Spain	27 Jul 1993
Pole vault	6.14 m (20 ft 1.73 in)	Sergei Bubka (Ukraine)	Sestriere, Italy	31 Jul 1994
Long jump	8.95 m (29 ft 4.36 in)	Mike Powell (USA)	Tokyo, Japan	30 Aug 1991
Triple jump	18.29 m (60 ft 0.78 in)	Jonathan Edwards (GB)	Gothenburg, Sweden	7 Aug 1995
Shot	23.12 m (75 ft 10.23 in)	Randy Barnes (USA)	Los Angeles, USA	20 May 1990
Discus	74.08 m (243 ft 0.53 in)	Jürgen Schult (GDR)	Neubrandenburg, Germany	6 Jun 1986
Hammer	86.74 m (284 ft 7 in)	Yuriy Sedykh (USSR)	Stuttgart, Germany	30 Aug 1986
Javelin	98.48 m (323 ft 1.16 in)	Jan Železný (Czech Republic)	Jena, Germany	25 May 1996
Decathlon*	9,026 points	Roman Šebrle (Czech Republic)	Götzis, Austria	27 May 2001

* 100 m 10.64 seconds; long jump 8.11 m; shot 15.33 m; high jump 2.12 m; 400 m 47.79 seconds; 110 m hurdles 13.92 seconds; discus 47.92 m; pole vault 4.80 m; javelin 70.16 m; 1,500 m 4 min 21.98 sec

WOMEN	RECORD	NAME & NATIONALITY	PLACE	DATE
High jump	2.09 m (6 ft 10.28 in)	Stefka Kostadinova (Bulgaria)	Rome, Italy	30 Aug 1987
Pole vault	5.01 m (16 ft 5.24 in)	Yelena Isinbayeva (Russia)	Helsinki, Finland	12 Aug 2005
Long jump	7.52 m (24 ft 8.06 in)	Galina Chistyakova (USSR)	St Petersburg, Russia	11 Jun 1988
Triple jump	15.50 m (50 ft 10.23 in)	Inessa Kravets (Ukraine)	Gothenburg, Sweden	10 Aug 1995
Shot	22.63 m (74 ft 2.94 in)	Natalya Lisovskaya (USSR)	Moscow, Russia	7 Jun 1987
Discus	76.80 m (252 ft)	Gabriele Reinsch (GDR)	Neubrandenburg, Germany	9 Jul 1988
Hammer	77.80 m (255 ft 3 in)	Tatyana Lysenko (Russia)	Tallinn, Estonia	15 Aug 2006
Javelin	71.70 m (235 ft 2.83 in)	Osleidys Menéndez (Cuba)	Helsinki, Finland	14 Aug 2005
Heptathlon†	7,291 points	Jacqueline Joyner-Kersee (USA)	Seoul, South Korea	24 Sep 1988
Decathlon**	8,358 points	Austra Skujyte (Lithuania)	Columbia, USA	15 Apr 2005

† 100 m hurdles 12.69 seconds; high jump 1.86 m; shot 15.80 m; 200 m 22.56 seconds; long jump 7.27 m; javelin 45.66 m; 800 m 2 min 8.51 sec

** 100 m 12.49 seconds; long jump 6.12 m; shot 16.42 m; high jump 1.78 m; 400 m 57.19 seconds; 100 m hurdles 14.22 seconds; discus 46.19 m; pole vault 3.10 m; javelin 48.78 m; 1,500 m 5 min 15.86 sec

ATHLETICS – INDOOR FIELD EVENTS

MEN	RECORD	NAME & NATIONALITY	PLACE	DATE
High jump	2.43 m (7 ft 11.66 in)	Javier Sotomayor (Cuba)	Budapest, Hungary	4 Mar 1989
Pole vault	6.15 m (20 ft 2.12 in)	Sergei Bubka (Ukraine)	Donetsk, Ukraine	21 Feb 1993
Long jump	8.79 m (28 ft 10.06 in)	Carl Lewis (USA)	New York City, USA	27 Jan 1984
Triple jump	17.83 m (58 ft 5.96 in)	Aliecer Urrutia (Cuba)	Sindelfingen, Germany	1 Mar 1997
	17.83 m (58 ft 5.96 in)	Christian Olsson (Sweden)	Budapest, Hungary	7 Mar 2004
Shot	22.66 m (74 ft 4.12 in)	Randy Barnes (USA)	Los Angeles, USA	20 Jan 1989
Heptathlon*	6,476 points	Dan O'Brien (USA)	Toronto, Canada	14 Mar 1993

* 60 m 6.67 seconds; long jump 7.84 m; shot 16.02 m; high jump 2.13 m; 60 m hurdles 7.85 seconds; pole vault 5.20 m; 1,000 m 2 min 57.96 sec

WOMEN	RECORD	NAME & NATIONALITY	PLACE	DATE
High jump	2.08 m (6 ft 9.8 in)	Kajsa Bergqvist (Sweden)	Arnstadt, Germany	4 Feb 2006
Pole vault	4.95 m (16 ft 2.9 in)	Yelena Isinbayeva (Russia)	Donetsk, Ukraine	16 Feb 2008
Long jump	7.37 m (24 ft 2.15 in)	Heike Drechsler (GDR)	Vienna, Austria	13 Feb 1988
Triple jump	15.36 m (50 ft 4.72 in)	Tatyana Lebedeva (Russia)	Budapest, Hungary	6 Mar 2004
Shot	22.50 m (73 ft 9.82 in)	Helena Fibingerová (Czechoslovakia)	Jablonec, Czechoslovakia	19 Feb 1977
Pentathlon†	4,991 points	Irina Belova (Russia)	Berlin, Germany	15 Feb 1992

† 60 m hurdles 8.22 seconds; high jump 1.93 m; shot 13.25 m; long jump 6.67 m; 800 m 2 min 10.26 sec

CYCLING (ABSOLUTE TRACK)

MEN	TIME/DISTANCE	NAME & NATIONALITY	PLACE	DATE
200 m (flying start)	9.772	Theo Bos (Netherlands)	Moscow, Russia	16 Dec 2006
500 m (flying start)	24.758	Chris Hoy (UK)	La Paz, Bolivia	13 May 2007
1 km (standing start)	58.875	Arnaud Tournant (France)	La Paz, Bolivia	10 Oct 2001
4 km (standing start)	4:11.114	Christopher Boardman (UK)	Manchester, UK	29 Aug 1996
Team 4 km (standing start)	3:56.610	Australia (Graeme Brown, Luke Roberts, Brett Lancaster, Bradley McGee)	Athens, Greece	22 Aug 2004
1 hour	49.7 km*	Ondrej Sosenka (Czech Republic)	Moscow, Russia	19 Jul 2005

WOMEN	TIME/DISTANCE	NAME & NATIONALITY	PLACE	DATE
200 m (flying start)	10.831	Olga Slioussareva (Russia)	Moscow, Russia	25 Apr 1993
500 m (flying start)	29.655	Erika Salumäe (Estonia)	Moscow, Russia	6 Aug 1987
500 m (standing start)	33.588	Anna Meares (Australia)	Palma de Mallorca, Spain	31 Mar 2007
3 km (standing start)	3:24.537	Sarah Ulmer (New Zealand)	Athens, Greece	22 Aug 2004
1 hour	46.65 km*	Leontien Zijlaard-van Moorsel (Netherlands)	Mexico City, Mexico	1 Oct 2003

* Some athletes achieved better distances within an hour with bicycles that are no longer allowed by the Union Cycliste Internationale (UCI). The 1-hour records given here are in accordance with the new UCI rules

★ WOMEN'S 500 M CYCLING

Anna Meares (Australia), on her way to winning the women's 500 m time trial (standing start) in a record time of 33.588 seconds at the UCI Track Cycling World Championship in Palma de Mallorca, Spain, on 31 March 2007.

SPORTS REFERENCE

FREEDIVING

MEN'S DEPTH DISCIPLINES	DEPTH/TIME	NAME & NATIONALITY	PLACE	DATE
Constant weight with fins	112 m (367 ft 5 in)	Herbert Nitsch (Austria)	Sharm el Sheikh, Egypt	1 Nov 2007
Constant weight without fins	86 m (282 ft 1 in)	William Trubridge (New Zealand)	Bahamas	10 Apr 2008
Variable weight	140 m (459 ft 4 in)	Carlos Coste (Venezuela)	Sharm el Sheikh, Egypt	9 May 2006
No limit	214 m (702 ft)	Herbert Nitsch (Austria)	Spetses, Greece	14 Jun 2007
Free immersion	108 m (354 ft 4 in)	William Trubridge (New Zealand)	Bahamas	11 Apr 2008
MEN'S DYNAMIC APNEA				
With fins	244 m (800 ft 6 in)	Dave Mullins (New Zealand)	Wellington, New Zealand	23 Sep 2007
Without fins	186 m (610 ft 3 in)	Stig Aavall Severinsen (Denmark)	Maribor, Slovenia	7 Jul 2007
MEN'S STATIC APNEA				
Duration	9 min 8 sec	Tom Sietas (Germany)	Hamburg, Germany	1 May 2007
WOMEN'S DEPTH DISCIPLINES				
Constant weight with fins	90 m (295 ft 3 in)	Sara Campbell (UK)	Dahab, Egypt	20 Oct 2007
Constant weight without fins	• 57 m (187 ft)	Natalya Avseenko (Russia)	Bahamas	8 Apr 2008
Variable weight	122 m (400 ft 3 in)	Tanya Streeter (USA)	Turks and Caicos Islands	19 Jul 2003
No limit	160 m (524 ft 11 in)	Tanya Streeter (USA)	Turks and Caicos Islands	17 Aug 2002
Free immersion	81 m (265 ft 9 in)	Sara Campbell (UK)	Dahab, Egypt	19 Oct 2007
WOMEN'S DYNAMIC APNEA				
With fins	205 m (662 ft 6 in)	Natalia Molchanova (Russia)	Maribor, Slovenia	5 Jul 2007
Without fins	149 m (488 ft 10 in)	Natalia Molchanova (Russia)	Maribor, Slovenia	7 Jul 2007
WOMEN'S STATIC APNEA				
Duration	8 min 0 sec	Natalia Molchanova (Russia)	Maribor, Slovenia	6 Jul 2007

• Please note that these records were still awaiting ratification at the time of going to press.

ROWING

MEN	TIME	NAME & NATIONALITY	REGATTA	DATE
Single sculls	6:35.40	Mahe Drysdale (New Zealand)	Eton, UK	26 Aug 2006
Double sculls	6:03.25	Jean-Baptiste Macquet, Adrien Hardy (France)	Poznan, Poland	17 Jun 2006
Quadruple sculls	5:37.31	Konrad Wasielewski, Marek Kolbowicz, Michal Jelinski, Adam Korol (Poland)	Poznan, Poland	17 Jun 2006
Coxless pairs	6:14.27	Matthew Pinsent, James Cracknell (GB)	Seville, Spain	21 Sep 2002
Coxless fours	5:41.35	Sebastian Thormann, Paul Dienstbach, Philipp Stüer, Bernd Heidicker (Germany)	Seville, Spain	21 Sep 2002
Coxed pairs*	6:42.16	Igor Boraska, Tihomir Frankovic, Milan Razov (Croatia)	Indianapolis, USA	18 Sep 1994
Coxed fours*	5:58.96	Matthias Ungemach, Armin Eichholz, Armin Weyrauch, Bahne Rabe, Jörg Dederding (Germany)	Vienna, Austria	24 Aug 1991
Coxed eights	5:19.85	Deakin, Beery, Hoopman, Volpenhein, Cipollone, Read, Allen, Ahrens, Hansen (USA)	Athens, Greece	15 Aug 2004
LIGHTWEIGHT				
Single sculls*	6:47.82	Zac Purchase (GB)	Eton, UK	26 Aug 2006
Double sculls	6:10.02	Mads Rasmussen and Rasmus Quist (Denmark)	Amsterdam, the Netherlands	23 Jun 2007
Quadruple sculls*	5:45.18	Francesco Esposito, Massimo Lana, Michelangelo Crispi, Massimo Guglielmi (Italy)	Montreal, Canada	1992
Coxless pairs*	6:26.61	Tony O'Connor, Neville Maxwell (Ireland)	Paris, France	1994
Coxless fours	5:45.60	Thomas Poulsen, Thomas Ebert, Eskild Ebbesen, Victor Feddersen (Denmark)	Lucerne, Switzerland	9 Jul 1999
Coxed eights*	5:30.24	Altena, Dahlke, Kobor, Stomporowski, Melges, März, Buchheit, Von Warburg, Kaska (Germany)	Montreal, Canada	1992
WOMEN				
Single sculls	7:07.71	Rumyana Neykova (Bulgaria)	Seville, Spain	21 Sep 2002
Double sculls	6:38.78	Georgina and Caroline Evers-Swindell (New Zealand)	Seville, Spain	21 Sep 2002
Quadruple sculls	6:10.80	Kathrin Boron, Katrin Rutschow-Stomporowski, Jana Sorgers, Kerstin Köppen (Germany)	Duisburg, Germany	19 May 1996
Coxless pairs	6:53.80	Georgeta Andrunache, Viorica Susanu (Romania)	Seville, Spain	21 Sep 2002
Coxless fours*	6:25.35	Robyn Selby Smith, Jo Lutz, Amber Bradley, Kate Hornsey (Australia)	Eton, UK	26 Aug 2006
Coxed eights	5:55.50	Mickelson, Whipple, Lind, Goodale, Sickler, Cooke, Shoop, Francia, Davies (USA)	Eton, UK	27 Aug 2006
LIGHTWEIGHT				
Single sculls*	7:28.15	Constanta Pipota (Romania)	Paris, France	19 Jun 1994
Double sculls	6:49.77	Dongxiang Xu, Shimin Yan (China)	Poznan, Poland	17 Jun 2006
Quadruple sculls*	6:23.96	Hua Yu, Haixia Chen, Xuefei Fan, Jing Liu (China)	Eton, UK	27 Aug 2006
Coxless pairs*	7:18.32	Eliza Blair, Justine Joyce (Australia)	Aiguebelette-le-Lac, France	7 Sep 1997

*Denotes non-Olympic boat classes

SPEED SKATING – LONG TRACK

MEN	TIME/POINTS	NAME & NATIONALITY	PLACE	DATE
500 m	34.03	Jeremy Wotherspoon (Canada)	Salt Lake City, USA	9 Nov 2007
2 x 500 m	68.31	Jeremy Wotherspoon (Canada)	Calgary, Canada	15 Mar 2008
1,000 m	1:07.00	Pekka Koskela (Finland)	Salt Lake City, USA	10 Nov 2007
1,500 m	1:42.01	Denny Morrison (Canada)	Calgary, Canada	14 Mar 2008
3,000 m	3:37.28	Eskil Ervik (Norway)	Calgary, Canada	5 Nov 2005
5,000 m	6:06.32	Sven Kramer (Netherlands)	Calgary, Canada	17 Nov 2007
10,000 m	12:41.69	Sven Kramer (Netherlands)	Salt Lake City, USA	10 Mar 2007
500/1,000/500/1,000 m	137,230 points	Jeremy Wotherspoon (Canada)	Calgary, Canada	18–19 Jan 2003
500/3,000/1,500/5,000 m	146,365 points	Erben Wennemars (Netherlands)	Calgary, Canada	12–13 Aug 2005
500/5,000/1,500/10,000 m	145,742 points	Shani Davis (USA)	Calgary, Canada	18–19 Mar 2006
Team pursuit (8 laps)	3:37.80	Netherlands (Sven Kramer, Carl Verheijen, Erben Wennemars)	Salt Lake City, USA	11 Mar 2007

WOMEN	TIME/POINTS	NAME & NATIONALITY	PLACE	DATE
500 m	37.02	Jenny Wolf (Germany)	Salt Lake City, USA	16 Nov 2007
2 x 500 m	74.42	Jenny Wolf (Germany)	Salt Lake City, USA	10 Mar 2007
1,000 m	1:13.11	Cindy Klassen (Canada)	Calgary, Canada	25 Mar 2006
1,500 m	1:51.79	Cindy Klassen (Canada)	Salt Lake City, USA	20 Nov 2005
3,000 m	3:53.34	Cindy Klassen (Canada)	Calgary, Canada	18 Mar 2006
5,000 m	6:45.61	Martina Sáblíková (Czech Rebublic)	Salt Lake City, USA	11 Mar 2007
500/1,000/500/1,000 m	149,305 points	Monique Garbrecht-Enfeldt (Germany), Cindy Klassen (Canada)	Salt Lake City, USA / Calgary, Canada	11–12 Jan 2003 / 24–25 Mar 2006
500/1,500/1,000/3,000 m	155,576 points	Cindy Klassen (Canada)	Calgary, Canada	15–17 Mar 2001
500/3,000/1,500/5,000 m	154,580 points	Cindy Klassen (Canada)	Calgary, Canada	18–19 Mar 2006
Team pursuit (6 laps)	2:56.04	Germany (Daniela Anschütz, Anni Friesinger, Claudia Pechstein)	Calgary, Canada	13 Nov 2005

SPEED SKATING – SHORT TRACK

MEN	TIME	NAME & NATIONALITY	PLACE	DATE
500 m	41.051	Sung Si-Bak (South Korea)	Salt Lake City, USA	10 Feb 2008
1,000 m	1:23.815	Michael Gilday (Canada)	Calgary, Canada	14 Oct 2007
1,500 m	2:10.639	Ahn Hyun-Soo (South Korea)	Marquette, USA	24 Oct 2003
3,000 m	4:32.646	Ahn Hyun-Soo (South Korea)	Beijing, China	7 Dec 2003
5,000 m relay	6:39.990	Canada (Charles Hamelin, Steve Robillard, François-Louis Tremblay, Mathieu Turcotte)	Beijing, China	13 Mar 2005

WOMEN	TIME	NAME & NATIONALITY	PLACE	DATE
500 m	43.216	Wang Meng (China)	Salt Lake City, USA	9 Feb 2008
1,000 m	1:29.495	Wang Meng (China)	Harbin, China	15 Mar 2008
1,500 m	2:16.729	Zhou Yang (China)	Salt Lake City, USA	9 Feb 2008
3,000 m	4:46.983	Jung Eun-Ju (South Korea)	Harbin, China	15 Mar 2008
3,000 m relay	4:09.938	South Korea (Jung Eun-Ju, Park Seung-Hi, Shin Sae-Bom, Yang Shin-Young)	Salt Lake City, USA	10 Feb 2008

★ MEN'S LONG TRACK 1,500 M
Denny Morrison (Canada) competing at the 2008 ISU Single Distances Speed Skating Championships in Nagano, Japan, on 8 March 2008. Only a few days later, on 14 March, Morrison broke the world record in the 1,500 m long-track event with a time of 1 min 42.01 sec back in his home country.

★ WOMEN'S SHORT TRACK 1,000 M

Wang Meng (China) competes in the 1,000 m semi-finals at the 2008 ISU World Short Track Speed Skating Championships on 9 March 2008 in Gangneung, South Korea. A few days later, on 15 March, she broke the world record for the 1,000 m when she clocked 1 min 29.495 sec in Harbin, China.

★ **NEW RECORD**
★ **UPDATED RECORD**

OFFICIAL WEBSITES

FREEDIVING:
www.aida-international.org

ROWING:
www.worldrowing.com

SPEED SKATING:
www.isu.org

SPORTS REFERENCE

SWIMMING – LONG COURSE (50 M POOL)

MEN	TIME	NAME & NATIONALITY	PLACE	DATE
50 m freestyle	21.64	Alexander Popov (Russia)	Moscow, Russia	16 Jun 2000
100 m freestyle	47.84	Pieter van den Hoogenband (Netherlands)	Sydney, Australia	19 Sep 2000
200 m freestyle	1:43.86	Michael Phelps (USA)	Melbourne, Australia	27 Mar 2007
400 m freestyle	3:40.08	Ian Thorpe (Australia)	Manchester, UK	30 Jul 2002
800 m freestyle	7:38.65	Grant Hackett (Australia)	Montreal, Canada	27 Jul 2005
1,500 m freestyle	14:34.56	Grant Hackett (Australia)	Fukuoka, Japan	29 Jul 2001
4 x 100 m freestyle relay	3:12.46	USA (Michael Phelps, Neil Walker, Cullen Jones, Jason Lezak)	Victoria, Canada	19 Aug 2006
4 x 200 m freestyle relay	7:03.24	USA (Michael Phelps, Ryan Lochte, Klete Keller, Peter Vanderkaay)	Melbourne, Australia	30 Mar 2007
50 m butterfly	22.96	Roland Schoeman (South Africa)	Montreal, Canada	25 Jul 2005
100 m butterfly	50.40	Ian Crocker (USA)	Montreal, Canada	30 Jul 2005
200 m butterfly	1:52.09	Michael Phelps (USA)	Melbourne, Australia	28 Mar 2007
50 m backstroke	24.80	Thomas Rupprath (Germany)	Barcelona, Spain	27 Jul 2003
100 m backstroke	52.98	Aaron Peirsol (USA)	Melbourne, Australia	27 Mar 2007
200 m backstroke	1:54.32	Ryan Lochte (USA)	Melbourne, Australia	30 Mar 2007
50 m breaststroke	27.18	Oleg Lisogor (Ukraine)	Berlin, Germany	2 Aug 2002
100 m breaststroke	59.13	Brendan Hansen (USA)	Irvine, USA	1 Aug 2006
200 m breaststroke	2:08.50	Brendan Hansen (USA)	Victoria, Canada	20 Aug 2006
200 m medley	1:54.98	Michael Phelps (USA)	Melbourne, Australia	29 Mar 2007
400 m medley	4:06.22	Michael Phelps (USA)	Melbourne, Australia	1 Apr 2007
4 x 100 m medley relay	3:30.68	USA (Aaron Peirsol, Brendan Hansen, Ian Crocker, Jason Lezak)	Athens, Greece	21 Aug 2004

WOMEN	TIME	NAME & NATIONALITY	PLACE	DATE
50 m freestyle	24.13	Inge de Bruijn (Netherlands)	Sydney, Australia	22 Sep 2000
100 m freestyle	53.30	Britta Steffen (Germany)	Budapest, Hungary	2 Aug 2006
200 m freestyle	1:55.52	Laure Manaudou (France)	Melbourne, Australia	28 Mar 2007
400 m freestyle	4:02.13	Laure Manaudou (France)	Budapest, Hungary	6 Aug 2006
800 m freestyle	8:16.22	Janet Evans (USA)	Tokyo, Japan	20 Aug 1989
1,500 m freestyle	15:42.54	Kate Ziegler (USA)	Mission Viejo, USA	17 Jun 2007
4 x 100 m freestyle relay	3:35.22	Germany (Petra Dallmann, Daniella Goetz, Britta Steffen, Annika Liebs)	Budapest, Hungary	31 Jul 2006
4 x 200 m freestyle relay	7:50.09	USA (Natalie Coughlin, Dana Vollmer, Lacey Nymeyer, Katie Hoff)	Melbourne, Australia	29 Mar 2007
50 m butterfly	25.46	Therese Alshammar (Sweden)	Barcelona, Spain	13 Jun 2007
100 m butterfly	56.61	Inge de Bruijn (Netherlands)	Sydney, Australia	17 Sep 2000
200 m butterfly	2:05.40	Jessicah Schipper (Australia)	Victoria, Canada	17 Aug 2006
50 m backstroke	28.09	Li Yang (China)	Hyderabad, India	19 Oct 2007
100 m backstroke	59.44	Natalie Coughlin (USA)	Melbourne, Australia	27 Mar 2007
200 m backstroke	2:06.62	Krisztina Egerszegi (Hungary)	Athens, Greece	25 Aug 1991
50 m breaststroke	30.31	Jade Edmistone (Australia)	Melbourne, Australia	30 Jan 2006
100 m breaststroke	1:05.09	Leisel Jones (Australia)	Melbourne, Australia	20 Mar 2006
200 m breaststroke	2:20.54	Leisel Jones (Australia)	Melbourne, Australia	21 Feb 2006
200 m medley	2:09.72	Wu Yanyan (China)	Shanghai, China	17 Oct 1997
400 m medley	4:32.89	Katie Hoff (USA)	Melbourne, Australia	1 Apr 2007
4 x 100 m medley relay	3:55.74	Australia (Emily Seebohm, Leisel Jones, Jessicah Schipper, Lisbeth Lenton)	Melbourne, Australia	31 Mar 2007

MEN'S 800 M FREESTYLE

Grant Hackett (Australia) won the gold medal in a time of 7 min 38.65 sec in the 800 m long course freestyle final during the XI FINA World Championships in Montreal, Quebec, Canada, on 27 July 2005. Hackett also holds the 1,500 m freestyle record.

★ WOMEN'S 50 M BUTTERFLY

A happy Therese Alshammar (Sweden) after swimming the 50 m long course butterfly in 25.46 seconds during the second leg of Europe's Mare Nostrum Series in Barcelona, Spain, on 13 June 2007.

★ NEW RECORD
✦ UPDATED RECORD

OFFICIAL WEBSITE

SWIMMING:
www.fina.org

SWIMMING – SHORT COURSE (25 M POOL)

MEN	TIME	NAME & NATIONALITY	PLACE	DATE
50 m freestyle	20.93	Stefan Nystrand (Sweden)	Berlin, Germany	18 Nov 2007
100 m freestyle	45.83	Stefan Nystrand (Sweden)	Berlin, Germany	18 Nov 2007
200 m freestyle	1:41.10	Ian Thorpe (Australia)	Berlin, Germany	6 Feb 2000
400 m freestyle	3:34.58	Grant Hackett (Australia)	Sydney, Australia	18 Jul 2002
800 m freestyle	7:25.28	Grant Hackett (Australia)	Perth, Australia	3 Aug 2001
1,500 m freestyle	14:10.10	Grant Hackett (Australia)	Perth, Australia	7 Aug 2001
4 x 100 m freestyle relay	3:09.57	Sweden (Johan Nyström, Lars Frölander, Mattias Ohlin, Stefan Nystrand)	Athens, Greece	16 Mar 2000
4 x 200 m freestyle relay	6:52.66	Australia (Kirk Palmer, Grant Hackett, Grant Brits, Kenrick Monk)	Melbourne, Australia	31 Aug 2007
50 m butterfly	22.60	Kaio Almeida (Brazil)	Santos, Brazil	17 Dec 2005
100 m butterfly	49.07	Ian Crocker (USA)	New York City, USA	26 Mar 2004
200 m butterfly	1:50.73	Franck Esposito (France)	Antibes, France	8 Dec 2002
50 m backstroke	23.27	Thomas Rupprath (Germany)	Vienna, Austria	10 Dec 2004
100 m backstroke	49.99	Ryan Lochte (USA)	Shanghai, China	9 Apr 2006
200 m backstroke	1:49.05	Ryan Lochte (USA)	Shanghai, China	9 Apr 2006
50 m breaststroke	26.17	Oleg Lisogor (Ukraine)	Berlin, Germany	21 Jan 2006
100 m breaststroke	57.47	Ed Moses (USA)	Stockholm, Sweden	23 Jan 2002
200 m breaststroke	2:02.92	Ed Moses (USA)	Berlin, Germany	17 Jan 2004
200 m medley	1:52.99	Laszlo Cseh (Hungary)	Debrecen, Hungary	13 Dec 2007
400 m medley	3:59.33	Laszlo Cseh (Hungary)	Debrecen, Hungary	14 Dec 2007
4 x 100 m medley relay	3:25.09	USA (Aaron Peirsol, Brendan Hansen, Ian Crocker, Jason Lezak)	Indianapolis, USA	11 Oct 2004

WOMEN	TIME	NAME & NATIONALITY	PLACE	DATE
50 m freestyle	23.58	Marleen Veldhuis (Netherlands)	Berlin, Germany	18 Nov 2007
100 m freestyle	51.70	Lisbeth Lenton (Australia)	Melbourne, Australia	9 Aug 2005
200 m freestyle	1:53.29	Lisbeth Lenton (Australia)	Sydney, Australia	19 Nov 2005
400 m freestyle	3:56.09	Laure Manaudou (France)	Helsinki, Finland	9 Dec 2006
800 m freestyle	8:08.00	Kate Ziegler (USA)	Essen, Germany	14 Oct 2007
1,500 m freestyle	15:32.90	Kate Ziegler (USA)	Essen, Germany	12 Oct 2007
4 x 100 m freestyle relay	3:30.85	Netherlands (Hinkelien Schreuder, Femke Heemskerk, Ranomi Kranowidjojo, Marleen Veldhuis)	Eindhoven, the Netherlands	9 Dec 2007
4 x 200 m freestyle relay	7:46.30	China (Xu Yanvei, Zhu Yingven, Tang Jingzhi, Yang Yu)	Moscow, Russia	3 Apr 2002
50 m butterfly	25.33	Anne-Karin Kammerling (Sweden)	Gothenburg, Sweden	12 Mar 2005
100 m butterfly	55.95	Lisbeth Lenton (Australia)	Hobart, Australia	28 Aug 2006
200 m butterfly	2:03.53	Otylia Jedrzejczak (Poland)	Debrecen, Hungary	13 Dec 2007
50 m backstroke	26.50	Sanja Jovanovic (Croatia)	Debrecen, Hungary	15 Dec 2007
100 m backstroke	56.51	Natalie Coughlin (USA)	Singapore	28 Oct 2007
200 m backstroke	2:03.62	Natalie Coughlin (USA)	New York City, USA	27 Nov 2001
50 m breaststroke	29.90	Jade Edmistone (Australia)	Brisbane, Australia	26 Sep 2004
100 m breaststroke	1:03.86	Leisel Jones (Australia)	Hobart, Australia	28 Aug 2006
200 m breaststroke	2:17.75	Leisel Jones (Australia)	Melbourne, Australia	29 Nov 2003
200 m medley	2:07.79	Allison Wagner (USA)	Palma de Mallorca, Spain	5 Dec 1993
400 m medley	4:27.83	Yana Klochkova (Ukraine)	Paris, France	19 Jan 2002
4 x 100 m medley relay	3:51.84	Australia (Tayliah Zimmer, Jade Edmistone, Jessicah Schipper, Lisbeth Lenton)	Shanghai, China	7 Apr 2006

★ MEN'S 200 M & 400 M MEDLEYS

Laszlo Cseh (Hungary) broke his own 400 m medley record with a time of 3 min 59.33 sec on 14 December 2007 during the European Short Course Swimming Championships. The previous day he had set a new record in the 200 m medley of 1 min 52.99 sec.

★ WOMEN'S 200 M BUTTERFLY

Otylia Jedrzejczak (Poland) swims the 200 m butterfly at the European Short Track Swimming Championships in Debrecen, Hungary, on 13 December 2007. She won in a record time of 2 min 3.53 sec.

WEIGHTLIFTING

MEN	CATEGORY	WEIGHT LIFTED	NAME & NATIONALITY	PLACE	DATE
56 kg	Snatch	138 kg	Halil Mutlu (Turkey)	Antalya, Turkey	4 Nov 2001
	Clean & jerk	168 kg	Halil Mutlu (Turkey)	Trencín, Slovakia	24 Apr 2001
	Total	305 kg	Halil Mutlu (Turkey)	Sydney, Australia	16 Sep 2000
62 kg	Snatch	153 kg	Shi Zhiyong (China)	Izmir, Turkey	28 Jun 2002
	Clean & jerk	182 kg	Le Maosheng (China)	Busan, South Korea	2 Oct 2002
	Total	325 kg	World Standard*		
69 kg	Snatch	165 kg	Georgi Markov (Bulgaria)	Sydney, Australia	20 Sep 2000
	Clean & jerk	197 kg	Zhang Guozheng (China)	Qinhuangdao, China	11 Sep 2003
	Total	357 kg	Galabin Boevski (Bulgaria)	Athens, Greece	24 Nov 1999
77 kg	Snatch	173 kg	Sergey Filimonov (Kazakhstan)	Almaty, Kazakhstan	9 Apr 2004
	Clean & jerk	210 kg	Oleg Perepetchenov (Russia)	Trencín, Slovakia	27 Apr 2001
	Total	377 kg	Plamen Zhelyazkov (Bulgaria)	Doha, Qatar	27 Mar 2002
85 kg	★Snatch	187 kg	Andrei Rybakou (Belarus)	Chiang Mai, Thailand	22 Sep 2007
	Clean & jerk	218 kg	Zhang Yong (China)	Ramat Gan, Israel	25 Apr 1998
	Total	395 kg	World Standard*		
94 kg	Snatch	188 kg	Akakios Kakhiasvilis (Greece)	Athens, Greece	27 Nov 1999
	Clean & jerk	232 kg	Szymon Kolecki (Poland)	Sofia, Bulgaria	29 Apr 2000
	Total	417 kg	World Standard*		
105 kg	Snatch	199 kg	Marcin Dolega (Poland)	Wladyslawowo, Poland	7 May 2006
	Clean & jerk	242 kg	World Standard*		
	Total	440 kg	World Standard*		
+105 kg	Snatch	213 kg	Hossein Rezazadeh (Iran)	Qinhuangdao, China	14 Sep 2003
	Clean & jerk	263 kg	Hossein Rezazadeh (Iran)	Athens, Greece	25 Aug 2004
	Total	472 kg	Hossein Rezazadeh (Iran)	Sydney, Australia	26 Sep 2000

WOMEN	CATEGORY	WEIGHT LIFTED	NAME & NATIONALITY	PLACE	DATE
48 kg	Snatch	98 kg	Yang Lian (China)	Santo Domingo, Dominican Republic	1 Oct 2006
	Clean & jerk	120 kg	Chen Xiexia (China)	Taian City, China	21 Apr 2007
	Total	217 kg	Yang Lian (China)	Santo Domingo, Dominican Republic	1 Oct 2006
53 kg	Snatch	102 kg	Ri Song-Hui (North Korea)	Busan, South Korea	1 Oct 2002
	Clean & jerk	129 kg	Li Ping (China)	Taian City, China	22 Apr 2007
	Total	226 kg	Qiu Hongxia (China)	Santo Domingo, Dominican Republic	2 Oct 2006
58 kg	Snatch	111 kg	Chen Yanqing (China)	Doha, Qatar	3 Dec 2006
	Clean & jerk	141 kg	Qiu Hongmei (China)	Taian City, China	23 Apr 2007
	Total	251 kg	Chen Yanqing (China)	Doha, Qatar	3 Dec 2006
63 kg	Snatch	116 kg	Pawina Thongsuk (Thailand)	Doha, Qatar	12 Nov 2005
	Clean & jerk	142 kg	Pawina Thongsuk (Thailand)	Doha, Qatar	4 Dec 2006
	★Total	257 kg	Liu Haixia (China)	Chiang Mai, Thailand	23 Sep 2007
69 kg	Snatch	123 kg	Oxana Slivenko (Russia)	Santo Domingo, Dominican Republic	4 Oct 2006
	Clean & jerk	157 kg	Zarema Kasaeva (Russia)	Doha, Qatar	25 Apr 1998
	★Total	276 kg	Oxana Slivenko (Russia)	Chiang Mai, Thailand	24 Sep 2007
75 kg	★Snatch	131 kg	Natalia Zabolotnaia (Russia)	Chiang Mai, Thailand	25 Sep 2007
	Clean & jerk	159 kg	Liu Chunhong (China)	Doha, Qatar	13 Nov 2005
	Total	286 kg	Svetlana Podobedova (Russia)	Hangzhou, China	2 Jun 2006
+75 kg	Snatch	139 kg	Mu Shuangshuang (China)	Doha, Qatar	6 Dec 2006
	Clean & jerk	182 kg	Gonghong Tang (China)	Athens, Greece	21 Aug 2004
	★Total	319 kg	Mu Shuangshuang (China)	Chiang Mai, Thailand	26 Sep 2007

* From 1 January 1998, the International Weightlifting Federation (IWF) introduced modified bodyweight categories, thereby making the then world records redundant. This is the new listing with the world standards for the new bodyweight categories. Results achieved at IWF-approved competitions exceeding the world standards by a minimum of **1 kg** will be recognized as world records.

★MEN'S 85 KG SNATCH

Andrei Rybakou (Belarus) lifts the bar to break the world record in the men's 85 kg snatch at the weightlifting World Championships in Chiang Mai, Thailand, on 22 September 2007. He succeeded in lifting 187 kg.

OFFICIAL WEBSITES

WEIGHTLIFTING:
www.iwf.net

WATER-SKIING:
www.iwsf.com

★NEW RECORD
★UPDATED RECORD

★WOMEN'S 75 KG SNATCH

Natalia Zabolotnaia (Russia) lifts the bar to win the gold medal in the women's 75 kg snatch at the weightlifting World Championships in Chiang Mai, Thailand, on 25 September 2007. She lifted 131 kg.

WATER-SKIING

MEN

MEN	RECORD	NAME & NATIONALITY	PLACE	DATE
Slalom	1.5 buoy/9.75-m line	Chris Parrish (USA)	Trophy Lakes, USA	28 Aug 2005
Barefoot slalom	20.6 crossings of wake in 15 seconds	Keith St Onge (USA)	Bronkhorstspruit, South Africa	6 Jan 2006
Tricks	12,400 points	Nicolas Le Forestier (France)	Lac de Joux, Switzerland	4 Sep 2005
Barefoot tricks	10,880 points	Keith St Onge (USA)	Adna, USA	17 Sep 2006
Jump	74.2 m (243 ft 5 in)	Freddy Krueger (USA)	Seffner, USA	5 Nov 2006
Barefoot jump	27.4 m (89 ft 11 in)	David Small (GB)	Mulwala, Australia	8 Feb 2004
Ski fly	91.1 m (298 ft 10 in)	Jaret Llewellyn (Canada)	Orlando, USA	14 May 2000
Overall	2,818.01 points*	Jaret Llewellyn (Canada)	Seffner, USA	29 Sep 2002

WOMEN

WOMEN	RECORD	NAME & NATIONALITY	PLACE	DATE
Slalom	1 buoy/10.25-m line	Kristi Overton Johnson (USA)	West Palm Beach, USA	14 Sep 1996
Barefoot slalom	17.0 crossings of wake in 15 seconds	Nadine de Villiers (South Africa)	Witbank, South Africa	5 Jan 2001
Tricks	8,740 points	Mandy Nightingale (USA)	Santa Rosa, USA	10 Jun 2006
Barefoot tricks	4,400 points	Nadine de Villiers (South Africa)	Witbank, South Africa	5 Jan 2001
Jump	56.6 m (186 ft)	Elena Milakova (Russia)	Rio Linda, USA	21 Jul 2002
Barefoot jump	20.6 m (67 ft 7 in)	Nadine de Villiers (South Africa)	Pretoria, South Africa	4 Mar 2000
Ski fly	69.4 m (227 ft 8.2 in)	Elena Milakova (Russia)	Pine Mountain, USA	26 May 2002
Overall	2,850.11 points**	Clementine Lucine (France)	Lacanau, France	9 Jul 2006

* 5@11.25 m, 10,730 tricks, 71.7 m jump   ** 4@11.25 m, 8,680 tricks, 52.1 m jump; calculated with the 2006 scoring method

★ **MEN'S WATER-SKI JUMP**
Freddy Krueger (USA) jumped a record 74.2 m (243 ft 5 in) on 5 November 2006 in Seffner, USA.

LONGEST SPORTS MARATHONS

SPORT	TIME	NAME & NATIONALITY	PLACE	DATE
★ Aerobics	24 hours	Duberney Trujillo (Colombia)	Dosquebradas, Colombia	26–27 Feb 2005
Archery	27 hours	Michael Henri Dames (South Africa)	Grahamstown, South Africa	8–9 Aug 2005
Baseball	32 hr 29 min 25 sec	St Louis Chapter of the Men's Senior Baseball League (USA)	O'Fallon, Missouri, USA	13–14 Oct 2007
Basketball	72 hours	Students of Holy Trinity Church of England Secondary School (UK)	Crawley, West Sussex, UK	13–16 Jul 2007
Basketball (wheelchair)	26 hr 3 min	University of Omaha students and staff (USA)	Omaha, Nebraska, USA	24–25 Sep 2004
Bowling (tenpin)	120 hours	Andy Milne (Canada)	Mississauga, Ontario, Canada	24–29 Oct 2005
Bowls (indoor)	36 hours	Arnos Bowling Club (UK)	Southgate, UK	20–21 Apr 2002
Bowls (outdoor)	105 hours	Lloyd Hotel Bowling Club (UK)	Manchester, UK	14–18 Oct 2006
Cricket	35 hours	Chestfield CC and Oakwood Homes (UK)	Chestfield, UK	8–9 Sep 2007
Curling	40 hr 23 min	B. Huston, C. McCarthy, G. Poole, K. McCarthy, K. Martin, M. Witherspoon, R. Martin, T. Gouldie, T. Teskey, W. From (Canada)	Brandon, Manitoba, Canada	9–10 Mar 2007
Darts (doubles)	25 hr 34 min	Richard Saunders, Derek Fox, Paul Taylor, Andrew Brymer (UK)	Hurst, Berkshire, UK	12–13 Jan 2007
Darts (singles)	26 hr 22 min	Chris Nessling and Mick Dundee (UK)	Hurst, Berkshire, UK	12–13 Jan 2007
★ Fistball (indoor)	24 hours	TG 1855 Neustadt bei Coburg e.V. (Germany)	Frankehalle, Neustadt, Germany	16–17 Apr 2005
★ Floorball	24 hr 15 min	TRM Floorball and Hornets Regio Moosseedorf Worblental (Switzerland)	Zollikofen, Switzerland	27–28 Apr 2007
Football	30 hr 10 min	FC Edo Simme and FC Spiez (Germany)	Erlenbach, Switzerland	8–9 Jul 2006
★ Football (five a side)	24 hr 30 min	Rossendale Mavericks and the Fearns Community Sports College (UK)	Waterfoot Rossendale, UK	23–24 Nov 2007
Futsal (indoors)	30 hours	Max Cosi/Quinny and Keo teams (Cyprus)	Limassol, Cyprus	19–20 Nov 2005
Handball	70 hours	HV Mighty/Stevo team (Netherlands)	Tubbergen, the Netherlands	30 Aug–2 Sep 2001
Hockey (ice)	240 hours	Brent Saik and friends (Canada)	Strathcona, Alberta, Canada	11–21 Feb 2005
Hockey (indoor)	32 hours	TF Farm Industries and Sandyhill teams (Canada)	Taber, Alberta, Canada	17–18 Aug 2007
Hockey (inline/roller)	24 hours	8K Roller Hockey League (USA)	Eastpointe, Michigan, USA	13–14 Sep 2002
Hockey (street)	100 hr 2 min	Blacks and Reds, Face-off for a Cure (Canada)	Winnipeg, Manitoba, Canada	13–17 May 2007
Korfball	26 hr 2 min	Korfball Club de Vinken (Netherlands)	Vinkeveen, the Netherlands	23–24 May 2001
Netball	56 hours	Airborne Netball Club (UK)	Bristol, UK	26–28 May 2007
Parasailing	24 hr 10 min	Berne Persson (Sweden)	Lake Graningesjön, Sweden	19–20 Jul 2002
Pétanque (boules)	40 hr 9 min	Bevenser Boule-Freunde (Germany)	Bad Bevensen, Germany	22–23 Jul 2006
★ Pool (singles)	50 hr 2 min	Alan Skerritt and Mike Tunnell (UK)	Stockton-on-Tees, UK	22–24 Mar 2006
Skiing	202 hr 1 min	Nick Willey (Australia)	Thredbo, NSW, Australia	2–10 Sep 2005
Snowboarding	180 hr 34 min	Bernhard Mair (Austria)	Bad Kleinkirchheim, Austria	9–16 Jan 2004
Spinning (static cycling)	175 hr 50 min	Joey Motsay (USA)	Greenboro, North Carolina, USA	22–29 Sep 2007
Table football	40 hr 30 min	Volker Lewedey, Karsten Link, Jakob Polzer and Christian Röhrer (Germany)	Spaichingen, Germany	14–15 Jul 2007
Table tennis (doubles)	101 hr 1 min 11 sec	Lance, Phil and Mark Warren and Bill Weir (USA)	Sacramento, California, USA	9–13 Apr 1979
Table tennis (singles)	132 hr 31 min	Danny Price and Randy Nunes (USA)	Cherry Hill, New Jersey, USA	20–26 Aug 1978
Tai chi	25 hr 5 min	Ken Dickenson and Kevin Bartolo (Australia)	Sutherland, NSW, Australia	17–18 Mar 2006
Tennis (doubles match)	48 hr 15 min	Brian Jahrsdoerfer, Michel Lavoie, Peter Okpokpo, Warner Tse (USA)	Houston, Texas, USA	13–15 Apr 2006
Tennis (singles match)	26 hr 26 min 26 sec	Rinie Loeffen and Ton Dollevoet (Netherlands)	Macharen, the Netherlands	23–24 Jun 2007
Tobogganing (steel)	56 hours	Michael Kinzel (Germany)	Kirchhundem, Germany	4–6 May 2002
Volleyball (indoor)	55 hr 3 min	OBEY (USA)	Lexington, Kentucky, USA	30 Jul–1 Aug 2007
Wakeboarding	6 hr 17 min	Ian Taylor (UK)	Milton Keynes, UK	1 Sep 2004

PLEASE NOTE: *GWR sports marathon guidelines are constantly updated – please contact us for information before you attempt a record.*

HOLLYWOOD HALL OF FAME

There's 300 to 400 films every year. Five of them get that phone call, and I've gotten it 18 times... I really feel fortunate.

Kevin O'Connell,
interviewed in 2006

MOST OSCAR NOMINATIONS WITHOUT A WIN

Sound mixer Kevin O'Connell (USA) has received 20 Oscar nominations for sound, starting with *Terms of Endearment* (USA, 1983) in 1984 and most recently with *Transformers* (USA, 2007) in 2008 – the longest losing streak in Oscar history! He is pictured below at his mantlepiece, where his Oscar statue will eventually go!

★ MOST LUCRATIVE MOVIE PARTNERSHIP

In terms of total box-office gross, the most successful partnership in Hollywood – not including sequels – is that of director Tim Burton (above left) and actor Johnny Depp (above right). Together, the duo have grossed $986.89 million (£500.73 million) from six movies: *Edward Scissorhands, Ed Wood, Sleepy Hollow, Charlie and the Chocolate Factory, The Corpse Bride* and *Sweeney Todd* (pictured).

I hate film premieres. The one thing I never do at them is smile – neither does Johnny Depp or Tim Burton. It's so phoney.

Christopher Lee

CHRISTOPHER LEE

The veteran actor with over 244 acknowledged film and TV movie roles out of at least 358 screen credits is also the actor with the most sword fights in a movie career (17). We caught up with the screen legend and asked what it felt like to be a Guinness World Record holder.
Well, the word "survival" comes to mind! Survival and privilege. Sometimes when I look at all the things I've done, I don't realize it was me. I was going through a list of everyone in this business that I've worked with – or even just met – and I worked out that I've met just about everyone you would have heard of – from the Goldern Era, at least – everyone except [Greta] Garbo.

Who's the greatest actor you've ever worked with?
The greatest *actress* I've worked with was Bette Davis [in *Return from Witch Mountain* (USA, 1978)], and the French actor Jean Reno [in *Crimson Rivers 2: Angels of the Apocalypse* (USA, 2004)] was terrific – such a generous man. The best *young* actor I can think of is [Leonardo] DiCaprio. I met him, and he was very nice, very quiet. Oh, and Viggo Mortensen is a wonderful actor, isn't he? And Johnny Depp – he's brilliant, and a good friend of mine.

Are you happy to have played the bad guy so often?
Well, they're much more interesting to play! But I haven't made what they refer to as – and I dislike, as did [co-star] Boris Karloff – a "horror" film since 1975. I was typecast for a while, but not any more.

Any advice for up-and-coming actors?
Don't expect to be a megastar overnight. I've always said that it takes ten years to become an actor. Far too many actors are far too young to handle major roles.

DANIEL DAY-LEWIS
Most Best Actor Oscar wins (2)*

MERYL STREEP
Most Oscar-nominated actress (14)

ANGELINA JOLIE
Most powerful actress in Hollywood

A GWR PRODUCTION

Hollywood

HALL O

THE RECORD-BREAKING MOVERS AND S

*RECORD SHARED WITH TOM HANKS, DUSTIN HOFFMAN, FREDERIC MARCH, GARY COOPER, MARLON BRANDO AND SPENCER TRACEY. DANIEL
JACK NICHOLSON AWARDED OSCARS FOR TERMS OF ENDEARMENT (1983) AND AS GOOD AS IT GETS (1998) • †BASED ON 68 MOVIES M
• THE GUINNESS WORLD RECORDS MOVIE POWER RATINGS ARE CALCULATED USING A COMBINATION OF EARNINGS, BOX OF

SIZE MATTERS

To fully ratify any height-related claims, Guinness World Records insists on taking six measurements of the claimant three times in one day – in the morning, afternoon and evening – both lying down and standing up. The final height is the average of the six figures.

There are, however, people who cannot be as thoroughly measured, for medical reasons. For example, sufferers of severe osteogenesis imperfecta, or OI ("imperfect bone formation") – a crippling genetic disorder characterized by congenital brittle bones – are unable to stand or lie flat.

Linn Yih-Chih of Taiwan (below right) is technically the world's **shortest living man** at 67.5 cm (27 in), but he is immobilized by OI, as is Madge Bester (South Africa, pictured being kissed), the **shortest living woman** at 65 cm (26 in).

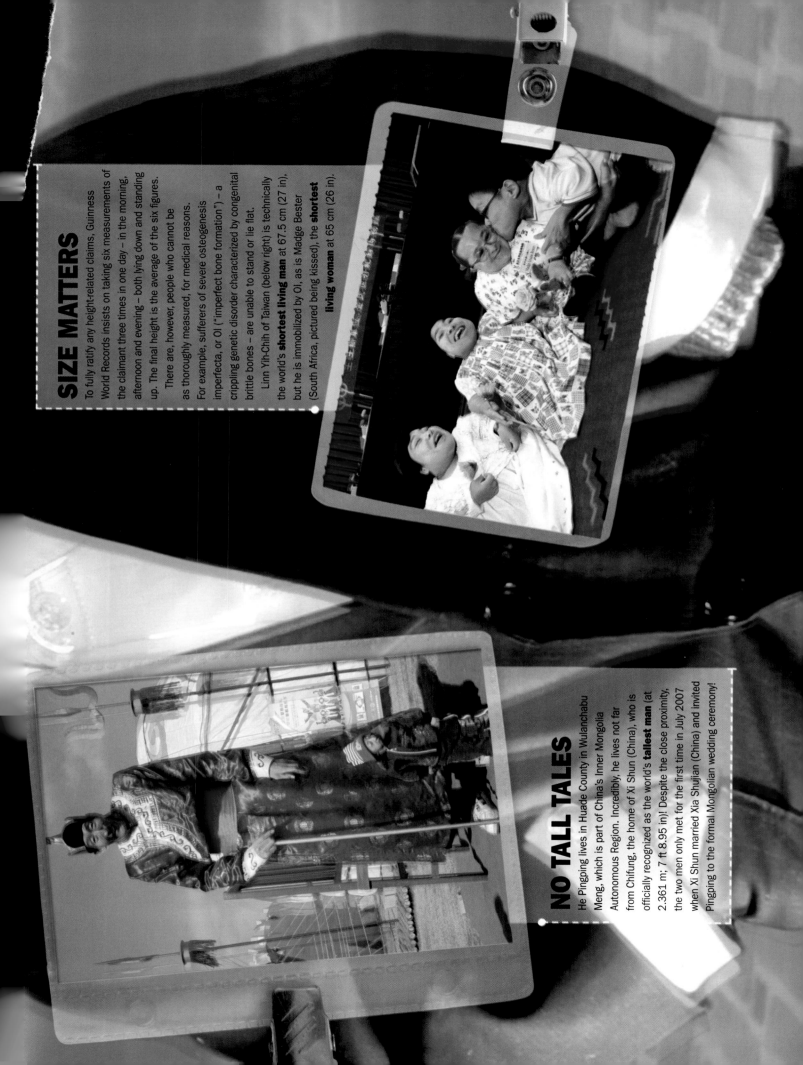

NO TALL TALES

He Pingping lives in Huade County in Wulanchabu Meng, which is part of China's Inner Mongolia Autonomous Region. Incredibly, he lives not far from Chifung, the home of Xi Shun (China), who is officially recognized as the world's **tallest man** (at 2.361 m; 7 ft 8.95 in)! Despite the close proximity, the two men only met for the first time in July 2007 when Xi Shun married Xia Shujian (China) and invited Pingping to the formal Mongolian wedding ceremony!

HE PINGPING

MEET HE PINGPING

He's from China and he's the **shortest (mobile) living man** to be officially authenticated by Guinness World Records. The minuscule 19-year-old from Inner Mongolia, China, measures just 74.61 cm (2 ft 5.37 in) and is seen here at his actual size!

To welcome Pingping to the Guinness World Records family, we've produced this fold-out feature – so, read on to discover more about this incredible new record breaker.

ACTUAL SIZE

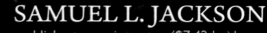

WOOD

SAMUEL L. JACKSON
Highest-grossing actor ($7.42 bn)†

JACK NICHOLSON
Most Oscar-nominated actor (12)
Most Best Actor Oscar wins (2)*

BRAD PITT
Most powerful actor in Hollywood

F FAME

HAKERS IN THE MOVIE POWER GAME

DAY-LEWIS AWARDED OSCARS FOR MY LEFT FOOT: THE STORY OF CHRISTIE BROWN (1990) AND THERE WILL BE BLOOD (2008);
ING STAR WARS: EPISODES I, II & III, JURASSIC PARK, THE INCREDIBLES, PATRIOT GAMES, S.W.A.T. AND PULP FICTION
E TAKINGS, AWARDS, WEB IMPRESSIONS AND PR. & MEDIA EXPPOSURE BETWEEN 1 MAY 2007 AND 30 APRIL 2008

THE MAGIC OF
HARRY POTTER

HARRY POTTER AND THE...

TITLE	BOOK SALES	CINEMA OPENING	CINEMA GROSS
Philosopher's/ Sorcerer's Stone	120 million	$90,294,621	$968,657,891
Chamber of Secrets	77 million	$88,357,488	$866,300,000
Prisoner of Azkaban	61 million	$93,687,367	$789,458,727
Goblet of Fire	66 million	$102,685,961	$892,194,397
Order of the Phoenix	55 million	$77,108,414	$937,000,866
Half-Blood Prince	65 million	n/a	n/a
Deathly Hallows	75 million	n/a	n/a

HARRY MAGIC

★ LARGEST ORDER OF FORESTRY-CERTIFIED PAPER

Almost two-thirds of the initial 16,700 tonnes (36.8 million lbs) of paper needed to print *Deathly Hallows* in the USA was certified by the Forest Stewardship Council (FSC), the global body responsible for forest management.

★ FASTEST-SELLING FICTION BOOK (24 HRS)

Deathly Hallows sold 8.3 million copies in the first 24 hours (or 345,833 books per hour) following its release in the USA on 21 July 2007.

LARGEST FIRST-EDITION PRINT RUN

The release of *Order of the Phoenix* in June 2003 marked the largest first-edition print run ever, at 8.5 million copies.

MOST ADVANCE ORDERS

Goblet of Fire received record advance orders of 5.3 million copies from around the world.

FASTEST-SELLING DVD EVER

The *Goblet of Fire* DVD sold more than six copies per second on the day of release in the UK on 20 March 2006 and has continued to sell more than three copies per second since. It also sold more than 5 million copies on the first day of release in the USA, on 7 March 2006.

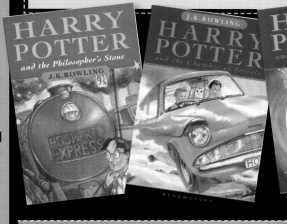

J. K. ROWLING

The Harry Potter series has sold 400 million copies worldwide and made its creator one of the wealthiest people in the world. We wanted to know which was her favourite book of the series...

Deathly Hallows remains my favourite book of the series. I hope that, even if it's not yours, you understand, at least that this was where the story was leading; it was the ending I had planned for 17 years, and there was more satisfaction than you can possibly imagine in finally sharing it with my readers.

Now that it's all over, how would you describe your time with Harry?

It's been one of the longest relationships of my adult life: my rock through bereavement, marriage and divorce, single motherhood, changes of country and also of joy – on the day Bloomsbury decided to publish it.

You support many notable charities. Why did you decide to start your own?

The Children's High Level Group was founded by, amongst others, MEP Emma Nicholson and myself when we were deeply moved by the poverty, sickness and maltreatment of children. The Children's Voice campaign wants to make life better for young people in care around the world.

RECORD HOLDER!

After repeated visits to the hospital for measurements and having satisfied all the other criteria, Pingping finally earned his Guinness World Records certificate. The average measurement takes into account the shrinking of the spine during a typical day – the spongy discs between the vertebrae become more compact, which is why you go to bed shorter than when you wake up! – but in Pingping's case, the variation was minimal. Welcome to the GWR family!

NELSON DE LA ROSA

The title of **shortest (mobile) living man** (see above) passes to Pingping from Nelson de la Rosa (Dominican Republic), who measured 72 cm (28.3 in). Before his death at the age of 38 in October 2006, this colourful character had carved out a successful media career for himself, including a role in *The Island of Dr. Moreau* (USA, 1996).

GUINNESS WORLD RECORDS

CERTIFICATE

The shortest (mobile) living man
is He Pingping (China. b. 1988),
who was measured in
Hohhot, China on
22 March 2008

GUINNESS WORLD RECORDS LTD

EYEWITNESS TESTIMONY

To verify He Pingping's final height, Guinness World Records' Editor-in-Chief Craig Glenday personally oversaw the six-step measuring process in a hospital in Hohhot, the capital city of Inner Mongolia. "The tallest and smallest human categories are among the most important records," he said. "Nothing should be left to chance or doubt."

ADULTS ONLY!

The average Chinese adult measures between 165 and 170 cm (5 ft 5 in–5 ft 7 in), but Pingping's height is equivalent to that of a one-year-old child. For this reason, it is important that we confirmed his age, as only people who are over 18 years old are eligible for this record. Pingping proved his age with his identity card (held by everyone in China over the age of 16, see picture below right), confirming that he had reached adulthood.

DEFINING HEIGHTS

When Pingping was born, his brother-in-law told us, he was no bigger than his father's palm. Doctors at the time diagnosed osteogenesis imperfecta (see "Size Matters" box, above right). However, his mobility now suggests that this is not the case.

There is no doubt that he has a dwarfism, but there are around 200 different types of that condition – so which one is it?

• Primordial dwarfism (PD) is a profound growth retardation that begins in the womb and continues after birth. There are many subtypes, which can be difficult to diagnose, but the umbrella term means "small from the beginning of life".

• Pingping also displays "proportionate dwarfism", as his legs, arms, head and body are the same size in relation to one other. The medical definition for this used to be "midget", although this is no longer considered an acceptable term; "person of short stature" or simply "little person" are now preferred. (The most common dwarfism is achondroplasia, which accounts for 70% of cases and results in shortened limbs or a shortened trunk.)

HALLOWED VOICES

In April 2007, actor Jim Dale (UK) created and recorded 146 different and distinguishable character voices for the US audiobook *Harry Potter and the Deathly Hallows* – the ★**most voices by an individual in an audiobook**. He shares the record with Stephen Fry (UK), narrator of the UK edition.

LARGEST READING

J.K. Rowling was one of three authors who read excerpts from their works to a record audience of 20,264 at Toronto's SkyDome stadium (Canada) on 24 October 2000. Rowling read from *Harry Potter and the Goblet of Fire*; readings were also given by Kenneth Oppel and Tim Wynne-Jones (both Canada).

MONEY MAGIC

GWR's entertainment consultant Thomasina Gibson spoke to the Hogwarts high flying trio and heard how they spend some of their hard-earned sickles and knuts.

Rupert Grint "Oh, I bought a proper Mr Whippy-type ice-cream van! It's really cool. It's got everything. Whipped ice-cream, treats, toppings – the lot!"

Emma Watson "I guess my biggest thing was I bought myself an Apple Mac, my little laptop, which I love. It's my pride and joy."

Daniel Radcliffe "I'm quite interested in artwork and things like that but I've never been into cars so I don't think I'm going to dash out and buy an exotic car any time soon like people expect me to."

DANIEL RADCLIFFE

Daniel Radcliffe talked to GWR about playing Harry Potter and the advice his parents gave him about handling his fame…

My mum and dad have just told me to enjoy it. There are a lot worse things that could happen than just being recognized.

What was the most memorable part of film-making, and the most nerve-wracking?

I'm not just saying this, but one of the best parts was working with Chris [Columbus], because he's a total inspiration. He really enjoys what he does, and it's a real honour working with him. The most nerve-wracking thing was the first day, because before that it had just been me, Rupert [Grint], Emma [Watson] and Chris, rehearsing in Chris's office. I got the call sheet for the first day, I looked under the cast and it said "Daniel Radcliffe, Emma Watson and Rupert Grint". So I thought, fine, I'm used to that. Then I turned over the page and it said: "Extras, 150." At that moment, I got quite scared…

RECORD-BREAKING CAST & CREW

The Harry Potter film franchise is among the most successful ever, grossing an average of $890 million per movie and attracting the cream of British and American talent both in front of the cameras and behind. Among those who brought the books alive are a selection of record holders:

Robbie Coltrane (Hagrid): Robbie Coltrane (UK, right) earned himself a record for the **most consecutive Best Actor BAFTA wins**, with three, playing criminal psychologist Eddie "Fitz" Fitzgerald in *Cracker* in 1994, 1995 and 1996.

Michael Gambon (Dumbledore, below): Equalling Coltrane's record for the **most consecutive Best Actor BAFTA wins** is Michael Gambon (UK), who won BAFTA gongs for *Wives and Daughters* (1999), *Longitude* (2000) and *Perfect Strangers* (2001).

Emma Thompson (Sybil Trelawney): In 1993, Emma Thompson (UK) won a Best Actress Oscar for her role in *Howards End* (UK, 1991) and was awarded Best Screenplay Written Directly for the Screen for *Sense and Sensibility* (USA/UK, 1995) in 1996, making her the **first person to win Oscars for both acting and writing**.

Julie Walters (Molly Weasley): The record for the **most Best Actress BAFTA wins** is three, shared by four British actresses, one of whom is Julie Walters (UK). She won for *My Beautiful Son* (UK/USA, 2001), *Murder* (UK, 2002) and *The Canterbury Tales* (UK, 2003). She also shares with Helen Mirren (UK) a record for **most consecutive Best Actress wins**.

John Williams (composer): Maestro Williams (USA) has had 45 Academy Award nominations from 1968 to 2006, making him the **most Oscar-nominated living person**. His first nomination was for Best Music, Scoring of Music, Adaptation or Treatment for *Valley of the Dolls* (USA, 1967), with his most recent for Best Achievement in Music Written for Motion Pictures, Original Score at the 2006 Oscar ceremony for both *Munich* and *Memoirs of a Geisha* (both USA, 2005).

★ **NEW RECORD**
★ **UPDATED RECORD**

HARRY SPELLS MAGIC FOR WARNER BROS.

The Harry Potter franchise has proved a highly successful one for Warner Bros. (USA). Today, all five Harry Potter movies feature in Warners' Top 10 most successful films ever. In 2005, the studio's gross profits came to $1.37 billion (£800.45 million), giving them the record at the time for the highest-grossing studio (though this has since been broken). The studio's most successful movie of the year was *Harry Potter and the Goblet of Fire* ($290 million; £159.5 million), followed by *Charlie and the Chocolate Factory* ($206 million; £113.3 million) and *Batman Begins* ($205 million; £112.75 million).

GAZETTEER

★LARGEST
CONSUMERS OF ENERGY

This photograph of the Earth at night is pieced together from satellite shots and shows the major conurbations of the world, clearly picked out by street lights.

The world's greatest consumer of electricity is the United States, which used 3,717 billion kW per hour in 2005. This figure is almost a quarter of the total net electricity consumption of the whole world, which in 2005 came to 16,282 billion kW per hour.

The ★ **greatest consumer of electricity per person** is Iceland, where 26,101 kW per hour per person were used in 2005. In the United States, 12,343 kW per hour per person were consumed over the same period. Seven of the 10 countries that use the lowest amounts of electricity are found in Africa.

CONTENTS

USA

Bun topped with Parmesan cheese and poppyseeds

Shavings of Perigord black truffles

Layered with horseradish, tomato confit, fresh tomato, red onion, and frisée lettuce

★ MOST EXPENSIVE HAMBURGER

The most expensive burger commercially available is the db Double Truffle Burger, created by Chef Daniel Boulud (France) and available on the menu of db Bistro Moderne in New York City for $120 (£64.70).

Ground sirloin steak patty...

... filled with boned and minced short-rib braised in red wine, truffles, foie gras, and a mirepoix of root vegetables

Chunks of foie gras

(Served with pommes soufflés)

AT A GLANCE

- **AREA**: 9,826,630 km² (3,794,083 miles²)
- **POPULATION**: 301.1 million
- **DENSITY**: 30 people/km² (79 people/mile²)
- **KEY FACTS**: The USA is the world's **most powerful nation state**, with a per capita gross domestic product (GDP) of $46,000 (£22,910). (Continued on opposite page.)

★ LARGEST MAMMAL EXPLODED

The largest mammal ever exploded was the 7.25-tonne (16,000-lb), 13.7-m-long (45-ft) carcass of a sperm whale that washed up south of Florence, Oregon. On 12 November 1970, the Orgeon State Highway Division placed half a tonne (1,000 lb) of dynamite around the decomposing, foul-smelling whale and detonated it. The dynamite was far more powerful than required and huge chunks of whale meat rained down on spectators.

One 0.9 x 1.5-m (3 x 5-ft) lump of whale crushed the roof of a Buick car 0.4 km (0.25 mile) away!

★ LARGEST OFF-LICENCE

The largest off-licence (liquor store) is Daveco Liquors owned by Henry Sawaged (USA) and situated in Thornton, Colorado. The store covers an area of 9,297.13 m² (100,073 ft²) – enough to accommodate 35 tennis courts! – and was opened on 18 November 2006.

★ FASTEST RAP MC

The fastest rap MC is Rebel XD (a.k.a. Seandale Price, USA), who rapped 852 syllables in 42 seconds in Chicago, Illinois, on 27 July 2007.

FASTEST RUN UP THE EMPIRE STATE BUILDING

At the 26th Annual Empire State Building Run-Up in New York, USA, on 4 February 2003, the fastest time was achieved by Paul Crake (Australia) in 9 min 33 sec. The course covers 1,576 steps up to the 86th floor. The **fastest woman to run up the Empire State Building** was Belinda Soszyn (Australia) in 1996, with a time of 12 min 19 sec.

★ HIGHEST ANNUAL GAMING REVENUE (CITY)

In the year 2000, the casinos and entertainment complexes of Las Vegas, Nevada, USA, generated a record $7,673,134,286 (£5,416,584,982) in gaming revenue.

★ LARGEST LINE DANCE

A total of 17,000 participants performed the Cupid Shuffle line dance for eight minutes at the Ebony Black Family Reunion Tour in Atlanta, Georgia, on 25 August 2007.

LARGEST LAND GORGE

The Grand Canyon, created over millions of years by the Colorado River in north-central Arizona, extends from Marble Gorge to the Grand Wash Cliffs over a distance of 446 km (277 miles). It reaches a depth of 1.6 km (1 mile), while its width ranges from 0.5 km to 29 km (0.3–18 miles).

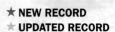

LARGEST INFLATABLE PARADE

Macy's Annual Thanksgiving Day Parade in New York City is the world's largest inflatable parade, seen by millions of spectators lining the streets and watching on television. On 22 November 2001, the famous parade celebrated its 75th anniversary with 30 larger-than-life balloon characters.

★ **NEW RECORD**
★ **UPDATED RECORD**

The USA spends more than any other country on **health** – $5,274 (£3,480) per person in 2002), **foreign aid** and the **military**; it is also home to the **most billionaires** (419 of the world's 946 total). US citizens are the **greatest consumers of calories** (3,774.1 a day) and watch the **most TV** (4 hr 32 min per person per day). They own the **most guns** (40% of homes have them) and **downloaded singles** (98% of singles were bought online in 2005). The USA also has the **highest national debt**: it stood at $9,372,485,723,263.83 (£4,716,285,558,172.72) as of 22 April 2008.

A great sporting nation, the USA has also won the **most Olympic medals** (975 from summer and winter games) and, in golf, the **most Walker** (34), **Solheim** (7) and **Ryder** (24) **cups**.

★ LONGEST ROAD NETWORK

According to the most recent figures (2007), the USA has 6,433,272 km (3,997,449 miles) of graded roads – enough to circle the Earth at least 160 times!

FACT

More than 2.5 million people line the streets of New York to see Macy's parade each year. An additional 44 million tune in to watch it on TV.

★ LARGEST CORN MAZE (TEMPORARY)

The largest temporary corn maze in the world measured 16.385 ha (40.489 acres) when opened to the public in September 2007 at Coolpatch Pumpkins in Dixon, California, USA. The record attempt was organized by Mark Cooley (USA).

GREATEST PRIZE MONEY WON AT A RODEO

The most prize money won at a single rodeo is $124,821 (£79,716) by Ty Murray (USA) at the National Finals Rodeo in Las Vegas, Nevada, in 1993.

GREATEST RANGE OF A LIGHTHOUSE

The lights with the greatest range are those 332 m (1,089 ft) above the ground on the Empire State Building in New York City. Each of the four-arc mercury bulbs is visible 130 km (80 miles) away.

HIGHEST ANNUAL SPORTS EARNINGS

Football: In 2005, the Atlanta Falcons' quarterback Michael Vick (USA) earned $37.5 million (£21.4 million). Vick signed a 10-year, $130-million (£67.9-million) deal on 23 December 2004, which included a $27-million (£14.1-million) signing bonus.
Basketball: The Miami Heat's Shaquille O'Neal earned an estimated $33.4 million (£19.1 million) in 2005.

MOST HIT SINGLES (US CHART)

Elvis Presley (USA) charted a record 151 hit singles on the Billboard Hot 100 from 1956 to 2003.

MOST RIAA CERTIFICATES EVER

The recording artist with the greatest number of Recording Industry Association of America (RIAA) certificates is Elvis Presley (USA), with 262 certified titles (148 gold, 82 platinum, 32 multiplatinum) for both albums and singles.

HEAVIEST STATUE

Liberty Lighting the World, a.k.a. the Statue of Liberty, on Liberty Island, New York City, was presented to the United States by France in 1886 to commemorate liberty and friendship between the nations. The 92.99-m-tall (305-ft 1-in) statue weighs 24,635 tonnes (54.3 million lb), of which 28 tonnes (61,729 lb) are copper, 113 tonnes (250,000 lb) are steel and 24,493 tonnes (53.9 million lb) make up the concrete in the pedestal.

MEXICO

ACTUAL SIZE

AT A GLANCE

- **AREA**: 1,972,550 km² (761,605 miles²)
- **POPULATION**: 108,700,891
- **DENSITY**: 55 people/km² (142 people/mile²)
- **KEY FACTS**: Mexico cradles the Gulf of Mexico, the world's **largest gulf**, at 1,544,000 km² (596,000 miles²) and with a shoreline of 5,000 km (3,100 miles). The 3,110-km (1,933-mile) border the country shares with the USA is the world's **most crossed border**: in 2000, over 290 million people crossed from Mexico into the USA. Just over 10 years ago, Mexico City, the capital, was the largest conurbation in the world, with a population of 16,908,000. Today, this record is held by Tokyo. *(See p.274.)*

MOST DEATHS CAUSED BY SCORPION STINGS

In 1946, a total of 1,933 people died in Mexico as a result of scorpion stings – more than in any other country in a single year. As many as 1,000 people, mostly children, still die every year.

LARGEST COLONY OF MAMMALS

The black-tailed prairie dog (*Cynomys ludovicianus*), a rodent of the family Sciuridae found in the western USA and northern Mexico, builds large colonies. One single "town" discovered in 1901 contained about 400 million individuals and was estimated to cover 61,400 km² (23,705 miles²) – almost the size of Ireland – making it the largest colony of mammals ever recorded.

SHORTEST PRESIDENCY

Pedro Lascurain (Mexico) governed his country for one hour on 18 February 1913 as successor to Francisco Madero (Mexico), who was murdered on 13 February 1913. The vice-president of Mexico was disqualified as he was under arrest at the time and thus Lascurain was sworn in, appointed general Victoriano Huerta (Mexico) as his successor and then resigned.

★ LARGEST TACO

A taco weighing 750 kg (1,654 lb) was made by the city of Mexicali and Cocinex SA de CV, in Baja California on 8 March 2003. A taco is a traditional Mexican dish: a rolled maize tortilla with a filling.

FASTEST LAND MAMMAL (LONG DISTANCE)

The pronghorn (*Antilocapra americana*) is the fastest land animal over long distances. These antelope-like ungulates have been observed travelling at 56 km/h (35 mph) for up to 6 km (4 miles). They are found in the western USA, south-western Canada and parts of northern Mexico. *(For the **fastest mammal on land** over short distances, see p.46.)*

LARGEST PYRAMID

In terms of volume, the largest monument ever constructed, and the largest pyramid, is the Quetzalcôatl Pyramid at Cholula de Rivadavia, 101 km (63 miles) south-east of Mexico City. It is 54 m (177 ft) tall and its base covers nearly 18.2 ha (45 acres). Its total volume is an estimated 3.3 million m³ (166.5 million ft³).

VISAS ★

CENTRAL AMERICA & THE
CARIBBEAN

RAREST LIZARD

The Jamaican iguana (*Cyclura collei*) is a critically endangered species, only rediscovered in 1990. With no more than 100 adult specimens existing, it is clinging to survival in southern Jamaica's remote Hellshire Hills – the only sizeable area of primary dry forest remaining on the island but under threat from charcoal burners.

LONGEST-SERVING HEAD OF STATE

Fidel Castro (Cuba), president of Cuba's Council of State, is the longest-serving non-royal head of state. He was Cuba's unchallenged revolutionary and political leader from 26 July 1959 (when his guerrilla movement, led by Latin American revolutionary Che Guevara, overthrew the island-state's military dictatorship) until his announced retirement on 19 February 2008 — a total of 48 years 208 days. (Castro became president of Cuba when the post of premier was abolished in 1976.)

Castro is also known for the **longest UN speech**. On 26 September 1960, he addressed the United Nations for 4 hr 29 min.

In 2006, Fabian Escalante (Cuba), a bodyguard assigned to protect Castro, announced that the president had survived 638 assassination attempts – the **most failed assassinations** on the life of any person.

MOST INTENSE RAINFALL

While rainfall readings for very short periods are difficult to collect, the figure of 38.1 mm (1.5 in) in one minute at Basse Terre, Guadeloupe, on 26 November 1970 is regarded as the most intense recorded using modern methods.

OLDEST ARTIST TO HAVE A MILLION-SELLER

Cuban singer/guitarist Compay Segundo sold over one million albums around the world after his 88th birthday in 1995. He first recorded in the 1930s, but found new fame as a member of the Buena Vista Social Club in 1996.

AT A GLANCE

- **AREA: Central America**: 523,780 km² (202,232 mile²); **Caribbean**: 127,753 km² (49,325 mile²)
- **POPULATION: C. America**: 44,934,014; **Caribbean**: 22,636,621 (2007 est.)
- **DENSITY**: 103 people/km²; 268 people/mile²
- **COUNTRIES: C. America**: Belize, Costa Rica, El Salvador, Guatemala, Honduras, Nicaragua, Panama; **Caribbean**: Anguila, Antigua and Barbuda, Aruba, The Bahamas, Barbados, British Virgin Is., Cayman Is., Cuba, Dominica, Dominican Republic, Grenada, Guadeloupe, Haiti, Jamaica, Martinique, Montserrat, Netherlands Antilles, Puerto Rico, St Barthélemy, Kitts & Nevis, St Lucia, St Martin, St Vincent & the Grenadines, Trinidad & Tobago, Turks & Caicos, US Virgin Isles.

DEEPEST BLUE HOLE

Dean's Blue Hole is a 76-m-wide (250-ft) vertical shaft that plunges 202 m (663 ft) at Turtle Cove near Clarence Town on the Atlantic edge of The Bahamas. Lying just a few steps offshore, it contains 1.1 million m³ (11.8 million ft³) of water and is the second largest water-filled cavern on the planet. Blue holes are found at or just below sea level and were once caves that filled with water as the icecaps melted and the water levels rose during the last Ice Age.

SHORTEST SNAKE

The very rare thread snake (*Leptotyphlops bilineata*), known only from Martinique, Barbados and St Lucia, has such a matchstick-thin body that it could enter the hole left in a standard pencil after the lead has been removed. The longest known specimen measured only 10.8 cm (4.25 in).

LONGEST CIGAR

A cigar measuring 41.2 m (135 ft 2 in) was hand-rolled by Patricio Peña (Puerto Rico) and his team from Don Ray Cigars in Fort Buchanan, Puerto Rico, from 13 to 15 February 2007.

OLDEST BRIDES & GROOMS

Of the 2,628 marriages in The Bahamas in 1996, 73.9% of the brides were aged 30 or over, as were 86% of the bridegrooms.

SOUTH AMERICA

AT A GLANCE

- **AREA**: 17,840,000 km² (6,888,062 miles²)
- **POPULATION**: 371 million
- **DENSITY**: 20.8 people/km² (53.8 people/mile²)
- **KEY FACTS**: The South American continent (which does *not* include Central America) covers 3.5% of our planet's surface.
- **COUNTRIES**: Argentina, Bolivia (home of the world's **largest land-locked navy**, with 4,800 personnel as of 2006), Brazil (the largest country in the continent, the world's **most forested country** and the only Portuguese-speaking country in the Americas), Chile, Colombia (infamously the country with the **highest rates of kidnapping** and the **largest producer of cocaine**), Ecuador (**highest murder rate**), French Guiana, Guyana, Paraguay, Peru, Suriname, Uruguay and Venezuela (**most wins of the Miss World beauty competition**).

LARGEST LAGOON

Lagoa dos Patos, located near the seashore in Rio Grande do Sul, southernmost Brazil, is 280 km (174 miles) long and extends over 9,850 km² (3,803 miles²). It is separated from the Atlantic Ocean by long sand strips, and has a maximum width of 70 km (44 miles).

★ FASTEST GUITAR PLAYER

José del Rio (Chile) played "Duelling Banjos" on the guitar at a speed of 250 beats per minute in Las Condes, Santiago, Chile, on 9 April 2006.

★ HIGHEST ALTITUDE CONCERT ON LAND

Musikkapelle Roggenzell – a group of 10 musicians from Germany and Bolivia – successfully staged the highest concert on land when they played at 6,069 m (19,911 ft) on Mount Acotango, Bolivia, on 6 August 2007.

★ LARGEST SWIMMING POOL BY AREA

The San Alfonso del Mar seawater pool in Algarrobo, Chile, is 1,013 m (3,324 ft) long and has an area of 8 ha (19.77 acres) – larger in area than 15 American football fields!

LARGEST ATTENDANCE AT A STADIUM

A crowd of 199,854 attended the Brazil v. Uruguay World Cup Final match in the Maracanã Municipal Stadium, Rio de Janeiro, Brazil, on 16 July 1950. Uruguay won 2–1.

★ LARGEST BINGO HOUSE

A game of bingo involving 70,080 participants took place at an event organized by Almacenes Exito S.A. in Bogotá, Colombia, on 2 December 2006.

FEWEST CINEMAS PER POPULATION

Suriname, with a population of 436,494, has only one cinema, which can be found in the capital, Paramaribo. In 1997, this cinema saw a total of 103,626 admissions.

HIGHEST AND LONGEST PASSENGER CABLE CAR

The Teleférico Mérida in Venezuela travels from Mérida City, at 1639.5 m (5,379 ft) above sea level, to the summit of Pico Espejo, at 4,763.7 m (15,629 ft), a rise of 3,124 m (10,250 ft).

HIGHEST FOOD CONSUMPTION

According to the latest figures published in the Britannica Yearbook 2000, Argentina has the highest food consumption, with each citizen consuming 183% of the United Nations Food and Agriculture Organization's (FAO) recommended requirement. This figure was recorded in 1996.

★ LONGEST MARATHON READING ALOUD (TEAM)

A team comprising Milton Nan, Silvina Carbone, Yolanda Baptista, Carlos Antón, Edit Díaz and Natalie Dantaz (all Uruguay) read aloud for 224 hours at Mac Center Shopping, Paysandú, Uruguay, between 13 and 22 September 2007.

★ MOST DANGEROUS ROAD

The road considered by many to be the most lethal in the world is the North Yungas Road that runs for 69 km (43 miles) from La Paz to Coroico in Bolivia. It is responsible for up to 300 deaths annually,

DRIEST PLACE

For the period between 1964 and 2001, the average annual rainfall for the meteorological station in Quillagua, in the Atacama Desert, Chile, was just 0.5 mm. This discovery was made during the making of the documentary series *Going to Extremes*, by Keo Films, in 2001.

MOST SURFERS RIDING THE SAME WAVE SIMULTANEOUSLY

Rico de Souza (Brazil) led 84 surfers riding the same wave simultaneously at Santos Beach in Santos, Sao Paulo, Brazil, on 2 September 2007.

MOST SOUTHERLY BIRTH

At the time of his birth, Emilio Marcos Palma (Argentina), born 7 January 1978 at the Sargento Cabral Base, Antartica, could claim to be the first and only child to be born on the icy southern continent.

MOST SOUTHERLY VILLAGE

Puerto Williams (pop. 1,600 in 1996) on the north coast of Isla Navarino, in Tierra del Fuego, Chile, is 1,090 km (677 miles) north of Antarctica.

MOST SUCCESSFUL LAWYER

Sir Lionel Luckhoo (b. 2 March 1914), senior partner of Luckhoo and Luckhoo of Georgetown, Guyana, succeeded in getting 245 successive murder-charge acquittals between 1940 and 1985.

TREE BEARING MOST DIFFERENT FRUIT SPECIES

In 2000, Luis H. Carrasco E. of Lo Barnechea, Santiago, Chile, grafted five different fruit species on to a single prune tree. The tree later successfully produced apricots, cherries, nectarines, plums and peaches.

which works out at 4.3 deaths per km (6.9 per mile). For the majority of the stretch, the single-lane mud road (with two-way traffic) has an un-barricaded vertical drop measuring 4,700 m (15,420 ft) at its highest. Not surprisingly, the road is at its most deadly during the rainy season!

WORST DESTRUCTION OF THE NATURAL ENVIRONMENT BY FIRE

Deliberately started forest fires made 1997 the worst year in recorded history for the destruction of the natural environment. The largest and most numerous were in Brazil, where they raged on a 1,600-km (1,000-mile) front.

★ FIRST PERSON SHOT BY A GUN IN THE AMERICAS

A young Inca, who is believed to have been shot by a Spanish conquistador during the siege of Lima (in present-day Peru) in 1536, is the earliest-known victim of a gunshot wound in the New World. (See box to right.)

FASTEST GOAL IN A WORLD CUP FINALS BY A SUBSTITUTE

Uruguay's Richard Morales scored just 18 seconds after coming on against Senegal at the 2002 World Cup in Suwon, South Korea, on 11 June 2002.

WIDEST ROAD

The Monumental Axis runs for 2.4 km (1.8 miles) through Brasilia, Brazil. The six-lane boulevard was opened in April 1960 and is 250 m (820 ft 2 in) wide.

★ MOST ENDANGERED TRIBES

According to a report published in August 2003 by Survival International, the worldwide organization supporting tribal peoples, the three tribes currently facing the greatest threat to their survival are the Ayoreo-Totobiegosode (pop. 5,000) of western Paraguay, the Gana and Gwi "Bushmen" (pop. 100,000) in Botswana and the Jarawa tribe, pictured right, (pop. 200–300) from the Andaman Islands in the Indian Ocean.

UNEARTHING THE VICTIM

Excavation work by archaeologists in Puruchuco, Lima, Peru, led by Guillermo Cock (Peru), unearthed the body of the young Inca (found with 71 others in a mass grave). Forensic examination of the victim discovered traces of iron on the edges of two holes in the skull, which was believed to be the iron of a musket ball, a weapon widely used by the conquistadors. Exit damage was also found in the face where the bullet left the head. The skeleton was discovered in 2004 and announced by *National Geographic* in June 2007.

★ **NEW RECORD**
 UPDATED RECORD

CANADA

AT A GLANCE

- **AREA**: 9,984,670 sq km² (3,855,102 miles²)
- **POPULATION**: 33,390,141
- **DENSITY**: 3.3 people/km² (8.6 people/mile²)
- **KEY FACTS**: Canada is the world's second largest country and one of the most sparsely populated – only about half of the country is developed, with the north still an untouched wilderness. Hudson Bay is the **largest bay** in the world, with a shoreline of 12,268 km (7,623 miles) and covering an area of about 1,233,000 km² (476,000 miles²), and the Davis Strait between Baffin Island in Canada and Greenland is, at 388 km (210 miles), the world's **widest strait**.

Beyond its natural wonders, Canada boasts the world's **largest shopping centre** – the West Edmonton Mall, with over 800 stores (see right) – and the CN Tower, the **largest freestanding tower** (see far right).

★ **NEW RECORD**
☆ **UPDATED RECORD**

LONGEST BOUNDARY

The boundary between Canada and the United States, when including the Great Lakes boundaries, extends for 6,416 km (3,986 miles), but excludes the frontier of 2,547 km (1,582 miles) with Alaska. If the Alaskan boundary is added, the Canada–USA boundary is 8,963 km (5,568 miles) long in total.

LARGEST SHOPPING MALL

The enormous West Edmonton Mall in Alberta covers 492,386 m² (5.3 million ft²) – the equivalent of 48 city blocks or around 115 football pitchs – and cost CAN$1.2 billion ($927 million; £700 million) to build. It features more than 800 stores and 110 food outlets.

The mall opened on 15 September 1981. Parking for over 20,000 vehicles (plus an overflow capacity for another 10,000) is provided in the world's **largest car park**.

The mall also includes Galaxyland, the **largest indoor amusement park**, which at 37,200 m² (400,000 ft²) holds 30 skill games and 27 rides and attractions, including *Mindbender*, a 14-storey, triple-loop roller coaster, and *Drop of Doom*, a 13-storey free-fall ride.

FACT
Officially known as the International Boundary, the Canada–USA border must be kept clear of brush and vegetation for 6 m (20 ft) – or 3 m (10 ft) on both sides of the line – as seen above.

★ LONGEST WINTER ROAD

The "Wapusk Trail" road is 752 km (467 miles) in length and is constructed each year between Gillam, Manitoba, and Peawanuk, Ontario. It gives road access for a few weeks to remote settlements around Hudson Bay until warmer March weather forces its closure. These settlements are normally only accessible by air.

LARGEST ISLAND MADE BY HUMAN INTERVENTION

The largest island created as a result of human action is the Ile Rene-Lavasseur in Manicouagan Reservoir, Quebec. It measures 2,020 km² (780 mile²) in size, so the whole of New York City could fit on to it 2.5 times. It was formed after a river was dammed, flooding a 210-million-year-old meteor crater. The central uplift of the crater forms the island.

LARGEST NATURALLY FROZEN ICE RINK

The Rideau Canal Skateway in Ottawa, Ontario, is 7.8 km (4.8 miles) long and has a total maintained surface area of 165,621 m² (1.782 million ft²), which is equivalent to 90 Olympic-size skating rinks.

TALLEST FREESTANDING TOWER

The CN Tower in Toronto rises to a height of 553.34 m (1,815 ft 5 in). Excavation work for the 130,000-tonne (286 million lb) reinforced, post-tensioned concrete structure began in February 1973, and it was finally "topped out" on 2 April 1975.

LARGEST ADMISSION TICKET

The largest admission ticket is 142 x 50 cm (56 x 19 in) and was created by Canada's National Arts Centre for entrance to the Hope and Glory concert in Ottawa on 8 February 2007.

★ FASTEST RUN ACROSS CANADA BY A WOMAN

Ann Keane (Canada) ran across the country from St John's, Newfoundland, to Tofino, British Columbia, in 143 days between 17 April and 8 September 2002. She covered a total of 7,831 km (4,866 miles).

FASTEST MARATHON SKIPPING

The record for the fastest marathon run while skipping with a rope is 4 hr 28 min 48 sec and was set by Chris Baron (Canada) at the ING Ottawa Marathon, Ontario, on 27 May 2007.

HIGHEST TIDE EVER

A tide range of 16.6 m (54 ft 6 in) was recorded at springs in Leaf Basin in Ungava Bay, Quebec, in 1953.

MOST ART ROSS TROPHIES

The Art Ross Trophy is awarded each year to the player who has scored the most points in National Hockey League regular season play. Wayne Gretzky (Canada) won an unprecedented 10 Art Ross Trophies between 1981 and 1994.

LARGEST SMOOTHIE

The largest smoothie contained 681.92 litres (150 gallons) of bananas, strawberries, sorbet, ice and fruit juice, and was made by Frank and Simon Voisin (both Canada) of Booster Juice juice and smoothie bar, London, Ontario, on 22 July 2006.

★ MOST CONSECUTIVE RENDITIONS OF A NATIONAL ANTHEM

The Canadian national anthem was performed 607 times consecutively by members of Magic Feet Canada at Harbourfront Centre, Toronto, Ontario, on 1 July 2000.

TOWER TREATS

The lofty CN Tower has hosted many record-breaking attempts over the years. The **longest descent down the side of a building** was one of 446.5 m (1,465 ft), by two teams of 12. All 24 people abseiled from the Space Deck of the Tower to the ground on 1 July 1992. The world's **highest wine cellar** is the Tower's "Cellar in the Sky", located 351 m (1,151 ft) above Toronto. Lastly, the **fastest time to pogo-stick jump up the CN Tower** is 57 min 51 sec, achieved by Ashrita Furman (USA) on 23 July 1999.

CN Tower - visitor's guide

- The Tower took 40 months to complete, finally opening to the public in June 1976. In total, 1,537 workers laboured five days a week, 24 hours a day, to get the job done.
- It can survive an earthquake of 8.5 on the Richter scale, and the upper reaches can withstand winds of up to 418 km/h (260 mph).
- On a clear day, visitors can see for more than 160 km (100 miles) from the observation deck - all the way to Niagara Falls and across to New York State.
- The 360 Restaurant, situated around two-thirds of the way up, makes a complete rotation every 72 minutes.
- The CN Tower is double the height of the iconic Eiffel Tower in Paris, France!

UK & IRELAND

★ LARGEST HIGHLAND DANCE

The largest Highland dance involved 1,453 participants from schools in the Nairn region of Scotland, UK, who danced the *Dashing White Sergeant* for an event organised by the Nairn Associated Schools Group to celebrate the Highland Year of Culture 2007 at Nairn Links, Scotland, UK, on 22 June 2007.

AT A GLANCE

- **AREA**: UK 244,820 km² (94,525 miles²); **Ireland** 70,280 km² (27,135 miles²)
- **POPULATION**: **UK** 60.7 million; **Ireland** 4.1 million
- **DENSITY**: UK 248 people/km² (643 people/mile²); **Ireland** 58.3 people/km² (151 people/mile²)
- **KEY FACTS**: The **United Kingdom** comprises Great Britain (England, Scotland and Wales) and Northern Ireland (occupying one-sixth of the island of Ireland). The country of **Ireland** (or Eire, to use its local short form) occupies five-sixths of the island of Ireland.

The British Empire was the **largest empire** of all time, covering 36.6 million km² (14.1 million miles²) – about a quarter of the earth's surface – at the height of its power (1917–22).

★ LONGEST REIGN (LIVING QUEEN)

The longest-reigning living queen is Her Majesty Queen Elizabeth II (b. 21 April 1926), who succeeded to the throne on 6 February 1952 on the death of her father, King George VI. Elizabeth II is Queen of the UK and head of the Commonwealth.

★ LARGEST MORRIS DANCE

A morris dance involving 88 participants was organized by The Moreton-in-Marsh Show in Gloucestershire, UK, on 1 September 2007.

★ MOST FILMS SEEN

Gwilym Hughes (UK) of Gwynedd, Wales, saw his first film, *King Solomon's Mines*, in 1953. Since then, he has kept a diary of all the films he has seen and has logged a total of 28,074 different movies as of 13 March 2008.

★ LARGEST BOWL OF PORRIDGE

A bowl of porridge weighing 81.6 kg (179 lb 14 oz) was served up at the Edinburgh Farmers' Market in Edinburgh, Scotland, UK, on 15 September 2007.

DID YOU KNOW?
Bruce made his 40,000th pub visit at the Bull's Head in Ranmoor, Sheffield, UK. The picture above was taken at The Red Lion pub in Hernhill, Kent, UK.

★ MOST PUBS VISITED

As of 9 December 2006, Bruce Masters (UK) has visited 40,000 pubs and bars since 1960, sampling the local brew where available.

★ MOST EXPENSIVE VETERAN CAR SOLD AT AUCTION

An anonymous British collector paid £3,521,500 ($7,242,916) for the world's oldest surviving Rolls Royce, numbered 20154, making it the most expensive veteran (pre-1905) car. The two-seater, 10-hp automobile, manufactured in Manchester, UK, in 1904, was sold by Bonhams in London, UK, on 3 December 2007.

FASTEST TAP DANCE

The fastest rate ever measured for tap dancing is 38 taps per second, by James Devine of Ardnacrusha, Co. Clare, Ireland, on 25 May 1998. Devine beat the record of 35 taps per second achieved by "Lord of the Dance" Michael Flatley (USA).

MOST TORNADOES (AREA)

Incredibly, the UK is the world's tornado hotspot, hit by a record of one tornado per 7,397 km² (2,856 mile²). The equivalent figure for the USA is one tornado per 8,663 km² (3,345 mile²).

★ LARGEST SAME-NAME GATHERING (SURNAME)

On 9 September 2007, 1,488 people with the surname Gallagher amassed in Letterkenny, Ireland – the largest gathering of the same surname.

★ TALLEST WINDMILL

St Patrick's Distillery Mill in Dublin, Republic of Ireland, has the tallest windmill in the world. Now without sails, the mill is 45.7 m (150 ft) tall.

LARGEST TRILITHONS

Stonehenge on Salisbury Plain, UK, boasts the world's largest trilithons (structures made from two large vertical stones supporting a third stone set across the top), with a series of sarsen blocks weighing over 45 tonnes (99,208 lb) each. The tallest upright stone in the prehistoric monument is 6.7 m (22 ft) high, with another 2.4 m (8 ft) below ground. The first stage in the building of the stone circle has been dated to 2950 BC.

★ LONGEST RIVERDANCE LINE

The world record for the longest "Riverdance" line was 216 achieved by CLRG Dance Schools, Leinster Province, at St Stephens Green, Dublin, Ireland, on 8 November in the celebrations for Guinness World Records Day 2007.

SMALLEST CRYSTAL BOWL

A crystal bowl made by Jim Irish (Ireland), a former master cutter at Waterford Crystal, measured 8.55 mm (0.33 in) wide, 4.6 mm (0.18 in) tall, 2.1 mm (0.08) thick and was made with 208 cuts.

LONGEST DANCE PARTY

Unique Events Limited (Ireland) organized a dance party at the Quay Front, Wexford, Ireland, that began on 27 October 2006 at midday with 40 dancers, and finished 55 hours later with 31 exhausted dancers still on their feet!

FASTEST TIME TO PLUCK A TURKEY

Vincent Pilkington of Cootehill, Co. Cavan, Ireland, plucked a turkey in 1 min 30 sec on RTE television in Dublin, Ireland, on 17 November 1980. Despite the 29 years that have passed since Vincent set this record, his achievement has yet to be bettered.

★ FIRST FEMALE BEEFEATER

The first female Beefeater is Moira Cameron (UK), who was appointed as Yeoman Warder of Her Majesty's Royal Palace and Fortress the Tower of London, UK, in January 2007. Historically a male role, Beefeaters are ceremonial guardians of the Tower of London whose traditional purpose was to look after prisoners being held there and safeguard the British Crown Jewels. Today, however, Yeoman Warder Cameron's duties include the Ceremony of the Keys (the nightly locking of the gates) and knowing the 1,000-year history of the Tower so she can conduct her own Beefeater Tours.

FRANCE

AT A GLANCE

- **AREA**: 547,030 km² (211,209 miles²)
- **POPULATION**: 60.8 million
- **DENSITY**: 111 people/km² (287 people/mile²)
- **KEY FACTS**: France is the world's **most popular tourist destination**, attracting 79.1 million international visitors in 2006. A total of 49,733 people applied for asylum in France in 2005, the **most applications received for political asylum by one country**.

France is a nation of wine lovers, so it is perhaps unsurprising that the **most expensive commercially available wine** is French – the Chateau d'Yquem Sauternes (1787), a sweet dessert wine from Bordeaux, priced at an average of $60,000 (£31,402).

And the **most expensive wine per glass**? Again, it's French: Robert Denby (UK) paid FF8,600 ($1,382.80; £982) for the first glass of Beaujolais Nouveau 1993, released in Beaune (from Maison Jaffelin), in the wine region of Burgundy, France. It was purchased at Pickwick's, a British pub in Beaune, on 18 November 1993.

★ FASTEST TRAIN ON A NATIONAL RAILWAY

A French SNCF modified version of the TGV called V150 (with larger wheels than usual and two engines) reached a speed of 574.8 km/h (357.2 mph) on 3 April 2007.

FIRST MANNED FLIGHT

Frenchman François Pilâtre de Rozier is widely regarded as the first person to have flown. On 15 October 1783, he rose 26 m (84 ft) into the air in a tethered hot-air balloon built by the inventors Joseph and Jacques Montgolfier (France).

FIRST CINEMA

The Cinématographe Lumière at the Salon Indien – a former billiard hall in the Grand Cafè, 14 Boulevard de Capucines, Paris, opened on 28 December 1895.

★ MOST EXPENSIVE WEAPON SOLD AT AUCTION

A sword used by the Emperor Napoléon Bonaparte fetched the sum of €4.8 million (£3.3 million; $6.5 million) at an auction held in Fontainebleau, on 10 June 2007.

HEAVIEST CHOCOLATE TRUFFLE

On 30 November 2001, Alain Benier (France) presented a chocolate truffle weighing 100 kg (220.4 lb) on the set of *L'Émission des Records*, Paris.

★ FASTEST MOVING WALKWAY

A high-speed moving walkway (or travelator) at Montparnasse metro station in Paris, moves commuters at 9 km/h (5.6 mph), around three times as fast as regular moving sidewalks. The 180-m-long (590-ft) walkway was installed in 2003.

DID YOU KNOW?

The **highest average speed by a train over a distance of 1,000 km** (621 miles) is 306.37 km/h (190.37 mph), by an unmodified SNCF TGV train between Calais and Marseille on 26 May 2001.

★ MOST NATIONALITIES SERVING IN ONE MILITARY FORCE

As of July 2007, the French Foreign Legion had 7,655 men serving in its ranks hailing from a range of 136 countries.

★ **NEW RECORD**
UPDATED RECORD

ITALY

★ LARGEST CAZÖLA

A cazöla is a traditional Italian dish much like a stew, comprising pork ribs, crackling, bacon, sausages and vegetables. The largest cazöla was created by 10 volunteers from the town of Ossona, and weighed 931.46 kg (2,053 lb 6 oz). It was displayed at the Piazza Litta, Ossona, on 24 August 2002.

BEST-SELLING CLASSICAL MUSIC ALBUM

In Concert – recorded by José Carreras, Placido Domingo and Luciano Pavarotti (all Italy) in Rome on 7 July 1990, during the 1990 World Cup Finals held in Italy – has registered global sales of 10.5 million copies to date.

★ LONGEST RADIO DJ MARATHON

Stefano Venneri (Italy) DJ'd for 135 hours on Radio BBSI in Alessandria, from 21 to 26 April 2007.

FASTEST GOAL IN A CHAMPIONS LEAGUE FINAL

Paolo Maldini (Italy) scored a goal for AC Milan against Liverpool in just 52 seconds in the Champions League final on 25 May 2005.

★ LARGEST FOOTBALL SHIRT

A football shirt measuring 68.50 x 71 m (224 ft 8 in x 232 ft 11 in) was created by ERREA for KONAMI to mark the launch of ProEvolution Soccer 2008 in an event organized by Brand2Live at the Arena Civica, in Milan, on 18 December 2007.

★ LARGEST PANCETTA

The Commune de Ponte dell'Olio and the Piacenza Chamber of Commerce, Piacenza, created a pancetta (a cured pork belly roll) weighing 150.5 kg (331 lb 12 oz). It was displayed at the Pancetta Festival in Ponte dell'Olio on 23 June 2002.

MOST F1 GRAND PRIX WINS BY A MANUFACTURER

The greatest number of grand prix wins in Formula One by a constructor is 201 by Ferrari (Italy) between 1951 and 2007.

LARGEST AMPHITHEATRE

The Flavian amphitheatre or Colosseum of Rome, completed in AD 80, covers an area of 2 ha (5 acres) and has a capacity of 87,000. It has a maximum length of 187 m (612 ft) and a maximum width of 157 m (515 ft).

OLDEST SCOOTER MANUFACTURER

Piaggio of Italy is the producer of the famous Vespa. The prototype Vespa scooter was tested and approved in December 1945, with production beginning in April 1946.

AT A GLANCE

- **AREA**: 301,230 km² (116,305 miles²)
- **POPULATION**: 58.1 million
- **DENSITY**: 192 people/km² (499 people/mile²)
- **KEY FACTS**: It's no surprise that Italy holds the record for the ★ **longest pizza**. A team of chefs led by Umberto Mosti (Italy), owner of the Pizzeria Fornaretto in Massa, Italy, created a 407.37-m (1,329-ft 11-in) pizza on 4 October 2007. *Il bel paese* is also home to Mt Stromboli, in the Tyrrhenian Sea, the **longest continuously erupting volcano**, which has undergone continuous eruptions since at least the 7th century BC. Its regular mild explosions of gas and lava – usually several each hour – have earned it the nickname "Lighthouse of the Mediterranean".

SPAIN

AT A GLANCE

- **AREA**: 504,782 km^2 (194,897 miles^2)
- **POPULATION**: 40,448,191
- **DENSITY**: 80 people/km^2 (207 people/mile^2)
- **KEY FACTS**: Spain is the world's **leading cultivator of olives**, producing a grand total of 970,000 tonnes (2.1 billion lb) a year. Principal olive-producing regions are Catalonia and Andalusia. Spain and Italy together account for 54% of the total amount of olive oil produced worldwide.

The Casa Botín in Madrid is regarded as the **oldest restaurant** in the world. It has been in operation continuously since it opened in 1725.

Continuing the food theme, Spain holds the record for the **largest paella**. Juan Carlos Galbis (Spain) and a team of helpers created a paella measuring 20 m (65 ft 7 in) in diameter in Valencia, on 8 March 1992. It was eaten by 100,000 people.

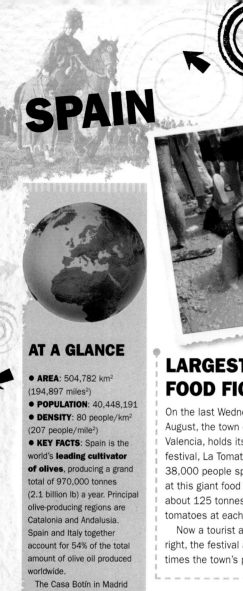

LARGEST FOOD FIGHT

On the last Wednesday in August, the town of Buñol, near Valencia, holds its annual tomato festival, La Tomatina. In 2004, 38,000 people spent one hour at this giant food fight, throwing about 125 tonnes (275,500 lb) of tomatoes at each other.

Now a tourist attraction in its own right, the festival attacts over three times the town's population of 9,000.

★ LARGEST COMMERCIAL JIGSAW PUZZLE

EDUCA of Barcelona manufactures a puzzle consisting of 24,000 pieces.

★ MOST PARTICIPANTS IN A ROLE-PLAYING GAME

A total of 483 people from the Irmandiños a Revolta group took part in a role-playing game in Monterrei, Spain, from 5 to 7 October 2007.

FACT
La Tomatina has been held every year since 1944. After the battle, participants walk to the riverbank, where makeshift public showers are provided.

★ LONGEST CHORIZO
A 110.15-m-long (361-ft 4-in) chorizo was created by mayor Manuel Alberto Pardellas Álvarez and the Concello de Melón, in Melón, Ourense, on 25 February 2007.

★ LARGEST CAFETIÈRE
Salzillo Tea and Coffee (Spain) created a cafetière measuring 230 cm (7 ft 6 in) tall and 72 cm (2 ft 4 in) in diameter in Murcia in February 2007.

LARGEST CASTANET DANCE (JOTA)
A total of 157 mixed couples performed the traditional folk dance *The Jota of Aragon* for eight minutes at Zaragoza on 18 May 2003.

LARGEST NIGHTCLUB
Privilege nightclub in San Rafael, Ibiza, can hold up to 10,000 people and covers an area of 6,500 m^2 (69,940 ft^2).

★ MOST BOTIJOS
Jesús Gil-Gilbernau del Río of Logroño has collected more than 3,000 botijos (traditional Spanish drinking vessels with two spouts and a handle).

★ LARGEST WATER-PISTOL FIGHT

A record 2,671 participants took a soaking in the world's largest water-pistol fight. The event was organized by the Coordinadora de Peñas de Valladolid in Valladolid on 14 September 2007 as part of the annual celebrations for the patron of Valladolid, the capital of Spain's largest province, Castile-Leon.

★ LARGEST SAND PAINTING

A sand painting measuring 859 m^2 (9,250 ft^2) was created in the Town Hall square of La Oratava, Tenerife for the Patron Saint day festivities on 13 June 2007.

PORTUGAL

MOST CORK FOREST

At 725,000 ha (1,791,514 acres), Portugal's cork-oak forests account for 33% of the world total. This represents 51% of global cork production.

MOST WIDELY SUPPORTED FOOTBALL CLUB

Sport Lisboa e Benfica, Portugal, has 160,398 paid-up members. The record was acknowledged on 9 November 2006 during celebrations for Guinness World Records Day.

★LARGEST POCKET KNIFE

Designed by Telmo Cadavez and handmade by Virgílio, Raúl and Manuel Pires (all Portugal), the largest pocket knife measures 3.9 m (12 ft 8 in) when open, and weighs 122 kg (268 lb 14 oz).

★LARGEST CAR MOSAIC

Realizar S.A. and Smart Advertising (both Portugal) co-produced a car mosaic comprising of 253 Smart cars at the Mundo Dakar on 9 December 2007. The event was organized by Euro RSCG for Jogos Santa Casa in Lisbon.

★LONGEST MEXICAN WAVE

On 12 August 2007, a Mexican wave involving 8,453 participants was organized by Realizar Impact Marketing at the Parque das Nações in Lisbon.

LARGEST ACOUSTIC GUITAR

The largest playable acoustic guitar measures 16.75 m (59 ft 11 in) long, 7.57 m (24 ft 10 in) wide and 2.67 m (8 ft 9 in) deep. The instrument was built by Realizar Eventos Especiais, Porto, and weighs 4 tonnes (8,818 lb).

LARGEST PATCHWORK QUILT

The world's largest patchwork quilt measured an impressive 25,100 m² (270,174 ft²) and is called Manta da Cultura (Patchwork for Culture). The project was carried out by Realizar Eventos Especiais, of Parque da Cidade, Porto, and completed on 18 June 2000.

LARGEST FIREWORK DISPLAY

Macedo's Pirotecnia Lda, presented a firework display consisting of 66,326 fireworks in Funchal, Madeira, Portugal, on 31 December 2006.

★MOST PAPER AIRCRAFT LAUNCHED SIMULTANEOUSLY

A total of 12,672 paper aircraft were launched simultaneously on 2 November 2007 at an event organized by Realizar Impact Marketing and FC Porto at the Dragao Stadium, Porto.

★NEW RECORD
☆UPDATED RECORD

AT A GLANCE

- **AREA**: 92,391 km² (35,672 miles²)
- **POPULATION**: 10,642,836
- **DENSITY**: 115 people/km² (298 people/mile²)
- **KEY FACTS**: With 2,351 m (7,711 ft) above the sea's surface and 6,098 m (20,000 ft) below, Monte Pico in Portugal's Azores Islands is the world's **highest underwater mountain**. The Crown Prince Luis Filipe of Portugal was technically King of Portugal (Dom Luis III) for approximately 20 minutes on 1 February 1908. His father was shot dead in the streets of Lisbon, and the Crown Prince was mortally wounded at the same time. Although it would have been little consolation, this gave him the record for the **shortest reign ever**.

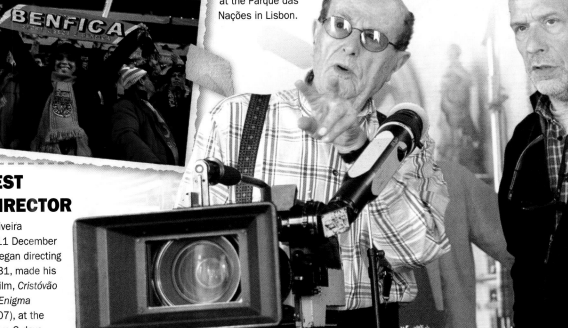

★ OLDEST FILM DIRECTOR

Manoel de Oliveira (Portugal, b. 11 December 1908), who began directing movies in 1931, made his most recent film, *Cristóvão Colombo – O Enigma* (Portugal, 2007), at the age of 99 years 2 days.

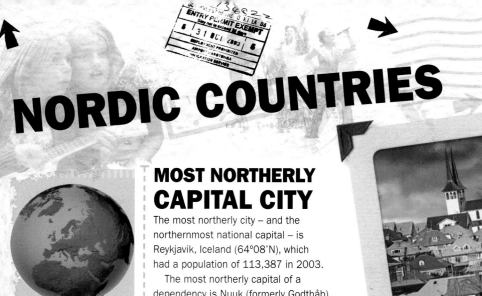

NORDIC COUNTRIES

AT A GLANCE

SWEDEN
- **AREA**: 449,964 km² (173,732 miles²)
- **POPULATION**: 9 million
- **DENSITY**: 20 people/km² (51 people/mile²)

FINLAND
- **AREA**: 338,145 km² (130,558 miles²)
- **POPULATION**: 5.2 million
- **DENSITY**: 15 people/km² (39 people/mile²)

NORWAY
- **AREA**: 323,802 km² (125,020 miles²)
- **POPULATION**: 4.6 million
- **DENSITY**: 14 people/km² (36 people/mile²)

ICELAND
- **AREA**: 103,000 km² (39,768 miles²)
- **POPULATION**: 304,367
- **DENSITY**: 2.9 people/km² (7.5 people/mile²)

DENMARK
- **AREA**: 43,094 km² (16,638 miles²)
- **POPULATION**: 5.4 million
- **DENSITY**: 125 people/km² (324 people/mile²)

MOST NORTHERLY CAPITAL CITY

The most northerly city – and the northernmost national capital – is Reykjavik, Iceland (64°08'N), which had a population of 113,387 in 2003.

The most northerly capital of a dependency is Nuuk (formerly Godthåb), Greenland (64°15'N). Its population was 15,047 in 2007.

★ LONGEST-LIVED ANIMAL

The oldest, non-colonial animal was a quahog clam (*Arctica islandica*) that had been living on the seabed off the north coast of Iceland until it was dredged by researchers from Bangor University's School of Ocean Sciences, UK, in 2006. On 28 October 2007, sclerochronologists from the university declared that the clam was 405–410 years old.

It was nicknamed "Ming", after the Chinese dynasty that was in power when it was born.

MOST VICTORIES AT LE MANS

The greatest number of wins by an individual at the Le Mans 24-hour race is seven by Tom Kristensen (Denmark) in 1997 and 2000–05.

★ HIGHEST CONCERT

Norwegian band Magnet (a.k.a. Even Johansen) celebrated the launch of his new album, entitled *The Simple Life!*, by performing at an altitude of 12,192 m (40,000 ft) on a flight from Oslo, Norway, to Reykjavik, Iceland, on 27 March 2007.

HIGHEST ANNUAL CINEMA ATTENDANCE

Iceland has a greater cinema attendance per capita than any other country, with 5.45 visits per person in 2004. The country has 46 cinemas, which in 2003 saw 1,531,000 admissions.

MOST FORMULA ONE FASTEST LAPS IN A SEASON

Mika Hakkinen (Finland) scored a total of nine fastest lap times in the 2000 Formula One season.

★ FASTEST DRIVE ON ICE

Four-time World Rally champion Juha Kankkunen (Finland) drove a Bentley Continental GT at 321.65 km/h (199.86 mph) on the Gulf of Bothnia frozen sea in Kuivaniemi, Finland, on 20 February 2007.

DID YOU KNOW?

Iceland is the country with the **lowest military spending per capita**. According to the CIA World Factbook, Iceland spent £0 ($0) on the military as of 2005.

MOST OLYMPIC ATHLETICS MEDALS (MALE)

Paavo Nurmi (Finland) won a total of 12 athletics medals (nine gold and three silver) at the Olympic Games of 1920, 1924 and 1928.

LARGEST PERMANENT TREE MAZE

Designed by Erik and Karen Poulsen (both Denmark), The Samso Labyrinten on the island of Samso in Denmark opened to the public on 6 May 2000 and has an area of 60,000 m² (645,835 ft²).

OLDEST CONTINUOUSLY USED NATIONAL FLAG

The current design of the Danish flag – a white Scandinavian cross on a red background – was adopted in 1625 and its square shape assumed in 1748. In Denmark it is called the "Dannebrog", or "Danish cloth".

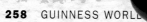

LARGEST UKULELE ENSEMBLE

"Ukulele 07", staged on Långholmen island in Stockholm, Sweden, on 18 August 2007, featured a ukulele ensemble comprising 401 participants.

★ LONGEST KNITTED SCARF

Over a 23-year period, Helge Johansen (Norway) knitted a 3,463.73-m-long (11,363-ft 11-in) scarf, finishing it in Oslo, Norway, on 10 November 2006.

MOST CONCURRENT MUSICAL PRODUCTIONS

As of February 2005, 12 productions of *Mamma Mia!* (music and lyrics by Benny Andersson and Björn Ulvaeus, both Sweden) were playing at one time: nine resident productions (London, UK; Las Vegas, USA; New York City, USA; Madrid, Spain; Osaka, Japan; Stockholm, Sweden; Stuttgart, Germany; Toronto, Canada and Utrecht, Holland) and three tours in Europe, South Africa and the USA.

★ DEEPEST UNDERGROUND CONCERT

Finnish group Agonizer performed a concert 1,271 m (4,169 ft 11 in) below sea level at Pyhäsalmi Mine Oy, Pyhäjärvi, Finland, on 4 August 2007.

★ LARGEST COFFEE MORNING (SINGLE VENUE)

On 6 June 2007, a group of 2,620 people gathered for a coffee morning at the Diocesan Festival in Kalmar, Sweden.

MOST OLYMPIC MEDALS FOR ALPINE SKIING (MALE)

Kjetil André Aamodt (Norway) won a total of eight medals (four gold, two silver and two bronze) at Olympic Games between 1992 and 2006.

★ MOST DOLLAR MILLIONAIRES

One in every 86 Norwegians claims a net worth of over $1 million (NOK5.8 million; £500,000) – excluding the value of their primary residences – according to a report by CapGemini and Merrill Lynch in July 2007.

KEY FACTS

● **LARGEST ICE VILLAGE:** A village of 140 igloos was built near the famous Icehotel at Jukkasjärvi, Sweden, to accommodate 700 employees of Tetra Pak International during a conference at the hotel in December 2002.

● **LARGEST WOODEN CHURCH:** The Kerimäki church in Kerimäki, Finland, is 45 m (147 ft 7 in) long, 42 m (137 ft 9 in) wide and 27 m (88 ft 6 in) high. Its dome is 37 m (121 ft 4 in) tall. It can accommodate 3,000 people seated or 5,000 standing.

● ★ **LARGEST FOREIGN AID DONATIONS (AS PERCENTAGE OF GDP):** According to the Organization for Economic Co-operation and Development (OECD), Norway donated $2.2 billion (£1.1 billion), or 0.9% of its gross domestic product (GDP), to poorer countries in 2004.

● **COUNTRY WITH THE HIGHEST TAX:** In Denmark, the highest rate of personal income tax was 62.9% as of June 2003.

● **LARGEST HOT SPRING:** The largest boiling river issues from alkaline hot springs at Deildartunguhver, north of Reykjavik, Iceland, at a rate of 245 litres (65 gallons) of boiling water per second.

GERMANY

AT A GLANCE

- **AREA**: 357,021 km² (137,846 miles²)
- **POPULATION**: 82.4 million
- **DENSITY**: 230 people/km² (597 people/mile²)
- **KEY FACTS**: Germany was home to the **first public electric railway**, which opened on 12 May 1881 at Lichtervelde near Berlin. The Germans are also the **biggest tourist spenders** while abroad; in 2004, they spent $71 billion (£38.7 billion) when on holiday in foreign countries. The fall of the Berlin Wall in 1989 (which separated West Berlin from the rest of East Germany for 28 years between 1961 and 1989) caused the world's **largest traffic jam**, as 18 million cars became gridlocked on the border. Lastly, Germany holds the record for the **highest paper recycling rate** – it recycles between 70% and 80% of its paper and cardboard per year.

★ FARTHEST-LEANING TOWER

The bell tower of the Protestant church in Suurhusen was found to be leaning at an angle of inclination of 5.1939 degrees when measured on 17 January 2007. It therefore claims the record previously held by the more famous Leaning Tower of Pisa in Italy, which tilts just 3.97 degrees.

★ LARGEST DIRNDL DRESS

On 21 June 2003, Gabriele Hein-Fischer (Germany) unveiled a dirndl dress that was an exact, scaled-up replica of the traditional Bavarian style, with the skirt measuring 2.9 m (9.5 ft) long and 9 m (29.5 ft) in diameter. Completing the look is a bodice, a wide skirt and 1.5-m-long (4.9-ft) sleeves!

★ LARGEST BLACK FOREST GATEAU

On 16 July 2006, Hans-Dieter Busch of the K&U Bakery in Rust made a Black Forest (cherry) gateau weighing 2,963 kg (6,532 lb).

★ NARROWEST STREET

Spreuerhofstrasse in Reutlingen, Germany, is 31 cm (1 ft) at its narrowest and 50 cm (1 ft 8 in) at its widest point. It was measured in February 2006.

★ HIGHEST COLD-WATER GEYSER

Geysir Andernach in Andernach blows water to heights of 30–60 m (98–196 ft). Unlike naturally occurring hot-water geysers, so-called "cold-water" geysers are formed by cold ground water dissolving large amounts of carbon dioxide (released through cracks from the Earth's upper mantle) and effectively "charging" the water; this charged underground water then erupts from a drilled well.

The Andernach well is 350 m (1,148 ft) deep and was re-drilled in 2001, following its closure in 1957 due to war damage. The highest recorded height, on 19 September 2002, was 61.5 m (201 ft 9 in). The average volume of water ejected per eruption is 7,800 litres (1,715 gal).

★ LONGEST TIME FLYING AN AIRSHIP

In November 1928, Hugo Eckener (Germany) flew the Graf Zeppelin for 71 hours and 6,384.5 km (3,967 miles), between Lakehurst, New Jersey, USA, and Friedrichshafen, Germany.

★ LONGEST STRUDEL

A 63.81-m (209-ft 4-in) strudel was made in Bitburg on 1 September 2007, by the two companies Freunde der Bütt and Bakery Flesch.

★ **NEW RECORD**
★ **UPDATED RECORD**

THE NETHERLANDS

LONGEST FLOTILLA OF TUG BOATS

On 16 June 2007, De Binnenvaart Association of Inland Shipping boasted a flotilla of 148 tug boats in Dordrecht, South Holland. They covered a distance of more than 3 km (1.86 miles).

★ LARGEST BROOM

On 12 September 2006, members of Kreateam 2006 made a huge broom in Sint-Annaland, Zeeland. The broom head was 32.65 m (107 ft 1 in) long and the handle was 20.85 m (68 ft 5 in).

★ MOST PEOPLE SPINNING PLATES SIMULTANEOUSLY

At the official opening of the Sportcampus in Utrecht, Ronstad on 25 September 2007, 1,026 people span plates at the same time.

TALLEST WORKING WINDMILL

De Noord Molen at Schiedam stands 33.33 m (109 ft 4 in) high.

★ LARGEST HAYSTACK

On 6 July 2006, at the Flaeijel Festival in Friesland, Frisia, a haystack was built measuring 9.51 m tall (31 ft 2 in) and with a diameter of 17 m (55 ft 9 in).

★ LARGEST GLASSES

The largest pair of spectacles were manufactured in December 2004 by Errold Jessurun (Netherlands), who is employed by Jess Optiek of Weesp, North Holland. The total width was 1.94 m (6 ft 4.25 in), with each lens 68 cm (2 ft 2.75 in) wide.

★ MOST DOMINOS TOPPLED BY A GROUP

After hundreds of builders from 13 countries worked for several weeks to install a total of 4,079,381 domino stones, they were toppled on 17 November 2006 at Domino Day 2006 in Leeuwarden, Friesland.

LARGEST CLOG DANCE

A group of 475 people took part in a clog dance at the Spuiplein in The Hague on 8 July 2006.

★ FASTEST HALF MARATHON BAREFOOT ON ICE/SNOW

Wim Hof (Netherlands) ran a half marathon barefoot in 2 hr 16 min 34 sec near Oulu, Finland, on 26 January 2007.

FASTEST CHAMPIONS LEAGUE GOAL

Roy Makaay (Netherlands) scored the opening goal for Bayern Munich against Real Madrid in just 10 seconds in Munich, Germany, on 7 March 2007.

AT A GLANCE

- **AREA**: 41,526 km² (16,033 miles²)
- **POPULATION**: 16.5 million
- **DENSITY**: 399 people/km² (1,033 people/mile²)
- **KEY FACTS**: The Netherlands is famed for its beer brewing and celebrates this fact with the record for the **most people in a beer race** – there were 928 participants in a beer race, a kind of beer drinking game, in Wageningen, Gelderland, on 1 February 2007. The city of Amsterdam is home to the world's **oldest stock exchange**. Founded in 1602, it printed shares for the United East India Company of the Netherlands.

EASTERN & CENTRAL EUROPE

AT A GLANCE

- **AREA**: 3,554,034 km² (1,372,220 miles²)
- **POPULATION**: 438 million
- **DENSITY**: 123 people/km² (319 people/mile²)
- **COUNTRIES**:

Central Europe: Austria (**highest proportion of organic farming**, where 10% of land is farmed organically), Czech Republic (**largest consumers of beer**, at 160.5 litres; 42.4 UK gallons per person), Germany (see p.260), Hungary (**most goals scored in a football World Cup tournament**: 27 in 1954), Liechtenstein, Poland (home of the **oldest purpose-built cinema in operation**, the Pionier, which opened in 1909), Slovakia (**largest collection of napkins**: 30,300 owned by Antónia Kozáková), Slovenia (**deepest natural shaft**: Vrtiglavica (meaning "vertigo") runs 643 m; 2,110 ft deep through Monte Kanin) and Switzerland.

Eastern Europe: Belarus, Estonia, Latvia (**largest shortage of men**: 53.97% of the population are female and 46.03% male), Lithuania, Moldova, Romania (**Largest dog shelter**: Ute Langenkamp can comfortably house up to 3,000 dogs) and Ukraine.

South-eastern Europe: Albania, Bulgaria, Bosnia and Herzegovina, Croatia, Greece (**first dictionary**, compiled by Protagoras of Abdera, 5th century BC), **first Olympic Games**: 776 BC), Macedonia, Montenegro, Romania, Serbia, Kosovo and part of Turkey.

MOST COUPLES KISSING SIMULTANEOUSLY

The greatest number of couples kissing simultaneously was 6,980 (13,960 participants) at an event organized by Radio Kameleon in Tuzla, Bosnia and Herzegovina, on 1 September 2007.

★ LARGEST HONEYCOMB

A honeycomb weighing 10.4 kg (22 lb 14 oz) – as heavy as a two-year-old child – was extracted from a beehive owned by Argirios Koskos (Greece) on 30 August 2007.

HEAVIEST BUILDING

The Palace of the Parliament in Bucharest, Romania, is constructed from 700,000 tonnes (1.5 billion lb) of steel and bronze with 1 million m³ (35 million ft³) of marble, 3,500 tonnes (7.7 million lb) of crystal glass and 900,000 m³ (31.7 million ft³) of wood.

★ LARGEST GATHERING OF TEST-TUBE CHILDREN

The largest gathering of children born as a result of artificial insemination was 1,180 at the ISCARE IVF Assisted Reproduction Centre in Prague, Czech Republic, on 15 September 2007.

★ SMALLEST PUB

The smallest permanent licensed bar is called the "Smallest Whisky Bar on Earth" and has a total floor area of 8.53 m² (91.82 ft²). The bar, owned by Gunter Sommer (Switzerland), is in Sta. Maria, Graubünden, Switzerland, and was opened in 2006 and measured in July 2007.

HIGHEST DENOMINATION BANKNOTE

The banknote with the highest denomination in the world is the Hungarian 100 million B-pengő (100,000,000,000,000,000,000 pengő). It was introduced on 1 January 1946 and withdrawn on 31 July 1946, when it was worth approximately $0.20 (£0.05).

★ HIGHEST PERCENTAGE OF FEMALE WORKFORCE (COUNTRY)

The country with the highest percentage of women in the workforce is Belarus, where 53.3% of workers are female. (In contrast, Pakistan has the ★ **highest percentage of men in the workforce**: 83.9% of workers there are male.)

MOST POINTS IN A DECATHLON (FEMALE)

Austra Skujyte (Lithuania) scored a total of 8,358 points in the decathlon in Columbia, Missouri, USA, on 14–15 April 2005. She bettered the previous record of 8,150 established by Marie Collonvillé (France) in the previous year.

★ LARGEST RADIATOR

The largest radiator measured 6.02 m (19 ft 9 in) high and 5.98 m (19 ft 7.4 in) long. It was manufactured by CINI Co. and displayed in Cacak, Serbia, on 23 April 2007.

★ LARGEST WALTZ

The largest waltz consisted of 115 pairs who danced in the Prater, Vienna, Austria. The record, organized by ORF Radio Wien, was set during the event Vienna Recordia in Vienna on 30 September 2007.

★ LONGEST CHAIN OF CONDOMS

The record for the longest chain of condoms is 3,269.46 m (10,726 ft 6 in) and was achieved by PSI Romania in Unirii Boulevard, Bucharest, Romania, on 28 October 2007.

★ LONGEST OCEAN SWIM

The longest distance ever swum without flippers in open sea is 225 km (139.8 miles) by Veljko Rogosic (Croatia) across the Adriatic Sea from Grado to Riccinoe (both Italy) from 29 to 31 August 2006.

★ LARGEST MATCHSTICK

A matchstick measuring 6.235 m (20 ft 5 in) long, with a cross section of 27.5 cm (10.8 in), was made by Estonian Match Ltd, and unveiled and struck at the Ugala Theatre, Viljandi, Estonia, on 27 November 2004.

LOWEST ROAD FATALITY RATE

Malta has the lowest fatality rate in road traffic accidents, with just 1.6 deaths per 100,000 population in 1996, according to the latest figures available. (The highest RTA rate is in Mauritius, with 43.9 per 100,000.)

★ LONGEST WEDDING-DRESS TRAIN

The longest wedding-dress train measured an incredible 1,362 m (4,468 ft 5 in) and was created by Andreas Evstratiou (Cyprus) for the bridal shop Green Leaf in Paphos, Cyprus, on 18 February 2007. When laid flat, the train stretches as long as 20 jumbo jets end to end!

LONGEST MOTORCYCLE WEDDING PROCESSION

Motorcycle enthusiasts Peter Schmidl and Anna Turceková (both Slovakia) had a wedding procession of 597 motorcycles when they tied the knot in Bratislava, Slovakia, on 6 May 2000. The event coincided with the Chopper Show 2000, which the majority of procession members were attending.

★ NEW RECORD
★ UPDATED RECORD

YOUNGEST CHESS GRAND MASTER

Sergey Karjakin (Ukraine, b. 12 January 1990) became the youngest individual to qualify as an International Grand Master on 12 August 2002, aged 12 years 212 days.

RUSSIA

AT A GLANCE

● **AREA**: 17,075,200 km²
(6,592,771 miles²)
● **POPULATION**: 141.3 million
● **DENSITY**: 8.2 people/km²
(21.4 people/mile²)
● **KEY FACTS**: Russia is the
largest country, representing
11.5% of the world's total land
area. It is also home to the
largest reservoir by volume,
the Bratskoye reservoir, which
has a volume of 169.3 km³
(40.6 miles³).

OLDEST LAKE

Lake Baikal in Siberia is 20–25 million years old and formed as a result of a tectonic rift in the Earth's crust. It holds more water than North America's Great Lakes combined and is host to the world's only freshwater seal.

LARGEST RUSSIAN NESTING DOLLS (MATRIOSHKA)

The largest set of Russian dolls is a 51-piece set hand-painted by Youlia Bereznitskaia (Russia). The largest doll measures 53.97 cm (1 ft 9.25 in) tall and the smallest 0.31 cm (0.125 in) in height. The set was completed on 25 April 2003.

MOST TV STATIONS

Russia had a staggering 7,306 television stations in 1998!

MOST GOALS SCORED IN A WORLD CUP FINALS MATCH

Oleg Salenko scored five goals playing for Russia against Cameroon in a 1994 World Cup finals match at Stanford Stadium, San Francisco, California, USA, on 28 June 1994.

GREATEST FLOOD

Roughly 18,000 years ago, an ancient lake in Siberia about 120 km (75 miles) long ruptured, causing the greatest freshwater flood in history. Research suggests the catastrophe unleashed waters 490 m (1,600 ft) deep and travelling at 160 km/h (100 mph). Scientists revealed the discovery in 1993.

MOST ORBITS OF THE EARTH

Russian cosmonaut Sergei Avdeyev completed 11,968 orbits of the Earth during his career. From July 1992 to July 1999, he spent 747 days 14 hr 22 min in space on three missions to the *Mir* space station.

LONGEST-OPERATING NUCLEAR POWER STATION

The nuclear reactor in Obninsk operated from 27 June 1954 until it was decommissioned on 30 April 2002. It was the **first nuclear reactor** in the world.

LONGEST UNINTERRUPTED TRAIN JOURNEY

The longest rail journey without a change of trains extends 10,214 km (6,346 miles) from Moscow, Russia, to Pyongyang, North Korea. One train a week travels the route, which takes in parts of the Trans-Siberian line.

FIRST MANNED SPACEFLIGHT

The earliest manned spaceflight was by Cosmonaut Flight Major (later Col) Yuri Alekseyevich Gagarin (USSR) in *Vostok 1* on 12 April 1961. The take-off was from the Baikonur Cosmodrome, Kazakhstan, at 6:07 a.m. GMT and the landing near Smelovka, near Engels, in the Saratov region of Russia, 115 minutes later. Gagarin parachuted to the ground separately from his spacecraft, landing 118 minutes after launch.

ISRAEL

LARGEST DANCE BY COUPLES

A dance featuring 552 couples took place on 9 May 2008 at Sportek Park in Tel Aviv, Israel; the participants performed Israeli folk dances for 30 minutes. The event was organized by Eddy Hassid and Gadi Bittonk and took six months to plan.

LARGEST MEZUZAH

A standard mezuzah consists of two written excerpts taken from Deuteronomy in the Old Testament, hand-written in Hebrew on a single piece of parchment, rolled up and placed in a container on the door frames of Jewish homes. The largest mezuzah parchment measured 94 cm (3 ft 1 in) long and 76 cm (2 ft 6 in) wide and its container measured 110 cm (3 ft 7.3 in) long on 19 May 2004. It was created by Avraham-Hersh Borshevsky (Israel).

★ LARGEST BANNER

On 23 December 2007, in Bar Yeuda, Massada, Grace Galindez-Gupana (Philippines) – President of HalleluYAH Prophetic Global Foundation Philippines – unveiled the largest banner, which combined the flags of Israel, the Philippines, North Korea and South Korea and measured 54,451 m² (586,103 ft²). The record attempt was organized by Sar-El Tours.

The industrious Ms Galindez-Gupana has also achieved several other world records, including the one for the **longest drawing** (5,007.36 m; 16,428 ft 3.76 in).

OLDEST ACTIVE FIGHTER PILOT

Uri Gil (Israel; b. 9 April 1943), a brigadier general in the Israeli Air Force, was a fighter pilot from 1964 to 20 June 2003, when he was 60 years 72 days old.

OLDEST SYNAGOGUE

A synagogue dating back to between 50 and 75 years BC was unearthed by archaeologist Ehud Netzer's team in 1998. The remains of the synagogue were discovered beneath the ruins of the Hasmonean winter palace, built by King Herod. The synagogue was destroyed by an earthquake in 31 BC.

LONGEST SIEGE

The longest recorded siege was that of Azotus (now Ashdod). According to the Greek historian Herodotus, it was besieged by Psamtik I of Egypt for 29 years in the period 664–610 BC.

DID YOU KNOW?

The Dead Sea on the Israel–Jordan border is the **lowest exposed body of water**, at an average of around 400 m (1,312 ft) below sea level. It is 80 km (50 miles) long and measures 18 km (11 miles) at its widest point.

LEAST EXTENSIVE METRO

The shortest operating underground system is the Carmelit in Haifa; it opened in 1959 and is 1,800 m (1 mile 626 ft) long. The only subway/metro in Israel, the Carmelit is a funicular running at a gradient of 12 degrees and has six stations.

LONGEST TIME TO SPIN A FOOTBALL ON ONE FINGER

Raphael Harris (Israel) spun a regulation-size football on one finger continuously for 4 min 21 sec in Jerusalem, on 27 October 2000.

OLDEST PLANT CULTIVATED FOR FOOD

In June 2006, researchers from Harvard University (USA) and Israel's Bar-Ilan University reported the discovery of nine carbonized figs, dated as 11,200–11,400 years old, in an early Neolithic village called Gilgal I, near Jericho.

AT A GLANCE

- **AREA**: 20,770 km² (8,019 miles²)
- **POPULATION**: 6.4 million
- **DENSITY**: 308 people/km² (798 people/mile²)
- **KEY FACTS**: Israel is the country with the **highest consumption of protein**, according to the United Nations, with an average of 128.6 g (4.53 oz) of protein per person per day. The world average is 75.3 g (2.65 oz).

  Israel is also the country with the **highest military expenditure per capita**, with $1,429.03 (£828.83) spent per person as of the latest figures available in 2005.

★ NEW RECORD
UPDATED RECORD

THE MIDDLE EAST

AT A GLANCE

- **AREA**: 7,158,624 km²
  (2,763,954 miles²)
- **POPULATION**: 334 million
- **DENSITY**: 46 people/km²
  (120 people/mile²)
- **KEY FACTS**: The **earliest coins** date from the reign of King Gyges of Lydia, Turkey, *ca.* 630 BC. The **sovereign countries with the least personal income tax** are Bahrain and Qatar, where the rate is nil. Iran is the country with the **youngest voting age** – just 15 years old.

- **COUNTRIES**: Bahrain, Egypt, Iran, Iraq, Jordan, Kuwait, Lebanon, Oman, Qatar, Saudi Arabia, Syria, Turkey, United Arab Emirates (UAE), Yemen. *(NB: as the Middle East is not a strictly definable region, we have opted to include the Gulf states here. For Israel, see p.265.)*

SANDIEST DESERT

The Arabian Desert covers nearly 2,600,000 km² (1 million miles²), of which about one-third is covered in sand. The desert occupies Saudi Arabia, Jordan, Iraq, Kuwait, Qatar, the United Arab Emirates, Oman and Yemen.

FIRST...

AUTOGRAPHS

Autographs made by scribes on cuneiform clay tablets from Tell Abu Salābikh, Iraq, have been dated to the early Dynastic III A period *ca.* 2600 BC. On one of these tablets, a scribe named "a-du" has added "dubsar" after his name, thus translating to "Adu, scribe". The earliest surviving signature on a papyrus is that of a scribe named Amen'aa. It has been dated back to the Egyptian middle kingdom, which began *ca.* 2130 BC.

CASTLE

Gomdan, or Gumdan, Castle, in the old city of Sana'a, Yemen, was built before AD 200 and once had 20 storeys.

ZOO

The earliest known collection of animals was established at modern-day Puzurish, Iraq, by Shulgi, a 3rd-dynasty ruler of Ur from 2097 BC to 2094 BC.

OLDEST...

CHURCH

An ancient church unearthed in the Jordanian coastal town of Aqaba by archaeologists from North Carolina State University, USA, is dated to between AD 290 and AD 300, making it the world's oldest purpose-built church.

DATABLE BRIDGE

The slab-stone, single-arch bridge over the river Meles in Izmir (formerly Smyrna), Turkey, dates from *ca.* 850 BC. Remnants of Mycenaean bridges dated *ca.* 1600 BC exist in the region of Mycenae, Greece, over the River Havos.

★ LARGEST KITE FLOWN

Abdulrahman Al Farsi and Faris Al Farsi (both Kuwait) made a kite with a lifting area of 950 m² (10,226 ft²). When laid flat, it had a total area of 1,019 m² (10,968 ft²) – approximately the same area as four tennis courts laid together. The kite was flown at the Kuwait Hala Festival in Flag Square, Kuwait City, Kuwait, on 15 February 2005.

LOVE SONG

An Assyrian love song to an Ugaritic god has been dated to *ca.* 1800 BC. It was reconstructed from a tablet of notation for an 11-string lyre at the University of California, Berkeley, USA, on 6 March 1974.

TALLEST PYRAMID

The pyramid of Khufu at Giza, Egypt, is the world's tallest. Also known as the Great Pyramid, it was 146.7 m (481 ft 4 in) high when completed around 4,500 years ago, but erosion and vandalism have reduced its height to 137.5 m (451 ft 4 in) today.

LARGEST PERCENTAGE OF POPULATION AT A FUNERAL

Official Iranian estimates gave the size of the crowds lining the 32-km (20-mile) route to Tehran's Behesht-e Zahra cemetery for the funeral of Ayatollah Ruhollah Khomeini on 11 June 1989 as 10,200,000 people – or one-sixth of Iran's population.

★ SHIPWRECK

A shipwreck located off Uluburun near Kaş, southern Turkey, has been dated to the 14th century BC.

LARGEST...

☆ BED

On 30 January 2007, the Dubai Shopping Festival and Intercoil International created a bed measuring 14 m (45 ft 11 in) long, 12 m (39 ft 4 in) wide and 2.10 m (6 ft 10 in) tall in Dubai, UAE.

CHANDELIER

Made from Swarovski crystal, the world's largest chandelier hangs in the Sultan Qaboos Grand Mosque in Muscat, Oman, and is 14.1 m (46 ft) tall, 8 m (26 ft) in diameter with 1,114 bulbs. Weighing approximately 8,500 kg (18,740 lb), it was built by Kurt Faustig SAS of Munich, Germany, in April 2000.

OLDEST WALLED TOWN

Following radiocarbon dating on specimens from the lowest levels of the town of Jericho, on the West Bank, archaeologists have revealed that a community of more than 2,000 people lived there as early as 7800 BC.

FACT

Ayatollah Khomeini actually had two funerals. The first was abandoned because the huge crowds damaged the wooden coffin in their eagerness to touch it. For the second funeral, security was boosted and the body was placed in a metal casket.

GOLD RING

The Najmat Taiba (which means "Star of Taiba") was created by Taiba for Gold and Jewellery Co., Ltd, of Saudi Arabia. The ring consists of 5.17 kg (11 lb 6 oz) of precious jewels set on a 58.686-kg (129-lb 6-oz) 21-carat gold ring. The total weight of the ring is 63.856 kg (140 lb 12 oz). It is 70 cm (27.5 in) in diameter and took 55 workers 45 days to build.

★ INFLATABLE SCULPTURE

The largest inflatable sculpture took the shape of a bottle and had a volume of 1,500 m³ (52,972 ft³). It was 25 m (82 ft) high and 11.9 m (39 ft) wide and was created by Japanese company Vitaene C at the Dubai Shopping Festival in Dubai, UAE, on 28 January 2007.

LARGEST ROYAL FAMILY

The house of Al-Saud of Saudi Arabia had over 4,000 royal princes and 30,000 royal relatives in 2002. The kingdom was established in 1932 by the patriarch, King Abdul Aziz, who had 44 sons by 17 wives, four of whom have ruled the kingdom since the King's death in 1953.

Saudi Arabia is the **country with the most siblings in government** – a total of six. The King, Abdullah bin Abdulaziz Al-Saud, is also Prime Minister and Commander of the Saudi National Guard. Between them, his five half-brothers hold the positions of Crown Prince, Deputy Prime Minister, Defence Minister, Interior Minister, Deputy Minister of Defence, Governor of Riyadh and Deputy Minister of the Interior.

AFRICA

AT A GLANCE

- **AREA**: 31,107,983 km² (12,010,859 miles²)
- **POPULATION**: 930 million
- **DENSITY**: 30 people/km² (77 people/mile²)
- **COUNTRIES**: Algeria, Angola, Benin, Botswana, Burkina Faso, Burundi, Cameroon, Cape Verde, Central African Republic, Chad, Comoros, Côte d'Ivoire, Democratic Republic of the Congo, Djibouti, Egypt, Equatorial Guinea, Eritrea, Ethiopia, Gabon, the Gambia, Ghana, Guinea, Guinea-Bissau, Kenya, Lesotho, Liberia, Libya, Madagascar, Malawi, Mali, Mauritania, Mauritius, Morocco, Mozambique, Namibia, Niger, Nigeria, Republic of the Congo, Réunion, Rwanda, Saint Helena, São Tomé and Príncipe, Senegal, Seychelles, Sierra Leone, Somalia, South Africa, Sudan, Swaziland, Tanzania, Togo, Tunisia, Uganda, Zambia, Zimbabwe.

RAREST CANID

There are believed to be fewer than 450 specimens of the Ethiopian wolf (*Canis simiensis*) alive. This endangered species is very vulnerable to the threat of rabies – indeed, at least 38 Ethiopian wolves have died from rabies since September 2003 in the Bale Mountains, Ethiopia, which is home to 300 individuals.

TALLEST MINARET

The minaret of the Great Hassan II Mosque, Casablanca, Morocco, measures 200 m (656 ft). The total construction cost of the mosque was 5 billion dirhams (£360 million; $513.5 million). The mosque can accommodate 25,000 worshippers in its prayer hall, which has a retractable roof, and a further 80,000 outside.

★ HIGHEST BIRTH AND FERTILITY RATES

Based on estimates for the period 2005–10, Niger is among the fastest-growing countries, with a predicted population rise of 41 million from 12 million (2004) to 53 million (2050). It also has the highest fertility rate, with 7.19 children per woman.

Niger also had 50.16 births per 1,000 population as of November 2007.

TALLEST TRIBE

Young adult males belonging to the Tutsi (also known as the Watussi) of Rwanda and Burundi, central Africa, average a height of 1.83 m (6 ft).

★ LARGEST BOWL OF COUSCOUS

The world's largest bowl of couscous was displayed at the International Fair of Algiers, Algeria, on 3 June 2004. It weighed 6.04 tonnes (13,315 lb) and was made by Semoulerie Industrielle de la Mitidja.

LARGEST PINK LAKE

Retba Lake, better known as Lac Rose (Pink Lake), is the world's largest pink body of water, measuring around 1.5 x 5 km (0.9 x 3 miles) at low water. A shallow lagoon, located 30 km (18 miles) north of Dakar, Senegal, the lake's unusual colour is the result of micro-organisms and a strong concentration of minerals.

LONGEST RIFT SYSTEM

The East African Rift System is approximately 6,400 km (4,000 miles) long with an average width of 50–65 km (30–40 miles). The escarpments around the edge of the valley have an average height of 600–900 m (2,000–3,000 ft). It begins in Jordan and extends to Mozambique in east Africa. This extensive rift system has been gradually forming for around 30 million years, as the Arabian peninsula has separated from Africa.

MOST VENOMOUS SCORPION

The Tunisian fat-tailed scorpion (*Androctonus australis*) is responsible for 80% of stings and 90% of deaths from scorpion stings in north Africa.

SOUTH AFRICA

LARGEST DIAMOND

A 3,106-carat diamond was found on 26 January 1905 at the Premier Diamond Mine near Pretoria, South Africa, and was presented to the reigning British monarch, Edward VII. Named The Cullinan, it was cut into 106 polished diamonds.

FASTEST LAVA FLOW

Nyiragongo is a volcano in the Virunga Mountains in the Democratic Republic of Congo. When it erupted on 10 January 1977, the lava burst through fissures on the volcano's flank, travelling at speeds of almost 60 km/h (40 mph). Up to 2,000 people were killed when the flow inundated the nearby city of Goma.

LARGEST MARIMBA ENSEMBLE

On 29 October 2004, at Bishops Diocesan College, Cape Town, South Africa, an ensemble of 78 musicians played the marimba (a percussion instrument similar to the xylophone) for over 10 minutes.

★ DEEPEST MINE

The Savuka Mine in South Africa is the largest gold mine, operating at a depth of 3,777 m (12,391 ft) as of 2005. At this depth, miners are able to extract rock that contains some 20 cm³ (1.2 in³) of gold in each cubic metre (35 ft³). The mine is in the Witwatersrand Basin, the world's **largest gold reserve**, which has produced over 42.5 billion grams (1.5 billion ounces) of gold since 1886.

LARGEST DESERT

Nearly an eighth of the world's land surface is arid, with a rainfall of less than 25 cm (10 in) per annum. The Sahara in north Africa is the largest hot desert in the world – it is larger than all of Australia. At its greatest length, it is 5,150 km (3,200 miles) from east to west. From north to south, it is between 1,280 km and 2,250 km (800–1,400 miles). The area covered by the desert is about 9.1 million km² (3.5 million miles²).

On 13 September 1922, the **highest recorded temperature** – 58°C (136°F) – was recorded in the shade at Al'Aziziyah in the Sahara Desert, Libya.

LARGEST POPULATION OF CHILDREN

Uganda had the highest population of children, with 50.8 % aged between 0 and 14 years old in 2003. The picture above shows children waiting in the street for the arrival of Prince Charles, the Prince of Wales (UK), in Kawempe Slum, Kampala, Uganda, on 23 November 2007.

YOUNGEST PERSON TO WIN THE MAN BOOKER PRIZE

Ben Okri (Nigeria) was 32 when he won the Man Booker Prize in 1991 for his novel *The Famished Road*.

The record for the **most Man Booker Prize wins** is shared by South African author J. M. Coetzee and Peter Carey (Australia), both of whom have won this prestigious prize twice.

LARGEST...

BIRD

The flightless elephant bird, or vouron patra (*Aepyornis maximus*), from Madagascar, died out about 1,000 years ago (although sightings were reported up to 1658). It grew to around 3–3.3 m (10–11 ft) tall and weighed about 500 kg (1,100 lb). (*For the **tallest bird ever**, see p.277.*)

ELEPHANT RELOCATION

In August 1993, the charity Care For The Wild International (CFTWI) moved more than 500 elephants in family groups some 250 km (155 miles) across Zimbabwe, from Gonarezhou National Park to the Save Valley Conservancy.

★ NEW RECORD
☆ UPDATED RECORD

CENTRAL & SOUTHERN ASIA

AT A GLANCE

- **AREA**: 3,600,292 km² (1,390,080 miles²)
- **POPULATION**: 1.5 billion
- **DENSITY**: 416 people/km² (1,079 people/mile²)
- **KEY FACTS**: Home to the **largest sea** (the Caspian, at 371,000 km²; 143,244 miles²) and Mount Everest, the **highest mountain** at 8,828 m (29,028 ft), located on the Nepal–China border.

- **COUNTRIES**: Afghanistan, Bangladesh, Bhutan, British Indian Ocean Territories, India, Kazakhstan, Kyrgyzstan, Maldives (**flattest country**; **highest divorce rate**, at 10.97 per 1,000 per year), Nepal, Sri Lanka (★**most cabinet ministers**, with 52), Pakistan, Tajikistan, Turkmenistan and Uzbekistan.

(Iran is considered south Asian only by the UN. The G8 regards it as part of the Greater Middle East – and so does GWR! For Middle Eastern records, please turn to pp. 266–67.)

HIGHEST RAINFALL

Mawsynram in Meghalaya, India, has an annual rainfall of 11,873 mm (467 in). The second rainiest place, at 11,430 mm (450 in) per year, is Cherrapunji, also in the state of Meghalaya. Most of the rain occurs during the monsoon season (May to September). Pictured is a Khasi woman taking her children to school on the outskirts of Shillong city.

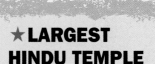

OLDEST KORAN

The Holy Koran Mushaf of Othman, owned by the Muslim Board of Uzbekistan, once belonged to Caliph Othman (*ca.* AD 588–656), third successor to the Prophet Mohammed. Only about half of the original 706 pages survive.

★ MOST REFUGEES

According to the United Nations High Commission for Refugees (UNHCR), Pakistan had received 1,085,000 refugees by 1 January 2006, more than any other country. This excludes Afghan refugees who live outside the UNHCR refugee camps, estimated at a further 1.5 million in 2005.

★ LARGEST HINDU TEMPLE

BAPS Swaminarayan Akshardham in New Delhi, India, has a total area of 8,021 m² (86,342 ft²). The temple was built within five years by 11,000 artisans. It measures 108.5 m (356 ft) long, 96.3 m (316 ft) wide and 42.9 m (141 ft) tall.

★ LARGEST CHAPATI

An Indian bread weighing 63.99 kg (141.07 lb) was made by the Shree Jalarm Mandir Jirnodhar Samitee organization at Jamnagar, India, on 15 January 2005.

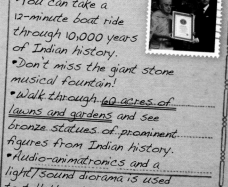

BAPS Swaminarayan Akshardham – visitor's guide

- Consecrated November 2005; GWR certificate presented to His Holiness Pramukh Swami Mahara in December 2007.
- Constructed in just <u>five years</u> entirely from Rajasthani pink sandstone and Italian Carrara sandstone – absolutely <u>no steel or concrete</u> allowed!
- Houses an 26 × 20 m (85 × 65 ft) <u>IMAX</u> cinema!

- You can take a 12-minute boat ride through 10,000 years of Indian history.
- Don't miss the giant stone musical fountain!
- Walk through <u>60 acres of lawns and gardens</u> and see bronze statues of prominent figures from Indian history.
- Audio-animatronics and a light/sound diorama is used to tell the story of Bhagwan Swaminarayan.

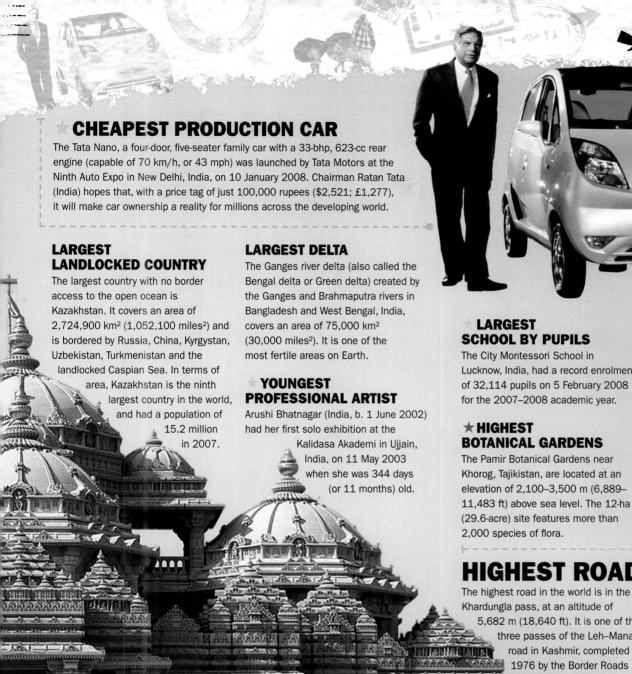

★ CHEAPEST PRODUCTION CAR

The Tata Nano, a four-door, five-seater family car with a 33-bhp, 623-cc rear engine (capable of 70 km/h, or 43 mph) was launched by Tata Motors at the Ninth Auto Expo in New Delhi, India, on 10 January 2008. Chairman Ratan Tata (India) hopes that, with a price tag of just 100,000 rupees ($2,521; £1,277), it will make car ownership a reality for millions across the developing world.

LARGEST LANDLOCKED COUNTRY

The largest country with no border access to the open ocean is Kazakhstan. It covers an area of 2,724,900 km² (1,052,100 miles²) and is bordered by Russia, China, Kyrgystan, Uzbekistan, Turkmenistan and the landlocked Caspian Sea. In terms of area, Kazakhstan is the ninth largest country in the world, and had a population of 15.2 million in 2007.

LARGEST DELTA

The Ganges river delta (also called the Bengal delta or Green delta) created by the Ganges and Brahmaputra rivers in Bangladesh and West Bengal, India, covers an area of 75,000 km² (30,000 miles²). It is one of the most fertile areas on Earth.

★ YOUNGEST PROFESSIONAL ARTIST

Arushi Bhatnagar (India, b. 1 June 2002) had her first solo exhibition at the Kalidasa Akademi in Ujjain, India, on 11 May 2003 when she was 344 days (or 11 months) old.

★ LARGEST SCHOOL BY PUPILS

The City Montessori School in Lucknow, India, had a record enrolment of 32,114 pupils on 5 February 2008 for the 2007–2008 academic year.

★ HIGHEST BOTANICAL GARDENS

The Pamir Botanical Gardens near Khorog, Tajikistan, are located at an elevation of 2,100–3,500 m (6,889–11,483 ft) above sea level. The 12-ha (29.6-acre) site features more than 2,000 species of flora.

HIGHEST ROAD

The highest road in the world is in the Khardungla pass, at an altitude of 5,682 m (18,640 ft). It is one of the three passes of the Leh–Manali road in Kashmir, completed in 1976 by the Border Roads Organization, New Delhi, India. Motor vehicles have been able to use it since 1988.

★ **NEW RECORD**
UPDATED RECORD

BOLLYWOOD BASICS

● Lalita Pawar (India) was the **actress with the longest Bollywood** career. She made her debut at the age of 12 and appeared in more than 700 films over the next 70 years.
P. Jairaj (India), who made his acting debut in 1929, had a career spanning 300 films and more than 70 years – the **longest career for a Bollywood actor**.

● The **most expensive Bollywood film** is *Devdas* (India, 2002), which cost an estimated 500 million rupees ($11.2 million; £5,740,911) to make.

● *Hum Aapke Hain Koun...!* (India, 1994), starring Madhuri Dixit and Salman Khan, is the **highest grossing Bollywood film**. It took over £40.4 million ($63.8 million) in its first year, breaking the record set by the curry western *Sholay* in 1975.

SOUTH-EAST ASIA

AT A GLANCE

- **AREA**: 4,495,553 km² (1,735,742 miles²)
- **POPULATION**: 574 million
- **DENSITY**: 128 people/km² (330 people/mile²)
- **COUNTRIES**: Brunei (boasting the **largest residential palace** in the world, with 1,788 rooms and 257 lavatories), Burma (home to the Padaung tribe, whose females have the **longest necks**, stretching up to 40 cm; 15.75 in), Cambodia, Indonesia (**largest Muslim population**, at 203 million), Laos (**most bombed country**, with 2.2 million tonnes; 5 billion lb; of bombs dropped between 1964 and 1973 during the Vietnam War), Malaysia (home to the 451.9-m [1,482-ft] Petronas Towers, the **tallest twin towers**), the Philippines, Singapore, Thailand (capital city Bangkok is the **longest place name** at 175 letters*) and Vietnam.

LARGEST BATIK

A batik painting called *The Batik on the Road* measuring 1,200 m² (12,916 ft²) was created by 1,000 participants on behalf of the Pekalongan Batik Community in Pekalongan City, Indonesia, on 16 September 2005.

LARGEST ANIMAL ORCHESTRA

The 12-piece Thai Elephant Orchestra at the Thai Elephant Conservation Centre in Lampang, Thailand, was founded by Richard Lair and David Soldier (both USA) in 2000 to help conserve the Asiatic elephant species.

LARGEST SHOE

Measuring 5.29 m (17.35 ft) long, 2.37 m (7 ft 8 in) wide and 2.03 m (6 ft 7 in) high, the world's largest shoe was created by the Marikina Colossal Footwear Team on 21 October 2002 in Marikina City, the Philippines.

MOST TREES PLANTED SIMULTANEOUSLY

In an event organized by Nurturers of the Earth, Children for Breastfeeding and the Department of Environment and Natural Resources (all the Philippines), 516,137 people planted 653,143 trees simultaneously along the National Highway of the Philippines on 25 August 2006.

HIGHEST POPULATION FOR AN ISLAND

The world's most populous island is Java, Indonesia, which had a population of 121,352,608 according to the 2000 census, all living in an area of 127,569 km² (49,254 miles²). That's more that 936 people per km² (2,463 people per mile²).

LARGEST TET CAKE

The world's largest Tet cake weighed 1.75 tonnes (3,858 lb) and was made by Saigontourist at Dam Sen Cultural Park, Ho Chi Minh City, Vietnam, to mark the traditional Tet festival in Vietnam from 18 to 21 January 2004.

*The shortened, 111-letter, six-word version of Bangkok is krungthephphramahanakhon bowonratanakosin

WORST MONSOON

Monsoons that raged throughout Thailand from September to December 1983 resulted in the deaths of 10,000 people. Up to 100,000 victims contracted water-borne diseases and 15,000 people were evacuated. More than $400 million (£275.6 million) worth of damage was caused.

★ NEW RECORD
☆ UPDATED RECORD

LARGEST BUDDHIST TEMPLE

The largest Buddhist temple is Borobudur, near Yogyakarta, central Java, Indonesia, constructed between AD 750 and AD 842. The 60,000-m³ (2,118,880-ft³) stone structure is 34.5 m (113 ft) tall and its base measures 123 x 123 m (403 x 403 ft). Having fallen into disrepair from the 14th century onwards, Borobudur was rediscovered by Sir Thomas Stamford Raffles in 1814, while he was British governor of Java.

HEAVIEST BELL IN USE

The Mingun bell in Mandalay, Burma, weighs 92 tonnes (202,825 lb) with a diameter of 5.09 m (16 ft 8 in) at the lip. The bell is struck by a teak boom from the outside. It was cast at Mingun in the reign of King Bodawpaya (1782–1819).

FACT

Monsoon rains also caused flooding in India's Bengal state during September 1978. With 15 million out of a population of 44 million made homeless, it represents the **worst flood disaster** in terms of homes lost.

LOUDEST NOISE

When the island-volcano Krakatoa in the Sunda Strait between Sumatra and Java, Indonesia, exploded in an eruption on 27 August 1883, the sound was heard 5,000 km (3,100 miles) away. The noise is estimated to have been heard over 8% of the Earth's surface and to have had 26 times the power of the largest ever H-bomb test.

LARGEST RELIGIOUS STRUCTURE

The Angkor Wat (City Temple) encloses 162.6 ha (401 acres) in Cambodia, making it the largest religious structure ever constructed. It was built to the Hindu god Vishnu by the Khmer King Suryavarman II in the period 1113–50. Its curtain wall measures 1,280 m (4,200 ft) and its population, before it was abandoned in 1432, was estimated to have reached 80,000. The temple forms part of a complex of 72 major monuments, begun ca. AD 900, that extends over 24.8 km (15.4 miles).

LARGEST GILDED BUILDING

The cone-shaped Shwe Dagon Pagoda in Rangoon, Burma, is 99 m (325 ft) tall, measures 137 m (450 ft) across at its base and is covered in gold plating. The Buddhist shrine has been rebuilt many times, but there is thought to have been a stupa (Buddhist monument) there for more than 2,000 years.

LONGEST ALPHABET

The language with the most letters is Khmer (Cambodian), with 74 (including some without any current use).

LARGEST FOUNTAIN

The Suntec City Fountain of Wealth in Singapore has a cast bronze superstructure weighing 85 tonnes (187,393 lb) and stands 14 m (46 ft) high, while the base of the fountain has a total area of 1,683.07 m² (18,117 ft²). It cost an estimated $6 million (£3.5 million) to build in 1997.

mahintharayuthaya mahadilokphiphobnovpharad radchataniburirom udomsantisug

FAR EAST

LARGEST GATHERING OF DANCING DRAGONS

A total of 55 dancing dragons assembled to take part in the opening ceremony of the 25th Luoyang Peony Festival of Henan Province, China, on 10 April 2007.

AT A GLANCE

- **AREA**: 11,795,031 km² (4,554,087 miles²)
- **POPULATION**: 1.55 billion
- **DENSITY**: 132 people/km² (341 people/mile²)
- **COUNTRIES**: China (the **most populated country**, with 1,323,345,000 citizens in 2005; also includes Special Administrative Regions [SARs] of Hong Kong and Macau). Continued on p.275.

★ DENSEST NETWORK OF ROADS

Macau, a Special Administrative Region of China, has 21.3 km (13.2 miles) of road per km² (0.38 miles²) of land area, according to *The Economist* in 2008.

★ LARGEST EMPIRE

The **largest connected empire** that ever existed was the Mongol Empire of 1206–1367, run by the Khan Dynasty. At its most powerful in 1279 under Kublai Khan, the empire ruled over 100 million people living across an area of 35.7 million km² (13.8 million miles²) – including areas in the present-day countries of China, Russia, Mongolia, central Asia, the Middle East and the Korean Peninsula.

★ MOST HEAVILY USED NETWORK OF ROADS

With 5,565,600 km (3,458,300 miles) driven for every kilometre (0.62 miles) of its road network each year, Hong Kong's roads are the most heavily used in the world.

★ LONGEST BOOM (TRUCK-MOUNTED)

Made by SANY Heavy Industry Co., Ltd (China), the longest truck-mounted boom is 66 m (216 ft 6 in) long. The multi-stage extensible arm is used in large-scale engineering projects.

★ HIGHEST CITY POPULATION

By 2007, Greater Tokyo, Japan, had a population of over 35 million, making it Asia's largest conurbation and the world's most populous urban agglomeration.

DID YOU KNOW?

The ★**longest dancing dragon** was 5,056 m (16,587 ft) in length and was made for the 25th Luoyang Peony Festival of Henan Province, China, on 10 April 2007.

★ LARGEST GYMNASTIC DISPLAY

The record for the largest gymnastic display involved 100,090 participants in May Day Stadium, Pyongyang, Democratic People's Republic of Korea, on 14 August 2007. The event was organized by Grand Mass Gymnastic and Artistic Performance "Arirang" State Preparing Committee of Democratic People's Republic of Korea.

★ MOST PANDAS BORN IN ONE YEAR

The most remarkable year for panda births was 2006, during which 30 cubs were born into captivity, some of which are shown here. Most of the cubs were born at Wolong Panda Research Centre in south-west China. The 30th cub was born at Adventure World, Wakayama, Japan, on 23 December 2006.

★ LARGEST RICE CAKE

A rice cake made by Kwak Sungho and staff of Han Bbang (South Korea) at the 12th World Rice Food Festival, Dongjin-gun, Chungnam, South Korea, on 7 October 2007 weighed 3.68 tonnes (8,113 lb).

★ LONGEST NOODLE

On 24 March 2007, Hiroshi Kuroda (Japan) made a noodle 548.7 m (1,800 ft 2 in) long and 3.3 mm (0.1 in) in diameter in Nasu, Tochigi, Japan.

★ LONGEST SUSHI ROLL

The Liaison Council of Japanese Postal Workers' Union in Gunma Prefecture, Maebashi City, Japan, created a 2,033.3-m-long (6,671-ft) sushi roll on 22 April 2007.

★ LARGEST KADOMATSU

A kadomatsu is a traditional Japanese New Year decoration that is placed in front of homes to welcome ancestral spirits.

★ LARGEST DISPLAY OF LANTERNS

On 24 February 2008, Tainan County Government organized a display of 47,759 lanterns at Solar City in the "Prayer for Peace" area of Tainan Science Park, Tainan, Taiwan – the greatest lantern display in a single venue.

The total area covered was 250 x 100 m, or 25,000 m² (820 ft 2 in x 328 ft 1 in, or 269,096.68 ft²). Seen from above, the completed arrangement of lanterns spelled out the words "Taiwan Peace" in Mandarin and English.

★ LARGEST PARADE OF BICYCLES

A parade of 2,152 bicycles was organized by Da Jia Jenn Lann Temple, Taichung County Government and Volvic Taiwan, in Taichung, Taiwan, on 1 March 2008.

★ LARGEST KICK-BOXING CLASS

A total of 986 people attended a kick-boxing class at an event organized by the charity HER fund at the MacPherson playground, Mongkok, Kowloon, Hong Kong, China, on 4 March 2007.

LARGEST PIGGY BANK

A golden piggy bank was made by Zhong Xing Shenyang Commercial Building Co., Ltd, and unveiled in Shenyang, China, on 2 May 2007. It is 5.6 m (18 ft 4 in) long, 3.96 m (12 ft 11 in) tall, has a circumference of 14.6 m (47 ft 10 in) and weighs about 3 tonnes (6,000 lb).

Two kadomatsu measuring 9.866 m (32 ft 3 in) each were completed in the Tachibana Park, Chijiwa-Nagasaki, Japan, on 18 December 2000. Sixty moso bamboos were used to create them.

Other countries: Japan (**largest population of centenarians**, with 25,606 people aged over 100 years old as of 2005), North Korea (the **most militarized country** per capita, with nearly 5% of the population in the military), Mongolia (the **most sparsely populated country**, with 1.6 people per km², or 4.1 per mile²), South Korea (boasting the **hardest-working citizens**, averaging 2,423 hours per person per year) and Taiwan (home to the world's **tallest building**, Taipei 101, at 508 m; 1,666 ft).

★ **NEW RECORD**
★ **UPDATED RECORD**

AUSTRALIA

AT A GLANCE

● **AREA:** 7,686,850 km²
(2,967,909 miles²)
● **POPULATION:** 20.4 million
● **DENSITY:** 2.6 people/km²
(6.9 people/mile²)

★LARGEST MARRIAGE-VOW RENEWAL CEREMONY

In an event organized by Virgin Money, Australia, 272 married couples took part in the largest marriage-vow renewal ceremony in Centennial Park, Sydney, New South Wales. The ceremony took place on 16 September 2007 and was presided over by celebrant Angela Miller.

★LARGEST BOTTLE OF WINE

At 1.95 m (6 ft 5 in) tall, the world's largest bottle of wine contained 290 litres (63.79 gallons) of red wine. The production of the bottle was organized by North Road Liquor (Australia), and it was filled at Plantagenet Wines (Australia) on 29 May 2006.

★MOST PEOPLE FIRE-EATING

A total of 171 members of the Chilli Club International (Australia) performed *Fire Storm Crossing Australi'* at the opening ceremony of the Sydney Olympic Games, on 15 September 2000.

MOST VENOMOUS LAND SNAKE

The small-scaled snake (*Oxyuranus microlepidotus*) measures 1.7 m (5 ft 7 in) and is found mainly in the Diamantina River and Cooper Creek drainage basins in Queensland and western New South Wales. The average venom yield after milking is 44 mg (0.00155 oz) but one male specimen yielded 110 mg (0.00385 oz), enough to kill 250,000 mice or 125 men. Fortunately, *O. microlepidotus* lives only in the arid deserts of central eastern Australia and no human death has been reported from its bite.

★MOST JOKES TOLD IN AN HOUR

Anthony Lehmann (Australia) told a total of 549 jokes in one hour at the Rhino Room club, Adelaide, South Australia, on 25 May 2005.

★LOUDEST DRUMMER

Col Hatchman (Australia) hit a peak reading of 137.2 decibels during a gig with his band, Dirty Skanks, at the Northern Star Hotel, Hamilton, New South Wales, on 4 August 2006.

LARGEST PRODUCER OF NATURAL DIAMONDS

Australia provides around 34% of the world's annual production of 110 million carats of natural diamonds.

LONGEST REEF

The Great Barrier Reef, situated off the coast of Queensland, is 2,027 km (1,260 miles) in length. It is not actually a single entity but consists of thousands of separate reefs. On three occasions – between 1962 and 1971, 1979 and 1991, and 1995 to the present day – corals on large areas of the central section of the reef have been devastated by the crown-of-thorns starfish (*Acanthaster planci*).

★LONGEST PINBALL-PLAYING MARATHON

Alessandro Parisi (Australia) played pinball for 28 hours at the Westland Shopping Centre in Whyalla, on 22–23 January 2007.

NEW ZEALAND

VISAS

MOST SOUTHERLY CAPITAL CITY

Wellington, North Island, with an estimated 2001 population of 165,278, is the southernmost capital city of an independent country (41°17'S). The world's southernmost capital of a dependent territory is Port Stanley, Falkland Islands (51°43'S), with a population of 1,989 (excluding service personnel) in 2001.

MOST SOUTHERLY VINEYARD

Westons Reserve Winery is located in Dunedin, South Island, south of Lat. 45°51'S, and is the world's most southerly commercial vineyard.

TALLEST EXTINCT BIRD

The *Dinornis maximus* – a species of moa (flightless birds native to New Zealand) – is believed to have attained a height of 3.6 m (12 ft) and weighed about 227 kg (500 lb). It had no wings, was ostrich-like and died out less than 10,000 years ago.

AT A GLANCE

- **AREA**: 268,680 km² (103,737 miles²)
- **POPULATION**: 4.1 million
- **DENSITY**: 15.3 people/km² (39.5 people/mile²)
- **KEY FACTS**: Research presented to the World Economic Forum in January 2006 revealed that the **country with the best environmental performance** was New Zealand. It is also home to the **world's tallest recorded geyser**, the Waimangu geyser, which erupted to a height in excess of 460 m (1,500 ft) in 1903.

★MOST PARTICIPANTS IN A SNOWBOARD RACE

A record 88 participants took part in a snowboard race at an event organized by The Rock FM and Mount Hutt at Mount Hutt in Christchurch, New Zealand, on 6 October 2007.

★LONGEST HANDSHAKE

The longest time that two people have shaken hands without interruption is 9 hr 19 min, achieved by Alastair Galpin and Jesse van Keken (both New Zealand) at Aotea Square Events Centre, Auckland, on 11 November 2006.

★MOST PEOPLE FIRE-WALKING

At an event organized by the New Zealand International Fire Festival, a total of 350 people attempted a fire-walk consecutively in a time of 1 hr 20 min at Dunedin, South Island, on 11 July 2004.

★LARGEST SPECIES OF WETA

Belonging to the order Orthoptera (grasshoppers and crickets) and confined entirely to New Zealand, the 70 species of weta include some of the world's most intimidating insects. The largest species of weta is the Little Barrier Island giant weta *Deinacrida heteracantha*, with a maximum recorded length of 11 cm (4.4 in) and a leg-span of over 17.5 cm (7 in).

★ NEW RECORD
★ UPDATED RECORD

ACKNOWLEDGEMENTS/CREDITS

Guinness World Records would like to thank the following individuals, companies, groups, websites, societies and universities for their help in the creation of the 2009 edition: Pedro Adrega (Fédération Internationale de Natation), American Paper Optics (John Jerit), BAPS Swaminarayan Akshardham, Bender Media Services (Susan and Sally), Betsy Baker, Luke and Joseph Boatfield, Ceri, Katie & Georgie Boulton, Alfie Boulton-Fay, Olivia Boulton, Box Office Mojo, Julie Bradshaw & The Channel Swimming Association (The CSA), Sir Richard Branson, Nikki Brin, Carlsberg, Stockholm, Peter Cassidy (Race Walking Association), The Cavalry & Guards Club, London, CCTV (Guo Tong and Wang Xuechun), Gene Cernan, ChartTrack, Edd & Imogen China, Roy Church, Ian Coburn, Paulo Coelho, Edouard Cointreau, The Costume Studio, London, Kenneth & Tatiana Crutchlow (ORS), Stacey Cusack, Elaine Davidson, Ceri Davis, Davis Media, David Donnelly, Terry Doyle, James Ellerker, Louis Epstein, ESPN X Games - Kelly Robshaw, Katie Moses Swope, Deb McKinnis, Europroducciones Spain and Italy (Stefano, Marco, Maria, Gabriella et al), Explorersweb, Factiva, Fall Out Boy (Andy Hurley, Patrick Stump, Joe Trohman, Pete Wentz, plus Bob Mclynn, Henry Bordeaux, Kyle Chirnside, Brian Diaz), Famitsu, Adam Fenton, Ian Fisk, Flix (Tam, Nic and Sharan), Forbes, Marion Gallimore (Fédération Internationale des Sociétés d'Aviron), The GFK Group, Brett Gold, Golden Tulip Hotel, Luxembourg, Google/YouTube (Theo), Louise Grant, Bexier Group, Jordan, Ryan and Brandon Greenwood, Victoria Grimsell, Debby de Groot, Kristopher Growcott, AJ Hackett, Tim Haines, Impossible Pictures, Peter Harper, Ray Harper, Andy Harris (International Water Skiing Federation), Stuart Hendry, Gavin Hennessy, Gill Hill (International Water Skiing Federation), Nigel Hobbs, Homewood School, Tenterden, Hospital Xanit Internacional, Malaga, Hotel Arts, Barcelona, Hotel Guadalpin, Marbella, ICM (Greg Lipstone, Heather Grayson), The Infamous Grouse and Sir Les (Jack Brockbank, Robert Dimery, Craig Glenday, Kaoru Ishikawa, Lucia Sinigagliesi, Nick Watson), Internet Movie Database, Tan Jun, Cathy & Bob Jung, Jefferson County Fairgrounds, Colorado, Jon Jeritt, Jon Adam Fashion Group, Joost (Alexandra and Symon), Mark Karges, Dr Haydn Kelly, Dr Theo Kreouzis, Department of Physics, Queen Mary University of London, Orla and Thea Langton, Christopher Lee, Lingfield Racecourse, Surrey, Helen Livingstone, Carey Low, Canadian Manda Group, Lula-Bell, Mad Max III (Claire Bygrave, Carol & Maureen Kane, Sam Malone, David Moncur), Manda, Canada, Mediazone (Gary), Clare Merryfield, Mora Siljan Airport, Sweden, MTV (Ritesh Guptah, James Montgomery), Derek Musso, National Geographic Kids magazine (Rachel Buchholz, Eleanor Shannah), NBA Entertainment (Patrick Sullivan, Karen Barberan, Jason Iodato), NBC (Craig Plestis, Jenny Ellis), Aniko Nemeth Mora (International Weightlifting Federation), Nationmaster, Liam Nesbitt, Norddeich TV Germany (Ollie, Melanie, Claudia, Jan et al), NPD Group, OANDA, Ocean Rowing Society, Michael Oram & CS&PF, Alberto Parise, Clara Piccirillo, Professor Theodore W. Pietsch, University of Washington, La Porte des Indes Restaurant, London, Fabrice Prahin (International Skating Union), He Pingping and family, Rob Pullar, Keith Pullin, La Quatre-Cats restaurant, Barcelona, R et G Productions, France (Stefan, Jerome, David, Jean-Francois, Julien et al), Red Lion Public House, Hernhill, Lee Redmond, Brian Reinert, Martyn Richards, Martyn Richards Research, Richmond Theatre, Surrey, RTL (Sascha, Tom, Sandra, Sebastian, Jennifer, Julia et al), Rebecca Saponiere, Tom Sergeant, Robyn Sheppard, Julien Stauffer (Union Cycliste Internationale), Bethan Muir Tame, Greenfield Media, Texperts (Tom, Sarah, Rhod and Paul), True Entertainment (Stephen Weinstock, Glenda Hersh, Bryan Hale, Shari Solomon Cedar), TSA/MAX Entertainment (Marcus, Belle, Alex, Christy, Ery et al), Twin Galaxies (Walter Day, Pete Bouvier), Jan Vandendriessche (International Association of Ultra Runners), Veoh (Emilia), VG Chartz, Jessica and Isabel Way (with support from Sean the Prawn), Carina Weirauch, Fran Wheelen, Royal Bath & West Show, Norman Wilson (International Association of Ultra Runners), Wookey Hole Caves, Somerset, YouTube.

End papers: Front (left to right), Longest sushi roll, Largest display of videos, Largest sirtaki dance, Largest Highland dance, Most Nicholaus boots filled up with gifts, Most titles of top-level sport championships represented at one venue, Largest collection of model coaches and buses, Most people performing synchronised swimming routine, Most knee bends on a Swiss ball in one minute, Longest ice cream dessert, Largest Christmas stocking, Longest carrot, Largest condiment sachet, Largest tuba ensemble, Fastest residential internet connection, Fastest cycle across Canada by a relay team, Most knee bends on a balance board in one minute, Largest bonfire, Most cocktails made in one hour, Largest decorated Easter egg, Largest paperclip, Farthest distance travelled on a skateboard in 24 hours, Most different makes of motorcycle in a parade, Longest sofa, Largest autograph signing by professional athletes, Most people inside a soap bubble, Most eggs held in the hand, Longest saree/sari, Most concrete blocks broken in one minute (male), Fastest car powered by dry-cell batteries, Largest stamp - special, Longest marathon singing by multiple singers, Longest "Riverdance" line, Largest serving of fried chicken, Longest graffiti scroll, Largest bed.

Back (left to right), Largest display of lanterns, Longest cigar, Largest Russian nesting doll ("matrioshkas"), Fastest time to row across the Atlantic east to west by a team of two, Fastest journey on foot across Australia (Perth to Sydney), Most slices of meat cut in 1 hour, Largest photo album, Heaviest pummelo, Largest chalk pavement art, Farthest distance pushing a scooter, Largest chestnut roaster, Most people shaving (single venue), Most eggs held in the hand, Heaviest kohlrabi, Fastest time to pop 1,000 balloons, Greatest distance walked balancing baseball bat on finger, Largest concert by town musicians, Longest reading aloud marathon by team, Largest collection of candles, Largest Japanese drum ensemble, Largest drum ensemble, Fastest time to complete GWR-Hasbro puzzle, Longest marathon radio DJ, Longest dog tunnel, Largest youth organization, Most participants in a snowboard race, Largest plastic duck race, Largest brick, Most people on space hoppers, Largest collection of model cars, Largest line dance, Largest caricature, Most snails on face, Largest robot dance, Largest bowl of soup, Largest speed dating event, Most hair donated to charity in 24 hours, Largest underpants.

IN MEMORIA...

Art Arfons, former land speed record holder; Bernie Barker, **Oldest male stripper**; Chris Bishop, GWR's military consultant; Hal Fishman, **Longest career as a newsreader**; Moses Aleksandrovich Feigin, **Oldest professional artist**; Steve Fossett, **Longest non-stop flight**, *inter alia*; Bertha Fry (b. 1 December 1893), third oldest person in the world at time of death; Wally Herbert, **First crossing of the Arctic**; Sir Edmund Hillary, **First ascent of Mt Everest**; Sarah Jeanmougin, **Oldest living twin**; Verity Lambert, founding producer of *Dr Who*, the **longest running sci-fi show on television**; Humphrey Lyttelton, organizer of the **Largest kazoo ensemble**; Eddie "Bozo" Miller, competitive eater; Yone Minegawa, **Oldest living woman** (and **person**) at time of death; Ellen Isabela Robertson, one of the **Oldest living female twins**; Charles Wright, **Oldest music teacher**.

PICTURE CREDITS

3 Richard Bradbury/GWR **4** Maximilian Weinzierl/Alamy; Alamy; John Wright/GWR; NASA; NASA; Charles Rex Arbogast/AP/PA; BBC Books/The Random House Group Ltd **5** David Dyson/Getty Images; John Wright/GWR; Samuel Golaya/Getty Images **6** BBC; **7** (UK) Ranald Mackechnie/GWR; (UK) Chris Capstick **8** (UK) Jason Lock **9** (UK) Lorenzo Dalberto; (UK) Chen Jie/GWR; (UK) Chen Jie/GWR; (UK) Ken McKay **10** John Wright/GWR **11** Andy Paradise/GWR **12** Paul Michael Hughes/GWR **14** The Art Archive; akg-images; Getty Images; PA **15** Rex Features; Stan Honda/Getty Images; NASA; Jack Smith/AP/PA; Emiliano Grillotti/Getty Images **16** NASA **18** Mark Garlick/SPL; Harvard-Smithsonian Center for Astrophysics; Mark Garlick/SPL **19** NASA; NASA/MAXPPP **20** Luke Dodd/SPL; NASA **21** NASA; SPL; NASA **22** NASA; SPL; Dept Of Geological Sciences, Dallas **23** ESA/DLR/FU Berlin (G. Neukum); SPL; Kees Veenenbos/SPL **24** NASA; NASA; Gordon Garradd/SPL **25** Detlev Van Ravenswaay/SPL; NASA **26** David Steele **27** Alan Dawson/Alamy; Santiago Ferrero; Joe Sohm/Photolibrary **28** Dave Lewis/Rex Features; European Space Agency; NASA **29** NASA/SPL; NASA; NASA/AP/PA **30** Photolibrary **32** Valerie Taylor/Ardea **33** FLPA; G Douwma/Getty Images; Doc White/Nature PL **34** Fred Hirschmann/Getty Images; George Grall/Getty Images; Mary Plage/Photolibrary **35** Mike Linley/Getty Images; Mark Carwardine/Nature PL **36** Richard Herrmann/Photolibrary; Steven David Miller/Nature PL; Jim Watt/Photolibrary **37** Tim Laman/Getty Images; Richard Manuel/Photolibrary; Alamy **38** Joe & Mary McDonald/Alamy; Eric Francis/Getty Images; FLPA **39** Samuel Aranda/Getty Images; Maximilian Weinzierl/Alamy; Peter Chadwick/SPL; Reuters **40** David Courtenay/Photolibrary; FLPA; J & A Scott/Getty Images **41** Bobby Haas/Getty Images; Frank Greenaway/Getty Images; Alamy **42** Duncan Shaw/SPL; Terry Whittaker/Alamy; Alamy **43** John Dransfield/Kew Gardens; Tony Craddock/SPL; Gerald Cubitt/NHPA **44** Bruce Beehler/AP/PA; Twan Leenders; Mark Carwardine/Nature PL **45** FLPA; FLPA **46** Martin Harvey/NHPA; FLPA **47** Daryl Balfour/NHPA; Ranald Mackechnie/GWR **48** Roy Toft/Getty Images; Nature PL; Rex Features; Andreas Lander/Corbis **49** Murray Cooper/Nathan Muchhala; Andy Rouse/NHPA **50** Alamy; Corbis; Corbis; Alamy **51** Sam Chadwick/Alamy; Corbis **52** Dietmar Nill/Nature Pl; Bruce Davidson/Nature PL **53** Rex Features; Andrew Parkinson/Nature PL **54** Ian Redmond/Nature PL; Matthias Breiter/Getty Images; David Scharf/Getty Images **55** Kim Taylor/Nature PL; Hugo Willcox/Getty Images **56** Ranald Mackechnie/GWR **58** Mary Evans Picture Library **59** Gray's Anatomy/Elsevier **60** Ranald Mackechnie/GWR; Phil Meyers/AP/PA **61** Sean Sexton/Getty Images; Tomas Bravo/GWR **62** Ranald Mackechnie/GWR **63** John Wright/GWR; Ranald Mackechnie/GWR **64** Manish Swarup/AP/PA; Paul Michael Hughes/GWR; Ranald Mackechnie/GWR **65** Li Zijun/Photoshot; Simon Smith/AP/PA; Ranald Mackechnie/GWR **66** Don Cravens/Getty Images; PA Photos; Daniel Berehulak/Getty Images **67** John Wright/GWR **68** Kiyoshi Ota/Reuters **69** Miguel Alvarez/Getty Images; Reuters; PA **70** Steve Dibblee/iStockphoto; Ranald Mackechnie/GWR **71** John Wright/GWR; RTL/Gregorowius **72** BBC Books/The Random House Group Ltd; John Wright/GWR; Drew Gardner/GWR **73** Ranald Mackechnie/GWR **74** Ian Cook/Getty Images; MAXPPP **75** Barbara Laing/Getty Images; Tom Strickland/GWR **76** Erik G Svensson **78** Richard Bradbury/GWR; Maxwells/GWR **79** BBC Books/The Random House Group Ltd; Getty Images **83** Paul Michael Hughes/GWR; Corbis; NASA **84** NASA; NASA; NASA; NASA; NASA; NASA; Photolibrary **85** NASA/SPL; NASA; NASA/Getty Images; Dorling Kindersley; Moonpans.com **86** John Wright/GWR **89** Craig Ruttle/AP/PA **90** Thomas Mukoya/Reuters; Ned Redway; China Photos/Getty Images **91** Chet Gordon/Times Herald-Record **92** John Wright/GWR; Pali Rao/iStockphoto **93** John Wright/GWR **94** Ranald Mackechnie/GWR **95** Charles Rex Arbogast/AP/PA; Ranald Mackechnie/GWR **96** Richard Bradbury/GWR; John Wright/GWR **97** Ranald Mackechnie/GWR **98** Colin Young-Wolff/Alamy; AP/PA; Peter Macdiarmid/Getty Images **99** Alen Dobric/iStockphoto; Marek Szumlas/iStockphoto; Georges DeKeerle/Getty Images; Bob Landry/Getty Images; Mike Kipling/Alamy **100** Richard Bradbury/GWR **101** John Wright/GWR; John Wright/GWR **102** John Wright/GWR; John Wright/GWR; John Wright/GWR **103** John Wright/GWR; Sukree Sukplang/Reuters; John Wright/GWR **104** John Wright/GWR; Manish Swarup/AP/PA **105** WENN; WENN; Jeff Spicer/Alpha/Channel Four **106** Fredrik Schenholm/www.schenholm.se **108** Fred Tanneau/Getty Images **109** Vincent Kessler/Reuters **110** William Garnier/ORS **111** Wolfgang Rattay/Reuters; Filip Singer/Getty Images; Getty Images **113** Carl de Souza/Getty Images; David Dyson/Getty Images **114** PA; PA; AP/PA **115** Ira Block/NGS; Corbis **117** Hiroyuki Kuraoka/AP/PA **118** Richard Bradbury/GWR **120** Claro Cortes/Reuters; Richard Bradbury/GWR **123** Ranald Mackechnie/GWR; Paul Michael Hughes/GWR; WENN; Alamy **125** Richard Bradbury/GWR; Chip East/Reuters **128** Richard Bradbury/GWR; Jay Williams/GWR **129** Maximilian Weinzierl/Alamy; Richard Bradbury/GWR **130** Rex Features; Cosmopolitan & Venus Breeze **131** Mario Anzuoni/Reuters **132** Alberto Roque/Getty Images; Sean Sprague/Panos Pictures; Mustafa Deliormanli/iStockphoto; Norman Chan/iStockphoto; Luca Da Ros/4Corners Images **133** Philimon Bulawayo/Reuters; AP/PA; Reuters **134** Natasja Weitsz/Getty Images; Tariq Mahmood/Getty Images; Eyevine **135** AP/PA; Shannon Stapleton/Reuters; Paula Bronstein/Getty Images; Martin Bureau/Getty Images **136** Christopher Herwig/Reuters; Sandy Huffaker/Getty Images; Getty Images **137** Eyevine; Getty Images; David Manyua/Reuters **138** Richard Bradbury/GWR **140** Yoshikazu Tsuno/Getty Images **141** CERN **142** Karl Shone/Getty Images; Randy Olson/Getty Images; Case Western Reserve University **143** David S. Holloway/Getty Images; Niels Bohr Institute **144** Swedish Institute; Corbis; Robert Galbraith/Reuters **145** Rex Features; Apple; DreamWorks Pictures (Paramount) **147** WENN; Justin Sullivan/Getty Images; Apple/Rex Features **148** Roland Gladasch/GWR; Robert F. Bukaty/AP/PA **149** M Roger/MAX PPP **150** James Davis/Alamy; Getty Images **151** Eitan Abramovich/Getty Images; Guang Niu/Getty Images; Adriana Lorete/Getty Images **152** Rabih Moghrabi/Getty Images **154** Rex Features; Kiyoshi Ota/Reuters; John Wright/GWR **155** Rex Features **156** Elaine Thompson/AP/PA **157** Georges Gobet/Getty Images; Jean-Bernard Gache **158** Getty Images; Reuters **159** Reuters; Reuters; Royal Navy **160** Rockstar Games **162** Getty Images; David Burner/Rex Features; Rex Features **163** Chris Jackson/Getty Images; Francois Guillot/Getty Images **164** Photolibrary; National Park Service; Ronald Grant; Ronald Grant; Universal Pictures; Paramount Pictures; Columbia Pictures **165** Warner Bros/Kobal; Warner Bros/Ronald Grant; Universal Pictures/Ronald Grant; www.moviescreenshots.blogspot.com; Ronald Grant; Columbia Pictures; New Line Cinema; Paramount Pictures/Ronald Grant **166** Sony RCA; Alex Grimm/Reuters; Getty Images; Matt Cardy/Getty Images **167** Rick Diamond/Getty Images; Sony RCA; PA **168** Rex Features; Kevin Westenberg/Getty Images; Evan Agostini/AP/PA **169** Dave Benett/Getty Images; Gary He/AP/PA; John Wright/GWR **170** Cate Gillon/Getty Images; Mykel Nicolao/GWR; Chitose Suzuki/AP/PA **171** Manish Swarup/AP/PA; DC Comics **172** Frank Micelotta/Getty Images; NBC-TV/Rex Features **173** Hanna-Barbera; NBC-TV/Kobal; 20th Century Fox/Rex Features **174** Richard Bradbury/GWR; John Wright/GWR **175** John Wright/GWR; Hermann J. Knippertz/AP/PA; Francisco Bonilla/Reuters; Francisco Bonilla/Reuters **176** David Stluka/Getty Images **178** Ludovic Franco/RedBull **179** Richard Eaton/Max PPP **180** David Stluka/Getty Images; David Stluka/Getty Images; Kai Pfaffenbach/Reuters **181** Ben Liebenberg/Getty Images; Jamie Squire/Getty Images **182** Kai Pfaffenbach/Reuters; Emiliano Grillotti/Getty Images; Koichi Kamoshida/Getty Images **183** Alexander Hassenstein/Getty Images; Brian Snyder/Reuters; Alexander Hassenstein/Getty Images; Torsten Silz/Getty Images **184** Michael Steele/Getty Images; Andreas Rentz/Getty Images **186** Rusty Jarrett/Getty Images; Kim Kyung-Hoon/Reuters; J. P. Moczulski/Reuters **187** John Harrelson/Getty Images; Jonathan Ferrey/Getty Images **188** Tengku Bahar/Getty Images; Grigory Dukor/Reuters; Joe Bryksa/CP Picture Archive **189** Stephen Cooper/Newspix; Phil Walter/Getty Images; Dominic Ebenbichler/Reuters **190** Mike Fiala/Getty Images; Jim McIsaac/Getty Images **191** Al Bello/Getty Images **192** Ints Kalnins/Reuters; Fernando Medina/Getty Images **193** Jeffrey Bottari/Getty Images; Joe Murphy/Getty Images; Barry Gossage/Getty Images **194** Gregory Shamus, NBAE/Getty Images; Joe Murphy/NBAE/Getty Images; Joe Murphy/NBAE/Getty Images **195** Joe Murphy, NBAE/Getty Images; Gregory Shamus/NBAE/Getty Images **196** Brendon Thorne/Getty Images; Paul Kane/Getty Images; Paul Kane/Getty Images **197** Craig Prentis/Getty Images; Lee Warren/Getty Images; Lee Warren/Getty Images **198** Yuruzu Sunada/Getty Images; Michael Steele/Getty Images; Jaime Reina/Getty Images; Yves Boucau/Getty Images **199** Jean Pierre Clatot/AFP; Samuel Golay/Getty Images; Getty Images; Getty Images **200** Carl De Souza/Getty Images; Carl De Souza/Getty Images; Paco Serinelli/Getty Images **201** Clive Mason/Getty Images; PA; Felix Ordonez/Reuters **202** Ranald Mackechnie/GWR; John Wright/GWR **203** Ranald Mackechnie/GWR; John Wright/GWR **204** Yang Enuo/PA Photos; Anthony Devlin/PA Photos; Donald Miralle/Getty Images **205** Scott Halleran/Getty Images; Sam Greenwood/Getty Images **206** Chris Trotman/Getty Images; Dave Sandford/Getty Images; Steve Babineau/Getty Images **207** Gregory Shamus/Getty Images; Getty Images **208** Ricardo Moraes/AP/PA; Javier Sorano/AFP; Ed Mulholland/Getty Images **209** World Wrestling Entertainment, Inc.; Rex Features; Toshifumi Kitamura/AFP **210** Anthony Phelps/Reuters; JM Hervio/AI/Reuters; Cameron Spencer/Getty Images **211** Cameron Spencer/Getty Images; David Rogers/Getty Images; Cameron Spencer/Getty Images; Chris McGrath/Getty Images **212** Brian Bahr/Getty Images; Odd Andersen/Getty Images; Clive Brunskill/Getty Images; Keith Hammet/AP/PA **213** Bobby Yip/Reuters; Cameron Spencer/Getty Images; Torsten Blackwood/Getty Images **214** Adrees Latif/Reuters; Damir Sagolj/Reuters; Grant Ellis/Getty Images; Andy Clark/Reuters **215** Lucy Nicholson/Reuters **216** Richard Bradbury/GWR; Ranald Mackechnie/GWR **218** IMG Media Ltd; IMG Media Ltd **219** IMG Media Ltd; IMG Media Ltd; Getty Images **220** David Callow/AP/PA; Tony Vu/ESPN; Jae C. Hong/AP/PA; Matt Morning/ESPN; Dom Cooley/ESPN; Tony Donaldson/ESPN **221** Jack Dempsey/AP/PA; Eric Lars Bakke/ESPN; ESPN; Tony Vu/ESPN **222** Reuters; Michael Steele/Getty Images **223** Michael Steele/Getty Images; Roland Weihrauch/AP/PA **224** Matthew Lewis/Getty Images; Andy Lyons/Getty Images **225** Bryn Lennon/Getty Images **227** Junko Kimura/Getty Images; Chung Sung-Jun/Getty Images **228** Jonathan Ferrey/Getty Images; Albert Gea/Reuters **229** Giampiero Sposito/Reuters; Michael Sohn/AP/PA **230** Sukree Sukplang/Reuters; Sukree Sukplang/Reuters **231** Mark Dadswell/Getty Images **232** Paramount Pictures; Stefano Paltera/AP/PA; Ranald Mackechnie/GWR **233** David McNew/Getty Images; Kevin Winter/Getty Images; Vince Bucci/Getty Images; MJ Kim/Getty Images **234** David Fisher/Rex Features; Michael Buckner/Getty Images **235** Chen Jie/GWR; Chen Jie/GWR; Chen Jie/GWR **236** Reuters; Reuters **237** Chen Jie/GWR; Chen Jie/GWR **238** Rex Features; Chen Jie/GWR **239** Bloomsbury; Marco Secchi/Getty Images **240** Ranald Mackechnie/GWR; Mario Anzuoni/Reuters; Warner Bros. Entertainment Inc. **241** Warner Bros. Entertainment Inc.; Dave M. Benett/Getty Images; Ronald Grant; Raine Vara/Alamy **242** NASA **244** Angelo Cavalli/Robert Harding **245** Hiroko Masuike/Getty Images; AP/PA; Getty Images **246** Achim Prill/iStockphoto; Patricio Robles Gil/Getty Images; Gary Vestal/Getty Images; Vladimir Pcholkin/Getty Images **247** Grey Villet/Getty Images; Adalberto Roque/Getty Images; Photolibrary; David McLain/Getty Images; Alamy **248** NASA; Miguel Mendez/Getty Images; Joel Sartore/Getty Images **249** Mauricio Lima/Getty Images; Elena Goycochea; H. John Maier Jr/Getty Images; Reuters **250** Joe Raedle/Getty Images; NASA; John Sylvester/Alamy **251** Reuters; Winston Fraser/Alamy **252** Ranald Mackechnie/GWR; PA; iStockphoto **253** Ranald Mackechnie/GWR; Shaun Curry/Getty Images **254** Francois Nascimbeni/Getty Images; Remy de la Mauviniere/AP/PA; Stephane De Satukin/Getty Images **255** OL Mazzatenta/Getty Images; AP/PA **256** P Desmazes/Getty Images; Ricardo Suárez; Xan G. Muras **257** Jose Manuel Ribeiro/Reuters; Clive Brunskill/Getty Images; Rex Features **258** Mitchell Funk/Getty Images; Marcel Lelienhof **259** Erlend Berge/Scanpix/PA; Gero Breloer/Corbis **260** Richard Bradbury/GWR **261** HNJ Van Essen/Getty Images **262** Amel Emric/AP/PA; Viktor Drachev/Getty Images **263** Michael Steele/Getty Images; Hideo Kurihara/Alamy; PA **264** A Nemenov/Getty Images; SPL; Stephen Dunn/Getty Images; Alamy **266** Bruno Morandi/Getty Images; Duncan Ridgley/Rex Features **267** Thomas Hartwell/Getty Images; Barry Lewis/Alamy; AA Rabbo/Getty Imag es **268** Fred Derwal/Corbis; Anup Shah/Getty Images; Franck Guiziou/Getty Images **269** George Mulala/Reuters; Chris Jackson/Getty Images; AP/PA **270** Corbis; Banaras Khan/Getty Images **271** Saurabh Das/AP/PA; Angelo Cavalli/Tips Images **272** Zhang Jun/Xinhua/WPN; Paula Bronstein/Getty Images; Ron Dahlquist/Getty Images **273** Alex Bowie/Getty Images; Juliet Coombe/Lonely Planet **274** AKG Images; Reuters **276** Jurgen Freund/Nature PL **277** Getty Images; Mary Evans; FLPA **286** Rex Features **287** Michael Buckner/Getty Images; George Burns/Harpo Productions; Paul Sanders **288** Gunnar Kullenberg/Rex Features

INDEX

This year's index is organized into two parts: by subject and by superlative. **Bold** entries in the subject index indicate a main entry on a topic, and entries in **BOLD CAPITALS** indicate an entire chapter. Neither index lists personal names.

STOP PRESS

★ MOST SPOONS BALANCED ON THE FACE

On 2 May 2008, schoolboy Joe Allison (UK) broke the record for balancing spoons on the face. His total of 16 spoons was one more than that of the previous world record, set by Tim Johnston (USA) in 2004.

★ LARGEST PICNIC BLANKET

A picnic blanket measuring 1,760 m² (18,944 ft²) was woven at the Melin Tregwynt Mill in Wales, UK, for Waitrose Ltd, and was laid out for the first time in Durban, South Africa, in April 2008.

THE GREAT GUINNESS WORLD RECORDS BANJO-OFF

Fast-fingered? Fancy your chances against our two banjo record holders? Here are the guidelines you'll need to follow:

● Guinness World Records will supply you – in advance of your attempt – with the music you *must* play. You *cannot* play a piece of your choice.
● The record is based on the speed (in beats-per-minute) at which the player can perform the entire piece.
● No speeding up or slowing down is permitted.
● A metronome must be used.
● The piece must be played without any errors – any mistakes will invalidate the attempt.
For full guidelines, apply at www. guinness worldrecords .com

★ FASTEST ASCENT OF MOUNT KILIMANJARO

Gerard Bavato (France) ran the 34 km (21.1 miles) from the base to the summit of Mount Kilimanjaro in 5 hr 26 min 40 sec on 26 October 2007.

★ YOUNGEST DRUMMER

Tiger Onitsuka (Japan) was just 9 years 289 days old when his debut album – *Tiger* – was released on 23 April 2008. Tiger is a jazz drummer and is signed to the Columbia label.

★ YOUNGEST PHOTOGRAPHER

Zoe Fung Leung (Hong Kong, b. 19 January 2006) was 2 years 70 days old when she exhibited and sold her work at Plaza Hollywood, Kowloon, Hong Kong, on 29–30 March 2008, making her the youngest professional photographer.

★ LARGEST FLAG DRAPED

The largest flag draped measured 22,813.293 m² (245,559.27 ft²) and was the national flag of the United Arab Emirates (UAE). It was created by Sedar Window Fashion (UAE) and presented, as a token of appreciation, to the Government of Sharjah in Sharjah, UAE, on 12 May 2008.

★ MOST ACCURATE ATOMIC CLOCK

The world's most accurate atomic watch, as of July 2006, is a prototype mercury optical clock which, if operated continually would neither gain nor lose a second in approximately 400 million years. The clock has been built and developed by the National Institute of Standards and Technology (NIST) in Boulder, Colorado, USA.

★ OLDEST COUPLE TO COMPLETE A MARATHON

Shigetsugu Anan (Japan), aged 83 years 11 days, and his wife Miyoko Anan (Japan), aged 78 years 71 days, finished the Ibusuki Nanohana Marathon in Japan, on 13 January 2008.

★ LONGEST DRIVEN JOURNEY

Swiss couple Emil and Liliana Schmid have driven a total of 626,960 km (389,574 miles) since 16 October 1984, crossing 159 countries and territories.

FASTEST BANJO PLAYERS

The year 2008 saw two banjoists competing for the title of world's **fastest banjo player**. Todd Taylor (USA, left) and Jonny Butten (UK, right) both have claims to the title, and each has held the Guinness World Record for a period of time. Both reached a speed that was impossible to judge under our old guidelines, so we have established a whole new set of rules to find out who truly has the fastest fingers. (*See above left.*)